THE INCREDIBLE

ESKIMO

LIFE AMONG THE BARREN LAND ESKIMO

by

Raymond de Coccola
& Paul King

Illustrations by James Houston

hancock

house

ISBN 0-88839-189-7

Cataloging in Publication Data

De Coccola, Raymond 1912-
The Incredible Eskimo
ISBN 0-88839-189-7

1. De Coccola, Raymond, 1912-. 2. Inuit — Northwest Territories —
Missions.* 3. Catholic Church — Missions — Northwest Territories.
4. Missionaries — Northwest Territories — Biography.
I. King, Paul, 1912- II. Title.

BV2813.D4A35 1986 266'.27192'0924 C86-091518-2

Edited by Jocelyn Cameron
Typeset by Hardip Randhawa
Design/Layout by Herb Bryce
Printed in Canada by Friesen Printers

Cover picture courtesy of
MUSEUM OF MAN
NATIONAL MUSEUM OF CANADA

Photographs supplied by:
National Museum of Canada
Geological Survey of Canada
Raymond de Coccola
Department of Mines and Resources

Published simultaneously in Canada and the United States by

HANCOCK HOUSE PUBLISHERS LTD.
19313 Zero Ave., Surrey, B.C. V3S 5J9
HANCOCK HOUSE PUBLISHERS INC.
1431 Harrison Avenue, Blaine, WA 98230

Contents

Introduction

For twelve years, (from 1937-1949) as a Corsican-born missionary and explorer, I have observed and recorded the attitude and way of life of the Krangmalit Eskimo scattered in the Canadian Central Arctic. I wrote this book to bring you, the reader, into closer contact with an extra-ordinary people, commonly called the Eskimo. I offer a true picture of the Barren Land with an unabridged accurate account of everyday Eskimo life as I have seen it and experienced it. It may be read for whatever intrinsic interest it possesses by young and old alike without offending their sensitivity and morality.

Looking on a map, you will notice that the Polar Sea, from the Pole ice belt, extends its gray cold waters in every direction and is enclosed by the American and Asiatic Mainland. In this frozen immensity is located the Eskimo population, the only people on our globe who can be compared, to a certain extent at least, with our ancestors of the glacial period. With the help of your imagination, you can place yourself far back in this time period and add life as well as reality to scenes that are actually routine for the Barren Land Eskimo. Thus you will gain an intimate contact with the polar region and its people who have been able to exist and also display for thousands of years a remarkable skill and endurance demanding sincere admiration.

It is possible that a few facts may seem not entirely accurate, in which case I can only say that this is not due to deliberate error, but rather to my inability always to convey directly the observations I have made. Moreover, I am describing the Krangmalit Eskimos or the People Beyond and not the Eskimos living in the Western Arctic or in the Eastern Arctic and Greenland. Concerning them, I have little knowledge, although I presume their way of life was or is practically more or less the same as the Krangmalit.

The Eskimo is therefore the hero of this book. I am only an observer. The land and the people are familiar to me for I have trudged and wandered with them for years, sharing their joys and sorrows in a long adventure I will never forget.

Raymond de Coccola
October, 1986

1

Naoyak, The Seagull

Angivrana was in labor. In the unsteady light of the stone lamp she looked worn and nervous, with her prematurely old face large, broad, and strong. She squatted on the *iglek*, the built-up snow platform covered with mattings of dwarf willow twigs and caribou skins, alternately moaning and murmuring to herself as she rocked gently back and forth. "My stomach is like the belly of a pregnant caribou cow. But why not? My husband is as potent as a rutting bull in the fall. *Eh! Eh! Eh!* I'm happy now. I'll give him another son," she chuckled softly.

Angivrana was not alone. To her left, ten feet away at the other end of the semi-circular *iglek*, minding her own blubber lamp, squatted a bent, shrivelled-up bundle of caribou fur, her mother Manerathiak. Seeing me enter the igloo, she dropped the flat bone she was using to scrape a caribou skin, stood up slowly as if she would break in two if she hurried, and moved towards me with outstretched, gnarled hands. A softening smile relieved her wizened, deeply lined face when our fingers touched.

"How are you?" I asked.

"I'm fine today," the stooped old woman replied through teeth worn to the gums.

"And how are you?" I turned to Angivrana, whose moaning had grown louder since my entry.

Several caribou and seal-skin satchels were slung over her belt to protect her and the unborn child against evil spirits. She placed her hand significantly on her abdomen. "Here inside, he's moving like a hare on the run! Come, feel for yourself."

"Looks as if you won't have long to wait," I parried, ignoring her invitation. "Just try to keep quiet for now. I'll go to my sled and bring back something to help you." I crawled out of the twelve-foot-diameter igloo through its low, narrow opening in the snow wall into the tunnel-like porch with its adequate headroom. Outside, I walked to my dogsled to get some bromide tablets, part of my meager medicine supply from the outside world.

After their 5-hour run here to the camp of Portage Bay from my Mission post in Burnside, thirty miles north of the Arctic Circle at the south end of Bathurst Inlet, my diligent dogs were tired. All nine rested in the snow, noses under their tails and collars chained to the dog line.

It was still as gray and cold as when I'd left the post at dawn. The rawness penetrated my bones through my double parka as I retrieved the needed tablets from my medicine bag in the grubbox. Back in the igloo, I said to Angivrana, "Here swallow this; it'll make you feel better." She rolled the pill between her finger tips, eyeing it with undisguised wonder.

"How can such a little thing make me feel better?"

"Just try it," I suggested.

She swallowed the pill, then, giggling and sucking the tips of her fingers, she said, "Thank you, Little Man!" It wasn't the first time my height had earned me this semi-patronizing, semi-affectionate nickname, so I took it as a small compliment.

After a few minutes, the drug quieted Angivrana. Meanwhile, her mother Manerathiak had brewed some tea in a kettle hanging from a driftwood rack above the blubber lamp. She licked the rim of an enamel cup clean before filling it with the hot drink. "Have some tea!" she offered. Then, motioning to a row of frozen caribou carcasses leaning against the snow wall near the entrance, she added, "Have some meat! You must be hungry."

Although I had eaten some dried caribou meat and fat on the trail, the morning trip had sharpened my appetite, so I cut off a piece of the lean, almost tasteless frozen meat with my pocket knife and bit into it with relish. Ever since I'd arrived in Burnside the year before, I'd liked it far more than strong-tasting seal meat, and had never grown tired of it.

Joining Angivrana on the *iglek*, I asked her out of curiosity, "Where is your husband *Nokadlak?*" Holding a teacup under her nose, she managed a smile. "Nokadlak—some people also call him *Pangnek*, the Bull—is hunting in the hills with our boy, Kudnanak." But the mention of her firstborn brought on a fresh

9

wave of self-pity. Looking down at her swollen belly, she confided, "I'll be glad when this one here is born. That's for sure! I crave raw meat during the day. But now Kirluayok, the shaman, says I must eat only in the morning and evening. Otherwise, bad luck will befall me. The Big Woman Arnakapfaluk, the Spirit of the Sea, would bring misfortune to us all. The shaman also told me that Nokadlak must not take me during the night. That's really too bad!"

I knew that, while childbearing is normally a simple experience for Eskimo women, certain prohibitions and dis-comforts have to be endured. The shaman or tribal sorcerer has decreed that once a child is well on the way, pregnant women must sleep alone in their own *krepik* (sleeping bag) and observe the immemorial laws of the Spirits of the Land and the customs of their ancestors. Also, they must not eat any raw meat or the tender parts of animals such as the liver, heart and kidneys.

Not long after taking the sedative I had given her, Angivrana's time finally arrived. She sat holding her caribou trousers between her legs writhing in pain and cried out, "I'm all wet!" Manerathiak, her aged mother, hurried to her side and pulled off Angivrana's parka and undergarments. She also spread out two caribou skins on the snow floor and assisted her daughter into a squatting position, with legs apart. Then the ancient woman spoke quietly to me, "Little White Man, come closer. I'll need you! Put on your mittens. I'll clean them afterwards. When the child comes, you give Angivrana a hand to pull him out. I'm too old, and my back is sore. I'll hold her now. She can rest her back against my legs."

As Angivrana's contractions increased, she called forth her long dead relatives: *"Ho! Ho!* Angak, my Father! Adjuk, my Grandmother!"* I understood this supplication to mean that the soul of the deceased, which could help her more than anyone else, was supposed to possess the new-born child who would then be named after that departed relative.

Gently rubbing her abdomen, Angivrana eventually expelled more fluid, whereupon the child's head began to appear, causing Manerathiak to tell me, "When the head is out, just hold it."

Straining hard and moaning louder, Angivrana mumbled words I couldn't understand. At last, her baby's tiny dark-haired head began to emerge. Gently but firmly I started helping it on its way. Manerathiak urged Angivrana to inhale deeply and breathe out heavily alternately. At this stage, Angivrana's hand sought out her child to help me complete the delivery. With practiced poise, Grandmother Manerathiak, as she was called, turned to using her sleeves for mopping the perspiration on

Angivrana's face, calmly humming "Ah! Ie, ie, ie, ie." And I helped by cautiously pulling on the baby's wet and bloodied body. Then, as I held her new grandchild in my outstretched arms, Manerathiak moved in beside me and grabbed the umbilical cord with her middle finger, saying "Lay the child on the caribou skin!" As soon as I did, she knelt on the snow floor and started licking the child's face, sucking the nose and the mouth, and stroking its back until the baby gave a vigorous cry.

Almost simultaneously, Angivrana, who was resting with her hands behind her back for support as she watched her baby, suddenly shouted in anguish, "It's too bad, too bad! It's only a girl!"

Manerathiak kept silent. Her attention was on the baby's cord. She tied it with a piece of caribou sinew, then cut it off with an *ulon*, the versatile half-moon-shaped Eskimo knife. With this vital link severed from her baby girl, Angivrana pressed hard on her own belly to expel the placenta. Manerathiak took the vascular organ in her hands and bit off the umbilical cord. She carefully placed a section of the cord in a small leather bag to later hang around Angivrana's neck as a safeguard against sterility. She then handed me the placenta to take to the porch where the ever-hungry pups would promptly consume it.

When I returned, she was wiping Angivrana clean with the soft fur of an Arctic hare, muttering to herself, "What a pity! Such a beautiful grandchild, but she is only a girl!" Regardless of her disappointment, the old woman helped Angivrana lie down on the *iglek* with the baby close to her breast beneath her parka. Angivrana lay back panting. Presently, her breathing returned to normal and she rested silently.

In my concern for Angivrana, I hardly had time to take a good look at her wailing female child. She had jet-black hair, slanted dark eyes (now partly closed), a tiny reddish body, and the bluish coccyx—a mark common to all Eskimos.

As I examined her tiny daughter, I detected distaste and self-pity in Angivrana's voice as she repeated quietly, "A girl! Only a girl!" Overhearing Angivrana's lament, Manerathiak mused audibly from her corner, "How will her father, Nokadlak, take the sad news? Had it been a little boy, he would proudly invite local friends to show off his latest man-child. 'Eh! Eh! no kidding!'they would giggle approvingly. 'A little boy, a small man!' And you know, Little White Man, before many winters came to pass the boy would be hunting and fishing at his father's side. And, in some future day, he would be the family's sole provider. But a girl! A useless mouth to feed for months and years until she is taken away by another man, possibly never to be seen again...."

"But Manerathiak, you are a woman yourself," I protested.

"Some day, maybe, you'll learn our ways," she rejoined, then abruptly dropped the subject. "Now I must rest for a while."

As her mind began to remember the past, she chanted in a tired, crackled voice:

"*Aye, aye, ie, ie, e, e, ...*
Attutiga talva, here is my song. *Aye, aye, ...*
I was born in the fall, *aye, aye, e, e*
When foxes turn white as snow
And waterfowl fly to the sun, *aye, aye, ie;*
I was born in a tent,
I was born a girl ..... only a girl,
Not abandoned to die, but
Promised to a hunter, *aye, aye, ie, ie, e, e,*"

I shuddered when I thought of what happens to so many Eskimo baby girls. A recent conversation with Anarvik, an unusually tall and big-boned woman I had occasionally seen at Burnside, stung my heart. Matter-of-factly, she had told me she did not raise a single girl in her family.

"What happened to your girls?" I inquired. She looked at me with transparent disdain, sizing me up as a slow-witted White Man.

"When a girl is born in winter we take her outside to freeze. If she is born in summer, we build a stone box near the camp and leave her there to die. Other times we choke her with caribou fur in her mouth, or we put her adrift on the ice."

"That must have been because you did not love your daughters as you love Poktok and Ungerlak, your sons," I ventured.

A smirk covered Anarvik's broad face as she surveyed mine. Her answer was quiet and steady as she answered with a single Eskimo word: *ayornaronarevok.* There is no English equivalent, but I understand it to mean "There is certainly nothing one can do about it. . . .It's truly hopeless. . . .It's our destiny."

My anxious mind also flashed back to Irkrarena, a strongly built girl from Taheriuak Lake, a true *Krangmalek,* or Person Beyond. In her last days of pregnancy, she and her husband Kraodluak left the camp to visit friends who were hunting on the Hanimor River. When Irkrarena returned to the camp a few days later, her figure was back to normal. She carefully avoided me, but I made a point of seeking her out. "You look so thin and pale, Irkrarena! Have you been starving on the trail?" I asked.

12

An odd expression came into her eyes, as a sad smile flickered on her full lips. "The trail was rough and she was a girl. Alas, only a girl ....."

I knew that for centuries native people of the Canadian Arctic and Greenland killed their girls at birth, but I could never accept it. Wherever I traveled in the Barren Land, I confronted men and women about this subject, but everywhere their answer was essentially the same. Hikhik, who had two wives, crudely summed up the Eskimo reasoning: "A girl is useless, like the droppings of a dog!"

Most of the Eskimo men and women I met, however, took Grandmother Manerathiak's slightly more positive approach: "A man knows that when he gets old, he cannot hunt anymore or provide adequately for his family. He will have a better chance to live a little longer and not be forced to commit suicide if he had sons to help him." She put significant emphasis on "sons."

Outside the igloo, my dogs began to howl. Nokadlak and his son Kudnanak were back from the hunt. As I walked towards their heavily laden sled, I found it difficult to guess Nokadlak's age. His strong features, burned brown by the rigors of Arctic life, expressed the impassive serenity of a man from the Barren Land. Although it had never felt a razor blade, his chin was almost clean and his upper lip carried only a trace of whiskers. A few strands of his tough, black hair escaped the hood, partly covering his thin, dark eyebrows beneath which two narrow slits betrayed jet-black eyes that glittered in the snowy whiteness.

Perhaps he was in his early thirties. If I'd asked his age, though, he probably would have laughed and retorted, "Do I look like a child, a young man or an old man? No, I'm a grown-up man! I don't know when I was born; some time in the past. Why do you want to know how many winters I have? What for?"

A better way to find out would have been to ask "How tall were you when a White Man who could speak like a Nethilit (someone from the Eastern Arctic) came this way from King William Land?" The visitor I meant was, of course, Knud Rasmussen whose expedition had hurriedly passed through Bathurst twelve years earlier in 1925. Then, raising his hand to indicate his height at the time, Nokadlak would have readily answered, "I was that tall—a young man."

Whatever his exact age, I was glad to shake hands with Nokadlak and meet his pleasant, alert young boy, Kudnanak. After we exchanged greetings, I told Nokadlak that his friend Kakagun had asked me to visit Angivrana because she was going to have a child. Nokadlak wasn't surprised. Looking straight at him, I added: "I helped Angivrana when the baby came this

13

afternoon. It's a girl. Your wife is asleep with her."

"A girl, eh?" he mused momentarily. Then, making no attempt to hide his disappointment, he blurted, "Too bad, only a girl!"

"I'll help you unload," I volunteered, to divert his troubled thoughts. And, noting his good catch I was about to compliment him on his hunting skill, when I remembered that to do so would be impolite Eskimo etiquette. Praise should come later, preferably after eating the hunter's game. Meanwhile, Nokadlak's weary dogs had to be tied to their line, and the sled's contents transferred to the igloo. This done, we shook the snow off our parkas and boots and entered the igloo. Old Grandmother Manerathiak must have awakened Angivrana because whe was sitting up. "The baby has come. It's only a girl," she said off-handedly.

"That's too bad," was Nokadlak's automatic reply. He took off his parka, shook it thoroughly to remove the remaining snow and ice and handed it to Manerathiak who hung it on the drying rack.

"It's cold outside," he commented to no one in particular, plucking off the icicles on his nostrils and his few chin hairs.

"It's freezing cold!" young Kudnanak readily added. Then he approached Angivrana, who was reclining on the *iglek* with his baby sister dozing in her arms, and sniffed at his mother's bulging breasts as a sign of filial affection as well as his appreciation for the breasts that had originally fed him. Whether by custom or taboo (I never did discover a definitive reason) Eskimos don't kiss on the mouth. Instead, they rub noses while inhaling at the same time. As crude as it may sound, it's not unlike canines sniffing each other's muzzles on first and subsequent encounters.

Kudnanak threw a cursory glance at his newborn sister and said mechanically, "It can't be helped! A little girl." He sat down on the *iglek* close to his father, pulled off his boots, hit them with a stick used to beat off snow, and gave them to his grandmother. Reaching for a dry parka and short caribou boots stored at the rear of the *iglek*, he put them on. Nokadlak did the same.

"Come and have tea!" proclaimed Manerathiak. She filled a cup and slowly brought it to Nokadlak, muttering "I'm an old woman," to explain her slowness and apologize for any sloppiness she caused. She served me next, then Kudnanak, Angivrana, and herself. Everyone ate some frozen fish and caribou meat with slabs of caribou fat set before us in a sealskin container.

Airing her uppermost thoughts, Manerathiak ventured

tentatively, "My mother was called Naoyak. Only one bears her name now. My mother could sew very well. She could snare weasels and ground squirrels, and. . . ."

Her subtle suggestion was instantly received. "Naoyak, Naoyak, we'll call her Naoyak!" declared Nokadlak.

Customarily, the husband decides whether or not to keep female newborns and now that was over, at least. I sighed with relief as I considered the name. Naoyak meant "seagull." It sounded fine to me; far better, in fact, than so many Eskimo names which originate in rank obscenity. And it seemed to be appropriate for the little girl, although—like other Eskimo names—it could just as easily have been used for a boy.

Great-grandmother Naoyak, I thought, now the aimless wanderings of your forlorn and lamented soul are over! According to your tribal beliefs, your refuge is in this newborn child. You are again a member of the group, and the spirits of all who bore this name in past generations will protect the little girl. But for how long? Her father had yet given no indication.

Politely waiting till her husband had made himself comfortable, and noticing traces of blood between his fingers and on his forearms, Angivrana said to Nokadlak, "I see you had good luck on the hills."

"It was not too bad. We traveled a lot. To Baillie Bay in the Arctic Sound the first day and visited Kakagun. On the second day we went inland, along the Hood River. We brought back enough for a few days," he concluded modestly.

"Father shot a musk-ox and a wolverine!" Kudnanak interjected excitedly.

With willing pride, Nokadlak began to describe the incident in a monotone of deliberate words, punctuated from time to time by Naoyak's crying.

"We had no luck at all on our first morning out," he recalled. "It was too windy. But in the afternoon, we saw wolverine tracks. I made a small tunnel with blocks of snow and put some caribou meat inside it. I tied one end of a length of sinew around the meat and the other end around the trigger of my old rifle, which I also hid in the snow tunnel. Then we drove off to look for game."

Eager to contribute, Kudnanak interjected, "Nuliayuk, the Spirit Mother of all wild creatures, was good to us. My father shot a fox that had just killed a hare. So we got them both with only one bullet!"

"That's so," confirmed Nokadlak, "and Kudnanak helped me shoot many ptarmigans along the river bank. They were feeding on willow buds and were very fat. But the next day was

15

stormy and we didn't leave the igloo we made on the river."

"Father and I thought we had offended Nuliayuk, so we hung ptarmigans' feet on our weasel-fur parkas that night. The Spirit Mother of all animals was good to us after that," said Kudnanak solemnly.

"Yes," acknowledged Nokadlak. "My old rifle killed the wolverine right between the eyes. It will make beautiful trimming for the hoods of our parkas."

"And on the way back we sighted a small herd of musk-oxen and my Father shot one of them. It was really big!" the youngster added irrepressibly, spreading his arms for emphasis.

"The Police might not like that," I interposed involuntarily, knowing full well, as did every Eskimo hunter in the Bathurst Inlet territory, that killing musk-oxen was forbidden by White Man's law. But nobody saw me. Besides, we didn't kill any caribou on this trip, so we needed food," said Nokadlak defending his illegal act.

Grandmother Manerathiak, who apparently had not missed a word, added this recollection: "I remember old Natkuhiak saying that musk-oxen were plentiful inland during his younger days. He told me they had lots of meat and fuel and skins then. But one summer the ice did not melt on the sea. A blizzard struck. Cold rain was followed by sleet; then heavy frost mantled the land. Ice, thick and slippery, encrusted everything—rocks, moss, and weeds. Musk-oxen drifted side by side with the caribou towards the sea. The terrible season pushed them clear off the land. They were not strong enough to break the ice and fill their bellies with grass. Hunger killed them right and left, and many of our people also died during that long winter. Since then we have often starved."

"Well, Grandmother, we are not going to starve today!" said Nokadlak brightly, and everyone laughed in appreciation.

I could well understand Manerathiak's viewpoint. Freezing and hunger are constant shadows that dog the Eskimos. This is the main reason they continually wander back and forth across the primeval and cruel Barren Land in an all-consuming search for food. In their desolate homeland of rocks, permafrost, snow, and freezing winds, the odds are heavily loaded in favor of nature's vagaries. The blizzard remains their chief enemy, although a spot of open water on the sea ice, the loss of a few dogs, or a bad shot from a rifle, can quickly also contribute to tragedy.

Angivrana listened with interest to our conversation as she fed her child and cleaned Naoyak's tiny reddish body with the silky fur of an Arctic hare, or simply with her tongue. At times she would tell her husband, "The child has messed up my back while sleeping," and Nokadlak would obligingly lick her back clean. Once, when she lifted the baby toward her face, I again saw the bluish spot at the base of the baby's spine. It was indubitably the Mongoloid mark, which sometimes spreads across the buttocks, but eventually fades or disappears in adolescence.

At one point, Angivrana wrapped her naked babe in the skin of a caribou calf and placed her on the furs covering the *iglek*. Then she donned her parka, stood up slowly, and used the conventional euphemism: "I think I shall get some fresh air." On her way to the porch she picked up a stick to fend off the young dogs who were always there, ready to clean up any feces.

After she returned to the *iglek*, Nokadlak reached the end of his proud narrative. Though he seemed to be tired and drowsy in the friendly glow of the blubber lamp and warmth of family life, he still retained his good mood as he turned and spoke to his wife, "Remember the good hunter Kakagun who helped us in the past when we had no food? He has a boy who ought to be a good hunter too, some day. Kakagun asked me once to keep a girl for his son. We will keep Naoyak for him."

I uttered a silent prayer of thanksgiving to God for preserving the little girl's life. I was especially glad to hear that Kakagun was to be the adopted father, for I knew he was one of the best hunters in the Central Arctic, as well as a fast friend. Whenever I met him, he would call out to me: 'Hey there, Little Man, come and stay in my igloo and tell me stories about God!' And in return, he would recount tales about the Spirits of the Land and the Souls of the Dead. His wife, Kablunak, an energetic, and proud woman with the fine fetures of white girl (as her name betokened), would take care of my clothes while teaching me words I couldn't understand and make me repeat them. Often she would laugh, and Kakagun would roar himself hoarse, because many of these words, I found later, pertained to intimate parts of the human body. But all this was done in good old-fashioned Eskimo fun.

Angivrana and the old grandmother seemed more relaxed now, but Kudnanak remained indifferent to his father's decision to bring up his little sister.

That night, as I crawled into my sleeping bag, after Angivrana, Nokadlak and Kudnanak had undressed and gone to sleep in their large family bag with the baby between them, I remembered the morning a native named Mangaluk came running into the Mission at Bathurst.

"*Fala, Fala!*" he cried when he saw me.

"What is it?"

"My child, my little child, he has lost his breath."

"You mean your child is dead? What happened?"

"He died in the night. I and my wife killed the Little Man without knowing it. We crushed his chest between us while we were sleeping. It's truly hopeless. He is dead."

Two years later Mangaluk and his wife "accidentally" killed another child in much the same way. This time it was a girl. But, in true Eskimo style, rather than accept responsibility, they attributed it to their inevitable destiny in the Barren Land. "There is indeed nothing we can do about it," they rationalized.

This terse dismissal of tragedy encompasses the stark hopelessness of the Eskimo philosophy. He simply accepts life as it comes. Death is everywhere; for to live here is to kill unsparingly, why couldn't it be as right to kill a man as to kill a caribou or seal?

Manerathiak was the last to get ready for bed, lingering by both stone lamps to lower their flames to a single wick. She reached into the excavation under the *iglek* for a musk-ox skull that served as a chamber pot, and took it over to her own corner. Mumbling and groaning to herself, the tired old woman undressed with pain and crept into her own bedding, using her folded parka as a pillow. "I feel worse every day," she soliloquized. "I feel like a woman with child. Oh, a child! Of what use am I now?" When she began to sing the song, though, little Naoyak had been kept alive:

> Yae, yae, ya, haya ...
> I'm but an old woman
> Remembering old times
> When I was willing and happy
> To be of use to my husband
> And nursing my little girl
> Spared from a sad death. Aye, yae, yae ...
> But who knows one's destiny?
> Here I lie, old and useless,
> With only my memories to help me. Ya, ya, yae ...

Although I'd had a fairly strenuous and eventful day, my anxiety for little Naoyak would not let me sleep; nor did the various sounds in the dimly lit igloo. Manerathiak's whisperings and incantations crescendoed in the gloom, but were drowned out occasionally either by the baby's wails or Nokadlak's heavy snoring, coughing, or spitting. I could see his head and Angivrana's close together resting on the edge of the *iglek*, a couple of feet above the packed snow floor. Steady streams of vapor rose from their mouths and nostrils in rhythm with their breathing. When the vapors hit the 10'-high dome of the igloo, they became tiny snow crystals that fell lightly on the sleepers. But the edges of their *krepik* (sleeping bag) were fringed with thick caribou fur that moved with their breathing and bodily movements, and shook it off, leaving their faces perfectly dry.

Conversely, the diuretic action of the tea affected everybody. Sooner or later someone would pick up a container, slip it carefully inside the *krepik* and urinate. The acrid smell from the makeshift chamber pots was anything but soporific. Only the cries of the newborn were reassuring.

Despite my weariness, I couldn't sleep. I lay inertly, half-dreaming, half-thinking about my own childhood and events that led me to become a missionary in this harsh, desolate land.

Unlike Naoyak, I was born the fourth of wanted children amid comfortable surroundings in the benign island climate of French Corsica, off the west coast of Italy. My birthplace was the hamlet of Coccola (which reflects our family name), built upon a rocky headland centuries ago, when native Corsicans were zealously independent. Like a watchtower, the high-perched Coccola commanded an immense view of the Tyrrhenian Sea and, whenever residents spotted pirate boats, their horn blowing and smoke signals gave ample warning to the neighboring villages.

Spending my childhood in semi-tropical splendor, I exulted in the island's seemingly endless white sandy beaches and tiny secret coves. I spied at its ancient towers and modern villas half-hidden from curious eyes by fragrant pine trees. Beyond them lay towering mountains with slopes of chestnut forests, orange groves, and terraced vineyards.

Our home was in the hamlet's centre. For miles around, the groves and vineyards belonged to my father. He often took me horseback riding over the verdant hills scented with rosemary, and during the spring and summer months, down to the seashore for a dip in the warm water. Mother did not accompany us on those idyllic rides. She remained home, keeping an eye on my three brothers and three sisters, busying herself with the many chores of a large household presiding over the servants, giving advice to the villagers, and helping my father administer the estate.

When I reached school age, I went to a lyceum in Bastia, the nearest town. Before my parents discovered that this boys' school could not control my independent spirit, I had spent much time getting into trouble. But when they did, they promptly transferred me to a boarding college at Thonon les-Bains in France's Haute Savoie Department, close to the shores of Lac Leman (Lake Geneva). This private school was operated by

19

the Jesuit Fathers, who are known the world over as conscientious teachers and strict disciplinarians.

In sharp contrast to the Eskimos almost total lack of parental discipline, the Jesuit Fathers supervised not only classes, but recess, 'home-work' sessions, play periods, meal times, church services, sports and recreation, and the dormitories.

We were awakened at 5 a.m. daily, except Sundays and holy days when we were allowed an extra two hours' sleep. On weekdays, we were given a half hour to wash and dress, and then taken to the chapel for mass until 6:30 a.m. After the church service, we were required to study until 7:20 a.m., when we vacated the study room and proceeded to the refectory for breakfast. This usually consisted of *cafe au lait* (coffee with milk), bread, butter, and cold meat.

At 8 a.m. we returned to our respective dormitories (there were two) to make our beds and prepare for classes at 8:30. These lasted until noon, with a half hour recess at 10:30 in the school yard. Dinner at mid-day was consumed in silence, broken only by one student reading a book, usually authored by an explorer or missionary, such as Father Armand David, a Lazarist missionary and veteran explorer-naturalist who traveled in China and Mongolia in the 19th century, discovering scores of plants and animals foreign to the West. Other writers who made their mark on my memory included Spanish monks and Jesuits in South America and the Central States. From the writings of more recent explorers we heard about the opening up of the Northwest Territories, as well as the exploits of Canada's *coureurs de bois* (forest runners of travelers), Arctic explorers, and missionaries. In short, we learned a lot while eating.

Formal classes resumed at 2 p.m. and ended two hours later. We were then given an hour for recreation, after which we were escorted back into the study room at 5 o'clock. Supper from 6 to 7 was succeeded by an hour's recreation, followed by a half hour's study.

It was prayers in the chapel from 8:30 to 9, and then bedtime. We were literally under the Jesuit Fathers' supervision around the clock.

French, my mother tongue, alternated with compulsory Latin and Greek languages in all our studies. Not a word of English—let alone Eskimo—did I learn at school. Actually, I picked up my first few English words aboard the *Empress of Australia* en route to Canada in 1937. With my oblate confreres, I always spoke French. It was years before I learned enough English from Arctic traders and policemen to get by. Reading some of their English books also helped me slowly build a fair understanding of their language. But without opportunity to practise, my 'foreign' accent remained. In truth, my frequent use of Eskimo also affected my English and even my French pronunciation that, when I would return to France ten years later, some people would question my nationality!

When I was almost through college, father moved our family to Paris so all my brothers and sisters could obtain a university education. I was reunited with my family there three years later, but did not enroll in a university. Instead, I resolved to make amends for my misguided youth by joining the Oblate Fathers, who specialized in the world's toughest missions, and I set my sights on the greatest challenge they offered—service in the Central Arctic.

By the sharpest contrasts, my training for such a rigorous assignment was based at *Notre Dame des Lumieres* (Our Lady of Lights) near the town of Avignon ('where everyone dances,' according to a popular French song). Situated in the most benign and beautiful part of Southern France—the Provence—it's blessed with such fascinating Mediterranean ports as Marseille, historic cities as Toulon, and boasts such tourist paradises as the *Cote d' Azur* (Azure or Sky Blue Coast) and the Riviera with their Cannes and Nice, a near-neighbor of renowned Monaco. Just as my native Corsica, *La Belle Provence* (the Beautiful Provence) is also long-famed for its mild sub-tropical climate, evergreen farmlands and forests, celebrated fruit orchards, vineyards and wineries, as well as its glorious rivers like the Rhone, its many delightful Mediterranean beaches, and its modern air, land, and sea communications.

When morning and reality finally came my nocturnal reverie ended, along with my needless worry about Naoyak's safety. Apart from waking to suckle, she had slept comfortably next to her parents warm bodies and was still very much alive.

Her Grandmother Manerathiak, who was tossing about fitfully during the pre-dawn hours, was the first to rise and busy herself with the stone lamp. After a while, she took her snow knife and went outside to fetch some fresh snow to melt in the kettle.

Since her family was together once more, I considered returning to my Mission after breakfast. Then I noticed that Nokadlak and Angivrana had also awakened and that Grandmother was welcoming them back to consciousness with cups of hot tea. Lying on his stomach, Nokadlak sipped his tea between bites on a big chunk of frozen meat also supplied by Manerathiak. He finished his breakfast in high spirits and he, Angivrana and

Kudnanak decided to get up. He pulled on his breeches, sat on the edge of the *iglek*, and began to pluck with his fingernails the few hairs growing on his chin, upper lips, and nostrils. I couldn't help laughing because he made such funny faces under the prickly pain. He looked at me, smiled, and said, "You should do the same. Then you wouldn't have ice on your face when you travel."

I knew that ice forms on eyebrows and whiskers in the intense cold, but brushed off his suggestion jokingly with "If I cut off my beard, I'll look like a girl!" He chuckled appreciatively, then made a gross remark that would have shocked a trooper. It included a word resembling my surname, which in Eskimo sounds close to one that denotes the sexual act. Frankly, that's why I never revealed my family name to the Eskimos. They had enough fun calling me variously by my nickname, the Little Man, "*Fala Kremo*" (The closest most of them could come to pronouncing Father Raymond), or simply '*Fala*' for short.

The Eskimo mind naturally gravitates to what, by our standards, is obscene. Their jokes, stories, and games all have a down-to-earth quality which they don't consider lewd. To avoid encouraging them, I shunned all opportunities, but can't honestly say I always succeeded.

Upon completing his facial depilatory, Nokadlak suddenly exclaimed, "Oh, but I had a wonderful dream last night! You should all hear about it." Then, sucking his fingers and belching with satisfaction, he warmed up to his story: "As I said, it was a beautiful dream. I was a young man again, and I was hunting musk-oxen. I spied one, a solitary bull, about the same time he saw me. He came charging at me, with his eyes aflame and his little tail in the air..." Nokadlak didn't finish his tale. Instead, as if awakening to reality, he asked his mother-in-law, "How is the weather?"

"I don't know," Manerathiak replied. "When I went out to get snow for the tea, it was blowing a bit. I'll have to look again." Taking the snow knife to cut her way through the outer entrance of the porch, she crawled out.

"The wind is rising" she reported. "The sky is cloudy. Drifting snow is blanketing the dogs. It doesn't look good."

If the old Grandmother was right, I thought, I'd better delay my return trip. Meanwhile, with another sudden Arctic storm in the offing, there was no time to waste.

Angivrana had nudged her son and told him to start dressing and help his father. When Kudnanak saw his father almost dressed, he obeyed sleepily and soon joined us outside.

We never did hear the outcome of Nokadlak's dreamy

encounter with the raging musk-ox. It was more important to us all that Manerathiak, like a reliable, old fashioned barometer, had correctly forecast an approaching blizzard.

2

Pirtok, The Blizzard

As the storm picked up its tempo in the depressing polar darkness, Nokadlak seemed apprehensive. Silently he studied the direction of the wind, already gusting fine snow along the frozen land. Then he began to cut blocks of snow with his knife and angle them like a shield onto the entrance of the igloo porch. The icy blasts and the driving snow would surely follow as soon as the blizzard reached its height.

Turning to Kudnanak, who was playing with a pup, Nokadlak said, "The *pirtok* is definitely coming. Check the dogs and cut snow blocks to shelter them. Then put away the guns, the ice chisel, and the scoop. And don't forget the harnesses!"

I thought it wise to take similar precautions with my dogs and equipment. Cutting three large snow blocks for each dog, I arranged them in a half-circle close enough to the animal to deflect the bitter wind.

Kudnanak had removed the rifles from his father's sled and stacked them in the shelter of the porch. He knew enough not to carry them into the igloo where condensation would form on the metal parts and they might rust or freeze when taken outside again. He then cut two snow blocks and put them ten feet apart to set the sled on top of them, thus ensuring it would not be snowed under. Also, as bidden, the boy collected all the dog harnesses and placed them on the sled beside a 10-foot long chisel and an equally long-handled scoop made of musk-ox horn. Later, like any other skilled Eskimo, he would make a hole in the thick winter ice with the chisel, and then clear out the ice chips with the scoop until water rushed to the surface. Over this indispensable equipment Kudnanak placed a large caribou-skin cover and lashed the bundle securely to the sled with long, narrow bands of seal hide.

I was going through a similar routine with my sled when I saw Grandmother emerge from the igloo and take the aired and dried caribou skins off the sticks planted in the snow. Normally Angivrana would look after this chore, but Manerathiak did so because of her daughter's baby. The old woman carried the skins into the igloo in bundles of four or five, making several return trips. No matter how long the storm might last, she, at least, would have plenty to do. Decidedly, she wasn't half as useless as she would have herself believe!

Nokadlak called to me: "Do you need some help with your sled?" "Yes, I certainly do!" I shouted back. My sled was twenty-two feet long and I didn't want to unload all my equipment. He came closer, suggesting we shove the sled atop the igloo where it was less likely to get snowed under. Who was I to argue?

With more prudent foresight, Nokadlak had cut several blocks of virgin snow which was the first snow to fall three months earlier. Mixed with lumps of frozen rain it had a greater water content. He handed one block to Kudnanak to take inside, then leaned the rest against the outside of the igloo. This would be the family's water supply at least during the *pirtok*. Finally, he blocked the porch entrance a couple of feet high to deflect drifting snow and joined the rest of his family. I followed him in.

Angivrana was nursing her baby. Kudnanak was munching a slab of dried fish. Manerathiak welcomed us with, "Have some dry fish. I'll make tea soon."

"We have taken care of everything outside," Nokadlak declared with evident pride in his foresight and concern for the family. "I didn't notice any chinks in the walls of the igloo. If any snow sifts through, I can patch them from here."

"I don't think anything will come through these walls," said Manerathiak flatteringly. "I remember how well you built this igloo. Angivrana and I helped to fill the few chinks. You laid the blocks tightly together."

Gratified, Nokadlak smiled. "My father was a good hunter and provider. He taught me how to built the best igloo in our land. Before he chose a site, he would say to me, 'Now, look. To find the best spot, go around and feel out the snow with the rod or knife, as if it were a living creature.' He would point out that the warmest place to built an igloo is over the ice, above a lake, or even a river, because the water there is not as cold as frozen ground. And if we were inland with no ice available, my father would then look for a deep snowdrift. It would keep the igloo off the ground.

"Even when I was a boy no older than Kudnanak, I tried to build igloos like my father. I remember one time a boy I knew challenged me to see who could make a better igloo. Not only did I build a better one, but I finished first and had a good laugh at his expense! Since then I have always been proud of my igloos." And he laughed. In fact we all chuckled with Nokadlak, and I, for one, felt his infectious confidence allay my misgiving in the face of the blizzard.

As he crowed on, I recalled my first impression of the inside of an igloo when I arrived in the Arctic fifteen months earlier. It was located at a place called Aniarhiaurvik, where four families lived in four separate igloos, joined together by high-arched passages with niches above ground for storing equipment, fish, and meat. In the glow of blubber lamps, the snow walls glittered warm and friendly, while children added life and laughter with their hide-and-seek games. Caribou skins were spread out on the *igleks* where most adults occupied themselves with sewing, scraping of caribou skins, or mending of dog harnesses. The remaining few rested, telling ribald stories in an atmosphere of good humored camaraderie.

More genteel tales were contributed by Milukhuk, a skinny woman with a tattooed forehead. Her chin and cheeks were scarred with deep vertical lines, not unlike miniature pressure ridges of Arctic ice. "One day *Orpik*, the Owl, decided to go hunting," she began. "He hadn't gone far from his nest when he saw the Ground Squirrel, standing in front of his entrance hole. The owl sat down and started to sing, 'Aye-aye-ye-ye. . .Come to me, my friend, come to me and bring me a present. . .Aye-ya-aye-ye. . .'

"As the Squirrel moved ahead to offer a present, the Owl hopped right in front of the Squirrel's hole in the ground. Not to be outsmarted, the Squirrel said flatteringly, 'You're a big, strong owl. Place your feet apart and show me the greatness of your chest!'

"Accepting the compliment, the Owl obliged. 'Wider, wider!' urged the Squirrel. Pleased no end, the Owl spread his legs as far as he possibly could, while inhaling more air to swell his chest. 'That's beautiful!' exclaimed the Squirrel as he darted between the Owl's legs, biting the latter's crotch before disappearing into his underground home."

Even though the plot was predictable, Milukhuk's listeners manifested delight, waiting patiently for the *pirtok* to blow itself out. And why not? They had no reason to rush anywhere. To them, time and distance didn't matter. They had lots of it to take things easily or go where they wanted to and eke out a living. Although the Arctic had conditioned them to a frigid existence I could see that the warm spark of humanity glowed brighter in them than people in more temperated climes.

I remembered being taken aback by the peculiar odor permeating the four igloos when I first entered them. I could not analyze it then, but eventually learned that it came not only from a mixture of furs, skins, dried fish, and game, but also from the acrid smell of burnt seal oil or caribou fat, and plain humanity. But there was no offending stench of unwashed bodies, offal, or excrements, either animal or human. The ever-present puppies took immediate care of that. Thus the word *tipartok*, meaning it stinks, was used only as a joke when someone passed gas.

And now Nokadlak's igloo was no exception. It had the same odors, but even a white man's nose eventually gets used to this effluvium. Instead, his sense of sight takes over. He notices the exact disposition of the blubber lamps and the drying racks above them, the masses of caribou skins and sleeping bags spread out on the *iglek*. He spies the pots and cups and other vessels lying askew around the soapstone lamp, the frozen caribou skins and seal carcasses heaped up on the floor near the tiny door, the bundles of frozen fish and dried meat, wasted bones and sundry pieces of fur and feather piled in a corner.

Snow serves as a carpet, and a slab of ice near the top of the igloo as a window. Blubber lamps supply most of what light there is, as well as heat for cooking. Because the inside temperature must be kept slightly above freezing, the lamp wicks are lowered with a flat bone resembling a spatula. If thawing begins, a piece of caribou fur stuffed into the ventilation hole in the igloo's dome is removed. Called the *krignak*, or nostril, by the Eskimos, this hole acts as a valve to control the igloo's temperature.

What struck me more than the physical appearance of an igloo was the friendly attitude of its occupants. The moment even a complete stranger entered the igloo, he became a welcome friend who could share whatever his hosts had for as long as he wished. Hot tea, hot broth or both were invariably served in unlimited quantities to help remove the depressing Arctic chill, and—so long as there was blubber or tallow or other food on hand—the guest became part of the family. I don't know of any other place in the world where you can tumble into people's houses without ceremony or warning and, merely by saying, "I have come from such and such a place. I was on the trail many days. My dogs are tired," you would at once be made the center of friendly greetings and open kindness. That was the way Nokadlak's family had accepted me and reciprocal feelings stirred within me. I wished I could somehow help them combat the storm. But, obviously, nothing could be done except sit it out in the igloo with my hosts.

Now and then, Nokadlak looked through a peephole and listened to the wind and the snow pattering on the frozen floor. "It is really drifting hard!" was his predictable comment. With the driven snow sifting relentlessly through minute chinks and weaknesses in the snow blocks, it seemed a superfluous observation. But his family accepted it as other North Americans might receive a radio weather report. Angivrana or her old Mother would add, "Yes, but I hope it won't last many days. Our meat supply is not very high." Though the danger of starvation during a prolonged storm is evident to the Eskimo, no one seemed particularly worried.

Nokadlak's wise, weatherbeaten face bespoke confidence and apparent unconcern towards the all-pervading terror of this frozen land—starvation. And yet there was something in his eyes I could not quite identify. Beyond his strength and self-assurance I thought I detected a hint of brooding depression, a hopelessness beyond redemption. Breaking through his thoughts, I asked, "Have you ever starved?"

Without a moment's hesitation he answered, "Little Man, this is part of our life. We always starve once in a while. The last time the caribou didn't come in the spring. Hilla, the Weather Spirit, took over. Storm after storm chased the caribou away. We nearly starved to death. My son Kudnanak was growing thinner and weaker all the time. Many of our people died that spring. And many dogs, too."

Nokadlak said little more as he quietly busied himself mending dog harnesses with caribou sinew and a triangular-shaped steel needle he had acquired at the trading post. He was not one to prostrate himself on the *iglek*, plunged into a sad stupor, as I've seen some Eskimos do during a *pirtok*. His even temperament prompted him to find some useful occupation to combat his restlessness and boredom. He acted like a true Inuk, supermen in their own estimation, men of excellence, tough and independent. He was a strong, happy, proud provider for his family no matter what hardships.

I excused myself and crawled into the porch for a closer look at the *pirtok*. In the polar semi-darkness and swirling snow I couldn't see a footstep ahead, so I wasted no time returning to comparative warmth of the igloo.

From my very first day in the Central Arctic shivering in

28

"summer" temperatures, I realized how inadequate my formal "preparation" was. I came to North America's cruel, primitive, and sparsely populated Land Beyond, knowing no English nor the language, customs, or traditions of the Inuit, its indigenous people, whom I was to serve as a missionary. I had no means of transportation until new pups were born in the spring. I had never seen a dogsled, nor had the dimmest idea of hitching and handling a dog team. In a land where every native male depended on his skill with firearms, traps, and spears to feed himself and his dependents, I hadn't a clue how to use these vital weapons. Why, I had never seen, let alone built even a small emergency igloo, the traditional nomadic Eskimo shelter, not to mention the family-sized igloo, such as the one whose expertly fitted snow blocks now protected Nokadlak's family and me from nature's vagarie.

Furthermore, my formal education had been regulated by seemingly medieval traditions, established by frustrated old men in Rome's high places, apparently with little inkling of the basic needs and longings of the human soul. How unlike their Master Who is all kindness, understanding and love.

So here I was—a "trained" missionary, ostensibly skilled in teaching Christianity—still learning the hard way how to survive among people I hoped to eventually understand and love.

On its first day the *pirtok* howled without let-up. We could barely step outside to feed the dogs. When we did, we carried our snow knives just in case we got lost and had to build ourselves a temporary shelter. To do so without a snow knife in such a blizzard—even a few steps away from Nokadlak's igloo—would be tantamount to courting untimely death.

Nokadlak had no conception of speed measurements, of course, but in an average Arctic storm (I found out in later years) wind velocities can exceed 80 miles an hour. Yet the *pirtok* is far less savage than the treacherous *uyaluk,* which is a sudden strike of hurricane-force winds over a few square miles. However, the oft-recurring *pirtok* with its persistent, inexorable pounding by snow-laden winds, is just as fearsome as the *uyaluk* to the People Beyond.

Like Nokadlak, her industrious son-in-law, Manerathiak kept busy as the storm continued. Squatting in a corner of the *iglek,* with a caribou skin secured between her knees, she was removing the remnants of fat and meat with a spoon-like scraper made of musk-ox horn. As she worked rhythmically with her right arm, her grandson crept up behind her, surprising her with, "Grandmother, tell me about Tarakapfaluk, the Spirit who lives at the Bottom of the Sea."

"Oh, it's you Kudnanak! I thought you were sleeping. So you want to know about the Spirit of Food who lives in the darkness of the sea. Her name was Tara. She was a little girl who didn't like men. But one day a bird of the sea came and took the form of a handsome man. And she fell in love with him.

"When Tara's father discovered this, he stole into her tent and took her away in his kayak. The bird got mad and blew up a big storm. Tara's father became frightened and threw her overboard. In terror she grabbed the side of the kayak, but her father cut off her arms with his snow knife, starting with her fingers, wrists, and forearms. As these pieces fell into the water, they turned into fish and seals. And as for Tara, she sank to the darkness of the sea and became the Spirit Mother of all Sea Food. She is still there. But now we call her Tarakapfaluk, the Big Tara. Oh, yes, I almost forgot. One day, when her father came to the bottom of the sea, she made him a Guardian Spirit in the Land of the Dead."

"*Goanna*, Grandmother," Kudnanak thanked her. "Now I can rest some more."

The old woman returned to her thoughts, interspersing her mutterings with monotonous songs about her lost children, her wonderful lovers of old, (Eskimo girls often have sex before marriage) and her deceased friends. In the relative stillness of the igloo her low humming was distinctly audible as she sang:

"I'm afraid and I tremble
When I remember my father and mother
Seeking the wandering game,
Struggling on the empty land
Weakened by hunger. *Eya, ya, ya. . .*

I'm afraid and I tremble
When I recall their bones
Scattered on the low land,
Broken by prowling beasts,
Their skulls swept away by winds. Eya, ya, ya. . .

I'm afraid and I tremble
When the Spirit of the Deep
Comes to see me at night
To take my soul away
To the Land of the Dead. *Eya, ya, eye, ya. . .*"

I glanced at Angivrana. With her baby fed and asleep in the hood of her parka, she was now returned to household chores. Having scraped the stiff, bluish spots caused by wetness off the

30

heavy parka her husband had worn on his hunting trip, she carefully checked every seam and, finding a couple of small tears, mended them expertly with a glove needle and caribou sinew. Her face showed no emotion as she said wistfully, "It won't be long before we give Naoyak away to Naodluak, the son of Kakagun. I wonder if the hunting is good where they are?"

"When I saw Kakagun at Kattimanek, he was doing well," Nokadlak told his wife. "There's usually game there, and he's a clever hunter."

"My father is a capable hunter, too," chimed in Kudnanak, suddenly animated as the conversation touched his favorite topic. "I'll have a good dog team soon to help him."

"Yes, certainly," agreed his Grandmother, smiling. "Your father is a great hunter. He has never let us starve to death." She left unsaid what this actually meant to her. For had Nokadlak not been a good provider, she would have been discarded on the trail long ago as a useless chattel.

By association, my thoughts turned to Naoyak. The baby had awakened and was crying for her next meal. Angivrana swung the child off her back under her left arm, and cradled her between her bulging breasts under the parka, all the while rocking back and forth, humming and singing this plaintive ditty:

> Eya, eya, ie, ie. . .
> Where did she go, where did she come from—
> Naoyak, the Seagull?
> She came from the rising sun,
> She came from the sea. Eya, eya, ie, ie. . .
> Alas! She will fly away soon
> To the land of happy hunting,
> Not to return again—
> Naoyak, the Seagull. Aya, aya, eya, ie, ie. . ."

I thought it was touching for Angivrana to give verbal expression to her natural love for the child. I, too, wondered how soon Naoyak might be delivered to Kakagun's family. Since the nomadic Eskimos seldom know ahead when they may see their friends again, a promised girl is often adopted by her future in-laws almost from birth. They bring her up as their daughter, with great care and love until their son decides to leave and set up housekeeping with her.

On the other hand, once their girl is adopted by another family, her natural parents are free to try to have a son right away. (It takes three to four years for an Eskimo child to be weaned.) Its mother will seldom have another child during that time and I speculated whether or not this fact of Eskimo genetics was a reward for the thousands of years they had suffered extraordinary abuse from their environment. Whatever the answer, every man knows that he faces limited years as an active provider and cannot wait indefinitely for male children to help him care for his family when his own strength deteriorates.

My presence and the family's did not seem to bother Naoyak at all as she fed contendedly on her mother's warm, rich milk. But while the infant snuggled comfortably up to her mother's bosom, oblivious to the world around her, her parents became more apprehensive. The seething *pirtok* seemed to be reaching new heights. No one spoke much any more. Nokadlak was paying less attention to mending the dog harnesses than to mending cracks in the walls as winds pounded on the igloo like freight trains, lowering the temperature and driving snow drifts before them.

We all drank tea more often to keep warm. But, unlike the native broths of caribou or fish heads, or animal bones with their abundant nourishment, the "glowing" effect of tea was passing at best, merely increasing our trips to the porch. The puppies out there were curled up like giant fur doughnuts, huddling close to each other and waiting for their next meal. They neither stirred nor bothered us, but watched us with understandable curiosity.

It was Nokadlak who broke the uncomfortable silence. Turning towards his son, he volunteered: "Kudnanak, I have a story to tell you. It's about the White Man and the Indians, and how they came to our land. Once upon a time, a girl call Minguyok refused to take a husband. Her father got very upset and took her and his dog in his kayak to a small island in Pelly Lake. He pitched a tent and left his daughter there alone with the dog. Minguyok had no choice of companions, so eventually the dog took her and she gave birth to many pups. Her father came to the island once in a while with fish and meat for them, so they would not starve. When the pups grew up, Minguyok said to them one day, 'Your grandfather is coming to bring us food. Swim out to meet him; then overturn his kayak!' The young dogs ran to the water, swam out to the kayak, and turned it upside down. Minguyok's father drowned, punished because he forced her to marry a dog. But now there was no one to bring food to the island dwellers. So Minguyok took off the soles of her boots, placed them in the lake and they promptly expanded into two boats. She put some of the dogs into one boat and told them to go into the world beyond and learn all they could. They sailed away to a faraway land, and became White Men. It is said that all White Men are descended from them."

Nokadlak paused to let the legend sink in, then continued, "Loading the rest of the dogs aboard the other boat, Minguyok told them, 'Go and kill all the Inuit (Eskimos) to avenge the wrong your Grandfather did to me!'

"These dogs sailed away to a land where trees grew like men, and they became the Indians, who like to kill our people. But the White Men came and brought peace to our land."

"Thank you, thank you for the story, Father," said Kudnanak appreciatively. "But now we don't have to worry about an Indian attack; we have a White Man with us!" With everyone's eyes on me, they all laughed, temporarily forgetting the great storm outside.

At irregular intervals, out of courtesy to me as their guest, Angivrana and Manerathiak filled an open sealskin bag with choice bits of fish, dried meat, and caribou fat, placing it on the floor where we could all reach it. In between these semi-formal meals we helped ourselves to slices of frozen caribou whenever we felt so inclined.

Towards evening on the second day of the *pirtok*, with its howling still unabated, Kudnanak anticipated the supper meal by announcing, "I have stored away many caribou legs!" This revelation elicited a round of "Indeed that is delicious!" from his elders, as the youngster headed for the entrance to fetch the piece de resistance. I followed him out to see what he meant to do with the caribou legs, as well as to stretch my own.

From a niche in the wall of the passage, Kudnanak pulled out a half dozen front and hind caribou legs, throwing them all on the hard snow underfoot. Then, taking one leg at a time, he crushed the bones with the dull edge of a short axe. The pups gathered round expectantly, hoping for chunks of meat to fly in their direction, not daring to bite into the whole animal legs for fear of getting kicked for the impertinence.

Outside, despite the rumbling wind and grating snow, the dogs started to howl, no doubt anticipating their daily meal. But, at the moment, Kudnanak had only the family supper in mind. He was crushing the bones for their frozen marrow, the Eskimo's butter. I helped him fill a bag with pieces of marrow, and we returned inside.

Satisfied and warmed by his meal of meat, fat, and marrow, Nokadlak said to his son, "I'm going to feed the dogs." Kudnanak automatically accompanied him to the porch where he held back the pups while his father axed spoiled caribou meat into nine chunks of about two pounds each. Then he dumped them into the sealskin bag Kudnanak had brought from the igloo.

With the bag under one arm and the snow knife in the other hand, Nokadlak ventured out into the blizzard with me almost literally on his heels. We moved slowly, nearly crouched, carefully balanced against the wind, our backs to its icy blasts. All our dogs stood up, yapping and howling in the storm. Nokadlak went methodically up and down the dog line, dropping a chunk of meat to each half-starved animal. I gave my dogs slabs of dried meat and lumps of blubber, their usual ration on a trip. Keeping their tails curled between their legs for added warmth, the huskies devoured their rations. I felt genuinely sorry for them and wished I could find a better place for them to rest. I stroked them gently, rubbed their noses, and called them by their names—"Cleo, Ceasar, Dragon, Napo, Bobby." They were my true friends. I could always talk to them in this lonely land, for often there wasn't a soul around for scores (and sometimes hundreds of miles.)

Nokadlak yelled to me, "Come on, Little Man, let's go in!" We hurried back from our respective dog lines as fast as we could. Once in the shelter of the porch, Nokadlak pulled his parka over his head, exposing his bare, muscular torso, shook the snow off his garment, and replaced it before re-entering the igloo. Inside he knocked the snow off his leggings and handed them to his wife to place on the drying rack. I did likewise. Just like the rest of us, Nokadlak was ready for bed.

Unaccustomed to howling blizzards, I slept only intermittently. Awake, I mused on leaving the comforts of France and my beloved family. In the nonpareil city of Paris, I bid them adieu on a warm June day in 1937 when I was only 24 years old. Besides my parents, my three sisters (who were then attending the Sorbonne University) and my three brothers (who were studying at the Polytechnic College and the Medical University in the Latin Quarter), had gathered at the Gare de l'Est, or East Station, to see me off on the train that would take me to my ship at the port of Le Havre.

For my Mother, it was a painful moment. Yet with noble courage she held me in a final embrace, saying through tears, "You are going to a new world far away, a world that's hardly known. But no matter where you go, my dear Raymond, remember I shall always love you and will be waiting for your safe return!" Time after time when I was losing hope for my work in the Barren Land, her caring words gave me the strength I needed to carry on.

On the wharf at Le Havre I first met my traveling companion-to-be, Father Leonce Dehurtevent from Brittany, France, who would accompany me to the Arctic Coast. We sailed across the Atlantic aboard the *Empress of Australia*, a Canadian Pacific steamship destined to sink in the Atlantic Ocean during

World War II.

Debarking in historic Quebec City, we caught the west-bound trans-Canada, I marveled at its vastness, particularly the endless prairies. During our five-day layover in Edmonton, Alberta's capital city, Father Dehurtevent and I stayed with the Oblate Fathers at their Parish of St. Joachim, and they showed us around. Most memorable was our visit to the town of St. Albert, northwest of Edmonton, because its founders were the great missionaries of Canada's early days, such as Bishop Grandin and Father Lacomb.

From Edmonton our train traveled so slowly that local passengers wondered out loud if its engineers were visiting their trap lines along its tracks. It took twenty-four hours to reach Fort McMurray and Waterways, approximately 250 miles north of Edmonton. In those days McMurray, as locals called it, was a small village, while nearby Waterways had a salt mine. A resident priest showed us vast fields of surface tar in the adjacent forest from which his local Mission post and the Roman Catholic Hospital obtained their firewood.

In McMurray we boarded the Hudson's Bay Company's paddle steamer which was to take us 225 miles north to Fort Smith in a few days, but we were laid up for ten, waiting for the June ice to melt in the Athabaska River. We then made an uneventful run another 225 miles to Fort Smith, punctuated only by a brief stop at Fort Chipewyan on the eastern boundary of Wood Buffalo National Park, to let off some optimistic mining prospectors.

Our lazy days on the steamship ended upon our arrival at Fort Smith, the regional administrative centre for the NorthWest Territories, where we spent a week helping the resident Oblate Fathers and Brothers load the 100-foot-long Mission barge with a 1,000-ton capacity. She would be pushed ahead for better control along the sand bars and the tricky river currents by the tugboat *Santa Anna*. The Brothers were engineers and navigation pilots taking supplies to all the Missions—from the Slave River to Fort Resolution on the southeast shores of Great Slave Lake, Hay River near the mouth of the said river, then down the formidable Mackenzie River to Fort Providence, Fort Simpson, Norman Wells, Fort Good Hope, Arctic Red River, and Aklavik.

At Aklavik, some 100 miles from the sea, we relieved the barge of all supplies destined for the Arctic Coast Missions, as "our" barge had to return to Fort Smith to pick up additional supplies for Missions along the Mackenzie River, as well as inland. In all, there were more than twenty-five Oblate Missions and outposts in the Arctic at that time, many of them also providing their own schools and hospitals.

At Aklavik, too, the Missions' schooner or masted tugboat *Our Lady of Lourdes* was waiting for us and being fitted for our journey to Tuktuyaktuk and thence eastward along the Arctic Coast to distant Burnside. Built at a cost of $25,000 in Vancouver, British Columbia, she had been transported to Tuktuyaktuk aboard another boat, the *Audrey B*, owned by a Mr. Watson, an almost legendary Arctic trader and trapper. We loaded *Our Lady* with basic supplies mostly coal and lumber intended for the main Mission depot at Tuktuyaktuk. The bulk of our cargo, however, would be delivered there at cost by Hudson's Bay Company's barges for subsequent transfer to *Our Lady of Lourdes*.

Although we arrived in Tuktuyaktuk the second week of July, owing to uncertain ice conditions in the Amundsen Gulf, we had to wait until August 10 before our skipper, Father William Griffin of Texas, gave the departure order for the first delivery of supplies to a new Mission post some 300 miles away, where Father Dehurtevent was to remain. Father Griffin's motley crew on *Our Lady of Lourdes* comprised the pilot, Bill Trasher (half-Eskimo, half-Black), a whaler from San Francisco; Brother Kraut, the engineer, from Germany; Bishop P. Fallaize, who had made the first overland contact with Coppermine Eskimos; Father Biname from Belgium, and, of course, Father Dehurtevent and me.

It took us two days to reach the Anderson River at a place called Stanton, where the new Mission was to be built by Father Dehurtevent, and we left it in polar summer light the same day we arrived and unloaded its supplies. Our next port of call, the Paolatok Mission at Letty Harbor, lay another 300 miles further east. On the second day out we encountered heavy drifting ice off Baillie Island, but our skipper managed to enter a cove at Cape Bathurst.

A few miles away the Hudson's Bay Company's schooner *Fort St. James* was less fortunate. She was crushed by ice. Nearby, the Royal Canadian Mounted Police's 104-foot-long wooden motor schooner *St. Roch* (pronounced "Rock") was also in trouble—stuck in the ice. In the following decade she would make navigational history by becoming the first-ever vessel to traverse the Arctic's Northwest Passage from west to east (Explorer Roald Amundsen's *Gjoa* was the first to accomplish this feat circa 1906, but in the opposite direction). Moreover, by the start of 1943 the *St. Roch* would not only become the first ship to span the Passage in both directions, but also the only one to circumnavigate the North American continent!

What saved the *St. Roch* from the tragic fate of the *Fort St.*

James was the shape of her hull. Resembling an elongated egg, she was lifted up by the ice, though not without some damage. The crew of the *Fort St. James* walked across the ice to the comparative safety of the *St. Roch*. Meanwhile from Cape Bathurst, we watched the doomed *Fort St. James* sink tragically in about five hours. Yet, even the next day, the crow's nest atop her main mast remained visible above the drifting ice. As for the redoubtable *St Roch*, she had to be taken out for repairs at the first opportunity, to resume her Mounted Police patrol duties and ultimately win worldwide acclaim for her daring nautical accomplishments. From the crew of *Our Lady of Lourdes*, I found out that the *St. Roch* was commanded by R.C.M.P. Sergeant Henry Larsen (who would guide her on all her future triumphs), while the ill-fated *Fort St. James* was skippered by "Shorty" Summers. Both men were from Vancouver, Canada, where the *St. Roch* is now preserved for posterity in that beautiful city's maritime Museum. Eventually, I met and became friends with both of these courageous men.

On August 20, our own good ship *Our Lady of Lourdes* succeeded in delivering her remaining supplies to the Letty Harbor Mission on the Parry Peninsula where our skipper, Father Griffin, had spent the previous winter and spring along with Father Biname. While helping others unload the supplies, I noticed that the Mission building was situated conveniently close to the "Smoky Mountains"—a mass of low grade coal that had been smoldering for centuries and was now being used to heat the mission post.

Aided by the action of the strong winds that had dispersed the ice fields across Amundsen Gulf, we made good time on our return run to Tuktuyaktuk, where we picked up a second load of provisions for the Missions of Coppermine and Burnside. The latter, some 900 miles to the east, was to be my temporary post.

Off the tip of Baillie Island—within sight of Cape Bathurst— we spotted a pod of giant sperm whales several hundred yards away. By the time our entire crew gathered on deck to gape at them in tourist fashion, these massive cachalots, with their huge and powerful tails, began surfacing only about a hundred yards from our schooner. We were at once awed by their mobility, immense size and strength. We were relieved however, when we realized they had no aggressive intentions, but were merely returning our curiosity.

A couple of days before August ended we arrived in the Coronation Gulf and made for Coppermine near the mouth of the Coppermine River. Several Eskimos, in addition to Fathers Roger Buliard and Louis LeMer, who had arrived the previous year from their native France, helped us off-load the Mission supplies. Also, because her propeller had been somewhat damaged in the heavy ice, our schooner had to be jacked ashore for repairs, which took half a day. Our hosts, however, made sure we wouldn't be bored. Fathers Buliard and LeMer turned out to be tough, but surprisingly considerate men. Full of Gallic fun, they went out of their way to treat us with their best caribou steaks and broiled Arctic char which they had caught in the productive Coppermine River.

We bid them *au revoir* on the second day of September and set our course for Bathurst Inlet and the Mission of Burnside 350 miles away, reaching our destination without incident in three days. Here we were welcomed and helped by Fathers Lucien Delalande, a Parisian, and Joseph Adam, a Belgian. By mutual agreement with the Hudson's Bay Company's local representative, they had built the Mission post close to the H.B.C. trading post on a narrow spit of land jutting out into the Burnside Bay. This arrangement, convenient for both parties as well as for itinerant Eskimos, was similar to ones made by the trading company and the police for their respective posts in the Arctic. The trader at the H.B.C. post in Burnside was Ralph Jardine, a young man who in time became a good friend of mine. God's goodness was evident when both Father Delalande and Father Adam were permitted to stay at Burnside until the following spring to "show me the ropes" and otherwise aid me on their good work in their assigned zone. They would visit occasionally in later years as valued friends and comrades.

All small lakes and ponds in the area were already frozen, and snow had started falling by the time Father Griffin and his crew of *Our Lady of Lourdes* left Burnside the next day. No one was surprised at their hasty retreat, since we all knew the skipper was anxious to gain the safety of the Tuktuyaktuk harbor before the seasonal onslaught of great Arctic storms.

No Royal Canadian Mounted Police (Mounties, for short) were on hand to greet me at Burnside, since their nearest outposts were at Coppermine and Cambridge Bay. However, two Eskimo families, who lived two miles away at Ayapapartorvik on the Burnside River and who, I was told, had almost starved the previous winter when they lost most of their dogs and therefore couldn't establish a trap line, appeared pleased to see me. But their children were far too shy to approach me at first.

It didn't take Fathers Delalande and Adam long to introduce me to their Mission post. It consisted of a 30' by 20' wooden building still unfinished and largely unfurnished. In fact, from Day One (or, rather, Night One) we slept on the floor in our sleeping bags spread on caribou skins, just as Nokadlak's family and I did in their *iglek*.

Our supplies for the long, severe Arctic winter, the good Oblate Fathers told me, comprised basic items common to all their Missions, namely several tons of coal, dimensional lumber for finishing the Mission building and storage shed, coal oil and gasoline, ammunition for various hunting rifles and a shotgun, different size fishing nets, animal traps, ropes, and twine.

Food supplies included bags of rice, beans, oats, cornmeal, flour, sugar, tea, coffee, tallow for cooking, hardtack or *pilote* bread (a hard, rich cracker, about half an inch thick and about the size of a small pancake), and relatively small quantities of dried vegetables or fruit for extra-special treats. For the most part, though, we were expected to live off the land and water around us—just like the native people—hunting, trapping, and fishing for more substantial food-stuffs.

Our two basic means of transportation consisted of a 16-foot-long clinker-built jollyboat and nine sled dogs. Father Delalande had obtained this dog team from a former Russian count-turned-trapper named Art Groblein just before he suddenly left for his homeland. In the team were two especially beautiful dogs of inexact origin, but obviously with some Malamute and Husky blood. Father Delalande had imaginatvely named them Ceasar and Cleopatra (Cleo, for short). Their progeny would become our dog teams in the years ahead, all large and strong, with long, thick fur, and strikingly handsome.

The day I arrived at Bathurst, Fathers Delalande and Adam had set their nets in the channel and along the sandbar in front of the Mission building. By helping them at that point I learned how to prepare or mount a net, how and where to set it in the water, how to remove the caught fish, and how to repair torn nets.

During the ensuing few days, herds of caribou started to return to the tree line for winter grazing and we spotted them occasionally swimming across "our" channel. We would shoot them from shore when needed, then row out in the jolly boat to pick them up and replenish our larder. On other days we'd row out to Koagiuk Island, about a mile away, and shoot several big caribou bulls for ourselves and our dogs.

I learned all I could from my two confreres, but, because they themselves were still novices at the hunt, needed much more experience before gaining proficiency in various methods of food procurement to ensure daily survival in Arctic weather and exigencies. Now a year later, my skills had improved considerably.

When the sporadic talk in his igloo returned to the *pirtok* on the third day, Nokadlak related yet another experience: "It happened as my friend Iktutok and I were checking our trap line. The *pirtok* began, but we thought we could get back to our camp without making a temporary igloo. Instead we got caught in a torrent of wind and snow. The freezing wind clawed at Iktutok like a hungry bear. I remember him saying repeatedly, 'It's cold, it's freezing!' He had only one thought—to get out into a warm stillness; to escape forever from the roaring evil spirits trying to destroy us.   Meanwhile, he was slowly freezing under the blizzard's numbing bite.

"I dug a hole in the snow and barely managed to cut and place a few snow blocks around us to ward off the gale. We tried to sleep there that night. It was impossible. But the following day the Good Spirits of the land helped us reach our camp. By then Iktutok's toes were frozen. I had to cut off all the toes of his left foot, and two on his other foot. After cutting each toe, I tied its blood vessels with caribou sinew.

"I don't know if Iktutok was lucky to survive or not. I do know that in his soul slumbers a restless dread of big winds. Narluk, the Storm Child of the Spirit of the Sea, has confused his head. That's why he is no good for traveling any more!"

Nokadlak made no reference to Iktutok's behavior during this brutal but vital operation without any anaesthetic, and I deemed it wiser to resist the temptation to ask. It was added proof that Eskimo indifference to physical pain is more than legendary; it's real!   Therefore, I assumed that Iktutok had enough native stoicism in him to take that kind of treatment without crying or yelling. In all likelihood he merely said, "It's painful indeed!" and ground his teeth.

As a poetic epitaph to Nokadlak's grisly tale, Grandmother Manerthiak chanted quietly in her high-pitched voice:

Ayolerama, I'm truly helpless, *aya, aya, aye*. . .
When I see the heavens
Full of naked spirits
Blowing up the great storm. *Aya, ya, ya, ie*. . .
Ayolerama, I'm truly helpless
When I hear Narluk, the Storm Child,
Shrieking through the clouds,
Raising the great *pirtok*. *Aye, ya, aya, ie, ie, ie*. . .

Iktutok's fearful experience affirmed my resolve to stay with Nokadlak and his family until the storm ended. At first, they were suspicious and perhaps a trifle fearful of me, but the *pirtok* changed that. Certainly, there was no privacy for anyone in the circular igloo whose *iglek*—raised a couple of feet above the

40

snow floor, protruded from the igloo walls some seven feet at its deepest. Granted, beyond its low "crawl-out" door was affixed a 20-foot-long porch or *torho* resembling a giant snow tunnel which served as a latrine during bad weather, and as a storage area for food and equipment, as well as a shelter for the pups. In these circumstances it wasn't surprising that I began to better understand how my hosts lived, how they thought and they felt.

3

Burnside Mission Post

Even though I had left my sled atop Nokadlak's igloo, I had to use a shovel to dig it out of the snow piled up on it during the storm. It was now the fifth day since the *pirtok* had struck, and there wasn't a cloud in the sky. But it was still unusually cold, and the snow skimmed the frozen floor like wisps of smoke out of a campfire. Large snow drifts surrounded the igloo, as well as our dogs, changing the contours of the landscape into even more desolation.

On top of the snow blocks, Nokadlak's sled was in far better shape than mine—only its runners were packed with driven snow. Kudnanak helped his father lower the sled and turn it over to prepare it for their next trip, now very urgent. The family's food stores had dwindled rapidly while we were prisoners of the *pirtok*. With their snow knives, father and son meticulously scraped off the white ice coating that lay next to the protective three-inch layer of frozen peat on the steel runners. When he was satisfied that the coating had been completely removed, Nokadlak said simply, "It's ready!"

This was the signal for the boy to fetch the kettle in which his mother had melted granular snow, as well as a square piece of white bear fur, or *nanurak*, from the igloo. Nokadlak took a mouthful of the lukewarm water out of the kettle and, finding its temperature adequate, spat it out on the *nanurak*, then quickly rubbed one of the upturned runners with the wetted rag. Successive applications of water, given with a rhythmic sweeping motion, made a smooth new ice surface for the runners. This done, Nokadlak scraped off the drops of water frozen to the sides of the runners, set the sled upright, and with Kudnanak's help dragged it back and forth to prevent snow from sticking to the new coating.

"That will be fine," he said, panting. "My rested dogs will fly over the snow with almost nothing to pull!"

I was using the same method to ice my sled's runners, a trick one learns early. It's normally done about every two hours when the runners begin to hiss from constant friction against the snow floor—a sure sign the sled is dragging and impeding the dog team. Of course Nokadlak and Kudnanak finished the job well ahead of me, and were now straightening the dog harnesses.

Like many of the Krangmalit people, Nokadlak had built his sled from trees obtained after a long arduous trip to the tree line. "Only once or twice a lifetime do we make a trip to the tree line," he told me one evening. "Some of my friends and I will get together in the early spring, when the days are getting longer, and travel for many days until we reach the forest. But we don't like it. We know that many spirits dwell among the trees. They are the Forest Inhabitants who Stand Upright. We can hear them at night, moaning and whispering. It is said, also, that many of our people have been killed by Indians who dwell in the forest."

Like generations of Eskimo's before him, Nokadlak had secured the sled's crossbars to the two heavy runners with strips of seal and caribou skin, and had equipped the runners with steel (obtained from the H.B.C.) for travel. Last fall he had chopped some peat out of the marshy ground and thawed it in a large cauldron above the blubber lamp. Together with seal or caribou blood, this mixture was kneaded into a soft paste and plastered lukewarm on the runners, high up on the sides and thicker in front to broaden their up-curving ends. When the peat coating was frozen solid, Nokadlak smoothed all the rough spots with his snow knife. Then he had dragged the sled across sandy ground to rub away remaining imperfections.

During the extremely cold months from December to May his peat runners, properly ice-coated, would minimize friction whereas metal or wooden runners would drag in the snow and exhaust the dogs. Nokadlak knew that whale bones made more durable runners for the winter snow, but whales are scarce in the frozen seas of the Central Arctic. Peat runners tolerated long trips too, even with heavy loads.

Travelers in the Arctic have dreamed of discovering the perfect runner—smooth-sliding, unbreakable with minimal maintenance requirements. Nobody has fulfilled that dream, although Father Joseph Adam and I thought we came pretty

43

close when we experimented with frozen porridge! Some Eskimos followed our example and went further by carrying small bags of rolled oats which they heated and used for patching their runners in the colder months.

Nokadlak knew instinctively how much abuse his sled could stand, and took every precaution to avoid crossing anything that might damage the peat runners or chip their ice coating. Wherever he went, his experienced eyes searched the trail ahead for stones, sand, dogs' fresh droppings, and glare ice. He iced his runners whenever necessary on his trips and always carried peat for emergency repairs.

By the time I had finished rigging my sled, Nokadlak was already loading his. He did it with precision both learned and inherited. First, he laid some heavy caribou skins upon the crossbars, folding them over the exact width of the sled. Then he spread a larger cover of caribou-cow hides over it, sewn to overlap the sled on either side. Onto this, he placed the heaviest items—grub boxes and dog line so the sled could be handled more easily on a rough trail. The rest of his equipment he piled evenly throughout the sled, with the sleeping bags in the center as a comfortable seat.

With the load aboard, Nokadlak and his boy folded up the hems of the cover, wrapping up the contents and tying them like a huge mummy. Finally they inserted their rifles, ice-chisel, shovel, and snow-scoop between the ropes within easy reach.

During these preparatory steps, Kudnanak had been helping his father without a word of instruction, but now Nokadlak ordered him gently, "Anchor the sled." This is the last detail to remember before harnessing dogs. Made of caribou antlers or old scraps of iron, or perhaps even a worn-out rifle barrel, the anchor, shaped like a double claw, is attached with a strong rope to the central pulling line in front of the sled. With his dogs excitedly anticipating a warm run after their long rest in chilly beds, Nokadlak wanted to make sure they would not pull the sled before he was ready to leave.

Starting with the dog team's leader, the hunter and his son placed the light harness on each of the nine. It was made of parallel straps with crossed leather bands attached to a back-bar so that the dogs could pull with their shoulders and breasts with the least effort and greatest efficiency. They leashed the dogs in pairs with two leashes, one short—from the collar to the central trace—and the other, five-feet-long—tied to the back-bar and the main trace—thus concentrating the dogs' combined pulling strength on the central trace. Only the lead dog was left on a 10-foot leash, free to move according to his master's commands.

These included *"Takke!"* for "Get going!," *"Djee!* (Right!)," *"Ah!* (Left!)," and *"Ho. . .ho. . .ho"* for "Stop." Curiously, using Santa Claus' energetic intonation of *"Ho! Ho! Ho!"* in a more urgent manner would also be an Eskimo's signal for the dogs to "Go!"

I had stayed much longer with Nokadlak's family than I intended and was anxious to return to my Mission post in Burnside, but it was with a feeling of regret that I left Grandmother Manerathiak, Angivrana, and her dark-eyed baby with whom I had become involved from the moment of her birth. Although I couldn't see Naoyak, I was certain she lay comfortably warm in her mother's parka hood resting against her back.

Finally, I thanked Nokadlak for his hospitality, adding, "See you some day. Meantime, good hunting! Don't wait for me, I'll be leaving shortly. Thanks for the musk-ox meat, too!" Clearly mindful of his officially illegal kill, he laughed goodnaturedly, but didn't reply.

Young Kudnanak was visibly relieved to hear nothing would delay their departure. He picked up the anchor and jumped on the sled. *"Ho!. . . Ho!. . .Ho!"* shouted Nokadlak in a pressing voice filled with joy, and his dogs took off in a hubbub of yelping and scrambling. With Angivrana and her mother standing near me, we watched the hunters head swiftly down a slope in a frenzy of reborn freedom. As they disappeared from sight, I heard Angivrana say quietly to Manerathiak, "Only Nuliayuk, the Spirit Mother of all Animals, knows what lies beyond the hills. . . ."

"Definitely so," agreed the "ancient" woman. "Nuliayuk knows how many caribou the hunter will kill, and so does Hilla, the Spirit of Earth and Air. But who else knows how successful their hunt will be?"

Perhaps it was just as well that Nokadlak and Kudnanak did not stay to witness my departure. In the mad rush of the take-off, one of my dogs decided to relieve itself. Dragging its rump on the snow it caused all the other dogs to get tangled up! It all happened so fast while I was trying to steer the sled clear of the droppings, that I did not have time to brake with the anchor. The sled careered ahead, jostling the dogs, causing the inevitable fight.

I'm sure a man like Nokadlak would have taken the incident in his stride. Lacking his experience, however, I was disconcerted every time my team got fouled up. I summoned all my patience and tried to untangle the mess with good humor, but it was not that easy. Several dogs seized the opportunity to settle their disputes in roaring scramble, with others joined on the fringe. I had to whip the chief offenders with a thin chain to separate them, or they would have fought until one was injured or killed.

Eskimos believe that a good beating at the right time makes dogs more faithful and more obedient to their owner. They use the chain because it bites into the animal's skin without damaging its bones.

My fingertips were almost numb by the time I was able to disentangle the ropes and harnesses. It was with relief that I eventually jumped on the load and shouted "*Takke, takke, Bobby!*" to my lead dog. The dogs pulled as a cohesive team again, as if nothing had happened, and the sled with its bow-shaped runners, glided easily along the hard snow. Here and there, though, snowdrifts blown by the wind into regular patterns, like waves on the sea, made the going rough. Still, I reckoned we were making five to seven miles an hour and at this rate I ought to be in Burnside, thirty-five miles to the south, by supper time.

Occasionally the trail led over hills that slowed the dogs to a walk, and then I gladly gave them a helping hand, pushing and directing the sled in the flat depressions of ground. The extra effort warmed me up, loosened my stiff muscles, and helped to break the monotony. Fortunately there were no greater obstacles to combat on this comparatively short run; no boulders of ice or plain broken ice piled up by the winds and currents, as may be encountered on the frozen sea, to tax the endurance and ingenuity of a man and his dogs.

So often, through the succeeding years, I had to face the back-breaking job of chopping my way out of rough ice with an axe. Or filled dangerous holes with snow, using a short handled flat shovel, to get the team and sled across them. This time, however, my dogs were spared the arduous, tortuous climbs over rocks or mountainous ice that only resulted in exhaustion and limited the day's progress to perhaps five miles. Those hazards are the common enemies of all travelers in the Arctic, but we were spared them on the way back to the Burnside Mission.

Early in the afternoon I called for a stop, and anchored the sled. All the dogs lay down, their forepaws stretched out and their tongues lapping the snow to quench their thirst. I lit the primus stove, a three-legged round tank the size of a dessert plate, with a burner in the center and three removable supports for a kettle. This stove used kerosene only, air being pumped from the side of its tank. If the kerosene congealed in the extreme cold, one knew that the temperature was -55°F to -60°F. In such cases the burner had to be primed with wood alcohol which does not congeal. A round cup, attached under the burner, was filled with alcohol and fired. Once very hot, the valve of the burner was opened and the stove worked.

While the snow was melting in the kettle, I turned over the sled on one side and prepared the runners for icing. Shortly the job was done, so with the remaining water I made myself a cup of tea to help push down the dried meat I was munching.

After my lunch break, the dogs took off at a moderate pace. We drove for awhile along the Burnside River, meandering in a desolate landscape, wildly beautiful with its crumbling serenity. The overwhelming silence was broken only by the deep-swishing sound of water running under the ice at Burnside Falls, a few hundred yards away, and periodically by the grating runners on the snow.

My sympathy went out to Nokadlak and his people. How dreadful their lifestyle appeared to me! It is a monotonous enough life within an igloo, but to brave the elements day after day, year after year, in the continuous struggle for barest survival—how do the Eskimos do it? Aren't there moments when even the most primitive of men must be tempted to give up?

These and other questions arose in my mind, but as yet I had no answers. Only in the ensuing years would I begin to comprehend part of the spirit which enabled the Eskimo people to endure their severe life.

A full moon shone on the snowy landscape when we descended via a creek to the sea floor and presently beheld the flickering lights of the Mission and adjacent H.B.C. trading post. I had helped Father Delalande complete the Mission building after my arrival last year, and had since added a porch and a smaller building for storing supplies.

It was nearly six hours since I had left Nokadlak's camp and I was glad to be back among familiar surroundings. The dogs, excited at the sight and scent of the buildings, covered the two-mile stretch from the mouth of the river to the Mission post seemingly in no time. During my absence, Father Delalande had been holding down the station, and he now had a cheery fire going in the kitchen's coal-fired range. After taking care of the dogs, we retired to the kitchen where he treated me to a delicious supper of thick caribou steaks, slices of half-dried Arctic char, homemade bread, and coffee.

"Voila!" said "chef" Delalande, "All we need now for a perfect dinner is French fries, a salad with a touch of Roquefort cheese, and a bottle of wine. Guess we'll wait a long time for that!"

During supper we exchanged our news of the past few days, and until two o'clock in the morning talked of many other things that came to our minds. It was virtually our first heart-to-heart talk since our initial meeting the year before.

"So, what happened during your visit with Nokadlak?" he inquired. I told him about the birth of Naoyak and my assistance in her delivery, Nokadlak's decision to keep the baby girl, and the big storm.

"I picked up a few things on this trip," I added. "For instance, Manerathiak told us some fanciful tales, such as the one about Tarakapfaluk, the Spirit who dwells at the Bottom of the Sea, and Nokadlak did, too. I took note of those stories and of Manerathiak's songs. Pity I couldn't understand every word; probably missed the finer points."

This was a decided understatement. While few of the veteran traders and other longtime White residents of the Central Arctic could boast mastery over the Eskimo language, they were able to get by with a minimal knowledge. But as an immigrant missionary expected to teach and help his Inuit flock, I had no choice but to learn their language as fast as I could. Since no formal courses were available, the seek-and-find route would surely take years of application. So as newcomer who didn't know a single Eskimo expression prior to coming to the Arctic fifteen months earlier, I had to scramble. Fortunately I was endowed with a facile memory and language dexterity which enabled me to get by in simple, everyday conversation in a relatively short time. But the learning process never ended.

Historically the Eskimo language was transmitted from generation to generation by word-of-mouth only. Foreign missionaries began studying it about a century ago in the Eastern Arctic where Bishop A. Turquetil, O.M.I. (Oblate of Mary Imaculate) eventually compiled the first Eskimo grammar for the benefit of his young missionaries. It was also he who introduced the Moravian syllabic script to the Eskimos which is still used in the Eastern Arctic. This script was invented by preachers of a religious sect in Moravia, a province of Czechoslovakia, and was taught in all Missions from Churchill to Pond's Inlet. Full contact with the Eskimos of the Central Arctic, where I was to live and work for twelve eventful years, was not made by the missionaries until the 1930s when they, too, began using Bishop Turquetil's grammar for "starters."

My colleagues and I, however, circumvented his syllabic script by retaining Latin letters and subsequently taught the Eskimos to write that way. In due time a "dictionary" was also prepared with each missionary contributing his share of Eskimo words, their meaning and pronunciation.

From Greenland to Alaska, all Eskimos basically speak the same language. To complicate matters though, individual native groups have their own dialects with their own distinguishable vocabulary and pronunciation. These dialects are commonly understood by the other groups because they all adhere to a root-word principle. If, for example, two sentences back, I had replaced the word "complicate" with, say, "muddify" (which is not a dictionary word), you—dear reader—would have clearly known what I meant. So much for dialect.

As for explaining the root-word, let's start by considering it as the basis of the Eskimo language. For example, take *nuna* (a noun meaning land) as a root-word. It may be declined (with cases similar to Latin) as follows: *nunab* (of the land), *nuname (on the land), nunamun* (to the land), and *nunamin* (from the land)—that is, with varying suffixes replacing our prepositions. Now, as in a cooking recipe, add three more ingredients: try *galluar* (nevertheless or however), *niar* (signifying future action), and *tunga* (indicating a first person verbal ending). Stir these components together with the root-word on top, and what do you get? A real tongue-twister at first sight: *Nunamungalluarniartunga!* Meaning: "I will go inland (to the land, if you insist) nevertheless in the future."

Is it any wonder then, that by our standards Eskimos appear to speak deliberately and slowly? While much of their talk comprises standard words and phrases—just as any other language—they do make up their own multi-syllabic words by juggling prefixes, infixes, and suffixes, as partly illustrated above. And that, obviously, takes a little more concentration and time.

Furthermore, Eskimo verbs are conjugated (i.e. inflected for person, number, etc.), again as in Latin! Let's try it with the very "to speak" *(okrartok).* Here's how an Eskimo would say: I speak—*okrartunga;* you speak (actually thou speaks)—*okrartutin;* he or she speaks—*okrartok;* we speak—*okrartugut;* you (plural) speak—*okrartuhe;* they speak—*okrartun.* As a bonus, there's a specially inflected form for two (and only two) persons speaking—*okrartuk.*

Similarly, there are different suffixes (word endings, usually syllables) to distinguish between numbers. For example: one woman is *arnar;* two women—*arnak;* several women—*arnain.*

Galluar—I mean "However"—there are not definite or indefinite articles (a, an, or the) in Eskimo to worry about, as in English and French. A small mercy, admittedly, but let us be thankful *galluar* (nevertheless)!

Another salient advantage of the Eskimo language is that its grammatical rules are just that—definite rules, not exceptions piled on exceptions.

Eskimos speak gutturally, but softly, not gratingly, the

frequent utterance of their "k" and "rkr" sounds coming from their throats. This does not make it easier for the average non-Eskimo listener. Once a White Man has mastered the Eskimo language and is able to appreciate its beauty, if not its actual derivation, he cannot help wondering about the true origin of the People Beyond.

"If I were you, I wouldn't worry about the stories you heard," Father Delalande assuaged me. "They are common to all Eskimos, and you'll, no doubt, hear them again. But why not tell me more about yourself? You know, we've never really had a chance to sit down together and chat at length about ourselves."

Taken aback by his question, I surveyed him momentarily. He was a big, well-built man, fully six feet tall—a veritable giant compared to me. His face was memorable not only for his clear, sky-blue eyes, but also for his short whiskers of unusual carrot color, topped by brown hair; and his slightly crooked mouth gave him an air of perpetual amusement. On the whole, he was the picture of a solid, good-looking man. And yet in his mischievous eyes of a Parisian street urchin I thought I detected a sad longing for companionship. Satisfied that he wasn't just being polite, but genuinely interested, I told him of unusual incidents in my life prior to becoming a fellow missionary.

"When I was nineteen, I was drafted into the French Air Force and was assigned to the Villacoublay Airfield near Paris (where my family had earlier moved from Corsica) for my basic training. Four months later I was moved with my Company to a special unit that took care of officers' transportation. By coincidence, it was located where you came from—La Banlieue Rouge (the Red Suburb of Paris). There were about fifty men in our unit, and our main duties were to drive high-ranking officers to their jobs or homes. In addition, we took turns at night guarding the fleet of automobiles. I was on night duty twice a week, from eight o'clock until midnight.

"My daring comrades-in-arms managed to arrange with each man on duty to sneak their girlfriends into the barracks during those hours. Since my cohorts knew I was going in for priesthood, they would comfort me with such assurances as, 'Don't worry, we'll make sure you won't get into trouble!' But one night our sergeant made his routine inspection earlier than usual and caught a bunch of girls (whom I had let pass at the gate) in beds and in limousines with their boyfriends!

"The following day the Captain had me arrested and paraded to his office. 'Well, well!' he began affably. 'I hear you're a seminarist and a future priest, who's been caught helping my men to be naughty!' Laughing at his own amusing remark, he added, 'Oh, I understand, of course; but I have no choice. You'll get ten days' detention, cleaning the yards and latrines, and you will be locked up at night in the compound's jail' "

Father Delalande grinned knowingly. "You can be sure, *mon ami*, that you have my utmost sympathy. You see, I was drafted by the Infantry and I, too, spent a good deal of the time in military jail! But tell me, please, was that the end of your problems with the Armed Forces?"

"Oh no! A few weeks later—no doubt as further punishment—I was posted to the Rue St. Dominique quarters of the Air Force, ostensibly to be trained in the Secret Service. Actually, my job was anything but adventuruous or exciting, as its locality might lead you to believe. It consisted of little more than filing officers' documents according to their religious beliefs and previous military records. Naturally, you know how strong anticlericalism was in France in those days. Officers practising their faith had a difficult time getting promotions because of it. Even General De Gaulle had problems with his advancement. You can easily guess to what use their files were frequently put."

"Did you have similar trouble advancing through the ranks of the Secret Agents?" he inquired half-seriously.

"I didn't stay there long enough to find out. At the end of six months in their Quatrieme (Fourth) Bureau, I opted for an additional four years of study at the Seminary."

"Well, let's have a sip of coffee to that!" Father Delalande proposed. After re-lighting our cigarettes, I asked him if he had a girlfriend before entering the Seminary.

"Oh yes, I had a good one, but I couldn't make up my mind whether I should marry her or not. I suppose I was looking for a greater challenge. . .for something out of the ordinary to satisfy my mind and soul and make my life even more worthwhile. I wavered for some time until one day I bid my girl goodbye and entered the novitiate of the Oblate Fathers. And here I am!"

"Have you ever regretted your decision?"

"At times, yes, since those are memories one never forgets. But more so because I feel restrained in my work by orders, regulations and restrictions that often make no practical sense. As we both know, they are imposed by our superiors who live thousands of miles away and who have no idea of the correct approach in dealing with Eskimos. They want us to impose on them the full strength of the Christian morality as well as their antiquated puritanical posture. They won't accept the simple reality that our native people here are eternally engaged in a bitter struggle with a harsh environment, often hanging on the

51

very edge of survival. Instead they expect us to change the Eskimos in a matter of months from a way of life that has been their source of preservation for the past five thousand years. Why don't they just forget it? We'll be lucky if we ever get a handful of converts!"

I nodded agreement. "What you've said is pretty close to what I was thinking at Nokadlak's place during the *pirtok*. It would appear that our Anglican counterparts have a smarter approach. They don't push the Christian morality down Eskimos' throats. They simply close their eyes to some of the native customs and take the Eskimos into the Christian fold the way they are. I'm sure that time and compassion is the answer."

"To change the subject to something more pleasant," I rejoined Father Delalande, "tell me, did you have a girlfriend, too?"

"Not really," I replied. "I did have a kind of puppy love for a girl whose name was Lison. But nothing serious came out of it because, like you, I was searching for an extraordinary adventure that would help make my life more useful by accomplishing something exceptional. I have an uncle in central British Columbia who came to Canada in 1875 to work with the Indians in the Kootenays. He has been my inspiration since I first met him in my youth in Corsica. His name is Father Nicolas de Coccola. He has done a lot for the Indians and the early White settlers of that region. He is now 84 years old, but is still going strong."

Father Delalande glanced at the kitchen clock, saying, "I guess it's about time we went to the Chapel for our night prayer and then to bed. I'm sure you must be tired and sleepy...Oh, yes, before we retire I should tell you that a young fellow named Otokreak arrived here after you left for Kagnekoguyak. He told me he's planning to go back to his camp at Admiralty Island and I expect he won't mind if you go along. You can speak to him in the morning, if you are interested."

"I don't believe I know this man, but since I've got to try to establish a station at Cambridge Bay sooner or later, perhaps I'd better travel in his company at least part of the way. I'll talk to Otokreak tomorrow, as you suggest. . .On second thought, if I were to go, what would you do without a dog team?"

"I understand Father Adam will be returning from Coppermine in a few weeks. He will stay with me until spring, at least. I won't be needing a team in the interim I intend to work on the translation of our Prayer Book into Eskimo. You know it won't be long before the Eskimos learn to read. I've already taught some of them to read a little and they like it. So, don't worry. Go and find out all you can about the people of Cambridge Bay!"

When Father Delalande referred to "our" Prayer Book, he was being self-effacing, for he was the driving force in translating the basics of the Roman Catholic faith from French into Eskimo. His only collaborator was Father Roget Buliard. Father Adam and I played a minimal role, merely supplying the odd Eskimo word or phrase for the text.

Interestingly enough, the preface to his modest little Prayer Booklet, typed unpretentiously on small sheets of inexpensive paper, has this dedication by its "Editeurs", that is, Father Lucien Delalande and Roger Buliard, minus the bracketed comments which are mine:

> Dedicated to the 'Big Kids' (that's us,
> the missionaries) of the (Arctic) Coast
> who—without experience in the past (our
> Seminary days), without consolation in
> the present (from our overseas super-
> iors), and without much encouragement
> (from the latter)— have done, and are
> always doing their best (for the Eskimos
> and for the Roman Catholic Church and
> its missions abroad.)

Ironically, too, below this unique foreword, Father Delalande's signature appears following the Latin words *Nihil obstat,* the Church censor's traditional non-objection to (or approval of) the publication so endorsed. It must have been tongue-in-cheek when he did so in his official capacity as the "Vicar for all the Arctic Coast Missions on behalf of the Most Reverend Gabriel Breynat, Archbishop for the Northwest Territories."

By this time I was so tired I nearly fell asleep kneeling in the small Chapel. I knew I had much to be thankful for, and hoped the Good Lord heard my prayers.

I retired to my small bedroom, adjoining Father Delalande's. It featured a moose skin brought in from one of the Mackenzie River Missions. It was stretched to its full length and attached with ropes to a 2" x 4" lumber bed frame to serve as both a spring and a mattress. On this taut hammock I placed my sleeping bag and promptly entered the Land of Nod.

I was unceremoniously awakened before daylight when the Mission's entire contingent of fifteen dogs and their pups echoed the melancholy howling of our visitor Otokreak's dogs and passing wolves. Because my watch told me it was almost six o'clock, I dressed and went into the kitchen to find that Father Delalande had beaten me to the breakfast table. After sharing some cornmeal, toast, and coffee with him, I walked over to

Otokreak's little igloo on the bank of the Burnside Channel, some two hundred yards from the Mission. Crawling inside, I noticed his lamp was out and the place felt very cold.

"Come and have tea!" I said loudly, knowing full well that if there is one call that will wake an Eskimo it's an invitation to drink tea.

Lying on the *iglek* (raised platform) in a sleeping bag which covered him up to his neck, the young man of about seventeen rolled over on his stomach and propped himself up on his elbows, exposing his powerful chest and arms. Gazing at me through half-closed eyes, he asked automatically, "How's the weather?"

"The weather's fine," I assured him. It was as impolite for either of us to introduce himself as it was to ask the other's name. Such petty formalities could await their turn. Talk of tea and the weather were properly more pressing.

The complete absence of heat in the igloo caused Otokreak to don his parka, breeches, and boots in record time. I realized that while traveling one had to be careful to save fuel. Staying in the comfortable sleeping bag as long as possible was the answer, but only for a limited time because the cold would numb and freeze the body.

Otokreak followed me quicky to the Mission kitchen, which Father Delalande and I had warmed up to our liking. That was far too warm for our young visitor. He sweated freely as he gladly accepted dried caribou meat and fat and drank several cups of unsweetened hot tea. He told us that he had come from his camp on Admiralty Island, which lies off the east coast of Victoria Island, about eighty miles northeast of Cambridge Bay. On his way he had visited relatives at Gordon Bay, some thirty miles northeast of Burnside. And now he wanted to return.

"Which way are you going back?" I asked.

"The same way I came—through the Kulugayuk River."

"Are you going to call on any friends at Cambridge Bay?"

"Certainly! I must stop there to pick up some things I traded at the post. Maybe I'll even get myself a woman there."

"Perhaps Father Delalande told you that I want to visit the people of Cambridge Bay, and that I'd like to go with you."

Although surprised and seemingly flattered that a White Man wanted to accompany him, Otokreak's native practicality surfaced. "I haven't enough food for my dogs. My ammunition is low. And I have little food left for myself," he complained.

"All right," I yielded, "I'll feed your dogs and bring along enough food for you and me on the trail. How's that?"

"That suits me fine," he acknowledged, beaming in undisguised transformation.

It was now up to me, the agreed provider, to assume the initiative. "If the weather's good, we'll leave early tomorrow morning," I said.

Otokreak rose to return to his igloo just as Father Delalande brought in a load of ice for our kitchen's water supply. After he had dropped two large chunks into the 45-gallon steel barrel standing by the stove, I told my colleague of our plans to leave the next day. "I'll help you prepare the necessary supplies," he said. "It might be wise for you to take enough grub for ten days; for both of you and the dog teams. You'll be traveling through uncharted land that, to my knowledge, has never before been crossed by a White Man. If you followed the coast line to Kent Peninsula and Dease Strait to Cambridge Bay, you could easily make the trip in four days, but taking the land route is another story!"

While I was cleaning my primus stove and pouring kerosene and wood alcohol into tin cans, the kind Father filled a large pot with chopped caribou meat and placed it on the kitchen stove. Into another pot he put beans and rice, added water, and let them boil. As soon as they softened, he mixed the vegetables with meat and caribou fat. Then he took the thick concoction out to the porch to freeze, spreading it two inches thick on canvas lightly powdered with flour.

Otokreak returned unexpectedly with my harnesses and lines. "Some of your ropes are worn out," he said offering to help me splice new ones, and added, "A few of the crossbars on your sled are loose and should be tightened for the long trip." His own few chores done and his sled ready, except for icing its runners prior to departure, he was looking for something else to do and I did not want to discourage him.

"There are ropes and seal lines in the storeroom. If you need new snaps for the harnesses and dog collars, you'll find them there, too," I hinted.

Meanwhile I couldn't help noticing that every time Otokreak stood up or sat down, he appeared to be in pain. "Are you feeling all right?" I asked. He answered by placing his hand under his crotch, saying, "Every time I have a bowel movement it burns. Have a look!" He pulled down his breeches and bent over. There was a round, bluish swelling, the size of a grape, at the anal margin. From my medicine bag I took a tube of vaseline and rubbed it on the swelling. "That should help you a little now," I told him. "Keep greasing it with blubber for awhile. Also, eat blubber often to prevent constipation."

Hemorrhoids are a commom affliction among Eskimos

living mostly on caribou meat, and, to a lesser extent, among those on a seal and fish diet. I could empathize with them because I suffered the same way during my first year in the Arctic.

Out on the porch, Father Delalande was using an axe to fragment the frozen stew he had prepared for me. "There's enough here to fill a gunny sack!" he noted with satisfaction. "Should hold you and Otokreak for at least a couple of weeks. And with a load of green frozen fish and dried meat, you two will live like princes!"

"Oh, one sack should be plenty, thanks! But don't you think I ought to take some extra kerosene?"

"Why not take five gallons? Crossing new territory at this time of the year is a gamble. You can expect to be stormbound for days."

"How much dog food will you carry, Fala?" interjected Otokreak.

"Enough for my dogs for twelve days or more, and I'll give you ten days' supply of dried meat for your team."

"That's fine," the young hunter smiled, adding, "Maybe we can visit the big camp at Taherkapfalluk. It's not far out of our way and I have friends there!"

As a typical young Eskimo, Otokreak had no concern about the passage of time since he had all his life to do whatever he pleased. "Not far" to him, for example, might mean up to three days' traveling. Aware of this, I did not commit myself, although I was curious to meet those Eskimos of Taherkapfalluk, the Big Lake. Despite its descriptive name, this lake was not on the traveling map I got at Fort Smith. It was a map of the Central Arctic, scaled at thirty-five miles to the inch, from Cape Dalhousie in the Western Arctic to Chantrey Inlet in the East. Banks, Victoria, and King William Islands to Boothia Peninsula, up to 72° latitude north, were included. The map was made four years earlier from surveys by the Topographical Survey of Canada, from aerial photographs by the Royal Canadian Air Force, and from information supplied by early British explorers in search of the Franklin Expedition. Although it was not exhaustive, I learned to cherish it because it saved my life on several occasions when I traveled long distances to unfamiliar destinations. As for Otokreak's wish to take the Taherkapfalluk detour, I must admit I'd heard of Big Lake from other Eskimos and its name alone intrigued me.

Ever thoughtful, Father Delalande reminded me to take my double caribou-fur sleeping bag, as well as some thick caribou hides to sleep on. "It must be terribly cold inland now," he observed. "Last year when I went up to Hanimor River, the cold was so intense, I could feel it burning through the soles of my boots!"

I was still fairly new to the Arctic, and it to me. Thus, despite Father Delalande's admonition, I looked forward to my trip through tracts unknown to the White Man.

Into the grub box I placed a few boxes of .22 long ammunition for small game, and some .30-30 for larger animals. In a card box I stored sinew, needles, and cut some soft toilet paper. (Eskimos use only handfuls of snow).

That evening in the Mission, I took a sponge bath using a large bucket of warm water. I sensed I would be deprived of such luxury for a long time. At the moment, however, no one, not even Father Delalande, could have convinced me that my cheerful anticipation would soon change into despair.

4

Taherkapfaluk, The Big Lake

With Otokreak's dog team leading, we left the Burnside Mission early next morning in the gloomy polar light. Although clouds covered the sky, it was bitterly cold. Within half an hour, skirted the small Koagiuk Island at the entrance of Bathurst Harbor and at noon crossed the solidly frozen Bathurst Inlet, only five-miles-wide at this point. We then headed for Gordon Bay or Hiorkretak, meaning "a nice sandy beach." That night we made camp in an abandoned igloo in the Umimaktok Range, foothills, named for the *umikmak* (musk-ox) hunted there.

We spent the entire next day in slow, tired climbing between gentle slopes of sedimentary and terrace-like trap rocks to reach the plateau, where my combination barometer-altimeter showed an elevation of 1,050 feet. Looking south, back towards Gordon Bay, we faced a desolation of countless hills eroded by time. Nevertheless, I felt elated because, as I knew, I was the first White Man to explore this land!

Descending gradually to the north, we could see the frozen Hiorkretak River not far below us. Otokreak had told me earlier we would be following this river to its source, the usually wind-swept Krimakton Lake. We reached the lake early in the afternoon and stayed on its western bank to avoid its treacherous glare ice. The narrow lake was about twenty miles long and lay at an altitude of 850 feet. I was able to plot it fairly accurately with my compass. Perhaps I should have thought to give it a White Man's name, but I didn't.

Despite the intense cold, we took advantage of the full

moon to push on a few more miles. Under the eerie glow of the moonlight we built our igloo, unloaded our night supplies and fed the dogs.

In preparation for our hot meal, I melted snow in a pot to thaw the frozen stew, while Otokreak stuck frozen green fish into the snow wall to thaw them a little before we ate them. As he did so, he kept repeating, "It's cold, it's cold, it's freezing!" Since he was born to this climate and I to Corsica's, my feelings were numbed to say the very least. As soon as the water boiled, I poured some into a small kettle, adding two spoonfuls of tea. To the pot over the primus stove I added more snow and a generous portion of frozen stew. Our appetizer consisted of chunks of half-frozen fish, downed with mugs of warm tea, sweetened with sugar. We ate in customary silence, periodically stirring the stew until it turned into a thick paste. That was our entree, served in tin plates with *pilote* bread. Otokreak called it *"krarkolak."*

Before going to sleep, I questioned him about the trail ahead, "Is there much more climbing left?"

"No. Tomorrow we shall reach Taherkapfaluk camp. Maybe in the afternoon, if the wind is not blowing too hard."

Taherkapfaluk, Big Lake, the largest discovered on our trip, was only hours away. I should have been excited, but somehow I wasn't. Aloud I said, "Whom do you expect to see at Big Lake?"

"I want to see my friend Paoktok. He came up last fall to hunt caribou and trap foxes. The hunting is usually good there."

"I suppose you are a fair hunter yourself?" I asked, smiling.

"I'm pretty good, because my father, the best hunter of all, taught me when I was young."

"What is your father's name?"

"Kakagun."

"Kakagun! What a surprise! I know your father. He is indeed a great hunter, and a fine, kind man, besides. But he never told me he had a son named Otokreak."

"Perhaps it was because I was not born to his proper wife, but to an exchange one," he chuckled. Then, in response to further questions, Otokreak explained what he meant. "It was a poor winter inland. *Pingak,* the Spirit Woman, Mistress of the Weather, must have been displeased with something our people had done, because they were starving. Kakagun's wife, Kablunak, was big with child when he decided to search for game in a distant part of the land. To help him tend the blubber lamp and mend his clothes, Kakagun took along Nivikhana, the wife of his friend Onyak. He left his own wife, Kablunak, in Onyak's care. That's one way our people sometimes help each other. For many days they traveled and lived together as if they were husband

and wife. I was conceived during that time. Kakagun adopted me and brought me up."

"One summer, while hunting seals in his kayak, Onyak drowned. Kakagun returned me to my natural mother, Nivikhana, so I could support her. Eventually my father moved away from Krikitakapfaluk (Admiralty Island) to Taheriuak, close to the River Haningayok (known among the White People as Back River in honor of the English explorer who discovered it). My mother, Nivikhana, was taken as a wife by the good hunter Talritok, and she is living now with the Nunatarmeun (People at the Back of the Earth). That's why I'm looking for a wife myself, so far without success. Maybe the Spirit *Pingak* is mad at me. Anyway, I'm going back to Krikitakapfaluk to look around for a mate among my friends there."

"I wish you better luck this time. Who knows, you may even find one at Taherkapfaluk!" I said encouragingly.

Despite Otokreak's pronounced snoring, I slept well that cold night.

We had not trekked far in the morning when our dogs sensed something ahead. Their heads up, they looked around inquisitively and pulled harder to satisfy their curiosity. When they finally sighted an oncoming team, they exchanged gleeful yapping with each other.

We stopped at a convenient distance between the lead dogs, anchored our sleds to prevent dog fights, and walked ahead to shake hands silently with the unexpected stranger, whom Otokreak recognized immediately as Kivgalo.

After we had admired each other's dogs, the customary social trail ice-breaker, I told Kivgalo we were headed for the Big Lake. He replied, "I left the Kulugayuk River two days ago. My wife Araliuk died the day before I left. Now I'm going to Kringaun to trade some furs and see my friends." I knew the *kringaun* meant "nose" in Eskimo and that he referred to the bluff close to the post which resembled a human proboscis. Kivgalo did not need to add that he would also be looking for another wife, because no Eskimo widower, to survive if nothing else, remains that way longer than he can help.

"Was your wife sick very long?" I inquired sympathetically.

In true Eskimo fashion he wrinkled his nose and grunted, "No, she was an old woman."

Kivgalo was still a young man, short and powerfully built like a wrestler. His face was smooth and almost square. His eyes two slits, like a cat half-asleep. He had cut his black hair short, thereby showing a receding forehead and a well-defined ridge across the length of his skull, common to the Eskimo race. His

60

breeches, were strikingly embellished with horizontal stripes and tassels of white caribou fur. His late wife Araliuk must have been a capable seamstress.

I made a mental note of her death, so that I could notify the Royal Canadian Mounted Police detachment at Cambridge Bay. It was a routine duty every Arctic missionary performed for the government.

Several months later Kivgalo's path and mine would cross again, but neither of us knew that now. We parted without saying good-bye, for the word is non-existent in the Eskimo language.

At noon Otokreak and I reached the western bank of Taherkapfaluk, the Big Lake. Except for the bitter cold, abetted by a slight breeze, the weather was perfect. The lake's expanse of glare ice, broken only by occasional snowdrifts, stretched eastward as far as one could see. To my knowledge no White Man had beheld this sight before and I felt unusually privileged.

Otokreak told me his friend's camp was at the opposite end of the lake. It took nearly five hours to traverse its 25-mile length along the north shore. Once there, we found five igloos clustered within a radius of about fifty yards, two of them linked together, their dim lights collectively piercing the obscure polar evening.

Otokreak identified the owners of the linked igloos as his friends Paoktok and Amiraernek, both from Cambridge Bay. I discovered later that the third igloo of the same size belonged to Makara, while the fourth, much larger than the rest, housed Hikhik with his two wives and children. To each name Otokreak added the suffix "kut", like Paoktokut and Hikhikut, meaning that each one of them had his own family, that is, wife and children.

Even from a mile away, we could hear the dogs at their camp. Sensing our approach in the still night, they howled in concert. Having already scented the camp, our dogs pulled with renewed energy, their bushy tails curled up on their rumps, as a sign that they were happy and not overly tired.

As soon as the camp's inhabitants heard their dogs' clamor, they streamed from their igloos and waited to greet us. We anchored our sleds close to the camp. Men and youngsters approached us first and shook hands. Everyone smiled, but no one spoke. Then came the women, looking a little shy, walking pigeon-toed circling my sled, as the custom required, to ward off the Evil Spirit they believed frequently accompanied a stranger. By walking round and round my equipage, they would encircle and lock in the Evil One, thereby preventing his escape from the spell and the sorrow or misfortune that would result.

This precaution taken, the women folk shook our hands, eyeing me curiously, then giggling and muttering to each other, "This is a White Man!"

Otokreak approached me with another young hunter, saying, "This is my friend Paoktok." Behind Paoktok was a woman carrying a baby girl on her back in her hood. "And this is Nuitek, Paoktok's wife." As she neared me, she smiled, shook hands without a word, then turned her head to the baby, pulled out her tiny hand, and said quiety, *"Attitoren,* shake hands!" The child's hand was very warm, and so were the hands of all the people I met at camp. What surprised me even more was how small and stubby everyone's hands were. I wondered whether their little hands, combined with the high-protein diet common to all Eskimos, helped protect them against the intense cold. They, of course, could not confirm my speculation. It was easier to determine that their men folk had recently returned from the trap lines, their sleds still laden with frozen fox carcasses and heaps of rusty traps. Presumably, they had not yet finished setting out all their traps. Most hunters place several hundred of them during the trapping season, November to March.

The men had attached all their dogs to the dog line and were refreshing themselves with tea when our arrival threw the camp into commotion. Now the women went dutifully back to the igloos to keep the tea hot for their husbands as they remained outside to help us silently with our dogs. Meanwhile, the children clambered excitedly over our sleds, chattering about our dogs and me.

"He is a White Man with bushy eyebrows! He's not at all like us. Look at his face—it's covered with fur!" some kept exclaiming in open wonder. I had become accustomed to such scrutiny and discrimination, and did not let that bother me.

With the help of Hikhik and Makara, I set up my dog line and transferred my dogs to it. "You'll come and stay in my igloo," said Hikhik matter-of-factly, as if he'd read my thoughts. I had been wondering who would invite me, for a single traveler is always welcome in a camp and does not have to build his igloo.

"Thank you very much," I replied. "I'm tired and would like to stay with you." From my sled I picked up my sleeping bag, a pair of caribou fur socks, and boots to change into for the evening while my traveling clothes dried on the rack. Aided by Paotok and Amiraernek, Otokreak made short work of his unloading chores, and headed for the twin igloos, talking and laughing with his friends.

These two igloos were connected by a short passageway

which simplified heating and enabled the two families to enjoy each other's conversation, songs, jokes, and stories, while preserving their respective privacy. Recesses on each side of the passageway stored food and equipment. The twin igloos had only one snow-porch. It was large and sparkling, with additional storage niches in its walls for both families.

As I walked into Hikhik's spacious igloo, I wondered whether his two wives gave him the kind of prestige a two-car garage might bring a white working man. I realized that his bigamy represented virility and, in the eyes of his fellow hunters, added to his stature as an extraordinary hunter and fisherman. Yet I couldn't help thinking that any man with two wives in a group noted for its scarcity of women could be inviting serious trouble and possibly even murder. On the other hand, I saw that Hikhik was not a run-of-the-mill Eskimo hunter. His tall and massive frame, like many of the Umikmatomeun and Krangmalit people who live largely on lean caribou meat, was undeniably attractive. (His face was smooth with protruding red cheekbones and a slightly hooked nose.) But, having previously met him, I considered his kindness his greatest asset. His smiling mouth and wide-set eyes reflected good humor and fun, adding immeasurably to his inner self.

Hikhik's older son Anerodluk, a tall, red-faced, mature boy of about fourteen—already the image of his father—followed us into the family igloo. The younger son chose to play around the sleds with his friends.

Hikhik's younger wife, whose name (I learned later) was Arluk, sat watching the kettle over the lamp, while his first wife, whom he called Kommek, was scraping a caribou skin on the commodious *iglek*. They were both bashful—neither spoke to me, but they looked furtively at me when they thought I wasn't watching. I laid my sleeping bag on the *iglek* and sat down for a while before taking off my outer parka, boots and socks. Obligingly, but silently, Kommek placed them on the rack to dry. While I put on my fresh pair of socks and boots, Hikhik and his older boy carried in slabs of half-dry fish and dry meat. In addition, they cut large slices of frozen meat from caribou carcasses leaning against the wall. Radiant in her early twenties, Arluk was now pouring hot tea into an enamel cup which she offered me as the household guest. Accepting it, I thanked her. Hikhik then urged, "Come on, Little Man, eat! You must be hungry after a long day in the cold." Actually I needed no encouragement. I was starved so I ate my fill.

My hosts all ate silently, watching me and smiling, obviously pleased that I liked their hospitality. Then Hikhik belched loudly—a signal for breaking the polite silence.

I began describing my visit to Kagnekoguyak where I helped Angivrana deliver her child. "It was a beautiful baby girl, and when Nokadlak came down from the hills where he was hunting, he decided to keep the little girl for Kakagun's son Naodluak, and called her Naoyak. Angivrana and Grandmother Manerathiak were both very happy."

"Yes, yes," chorused Arluk and Kommek, "it's good, once in awhile, to keep a baby girl!"

Seated next to me on the edge of the *iglek*, Hikhik seemed more interested in Nokadlak and Kakagun. "They are great hunters," he acknowledged. "We shall visit them in the spring when we all go down to the sea to hunt seals." As we talked, Arluk poured more tea into our cups.

"Did you see many tracks of caribou, wolves, foxes, or anything else?" Hikhik inquired.

"It was difficult to see tracks as we climbed from Hiorkretak to Krimakton Lake," I answered, "particularly because the *naterorvik* (ground wind) was blowing and covering most marks with snow. However, this morning, soon after we left our igloo, we met Kivgalo. He was traveling from the Kulugayuk River to Kringaun (Burnside). He told us his wife Araliuk had died and he was going to trade at the White Man's post and visit his friends there."

At the mention of our chance meeting with Kivgalo, the two wives of Hikhik pricked up their ears. I detected a special interest on Kommek's face when I spoke of Araliuk's death. Six months would pass before I recalled and wondered again about that momentary flash in her dark eyes.

Surfeited with play, Kommek's youngster she called Ukayaluk and one of his playmates joined us in the igloo. Over their noisy, playful babbling, another young voice yelled outside: *"Teatorithe!"* It was a polite reminder that refreshments also awaited me in the twin igloos of Paoktok and Amiraernek. I picked up some candies from my grub box in the porch, gave a few to the two boys, and took the rest with me for the other children in camp. "It's very good, thank you!" they chorused happily after popping candies into their mouths.

Thanking my hosts for their hospitality, I told them I was going to feed my dogs and then visit their neighbors.

As I began to feed my dogs with dry fish and chunks of blubber, the other dogs howled, fearful of being neglected, and soon all the men emerged with bags of frozen caribou meat for their teams.

With Otokreak and his friends, accompanied by Hikhik, we

entered the double igloo through the single tunnel serving both. I was fascinated by two or more igloos joined together. Perhaps it was the rhythmic arrangement of domes and arch-ways increased in effect by its many component snow crystals. Three or four linked igloos gave me the impression of looking into several mirrors reflecting images of shimmering white hemispheres attached by round arches. "What you see today," I thought "has not changed an iota from at least five thousand years ago. These Eskimos live the same way their earliest predecessors did—in small, seasonally nomadic groups. They live in little camps of caribou-skin tents during summer; they find shelter from September's freezing rain and snow in small peat houses, built of peat blocks piled up about six feet high and covered with watertight seal skins; then, as the snow hardens in mid-November, they move into their beautiful igloos. Today I have merely stepped back into yesterday."

Aloud I said admiringly to Paoktok and Amiraernek, "It's roomy and nice here!" They beamed proudly. Their wives were both in the first igloo, which belonged to Paoktok. Fussing with the preparation of tea and meat, they customarily would not enter the conversation until later.

Having already informed his friends about the various camps he had visited since he left home and of my visit to Nokadlak's place, Otokreak started poking good-humored fun at my behavior on the trail.

"Fala was half-asleep on his sled, so sometimes he did not see the dogs' droppings. I had to help him unload it and clean and re-ice the runners!" Everyone giggled politely.

Rocking her sleeping baby girl on her back, Nuitek kept her eyes on Otokreak, who was far better looking than her husband Paoktok.

Encouraged by the initial attention, my young guide continued, "The day after we left Kringaun, we spotted a wolf in the valley. Fala said he'd go and shoot it. He took his rifle and went after the animal. I watched him get quite close to it. He sat down, fired, and the wolf fell dead. Fala was very proud of his marksmanship and ran to the wolf as fast as he could. When he got to it, he saw that the animal had a collar. It wasn't a wolf at all—it was an abandoned old dog!"

This time even the women guffawed, their shyness all gone. "Heh, heh, heh! He mistook a dog for a wolf! What a good joke, heh, heh, heh!" Their laugh was so infectious I laughed too.

While more tea was being poured, Otokreak told his friend Paoktok, "I've been traveling for a long time, but nobody has offered me his wife." Paoktok's reaction was immediate: "You are my friend and Nuitek likes you. She will be glad to share your *krepik* with you tonight," he said levelly. This casual arrangement, made openly in front of others, is a matter of everyday convenience, a part of necessary sharing, and did not in any way disrupt the conversation in the igloo. Amatory jealousies exist, of course, among the Eskimos, but in the main they know that sharing their food, abode, and other creature comforts is an integral part of their daily struggle for survival.

Paoktok and Amiraernek had two children each, and Amiraernek's wife Malrukhak was expecting a third. With the other children in the camp, Paoktok's boy and Amiraernek's two were joyfully running in and out of the different igloos. No one minded nor interfered with their play. Here was freedom largely beyond that enjoyed by our civilization, I thought. These happy youngsters could dash into any igloo any time and play or watch its occupants and nobody would hush them or shoo them away. That wasn't only because they could not bring mud or dust into the dwellings; it was simply because from what I saw, Eskimo children are free to do whatever they like as soon as they are able to walk. In fact, they are seldom rebuked and never beaten. Seemingly, the only parental restriction is that in stormy weather they are told to stay inside. And yet, when one of Amiraernek's boys silently accepted candy from me, and I heard his mother say, "Give thanks!" he immediately obeyed.

Having partaken of tea, raw frozen caribou meat, and slices of blubber which my hosts had obtained from Bathurst Inlet seals last fall, Otokreak, Hikhik and I adjourned from Otokreak's igloo to Amiraernek's side of the duplex.

Here, again, I could not offend the hostess by refusing tea. Malrukhak, Amiraernek's wife was small, with a full-moon face and slanted eyes. She had a wide mouth with a perpetually amused expression. I was curious about the origin of her name which translated into "Almost Two." It surely didn't refer to the hour she was born, I thought. Was it likely that her mother gave birth to twins? Although I eventually got to know all the families in the Central Arctic, I never heard that any of them kept twins. Later that evening I asked Hikhik if he knew of any female who had twins. He laughed as he answered, "Sure! Caribou cows have twins; women have twins. But, you know, Little Man, there is room only for one baby in the mother's hood. So the other one has to go. Sometimes one is adopted, but the Spirits don't like that."

Impromptu entertainment was now provided by three boys who took turns swinging and stunting on a wooden trapeze bar, suspended by two ropes from the center of the igloo's dome.

The ropes had been put right through the roof and were held securely by another piece of wood. The igloo's expertly shaped snow blocks had long since frozen into a single convexity whose structural strength could support far greater weights than that of a boy or man exercising on a trapeze. One of the youngest boys who swung on the trapeze was no more than five years old. He wore the adaptable breeches that practical mothers make for their tots. Such pants feature a loose fur-folded opening in the seat, so that, when their wearer stands, the folds close like pursed lips; but when the child squats to relieve himself, the folds open wide. This sartorial feature was promptly noted by the adult onlookers. Each time the youngster's naked posterior showed through, they giggled and made ribald remarks. The little lad lapped up their attention. As for me, I was surprised how clean he was. Obviously, he had been trained early to wipe himself with snow.

Urged to match or better the boys' acrobatic feats, the men doffed their parkas and showed off. They mocked and teased each other, but always approved well-executed stunts with appropriately vigorous exclamations. They were all well-built specimens with powerful torsos and arms, but Hikhik and Otokreak were outstanding.

"You too, Little White Man! Come on, come on!" they chorused anticipating another belly-laugh at my expense.

I did not have a large frame, but throughout my youth at school and college I was interested in gymnastics and felt at home on a trapeze. At the moment, though, I was full of liquid and food. Otokreak and my hosts took my hesitation to mean that either I did not know how to use a swinging bar, or else I was afraid of it. This made them feel superior to me, the Little White Man, and made them more insistent.

"You are a *Kablunak*. Show us what you can do!" persisted Otokreak.

"My stomach is filled with your good food, and I'm tired from my trip, but I'll try to show you one or two tricks," I agreed at last. Bare to the waist, I repeated the hardest presses, swings, dips, and stands of the four well-muscled young men, dismounting with a fancy somersault to the incredulous delight of all present.

"He is truly capable, the Little Man!" they kept repeating in amazement, gleefully gathering around me. I stood panting heavily like a winded prize fighter, but I was inwardly pleased with my unscheduled performance. The males felt my biceps, while Malrukhak and Nuitek stroked my back and chest, giggling and gushing, "His skin is as smooth as a child's and as white as the

67

milk of a caribou cow!" Their expressions of surprise and admiration were summed up by the older Hikhik, who up to now, had remained a cool spectator, "Eh! A man you are! You're small, but strong and capable. You should have a woman."

I let his suggestion pass, busying myself by wiping the sweat off my upper body and then replacing my parka. With all the acrobats sweating freely, the acrid smell of wet caribou fur and burnt seal oil permeated the place. As quickly as I could, I expressed my thanks to Amiraernek and Malrukhak and told them I was going to visit Makara. The men trooped out with me, leaving the women behind to clean up the makeshift gymnasium.

Despite my repeated attempts to change the subject, my companions detailed my prowess on the trapeze to the squat, round-faced Makara. His hair was cut very short, except for a tuft above the forehead. His impassive wife Paniyuak was tending the lamp and setting the tea cups ready, while their two boys and a girl stood shyly in a corner, staring at me with reverential wonder.

As the men continued jesting and laughing, Makara and ultimately his wife joined in their merriment and soon everyone's shyness vanished. While Paniyuak served tea, the men's conversation gravitated to their recent trips to their respective trap lines, and Makara added that he had spotted a small herd of musk-oxen in the distance along the Angnimayok River, north of Krimakton Lake.

Finally, over yet another cup of tea, reinforced with slices of meat, Hikhik turned to me and said, "I'll start with you tomorrow for Cambridge Bay." This sudden decision by their unofficial leader would involve everyone, but it received general approval. Otokreak's friends went back to tell their wives and prepare for the journey.

Outside it was very cold and the sky was altogether clear except for a halo around the half-moon. A slight breeze raised powdery snow along the shore of the Big Lake. But Hikhik didn't like that halo. "The weather is changing. We may get a storm," he forecast unequivocally. To me there was nothing in the air to indicate a drastic change in the next twenty-four hours, and I was prepared to turn in with a loaded stomach and a light heart.

Everyone was still up in Hikhik's igloo when he and I returned, for the entire Eskimo family habitually goes to bed at the same time. My composure was promptly ruffled when Hikhik asked me hospitably, "Which one of my two wives would you like for the night? You are my friend and it will please me if you choose one. Be happy, Little Man!" The tall, shapely, good-looking Arluk, and the more mature, but none-the-less attractive Kommek giggled at the proposal—not because it was out of the ordinary run of Krangmalit hospitality, but rather they had never had the opportunity to sleep with a White Man before. I did not wish to offend Hikhik nor to insult the two ladies present, especially the red-cheeked Kommek, who apparently thought I was going to choose her. In my opinion they were both desirable and could command the attention of many men.

Carefully choosing my words and using my politest tone, I replied, "I am an *Angakuk,* a priest in my country, and I am forbidden to accept such a wonderful invitation, not even from as good a friend as you, Hikhik." He did not expect my response and seemed perplexed.

"But our *Angakuk* (by this he meant their shaman, medicine man, or sorcerer) takes women in his *krepik* (sleeping bag) all the time," Hikhik persisted. "Why not you? You are a man; you need a woman. Even caribou, seals and birds must have females."

Arluk and Kommek were openly disappointed. "He is crazy. Such a waste of a nice-looking man!" was their consensus.

I was sorry to shatter their expectations, but I couldn't fly off on such a tangent and jeopardize my work.

Time proved me right. In succeeding years I would receive many similar offers from different Eskimo husbands and often directly from their women folk. By consistent refusal, I kept out of trouble. But is wasn't easy. As Hikhik put it, "A man needs a woman."

To this day, with all the experience I have had dealing with human nature, I sometimes wonder if the law of celibacy isn't contradictory to what God intended because according to the Scriptures, "Male and female He created them (the first man and woman). . .and God said unto them, 'Be fruitful, and multiply, and replenish the earth'," (Genesis 1:28).

Predictably, conversation lagged after my unequivocal refusal, so I seized the opportunity to undress and slip into my bag. The children also stripped and lay down to sleep. The rest of the family did likewise, shy in their nudity. Arluk crawled into Hikhik's family-sized *krepik,* while Kommek took with her the younger child, Ukayaluk, then put out the blubber lamp, leaving only a tiny flame burning for the night. She kept looking at me stealthily from her *krepik,* presumably expecting me to change my mind. I was left to my resolution and solitude with mixed emotions, accentuated by a gnawing in my stomach which, I suspected, resulted from overeating and over-exertion on the trapeze.

Intermittently through the night, the ice under the igloo exploded in long, booming sounds like rolls of distant thunder, caused by expanding frozen water in the intense cold. When I ultimately surrendered to sleep, it was transitory, punctuated by weird dreams. In one of them I was back at Burnside, airborne in a small plane above the cemetery. Peering below, I distinguished many broken human bones and skulls left by wolves and foxes. I was very hungry, and descended among the graves. Sitting on the frozen ground, I grabbed the skulls with flesh still left on them and started gnawing at them until I was full.

I woke up early in the morning, well ahead of everyone else, only too cognizant of an intense stomach-ache. . .

My infrequent mention of the Arctic dawn, morning, or its polar night may need some explanation. Here's why. North of the Arctic Circle, the sun disappears completely in October, and even sooner at the higher latitudes. That's when the polar night takes over. Each 24-hour day then consists of approximatley four hours of light (without the sun itself being visible), followed by twenty hours of night. Happily, the long polar nights are seldom, if ever, completely dark because the ubiquitous snow reflects the shine of the moon, the stars, and the Northern Lights.

Above the 71st parallel, roughly north of Victoria Land, the first rays of sunshine will appear for a few minutes each day on the eastern horizon about mid-January. The sun continues to climb progressively higher above the horizon as the days roll by until the end of July when the long Arctic days temporarily replace the nights. Then, slowly but relentlessly, the polar day will begin its inevitable swing back to the awesome polar night.

With this explanation, it should not be surprising that the morn preceeds the dawn, in the same manner as this narrative.

5

Across Unchartered Land

The entire camp bustled with travel preparations next morning. All igloos had been emptied of caribou skins, blubber lamps, sleeping bags, pots and kettles, fishing and hunting gear. Women and children helped the men load the long dogsleds with bundles of dry and green fish, dry meat, bags of blubber, cans of kerosene, primus stoves, wolves' and foxes' skins for future trading, and other necessary baggage.

Each family providently stowed away carcasses of caribou, bundles of skins, and other paraphernalia unessential for the immediate trip in their own igloos. They sealed their porch entrances with large snow blocks to keep out foxes, wolves, and wolverines. As a further deterrent, traps were set inside each porch to catch any venturesome predator bent on burrowing to the cached food.

Working methodically, the adults took their time, concerned only with the present. Who could blame them? In a way their imminent move was festive. Soon they would be at Cambridge Bay to enjoy the company of friends they had not seen since spring, and even swap animal pelts for goods at the local Hudson's Bay Company trading post.

Although most people—including those in neighboring Canada and the United States—were still coping with the economic and emotional devastation of the man-made Great Depression, the hardy Arctic nomads, dependent only on Mother Nature, were less affected. By 1938, the year after my first

71

glimpse of the Barren Land, native trappers and hunters felt they were being adequately rewarded for their trap line labors. And Arctic trading posts prospered accordingly.

The pelt of a common red fox, in 1938 for example, brought the Eskimo about $15 worth of merchandise at the trading post, or approximately half the retail market price in Vancouver, British Columbia (the nearest and largest international port, rail and air terminus).

A white fox would trade for about $40. To an Eskimo this represented three boxes of twenty rifle shells in each box, or ten yards of calico for his wife's sewing or twenty-five pounds of flour and a pound of tea or tallow to boot.

A cross fox—so named for its red and black fur, with the black areas forming what is considered a cross on the animal's shoulders and spine—traded for some $60. Each silver fox, actually having black fur mixed with white, meant the equivalent of about $75 Canadian to its captor and retailed for double that amount.

A mounted white fox would carry a retail price of at least $150. On an average, for every hundred white foxes one blue or platinum fox would be born. They bought about $120 worth of Hudson's Bay Company's goods for the Inuit hunter or trapper and retailed for $300 Canadian in Vancouver. However, I recall an exceptionally fortunate constable of the R.C.M.P. (Royal Canadian Mounted Police) acquiring a white fox from an Eskimo trapper in exchange for a pack of needles—few professional traders were that sharp!

We missionaries, having taken the vow of poverty, largely depended on our own hunting and fishing ability in good times or bad, as well as on the Missions' benevolence. The Missions were financed through the Society for Propagation of the Faith which received funds from Catholic church collections throughout the world, as well as from Papal Charities and our own efforts. Mission hospitals and schools, however, were subsidized jointly by Canada's Federal Government, the Oblates, and Papal Charities.

Some women rounded up their children for the impending departure with shouts of "Come here! Stay close!" Others set up primus stoves and melted snow for a last cup of tea before harnessing the dog teams. The four families had come to Big Lake the previous fall from Kiluiktok (Western River) at the extreme end of Bathurst Inlet. They had camped at Krimakton Lake until the following summer and then traveled overland on foot to the present camp. This was their first move in five months. They had built their igloos in early November, making them almost two months old—the maximum life of even a well-built igloo.

My stomach-ache had kept me awake most of the night, and by morning I was making frequent sorties to a snow drift. My new friends were amused to notice that I had developed piles. Swirling in the wind, the bloodied tissue paper was a dead giveaway. What neither they nor I knew then was that these hemorrhoids would stay with me for the next decade, weakening my system to the point that I couldn't bear them any more, ultimately causing me to return to civilization.

At daybreak, with all six sleds ready and loaded, their dogs harnessed and everyone seated, we took off at a fast clip, led by Otokreak on his lighter sled. Hikhik's team and mine were close behind him, with Paoktok, Amiraernek, and Makara following us in that order.

Travel in the bitter cold and wind made my ailment worse. I had to stop more often, holding up the entire caravan. Hikhik's son Anerodluk, who accompanied me on my sled, would call out to his father, "The White Man has to relieve himself. Wait for us!" Although these extra rest periods slowed our progress, they enabled others to tend their own needs, especially the mother's with their children.

To avoid the surrounding hills and difficult terrain, for twenty miles we followed the same route as Otokreak and I did to reach the camp the day before. Eventually the land flattened out on all sides and we veered sharply to the north at the source of the Angnimayok River. We had traversed only a few miles on the riverbed when Otokreak pulled up his team, anchored his sled, and ran towards Hikhik waving his arms, signaling him to stop too. The rest of us followed suit, sensing that our young leader had spied something out of the ordinary. Excitedly Otokreak yelled out to us, "Just ahead are many fresh musk-ox tracks!"

Hikhik and Makara (who had mentioned only the previous day that he had seen a small herd of musk-oxen while setting his trap line) picked up their rifles at once and followed the tracks. The women took advantage of this unexpected break to melt some snow for tea. Only Amiraernek's wife Malrukhak, now in her last month of pregnancy, was moving around with difficulty.

Close together for warmth, we kneeled on the snow, our bare hands grasping the warm enamel tea cups. Suddenly, we heard distant rifle reports. Our dogs stood up at once, howling in unison, breaking the polar nights gloomy silence.

"A big noise can be heard!" the children cried expectantly. Downing their tea, the men returned to their sleds for their knives and guns, then headed toward the shots. In an hour or so they were back, carrying portions of quartered musk-oxen. Two skins were filled with the edible parts of animal entrails. Their rib cages were carried with the aid of tumplines, while the rumps and hind legs were slung accross the men's shoulders. Thus each man was heavily-laden with illegal game.

Everyone appeared happy, especially the children, who enticed each other by saying, "Quick, quick, come and see the musk-oxen's heads!" Contentedly, with the meat securely loaded on the sleds, we resumed our trek.

Dark, sinister clouds began to form in the west, shrouding the faint light on the horizon as they floated directly towards us. An hour later a sudden fierce wind enveloped our teams with a swirling blanket of snow. Still we plowed on, the tinkle of the lead dogs' bells drawing us together. But soon we had to admit it was futile and unsafe to fight the storm. Accordingly, the men built two large igloos on the west bank of the river, where they would be sheltered somewhat from the wind. I wanted to help them, but I had lost so much blood that it was all I could do to care for my dogs. How my friends were able to construct their igloos in the face of onrushing, biting snowflakes, only an Eskimo could explain!

Trouble was added by masses of snow cascading periodically from the top of the riverbank, covering them in a huge white shroud. While they struggled, the women with crying youngsters huddled together in a vain attempt to keep warm on the lee of their sleds. The unencumbered women and boys braved the merciless wind to unharness their tired, shivering animals to the dog lines. Then they shuffled over to the slowly rising igloos and filled the cracks between the snow blocks.

Hikhik was putting the blocks together on one igloo and Otokreak on the other. Makara, Paoktok, and Amiraernek were cutting blocks out of the snow and passing them on to the builders. Their faces almost hidden with frost and flying snow, they all worked steadily, without rushing, yet quickly, methodically, and with consummate skill.

When Hikhik's igloo was ready, his family and Makara's family got the blubber lamps going inside and carried in the furs, sleeping bags, fish, and meat. Paoktok, Amiraernek, their families, and I followed suit as Otokreak's igloo was completed. With ten of us in each igloo, our accommodations would be crowded. Slabs of dried meat, frozen fish, and meat were passed around, as usual. Children got the most tender morsels of caribou meat and small chunks of blubber with a rancid smell. On the rack above the blubber lamp mittens and fur socks were placed to dry.

Nuitek, Paoktok's wife, served tea as her baby girl, wrapped in soft caribou fur, slept in a corner. Few words were exchanged. In a tired voice Amiraernek said, "Nuliayuk, the Spirit Mother of all Beasts, gave us food for a few days. Hikhik and Makara shot two musk-oxen. Makara was wearing wolverine claws on his sleeves for good luck."

Jammed side by side on the *iglek*, we kept reasonably warm, though not entirely comfortable. Seeing my poor state, Otokreak offered to tend my dogs when he and his friends went out into the raging storm to tend theirs and I gladly accepted his kindness. So weak and tired, I didn't know or care who lay next to me. No one actually enjoyed a restful sleep that night. There wasn't room to turn. It was cold. The younger children cried often. As the wind increased with time, Paoktok echoed everyone's misgivings, "It's cold here. We built the igloo hurriedly. The snow was too soft. I wonder if the blocks will hold as the wind gets stronger." His speculation only abetted my insomnia. But the hunters' concern for their shelter never reached the point of worry or fear. To them it was just another bad storm and they would wait it out, just like countless other times.

Quietly they talked back and forth about the trip. "The dogs didn't have much trouble pulling sleds. The snow is just fine. It's the wind that makes it difficult for us all," said Amiraernek.

"A good thing the wind was blowing in our direction! The musk-oxen didn't get a whiff of our scent. Now we'll have fresh meat for awhile," Otokreak rejoined from his *krepik*.

"We'll have a good feed tomorrow night if we stop early enough," contributed Malrukhak pleasantly. "The baby in my belly is moving like a weasel. He is rolling up and down. He did that all night," she added laughing. I silently coveted her sense of humor to help me in my own physical distress.

Before long, I was dressing for another trip outside. My fellow travelers poked more fun at my misery teasing me with "Where are you going, Little Man? To feed the pups again?" On the other hand, as I crawled out shakily through the small opening hung with caribou skin which served as an inner door, I heard Nuitek, Paoktok's wife, sympathize with me, "He is suffering, it's too bad!" Their kindness always overshadowed their playfulness. Frequent were their expressed concerns for my well-being, their offers of help, and such practical advice as "Drink a lot of tea! Don't run alongside the sled! We'll have musk-ox meat and broth later; you will feel like a young caribou!"

Towards day the wind seemed to lose some of its earlier fury and Otokreak suggested to Paoktok and Amiraernek that they might consider pushing on. "We will wait for Hikhik and Makara to rise. Then we'll talk it over with them. But we should prepare ourselves now if we decide to travel today," answered Amiraernek. He spoke slowly and carefully, as most sensible Eskimos do.

We were still about a hundred and fifty miles from Cambridge Bay as the crow flies, or approximately two hundred miles by dog team—five or six days' travel time with our heavy sleds over uneven inland trails. That is, according to the Eskimos, provided we had Hilla, the Spirit Weather, along with us as a friend. Otokreak's reason to resume the trip in spite of the storm was that the longer we waited, the less food would remain for the dogs. Feeble from hunger, they would be unable to pull our sleds and, lacking resistance, likely freeze in their sleep.

Once Paoktok and Amiraernek surveyed the situation outside, they both predicted that the storm would continue for several days. "There are no stars showing in the sky. No moon is to be seen. Nor any light where the sun rises in the spring." They were against moving until the weather cleared a little.

Hikhik and Makara joined them as they summed up their observations. "And what about the children?" Makara asked rhetorically. "Will they be able to stand the cold and the wind? Will they not freeze their noses and cheeks on the sleds if the wind grows stronger again? Or a child may fall from the sled and get lost in the *pirtok* (blizzard) and freeze to death as little Tautiak did, remember?"

Hikhik was silent up to this point. Instead, his experienced eyes minutely surveyed the snow-bound surroundings from the top of the river bank where all the men had gathered. Presently he walked off in a northeasterly direction for a few hundred feet, looked about him deliberately, then motioned the others to approach him.

"Look," he said to the four men, "this creek points toward the Kulugayuk River. I have traps all along it. If we follow it, we should reach the river in two days. Its high banks will give us more protection from the wind. And we'll be able to travel faster along its shoreline."

Only Makara, who was older than the others, could confirm Hikhik's identification of the frozen-solid creek. Its meandering was well-defined by a trough of packed snow, which showed no trace of dwarf willows or withered grass constituting the Arctic tundra. Here and there granitic rocks dominated the desolate land to give it a semblance of life.

After quiet cogitation, Makara spoke, "Hikhik is wise. We will follow him!"

Hearing no objections from his friends, Paoktok and Amiraernek, Otokreak declared, "Let's go!"

Like gray ghosts in the flying snow and howling wind, the hunters walked back to the igloos. Told of their decision, the women fed us all as much tea, dried fish, meat, and fat as we could consume, anticipating the long hours of sled-sitting and running that lay ahead.

It took strenuous effort to rouse the dogs action. Whipped along by the wind, the snow had piled up in the riverbed and spilled over on the dogs. They lay curled up, showing only a little of their fur. They didn't move until the moment they were harnessed, reluctant to believe their masters would travel in such abominable weather.

The younger children, in their soft fawn-skin parkas, looked like bear cubs who had been rolling in the snow. But they were not gamboling now. Their backs to the gusty wind, they sat quietly, almost motionlessly, on the sleds between their parents, as the teams pulled away from the temporary camp.

Driven by the wind, the snow clung to our eyelashes, sometimes so gluing our eyelids shut that we could only open our eyes by rubbing them with our mitts. Sitting behind me on the sled, Hikhik's son Anerodluk thoughtfully offered to sit in front, yelling in my ears, "Let me help you! You can rest behind me." As we changed positions, I noticed that my two wheel dogs (the ones closest to the sled) were bleeding from the jaws—an unmistakable sign of extreme cold. When temperatures drop below minus forty degrees, their bodies dehydrate faster and they bite more frequently into the hard snow for moisture. In doing so, they sometimes scrape their lips, drawing blood. Such unfortunate canines certainly had my sympathy.

Before leaving the igloo I had forced myself to eat with my friends to maintain my stamina and inner warmth. But my malaise was further aggravated by exposure to the storm. I couldn't warm up. Holding on to a rope tied to the sled, I tried running alongside, but that didn't help much. In my dejection and misery I cursed in French, "Nom d'un chien" (In a dog's name)! Then I prayed silently, I really hope You are in heaven, Good God, and have a place for me and all my Eskimo friends. Had He let me, I think I would have gladly lain down in the snow and gone to sleep forever. Yet somehow I managed to survive the nightmarish ordeal.

Early in the afternoon we discovered sled tracks and frozen dog droppings. The weight of the sleds had packed and frozen the snow where the runners had passed, so their tracks remained while the wind swept the softer snow to the sides. Here and there the tracks were broken and we could not tell when they were made. The mere sight of them, however, gave us needed courage and even our exhausted dogs pulled with renewed vigor.

Two hours later Hikhik; who had taken the lead, sighted black dots against the distant snowy backdrop. "Men, men, a lot of them!" he yelled encouragingly above the storm.

Three families in as many igloos were in a camp situated on the shore of a small lake, and we spent that night with them. Our host, Avalekrak, told us they had moved up in early winter from Krikirtariuak, (Melbourne Island) five miles north of Labyrinth Bay in Queen Maud Gulf. They had come here to retrieve caches of caribou they had killed in the fall and were living off them now.

"We will take back the rest of the caribou," explained Avalekrak. "We killed a large number of them. We will trade whatever you need."

Hikhik and his associates appeared pleased. "We killed two musk-oxen yesterday. We'll take a few caribou carcasses with us to Ikalututiak (Cambridge Bay)" Hikhik said, speaking for us all. Avalekrak thought it over, then said "We shall go with you to Ikalututiak to trade some foxes. We would also like to see our friends there." His impulsive, almost spontaneous decision to pick up and move was not atypical of Eskimos. It merely confirmed my earlier realization that the Inuit People Beyond were truly creatures of the present.

And for me this unexpected turn of events could not have been better. At the slow rate we were progressing, my diminishing supplies of dog food had me worried. I asked Avalekrak if he could spare some carcasses of caribou, offering him a case of *krakolak*, or hardtack bread, in trade, with further payment once we reached Cambridge Bay. "For my children I can use the *krakolak*," he answered. "And I shall come to your igloo in Ikalututiak for some calico for the wife."

The deal struck, Avalekrak piled six headless and legless frozen caribou carcasses on my sled and helped himself to my pilote bread.

Later that evening Otokreak, his face betraying inward satisfaction, sat down beside me and said with optimism, "Our dogs will be well fed from now on. Right now mine are getting so thin, they look like shadows."

"Did you trade some meat?" I asked.

"Yes, indeed," he grinned. "Avalekrak gave me three caribou carcasses for nothing!" I read between the lines and laughed. I was paying for nine instead of six carcasses!

The storm had turned into a ground drift, the *naterorvik*, a huge mass of whirling snow sweeping the barren floor and lifting the snow granules twenty or more feet above the ground. Our visibility was reduced to a few hundred feet in the polar night's opaque milky light.

I was confined to Avalekrak's igloo for two days and three nights. The men built an addition to the three igloos to reduce the overcrowding and make it more comfortable for everyone. The forced stop gave me a chance to rest my wasting body. The women boiled large quantities of musk-ox meat and served more broth than tea. When we were eating in Hikhik's igloo, I was surprised to hear his younger wife Arluk address me, *"Little* Man, I have boiled a musk-ox tongue for you!" Looking a little shy, but happy, smiling, and very attractive, she brought it to me. "Thank you, *Little* Arluk," I responded as everybody laughed, appreciating my word play. Her name also designated the beautiful blue-black wolf, a prized rarity in the Barren Land.

To while away the wakeful hours, I talked at length with Avalekrak's mother, Itireitok. She seemed incredibly old for an Eskimo woman. Her face was crisscrossed with deep wrinkles and bluish tattoo lines, three vertical ones on the chin, two horizontal ones on each cheek, and one—in the shape of a wish-bone—on her forehead. Despite her advanced age, her hair was still black showing only a faint gray line at the temples. A mixed expression of joy and sorrow showed in her black eyes, and she bubbled with energy and good humor, reminding me of "ancient" Manerathiak. Because I paid more attention to her story telling than her family did, she talked to me without reservation. In fact, I learned a lot more from older Eskimos than from younger ones. The oldsters had stored away many tales and sincerely resurrected them.

"Do you know the big Bay of Kattimanek?" she asked me by way of introducing one of her stories.

I nodded, recalling my numerous trips to the Arctic Sound en route to Coppermine.

"A long time ago a man lived there all by himself. He did not have a wife to look after him. No friends to visit him. But he was not lonely. He possessed a strange power not given to ordinary hunters. One day he went down to the seashore, saying to himself, 'Let's see if there is anything moving in the water.' He walked for a long time along the shore, peering into the clear water. But all he could see were smooth rocks and pebbles. On the beach, though, he found a piece of drift-willow and sat down to carve it with a knife. He cut out shavings of various shapes, leaving bark on some of them. Then he threw those shavings with bark on them into the water and called them *ikalupik* (Arctic char). To the smaller, barkless bits of wood he gave names like *kapielik, pikuktok,* and *aogak.* These large white fish we now find swimming in our lakes, rivers, and the sea."

Itireitok's legend reminded me of Manerathiak's myth about the Spirit who dwells in the dark depths of the sea, and—more remotely—of Greek mythology. Frequently the message these legends or fables originally communicated has been lost over the generations; but this one was refreshingly different. It certainly sounded clearer than some of the bizarre Krangmalit stories which often start nowhere and end nowhere.

Generally speaking, the people of the Barren Land do not try to analyze the universe around them. They simply accept it. They are basically unemotional fatalists inclined to reduce their fundamental philosophy to a single expression: "Ayornartok (It can't be helped)." Life for them is short and too much of a daily struggle against cold and famine, as it is. Glances into the indefinite past by old people like Itireitok and Manerathiak provided fantastic notions about their world. For them, as for other older Eskimos of the Central Arctic, the land is inhabited by supernatural beings. Some of them are good and harmless—souls of the dead who roam the land to help until they come to their final rest in a place of happiness called Heaven. They always protect the tired and sick against evil spirits and ghouls. The ghouls delight in misleading the unwary traveler during stormy weather and causing distress.

"They are around all the time," Itireitok assured me. "We call them *Tupilain.* They may be shy or fiendish. They are always breathing and whispering, like the wind itself. Sometimes they look like men. Sometimes like animals or mysterious hybrids. Raised out of nowhere, like the hills and mountains, the rivers, lakes, and seas."

The old woman paused to reflect on what she had told me, then continued, "Little Man, all things you see around you—on earth, in the sky, and in the waters—have life in them. Like musk-ox and caribou, plants and snow, rocks and ice, fish, and birds. The Spirits live in some of them, as they do in the mountains and the sea. Wolves and foxes—yes, all animals are inhabited by Spirits. Their breath or soul remains when they are killed or die."

Itireitok used the same word *anernek* to denote breath, soul, and spirit, because her own soul was living and breathing, capable of survival after death. Without knowing it, she was explaining her belief in animism, the doctrine that natural phenomena, animal life, and inanimate objects have souls.

"Tell me, what happens to the soul of a dead animal, such as a killed seal, musk-ox, or caribou?" I asked her.

"I don't know," she uttered, seemingly perplexed. "The *Angakuk*, our Shaman, tells us that its soul remains behind. That's why we must be careful when we kill a caribou. We cannot sew the skin, we cannot scrape it or dry it when live caribou are present. Otherwise they will run away and never return. Our *Angakuk* says we must give a piece of the liver to its soul right away and cut up the carcass on clean snow if it is to be taken into the igloo."

I knew that each shaman has his own methods of imposing taboos on his people. And, because they know that many things do go wrong in any venture, they capitalize on that by purporting a broken taboo.

Noticing that Itireitok was still in a talking mood and was apparently enjoying our conversation, I continued my questions. "What happens to the soul of a man when his body dies?"

"Who knows for sure?" she parried. "All we know is that we will live on forever. If we die old, we remain forever old. If we die young, we remain forever young. The *Angakuk* says that the soul stays close to the corpse for a few days. That's why we leave the body wrapped up in its *krepik* (sleeping bag)—on top of the igloo in winter and beside the tent in summer—just for a while. Then we take it away on the sled to a spit of land or a hill and we leave it there with some of the departed's belongings. The soul will roam the land until its name is given to a child or a dog. Then it'll go to the Land of the Dead, where it will live happily with plenty of food, playing games with other souls. Some souls go to the Land of the Day, so we call them the People of the Day. They are those who have been killed or died while hunting, and those who died in the *krepiks*. Some other souls go to the bottom of the sea. These are the souls of people who have drowned. They are the People on the Point of Land."

Try as I might, I could not get Itireitok to tell me whether the human soul is judged or punished, if found wanting; rewarded, if considered deserving. To her knowledge, all souls, including those of murderers, went to the same place of joy and good times. She believed in the immortality of the human soul, and that it is linked to a name as long as it is employed from generation to generation. Other souls with that same name linger with the current bearer bestowing their good qualities upon them.

Then she volunteered, "Departed souls can be so troublesome! I am afraid of them. It is no good for them to be wandering about, forlorn and unattached. That is why we name a dog after the dead person when no newborn child is in the family to receive that name."

I knew of several such dog namings. These animals received no special treatment in the bargain. They were beaten with the rest of the team when necessary and starved when their masters ran out of food. However, they were never killed by their owners. They had to die naturally so that their given names could be respectably transferred to other humans or canines.

I learned about that during my first year in the Arctic. One morning as the sun hung low over Kringaun, the mountain southeast of Burnside, I saw a dog crouching in the snow on the slope to the channel. As I drew closer, I realized it was dying. His ribs were sticking out through his thin fur. There was no flesh on him, just bones. I tried to make him walk with me, but he would not even rise. I hated to see the poor old dog suffer a slow death, so I put an end to his misery with a rifle shot. It was deep twilight when a tall, powerfully built Eskimo entered the Mission building. He came straight to the point. "Why did you kill Manillak?"

"Manillak?" I echoed in surprise. "Who is he? I've never killed anyone in my life!"

Father Delalande, who was nearby, knew I had shot a dog that morning. He told me that I'd made a bad mistake and offered to talk to the dog's owner should he come to the Mission. And here was the stranger, boiling angry, with a grim look in his black eyes. I couldn't understand everything he said, so Father Delalande summed up his complaint for me in French. "He knows you killed the dog, and says that Manillak was his late grandfather and the dog was named after him. I explained this Eskimo custom to you earlier in the day. But don't worry, I'll take care of the matter!"

Within a few minutes he had the man calmed by explaining White Man ways and smiling. The three of us went amicably into the kitchen and had tea. That was my introduction to Kakagun, undoubtedly the greatest hunter among all the Krangmalit that I would meet during my twelve years in the Arctic. Our paths would cross many times after this initial misunderstanding. Before he left our Mission post that night, Kakagun put his hand on my shoulder and said with an appreciative smile, "Little Man, you are a good shot!"

Towards the third night the storm played itself out and everyone spoke happily about resuming the interrupted trip on the morrow. I was feeling better and was able to feed my dogs myself. It was still extremely cold, but the clouds had vanished and the sky glowed with the Northern Lights. After storm and stress, they seemed more beautiful than ever. From a dusky line of diaphanous haze a few degrees above the horizon, the multicolored streaks ascended towards the heavenly zenith, assuming kaleidoscopic shapes and shades in their dazzling, quivering motion.

Hikhik, Otokreak, and the other men hardly gave them a glance, and I knew from experience that commenting on their beauty was a waste of time. They regarded the shimmering curtains with mixed feelings of fear and wonder, shunning any discussions of this remarkable phenomenon. Perhaps they were intimidated because they could neither comprehend nor fully enjoy it as it frequently indicated falling temperatures. In the intensely cold silent air, without any breeze or wind, the snow would expand, creating crackling sounds that seemed somehow to originate from the Northern Lights.

"The Heavenly Spirits are dancing!" they would observe automatically, and say no more. Characteristically, too, whenever there was a brilliant display of shooting stars, they were far less poetic. "Look," they'd exclaim, "the Spirits of the Heavens are excreting all over the sky!" Nevertheless, they were pleased to see the Northern Lights since they brightened the long, gloomy polar night.

What had begun as a caravan of two sleds from Burnside, was now an exodus as the families of Avalekrat, Igutak, and Avadluk joined us in the morning. To combat the cold, the men wore double breeches and double parkas, while the women donned breeches and double parkas that fell below their knees, making us look like huge apes.

Well-rested, our dogs pulled eagerly as we traveled in a northeasterly direction. By noon we were able to reach the banks of the Kulugayuk River, now at an altitude of 450 feet. We descended its snow-covered embankment to protect ourselves from the snarling westerly wind sweeping the barren floor above us. But the ideal snow we had hoped for was not there. Sheltered from the wind, the snow lay soft in drifts. It was so sticky that the sled runners had little chance of sliding through.

Time after time Grandmother Itireitok was told to walk ahead of Avalekrak's team. She was now excess baggage that could be discarded if need be. Bent over her long walking stick, the poor old woman resembled a scarecrow in an incongruous Arctic setting. I wanted to help her, but couldn't for two reasons: Not only was my sled already heavily laden, but—more significantly—it would have been improper for me to interfere in a family matter. With her indomitable spirit, Itireitok plodded on. She didn't complain. Knowing that she was altogether dispensable, she acted accordingly. When the going got tougher still, the other women were also compelled to walk alongside the dogs, while the male drivers and children remained on the sleds.

Recurrently we had to stop for other reasons. Particles of the soft snow easily attached themselves to the hair between our dogs' paws, freezing into icy balls that irritated and cut the helpless quadrupeds. Whenever he saw one of his dogs trying to bite its paws for that reason, Hikhik (who had taken the lead) would stop his team and walk over to the afflicted animal. When he called it by name, it would lie on its side and extend its aching paws to him. Down on his knees, Hikhik raised the paws to his mouth and bit off the icy pellets as children bite hard candy. Simultaneously drivers of the other sleds, assisted by members of their families, emulated Hikhik by examining all their dogs' paws and biting off accumulated ice. Despite this serious precaution, they did so with usual Eskimo good humor and crude jokes. Their consistently positive attitude in the face of difficulty helped me forget my own troubles.

Igutak's wife Oviluk, a short and chubby young woman with eyes so slanted they seemed almost closed, utilized these periodic stops to take two newborn pups to their mother for feeding. Picking them out of a caribou bag tied to the sled, she carried the yelping pair to the bitch, unharnessed her and spread a caribou skin for her to lie on. These puppies were the only survivors of a litter of eight; the rest had been discarded on the snow to freeze because they were supernumerary.

This time Oviluk noticed that the pups kept poking and pulling at their mother's teats without success. Suspecting the worst, she felt the breasts. They confirmed her fears. In the turmoil of the morning's preparations for the trail, she had forgotten to attach the apron-like blanket of caribou skin over the dog's belly. Almost devoid of hair around the teats, the enlarged breasts froze solid.

Oviluk called over her husband Igutak, a man in his late teens, tall and well-proportioned, whose long face seemed to be fixed in perpetual amazement. "That's really too bad! What shall we do with the pups?" he wondered aloud.

"I have enough milk in my breasts for our child and the pups," she replied without hesitation before returning to the sled with them. Lifting her double parka, she gave her breast first to one pup, then to the other, as naturally and unconcernedly as she did to her four-year-old daughter, the youngest of her three children.

Meanwhile, Igutak re-harnessed the pups' mother, picked up the rug, and took it back to the sled. To Avalekrak and Avadluk, who came to inquire what happened, he simply said, "We forgot to cover the bitch this morning. Her breasts are frozen. Tomorrow, before we pull away from camp, we'll know just how badly she is frozen." Word of this misfortune spread quickly to all the sleds, and the resigned comment was always the same, "It's certainly too bad."

The high embankments narrowed as we progressed, and the huge granite rocks, partly covered with snow, lay in our path. The hunters stopped their teams when Hikhik shouted to them, "It's getting dangerous! The women and children should walk on the bank." He was promptly obeyed. Ahead lay frozen rapids, boulders, and seepage through ice. Like a long, twisting snake, the dog teams followed one behind the other, the men skillfully maneuvering the sleds to avoid damage to the runners. Some of the dogs kept losing their footing on the glare ice and were dragged along on their bellies by the rest of the team.

Malrukhak, Amiraenek's wife, heavy with child, and old Itireitok intoned monotonously as they trudged stoically alongside the other women. They were all tired, but none of them grumbled. That was their lot and they took it in stride, lightening their desperation with gossip and even laughter.

"Look at Makara," one of them suggested. "He must be getting old—he nearly upset the sled!" They all giggled, including his wife Paniyuak, who added with a wide smile, "He's not so old in the *krepik!*" Like children, they saw humor in everything.

As we passed the rapids, we halted the teams to let the women catch up to us. The dogs were busy sniffing about, having discovered frozen droppings of wolves, wolverines, and foxes which must have been attracted to the river by the carcasses of drowned caribou, now partly submerged by the river's frozen overflow.

"Why are there so many dead caribou here?" I asked my sled companion, Anerodluk, pointing to the bleached bones showing through the ice.

"Last fall the caribou tried to cross the river near the rapids to get better footing on the rocks. The young ice gave way. They were swept under by the currents."

It was much the same all the way to the sea: glare ice, boulders, soft snow, and shortcuts through frozen rapids. Intermittent stops to rest the dogs and re-ice the runners continued throughout the afternoon.

While the women melted snow and heated water over primus stoves, the younger men—Otokreak, Paoktok, Amiraernek, Igutak, and Avadluk—scouted the sparsely willowed banks ahead for ptarmigan and *ukalek*, the big Arctic hare. Although they had little time for such hunting, they seldom came back empty-handed. The gizzards of the white-plumed ptarmigans, or Arctic grouse, they ate raw. Though rather tough for the children, they enjoyed grinding it with their teeth. The adults chomped on two or three gizzards at once, sounding like horse masticating grain. The Arctic hare pleased the women's taste buds the most, however. Although its meat was boiled slowly on the primus stove along with the ptarmigans', they welcomed it as a treat after their steady diet of caribou meat. In addition, the hare's pure-white, silky fur was kept by the women for their monthly discomforts or for cleaning their babies.

Each sortie of the hunters to bag ptarmigan or Arctic hare brought enjoyment to us all. There was emulation among the hunters, and even some of the women who had .22 rifles went along the riverbanks to do some shooting.

"I got more!" Paoktok proclaimed proudly, waving a hare by its ears in front of Otokreak who had managed only four ptarmigans, and both laughed.

We found four good-sized igloos to accommodate us that night and in the morning Otokreak announced that he had slept like a *Hikhik*.

"Why like a Hikhik? Because he is a big man?" I asked naively.

Otokreak exploded with laughter. "No, *Fala*, not like Hikhik, the hunter. Like *hikhik*, a ground squirrel who makes a noise like this: *tch, tch; tch, tch!*"

That morning we finally sighted the sea. It was still several miles away, but in the dim light of the polar night its wide expanse of level whiteness was unmistakable, broken here and there by small dark islands jutting out of the ice. The mere sight of it brought hopes of easier traveling to our band. Everyone's spirits rose, including those of old Itireitok who started a chant copied by the rest:

> "Where to. . .Down to the sea I went
> Where seals breathe through the ice.
> Surprised, I heard: *Hai-ie-ya, hai-ie-ya, ee-ai, ee-ai, ee-ai!*
> The song of the sea
> And the wail of the young ice: *Hai-ee-ya....*
>
> "Where from. . . ?
> From the bottom of the sea they came,
> The great black whales.
> Surprised, I heard: *Hai-ee-ya-ee-ya. . . .*
> The rumbling of the ice floes
> And the clamor of the sea gull. *Hai-ee-ya. . . ."*

Their masters' heightened feelings infected the dogs. They

pricked up their ears and pulled all the harder, sensing more open country and the prospect of food and rest. But as the land flattened out and we left the banks of the Kulugayuk River, we again felt the bite of the westerly wind. Spurning the cold, we headed for Labyrinth Bay, dotted with several small islands. My pains returned and I was once more forced to stop. Anerodluk beckoned his father Hikhik, who came with Otokreak and Avalekrak. They gathered around to shield me from the icy blasts. They did not joke anymore about my condition.

That night we made camp near Melbourne Island. It was so piercingly cold that we had to prime the primus stoves with alcohol. The coal oil had almost gelled.

Hoping to reach Cambridge Bay the following evening, we agreed to break camp early in the morning. It was gray, and fine powdery snow was falling as we left. Luckily, the wind had moderated and we made fairly good progress.

We were still about thirty miles from Cambridge Bay by early afternoon when we ran into a field of broken ice, formed in the fall by local winds and currents. Hikhik signaled us to stop our sleds, and strode ahead to reconnoitre. He subsequently reappeared from behind the jagged slabs and motioned us to follow his team.

If he can get through, so can we, I thought hopefully. But the difficulties we had surmounted along the Kulugayuk River paled beside the hazards that now beset us. Masses of ice rose at every step. Our sleds bumped and slithered, often toppling over and falling into deep holes. To set them right again meant endless unloading and reloading, then filling the holes with snow to make a passageway. It was heartrending to see the dogs exert such desperate efforts to get out of the frozen fissures. As for us, we lifted, pulled, and pushed the sleds till we were drenched in sweat, in spite of the chilling wind.

Tossed and shaken in the struggle, Amiraernek's wife, Malrukhak, began to moan from the onset of labor pains. Amiraernek had no trouble persuading the other hunters to stop and make camp. We found four level spots on which to construct our igloos. When the igloos were almost finished, I noticed that old Itireitok and Kommek, Hikhik's wife, were supporting Malrukhak as she knelt on caribou skins. The other women and the younger children gathered around them to shield Malrukhak from the wind. Bent forward over her knees, Malrukhak moaned so loudly that even the panting, played-out dogs began to howl, as if in orchestrated sympathy.

To everyone's relief the curtain was presently lowered on the pathetic scene as Kommek, her hands under Malrukhak's long parka, delivered the child. In her soft, worn voice Itireitok entreated the Good Spirits of the Earth to protect the baby against Nananuak, the powerful Evil Spirit.

Nananuak was feared by the Krangmalit because she was a murderess who had sojourned in the Land of the Dead. While there, she had been transformed into a man and was instructed to return to her husband in the Land of the Living. When she did, she refused to sleep with him because she had been changed into a man. Her husband was so upset that he decided to kill her. But she was a step ahead of him. When he came through the low door of the igloo, she stabbed him to death. Since then Nananuak had been turned into an Evil Spirit.

"It's a little boy, a strong little boy!" Kommek announced with satisfaction, wrapping the tiny body in the fur of a caribou fawn and hurrying him off into the first of the completed igloos.

Recalling the birth of Naoyak, the Seagull, I couldn't help wondering what Amiraernek would have done if Malrukhak had presented him with a daughter. I wondered, too, how Nokadlak and his family had weathered the storms since I left them.

Supported by Itireitok, Malrukhak lay down on the *iglek* to rest, amid general rejoicing that another little man was added to the People Beyond. "Kommek will clean your boy as soon as the water is warm," the old woman told Malrukhak. "Rest now, and I will get you hot water so that you can wash too."

Kommek and Hikhik's other wife, Arluk, remained with Malrukhak, while Itireitok joined her son Avalekrak in another igloo, and the other women left to help their men unload the sleds and prepare for the night.

I took my sleeping bag to Igutak's igloo where Oviluk, his wife, was tending the blubber lamp. The two newborn pups were whining for their next meal and, having scented their mother's presence in the igloo, were struggling to get out of the bag. Oviluk took one of the pups to the bitch, but the dog would not let her burning breasts be touched. Oviluk, whose own breasts were always full because her four-year-old daughter had not been weaned, again let the pups have her milk.

By morning there was obviously no hope for the pups' mother. Her breasts were raw masses of red pulp, which she tried in vain to soothe by licking. Igutak did not harness her, letting her follow the sled when we moved off. The poor animal did not last long. The ice field taxed the strongest dogs. The sick had to be abandoned when they could not continue. The Barren Land took care of the luckless creatures in its own impersonal, pitiless way.

Night was falling when we finally surmounted the ten-mile-wide ice field and, after a seeming eternity, stood again on smooth snow. So weary was everyone that we barely had strength to build our igloos and crawl in to sleep.

To me the most astonishing fact during our crossing of the broken ice field was the overnight transformation of Malrukhak. When the going became a bit rough, she would dismount from the sled with her newborn son and proceed to walk, cheerfully humming to herself:

"*Eya-eya-eyee-eyee*... I am happy
For the man-child I carry in my hood.
He will not be taken away,
Like my baby girl of old. *Eya-aya-eyee-eyee.*"

Some of the other women, walking and stumbling along their sleds, picked up her song, "*Eya-eya-eyee-eyee*...I am happy..."

The low bluffs of Victoria Land were clearly visible when we started on our last leg in the morning.

At noon—fifteen days after Otokreak and I left the Mission at Burnside—we touched on the low coast of Victoria Land near Cape Colborn. That evening we saw twinkling lights and white smoke rising against the overcast sky in the little cove of Cambridge Bay.

6

Ikalututiak—Cambridge Bay

The hub of Cambridge Bay was the Hudson's Bay Company's trading post operated by Scotty Gall, whose kitchen lights beckoned our approach. Storm lamp in hand, Scotty came out to welcome me with a warm smile wreathing the pipe in his mouth. "How are you, Father? I got a shortwave report that you had left Burnside over ten days ago, and the Police lads and I were beginning to wonder what was holding you up. Come inside and tell me about it!"

As we strolled arm-in-arm to the large, well-constructed H.B.C. building, two men marched toward us. They were Constables Scott Alexander and Reggie Goodie, who had left their R.C.M.P. Post at the end of the Bay, a mile away, to spend the evening with Scotty. I was glad to renew their acquaintance in Scotty's comfortable quarters. He had a tastefully furnished living room with a sofa, two chairs and a coffee table, but we preferred his cozy kitchen.

"You must be tired and cold. Let's have a cup of tea," said Scotty. "By the way," he added, trying to sound casual, "I got married last summer while visiting my home in Scotland. You must meet my Isabelle, Father!" Before I could congratulate him, he called out, "Honey, we have visitors! Can you come, please?"

A woman with a pleasant face appeared from one of the bedrooms. Her arms extended, she came toward me and hugged me. "Father Raymond, I have heard a lot about you from Scotty and these two fine gentlemen. Welcome to Cambridge Bay!" Her voice was full of kindness. We chatted briefly and then she left us menfolk.

"What do you think of my bonnie wife?" Scotty asked me. "She was a school teacher before I got her out of the classroom to see the world!"

"Isabelle is a real honey, as you call her," I told him honestly. "You are definitely a lucky man, Scotty!"

As we drank tea, Constable Scott Alexander studied my face momentarily, then put his thoughts into words "You don't look as well as when you came here last spring, Father. You must have had a tough trip."

"You're right, Scott. I was fine when we left Burnside, but I got sick at Taherkapfaluk, then grew worse along the Kulugayuk River. I think I'll survive, though."

Isabelle returned with a bottle of Scotch whiskey and a large kettle of hot tea. Everyone drank to my health and Scotty remarked, "What puzzles me, Father, is why you didn't come up through Melville Sound? Doubtless it would have been much easier than going overland." Scotty was not an adventurer (in the strict sense of the word). Of slender build, he stood five feet six inches and—despite his thirty-four years—still retained the face of a teenager. His blue eyes glistened when he spoke.

I told him about Otokreak and his friends that he, my guide, wanted to call on Big Lake. "In all my days in the Arctic I've never heard of any white men traveling across that country," Scotty persisted, "not even government surveyors. And I haven't heard of Big Lake, although, of course, there are millions of lakes in the Territories and no one could possibly hear of them all. Did you know that there are more lakes in Canada than in the rest of the world combined?" Without waiting for an answer, he turned to Scott Alexander, who was Reggie Goodie's senior by about eight years. "Have any of your fellows been over Father's trail?"

"Let's have a look at your map." Constable Alexander was not one to give quick answers. Scotty brought in a topographical survey map from the living room and spread it out on the wooden kitchen table. Dated 1932, it showed the mainland coast and its off-shore islands, but was mostly unchartered inland, from the Arctic Circle to the North Pole.

"This is the trail we took," I indicated, tracing it with a pencil and sketching in Lake Krimakton and Taherkapfaluk, the Big Lake, while describing the approximate size and shape of each.

"You sure took a chance, didn't you, Father?" suggested Scotty.

But before I could reply, Scott Alexander expressed his feelings. "I wish I had been along with you! So far as I know, no Mountie ever set foot there." Scott was an inveterate traveler and I knew he was genuinely sorry to have missed that trip.

"Think of it this way, Scott," his sidekick Reggie Goodie smiled as he consoled him, "the Air Force estimates that human efficiency decreases by two percent for every degree below zero. So what could you do at -50° F? Look at Father. He's just coming out of it and he is a tough little guy!"

When the party broke up, Scotty, always a kind host, asked if I would like to sleep in his quarters that night, but I declined his thoughtful invitation, explaining that I had planned to use my own hut.

"In that case we'll see you later," he said. "In the meantime I guess I'd better stick around because your traveling companions will be coming in soon for a cup of tea."

"We'll give you a hand with your dogs, Father," offered Scott Alexander when we stepped out into the freezing night air. My dogs, lying in the snow, raised their heads, no doubt anxious to be unharnessed and fed.

"Thanks a lot! I won't say no to that." We climbed aboard the sled to cover the four hundred yards to my little cabin on the west side of the Bay. A former trading post of the Can-Alaska Trading Company, it now belonged to the Hudson's Bay Company. I rented it, complete with its simple furnishings, from Scotty Gall (representing H.B.C.) for a yearly fee of a pair of fox pelts. It was a two-room 24' x 16' frame building, with the living room and kitchen forming one room, separated from the bedroom by a wallboard partition. No one had been in it since I vacated it the previous summer, so its musty smell was overwhelming. I lit both the coal heater, strategically cut into the partition to serve the living room and bedroom, and the old McClary range in the kitchen.

When I went outside, the two Constables had already put my dogs on the line, and Scott asked, "Do you have enough dog food, Father? If not, I'll bring you some tomorrow." "You're very kind," I replied, "but I have enough for a few days. Thanks just the same."

After feeding the dogs, we brought all my gear off the sled into the kitchen and left it on the floor to thaw. The mildewy odor still lingered, but the place was much warmer and more cheerful, especially with the kettle singing on the stove. To clear the air at least partially, I opened the door and the Arctic cold rushed in. I brewed some coffee for my guests and then closed the door so we could relax in relative comfort.

Scott Alexander, I noticed, had not changed since my last visit to Cambridge Bay. Thirty-four years old, he stood almost six feet and had an angular, clean-shaven face dominated by a long,

92

narrow nose. Never reluctant to pick on one's distinguishing trait, the Eskimos referred to him as *Avik*, the Knife, but—to my knowledge—he wasn't aware of it. His comrade-in-arms, Reggie Goodie, was nearly the same height as Scott, but stockier. His face was notable not only for its smooth, unblemished skin but also for its pleasant expression that quietly reflected his good sense of humor. Like me, Reggie was in his mid-twenties.

"I can't remember ever hearing of your young friend Otokreak before," Scott addressed me. "Who is he, Father?"

"He tells me he's from Admiralty Island, and that his father is Kakagun, the great hunter!"

"You know my friend Kakagun?"

"Know him! The year before you arrived at Burnside, Father, I was sent there to make a report on the Eskimos of Bathurst Inlet. As you know, practically every native fancies himself a fairly good hunter. So I was naturally surprised to find that wherever I went everyone agreed that the best hunter among the Krangmalit was Kakagun. I thought to myself, We'll see, the first chance that comes along."

"Did you get that chance?"

"You bet! The day Kakagun arrived in Burnside, your predecessor, Father Delalande, drew my attention to a lone wolf skirting the post. I said to him, 'I hear the great hunter Kakagun pulled in today. How would you like to call him, so we can see how good he is with his rifle?' 'I'll be glad to oblige,' said the Father. 'Kakagun is a fine fellow. I don't think he'll disappoint you.' And off he goes to fetch him, down the channel where he had built his igloo."

"While Father Delalande was gone, I studied the wolf through my field glasses, far off from where I stood. He was a lean, long-legged fellow, and he kept moving around as if he was following a scent. Father returned with Kakagun and I quickly told him what my intentions were. The big hunter smiled and said quietly, 'I'll try a shot.'"

"I kept my glasses on our distant quarry while Kakagun sat down on the snow, crossed his legs, rested his elbows on his raised knees, took steady aim, and fired. I didn't need binoculars to see that he'd scored a bull's eye! The wolf leaped into the air on impact, came down, tottered, and lay still. That was proof enough for me. I've been an admirer of Kakagun's skill ever since."

Noticing I was getting drowsy, Reggie Goodie, said "It's time we let Father hit the sack. It's been a long day for a young fellow." On parting, Scott asked me if I would be saying Mass in the morning, adding, "If you are, I'd like to come." "Sure," I answered, "come around nine and you'll be the altar boy."

Compared to the freezing igloo temperatures of the past two weeks and their hard, often crowded *iglek*, my heated bedroom with its double bed and an old, spring mattress, felt like the height of luxury. I fell asleep as soon as I got into my bag.

That night's comfortable sleep made me tremendously refreshed and stronger than I'd been for some time. Scott Alexander came a little before nine, glanced at me and commented on my transformation. Not surprisingly, I said Mass with renewed ardor. After the service Scott reminisced, "The last time I was an altar boy was in Regina, when I was training at the R.C.M.P. College. I used to go to Mass during the week whenever I could, and helped the priest."

We breakfasted together on toast and jam, Scott having brought a loaf of bread that Reggie Goodie had baked the day before. It was a distinct treat and a welcome change from the usual Inuit morning fare. After breakfast Scott said, "I must go now. Come up for dinner, Father, when you've finished your work. We'll relax and chat." I thanked him for all his favors and gladly accepted his mid-day invitation.

My shack was long overdue for a thorough clean up. After taking all the bedding, caribou skins, and parkas outside, I swept, washed, and dusted to give the place a semblance of neatness. Then I went out along the dog line, patted each one of my dogs and checked them for frostbite along their fleshy sides, between the ribs and the hips. These parts of a dog freeze fairly often in a cross wind because canines normally have less fur there. To my relief, the check showed no ill effects. By noon I was ready to return to the Constables' visit.

Their barracks were a quarter-of-a-mile away, sited on the river bank of the Ikalututiak River. Behind their quarters I could see the small belfry of St. George's Anglican Mission. Further north, four miles away, Mount Pelly marked the edge of the barrens. It was the only guiding beacon in this monotonously flat land.

Befitting his social standing as a great hunter, my friend Hikhik had set his igloo in the place of honor, which is near the R.C.M.P. buildings. My other traveling companions strung out their igloos between Hikhik's large igloo and my cabin.

Two dog teams overtook me as I strode toward the Police post. They were driven by Otokreak and Amiraernek. When they pulled up alongside, Amiraernek spoke to me. "Malrukhak, my wife, did not sleep well last night. She had a backache and the baby cried a lot." He spoke flatly, without any display of emotion.

94

"Are you also going to the Police place?" I asked, taking their answer for granted. But Otokreak and Amiraernek had other plans. "We are going to the sunken ship. We heard there is still lots of iron left on it," said Otokreak.

He was referring to the partly submerged hull of Roald Amundsen's abandoned *Maud* which lay on her side in the east bank of the Bay almost equidistant between the H.B.C. buildings. Old lady *Maud* had experienced a relatively brief, but note-worthy career. Her main claim to international fame came between 1918 and 1920 when Amundsen, the Norwegian explorer, sailed her through the Northeast Passage across the top of Asia. Following that historic voyage, she was converted into a freighter by the Hudson's Bay Company and became the *Bay Maud*. But because she couldn't take the rough seas and drifting ice floes of the oft-stormy Arctic, she was abandoned at Cambridge Bay, stripped of her vital parts and accoutrements, and left to die. Several decades later the Radio Aids to Navigation and a Radar Station would occupy the land above the *Maud*.

Not having boarded her before, I said, "I'll come and see it with you," and climbed on Otokreak's sled to satisfy my curiosity.

Only the wheelhouse remained above the icebound *Bay Maud*. Her two masts had been cut down and removed, along with everything else of value to the White Man. But the inventive Eskimo hunters had discovered that the innumerable spikes, set through her narrowly-spaced ribs and the heavy planking, made strong spear-heads and useful hunting knives. The strips of steel, also overlooked by the *Kablunak*, could be fashioned into versatile *ulon* knives and, if they were long enough, into runners for sleds.

As it turned out, Otokreak and Amiraernek were too late. Despite their thorough search, all they could salvage were a few long spikes. Even with tools borrowed from Scotty Gall, it took them most of the day to dislodge the bent metal from its oaken bed.

I did not stay long with them, but continued on to the Police buildings. Of these there were three: the barracks or station itself; a one-room cabin for the Eskimo couple who acted as interpreters, guides, and caretakers; and a warehouse. The warehouse contained a jail built like a circus lions' cage, its flat vertical steel bars, covered with red anti-rust paint, joining the steel floor and ceiling. I wondered if this jail had ever been used.

In their five-room bungalow Scott Alexander and Reggie Goodie were surrounded by many comforts of home. They had separate bedrooms, a spacious living room with a three-piece chesterfield suite and cabinet radio, a compact office, and a large, rectangular kitchen with ample dining space. Adequate lighting was provided by Coleman gas lanterns. But with no practical access to water because water pipes would freeze, the house had no plumbing, necessitating an adjacent outhouse. The main house was very warm, as it should have been with the twenty-four tons of coal each year that heated it.

"Welcome to our Royal Hilton!" Scott ushered me in. "Make yourself at home. We'll have a wee drink before we eat. Reggie's in the kitchen; it's his turn to handle the cooking and serving. Speaking of the cook and chief bottle washer, here he is!" he nodded towards the kitchen door. Adorned and protected by an apron, Reggie smiled shyly into the living room. "There's just one thing we'd like you to remember, Father: This is a well-regulated community with a curfew law enforced by His Majesty's Royal Canadian Mounted Police," he kidded me.

The dinner menu was superb with fried Arctic char and rice, thick caribou steaks and mashed potatoes (made from dehydrated spuds), and a pie Reggie had baked using dried apples. "If this is a sample of regular Scarlet and Gold fare, I'd sure like to board here," I said, raising my wine glass to Reggie, who grinned and, I thought, blushed.

I couldn't help singling out the char for special praise. "I don't know about your tastes, gentlemen but when it comes to choosing fish for the table, I definitely share the Eskimos' preference for salt-water Arctic char over all other fish I've ever eaten. What's your opinion?"

"No argument, Father!" they chorused, as if rehearsed. Actually, I didn't expect any. Generations ago the Eskimos had discovered that it was their best-tasting native fish and I agreed the first time I tried some when I arrived. Like Atlantic salmon in appearance, although it does have red flesh, an adult Arctic char weighs from six to twenty mouth-watering pounds. Where access to the sea has been cut off, however, it becomes a fresh-water denizen the Inuit call *ivitaruk,* and may weigh up to thirty pounds with its flesh even more vividly red. I fished Arctic char with nets, using four, five and six-inch mesh nets, sometimes catching fifty-pounders with the six-inch mesh. Whatever its size, though, I always found that char had more oil than its drier cousin salmon and possessed a flavor superior to any other fish in Europe or North America.

Soon after we adjourned to the living room, an Eskimo woman came in to do the dishes. She worked quiety and efficiently, using hot water from a large, aluminum pot in a generous-sized dishpan. When she finished washing the dishes,

Naoyak, the seagull.

Manerathiak.

Father Raymond de Coccola, on the Mackenzie River en route north in 1937.

This is some of the barren land in the Central Arctic.

The men unload *Our Lady of Lourdes* at Coppermine, 1940

RCM schooner *Our Lady of Lourdes,*
at Coppermine, 1940

The Mission schooner anchored at Tuktuyaktuk.

This is one view of Raymond de Coccola's Burnside Mission

A quiet summer moment with a friend at Burnside in 1938.

Leo Manning of the Hudson's Bay Co. and family visit Father Raymond

Father Raymond surveys the Burnside "kingdom."

Father Raymond takes a moment to ponder his mission.

Common Eskimo sleds "parked" on snow
blocks and igloos with front porches.

An Eskimo lays the foundation for an igloo a
Coronation Gulf.

Here the porch begins to take sh
for a completed ig

"Dog train" takes a rest on its way to the trading post with furs, near Cape Krusenster

A group of visitors arrive at Burnside by dog team in 1937.

These two small sleds are loaded with an Eskimo's entire possessions.

Drilling for water on Victoria Island with driftwood shank and metal tip. Note sealskin buckets.

Arctic fox furs being sunned outside snow houses to ready them for trading.

This Eskimo camp in late May, features three igloos with common entrance.

Overleaf: Life inside an igloo, with sleeping platform on the left and cooking platform on the right.

Jigging through crack in ice for Arctic char. Note driftwood sunglasses.

Top Right: Missionary visits the
             Eskimos at Read Island.

Center Right: The dogs rest as the me
                prepare to move out for a seal hur

Bottom Right: Loading the season's cato
              for the trip to the trading po.

A spring tent is pitched in early May and is buttressed with snow-block wall and porch

An Eskimo sings and plays the *katuk* (drum) to tune up before the dance.

The dance takes place inside a Copper
Eskimo big igloo. . .

Right: An Eskimo and his wif
in gala dress of caribou fu

. . .at Coronation Gulf, and the *katuk*
(drum) is passed around

Temporary shelter is made of musk ox skin.

Even the dogs carry loads as the family moves to a new camp in July.

Tree River Eskimo adjusts his wife's pack as they move camps mid-July.

Caribou tents shelter Bernard Harbor Eskimos as they peg out more skins to dry.

Tree River Eskimos load up their homemade *umiak* in mid-July.

The caribou herds are on the move in late spring.

The barren view from a "hilltop" in mid-summer.

Musk oxen rest and graze on the great barren land.

Man shares the land. Here an Eskimo and wife make a tent of caribou hides.

The land of the midnight sun: Arctic midnight sun along the 70th parallel.

Only four dogs can pull sled, with peat runners, along the ice pack.

Copper Eskimos get ready for an expedition, as the dogs wait.

The shaman, or sorcerer is an important person among the Copper Eskim

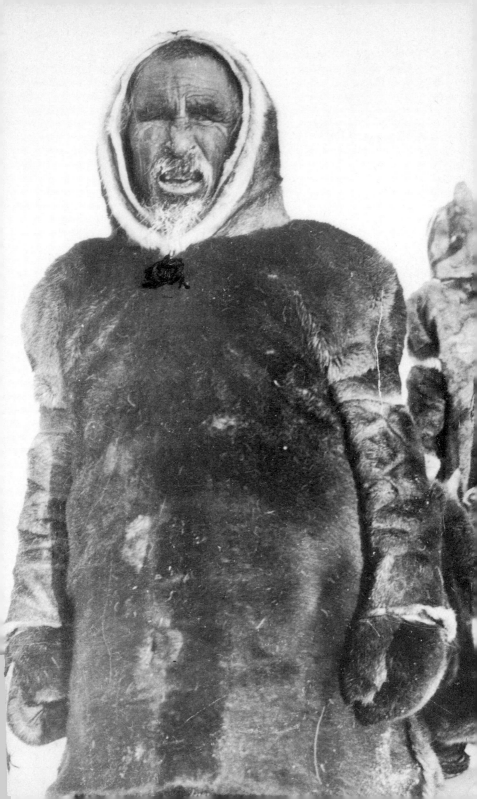

A young girl is all dressed up and ready to go—to the dance. Notice the amulets on the front.

The Lone Wolf Hunter—and son.

A group of women take a rest along the trail.

The cut shows the thickness of the blubber on this freshly killed seal.

This is part of Father Raymond's winter seal supply for dog food at Holman Island, 1

Our Lady of Lourdes **plies the ice fields in Coronation Gulf. . .**

. . .and meets up with *The Margaret A.*

Arctic char are hung out to dry in the summer sun at Bernard Harbor.

This is peaceful Bloody Falls on Coppermine River, the scene of many murders.

Hinnihiak, one of the murderers of Fathers Rouviers and Le Roux.

Kirluayok, the sorcerer at Burnside, 1937.

Eskimo with white hair is considered
rare (wooden goggles are not).

This woman's full-length parka is
made of ground squirrel fur.

Raymond de Coccola sets out from Burnside to visit the nets.

Ulukhak, one of the murderers of Fathers Rouviers and Le Roux.

An Eskimo woman wearing typical parka with a *maon* (hood) for newborn baby.

The Roman Catholic Mission stands stark and alone at Holman Island.

Father Raymond takes a friend fishing at Holman Island in October, 1948.

Parishioners gather around the Holman Island Mission in 1947.

Burnside Cemetery, final resting place for the "Great Disaster" victims.

A view of the Holman Island Mission at the entrance of the bay...

...and a view of the mission from Holman Island's King's Bay.

Raymond de Coccola with parishioners at Minto Inlet, in 1939.

Raymond and friends at Coppermine, 1940

Fathers Raymond de Coccola, R. Buliard and Louis Le Mer, at Coppermine, 1939.

Father Franche's dogs take a well-deserved rest at Tuktuyaktuk.

The H.B.C. *Fort Ross* wintering at Tuktuyaktuk, 1948.

Right: R.C.M.P. Frenchie Chartrand, sealing in spring.
Frenchie died on *The St. Roch* at Terror Bay.

Father Franche and Raymond de Coccola together in 1948.

The Mission at Minto Inlet (March, 1939) sits at 71° lat. N.

Moving out to the great seal hunt, in migration formation.

Police patrol uses regular team of nine dogs on the trail.

Copper Eskimos going inland after the great disaster; only a few dogs are left.

An Eskimo repairs his bow with caribou sinew in the Colville hills.

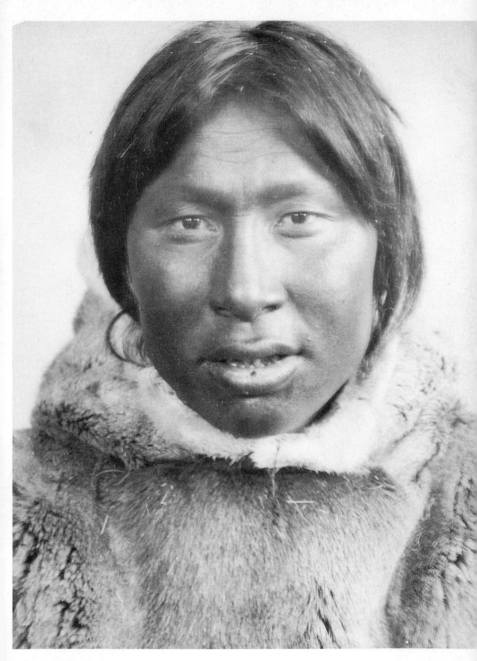

Ugiuk (Big Seal) who murdered a fellow Eskimo, Pelly Bay.

Inukut, or Cairn, on location of the caribou drive.

"Members of the family" at Ellice River.

Eskimos dry fish in their summer campsite at Burnside in 1945.

Burnside River Falls, with visitors, in 1945.

Raymond at Burnside—1938.

Raymond at Tuktuyaktuk—1948.

krenak, Raymond's faithful guide, out on a summer seal hunt.

Father Raymond de Coccola takes time to record a Burnside Mission moment, in Bathurst, 1938.

Bishop Fallaize and Father Raymond aboard *Our Lady of Lourdes*,
Amundsen Gulf, 1937.

Father Raymond at Melbourne Island, 1943.

**Crossing Amundsen Gulf to Coppermine
with Billy Trasher and Father Delalande.**

Father Raymond visits the trapline near the Mission at Burnside, 1941.

Father Raymond near the end of his time in the Central Arctic, at Holman Island in 1948.

pots, and pans, she poured the dishpan water into a slop-bucket and took it outside. She returned carrying a big block of ice which she lowered into the barrel beside the range to augment the water supply.

"How are you coming along with that district census you started last year?" I asked Scott.

"It's all done except for the people around Ellice and Perry Rivers to the Back River. That's a long way—about 250 miles. I've already visited five families inland around MacAlpine Lake, but I've heard since that there are more."

"Do you think you could let me have the names on your list so I can visit some of them before the break up?"

"Sure thing, *mon vieux* (my dear old friend)," Scott replied, using one of several French phrases he had picked up from Father Delalande. It took Scott only moments to fetch a copy of his list from the den and hand it to me. Although he had carried out his census through an interpreter, the survey surprisingly contained not only the names of the hunters, their wives and children, but also pertinent facts about their background and police record, if any. I complimented him on his fine job and assured him I would keep his information confidential.

"In return for that, Scott, I'll try to get you all the information I can on the people around Ellice River and Perry River. My understanding is that the people of Bathurst Inlet and Kent Peninsula come under the jurisdiction of the R.C.M.P. at Coppermine. I don't know how far your own district extends, but you might want to note a death that occurred during my trip. Araliuk, wife if Kivgalo, died—apparently of old age."

"Thanks, Father. When we share the necessary patrolling of Bathurst, any information we get helps a lot. We know little about the Eskimos of this region and, frankly, I sometimes wonder if my interpreter is hedging and not passing my message to the people. For instance, I've noticed he often uses the word *amakro* when he translates for me and snickers at the same time."

"That's one of the problems with a native interpreter," I smiled. "To protect his own skin, he will keep to himself much of what he hears or knows. He is not likely to go snitching on his own people. To him, and to all Eskimos, you are an *amakro*, or wolf, who has come to disturb their immemorial way of life. You're not the only ones to be so branded. Did you know that we missionaries have been charitably dubbed *Akortuyoaluk*, the Long Robe? It may merely be another manifestation of suspicion and possibly even a little fear of ways not their own.

Kitchen tidied, the interpreter's wife asked Scott if there was any other cleaning or washing he wanted done and, receiving a negative answer, she smiled her way out.

"Did you hear what happened to her mother, Alunak, a couple of weeks ago?" Reggie asked when the woman had left. I shook my head.

"If you remember Alunak she was not only getting on in years, but her eyesight was fading and she couldn't sew anymore. As a result, everybody kidded her about being helpless. Her infirmities and that constant teasing must have prayed on her mind until she found it unbearable, because one evening—after visiting friends near the trading post—she went out into the storm and was never seen again."

"That was the oddest thing, Father!" added Scott. "About an hour after she left her friends, Alunak's grandson arrived by sled to take her home. He was told his grandmother should have reached the barracks long ago, as it's only a mile along the Bay. So the kid doubled back here to sound the alarm. Then everyone in camp began looking for poor old Alunak.

"We spotted her footprints in the snow a few hundred yards away from our barracks. The footsteps led toward Ikalututiak Lake which, as you know, is another four miles away. Then the prints suddenly vanished in the drifing snow. Because the storm had reached its full strength, we abandoned our search until morning. But we never found another trace of her."

"What do you think might have happened?" I asked Scott.

"I imagine that she fell from exhaustion and was covered by the snow. We might find her remains in the spring."

"I doubt you'll ever find them when the snow does disappear. The foxes and wolves will find her body before that. The only part of her that might survive would be her skull. It's too big for them to crack. But why Alunak decided to walk out into the storm is sure puzzling. As a rule, young Eskimo couples try hard to lighten the unenviable existence of their old parents during normal times. Alunak's family wasn't starving. Her daughter was working for you. So she was better off than most aging Eskimos. Yet, she may have had a feeling, heightened by her friends' taunts, that it was time to get out of the way. On the other hand, since she was half-blind, she could conceivably have lost her way in the storm and frozen to death in a snowdrift, as you presumed."

"Speaking of weird happenings," I continued, "did Father Delalande ever tell you of an old couple at Bathurst who supposedly got lost together in a storm near a place called Kraomavaktok? No? Then I will. One day, while visiting the post at Burnside, the old couple's son casually mentioned to Father Delalande that he had taken his father and mother on the ice during a *pirtok*. 'They were so old,' the young Eskimo added.

" 'Why did you do that?' Father Delalande asked him.

" 'Nauna, I don't know,' was all he received in reply.

"I certainly agree with Father Delalande that an Eskimo's behavior is often unpredictable, quickly changing from one extreme to another. He may suddenly decide that a dastardly deed is a good idea, so he follows through. Sometimes his ignorance is considered his excuse."

My Mountie friends nodded agreement, and Scott said animatedly, "Here's another case, Father, to support your viewpoint. This one is almost a crime classic! A native woman named Mapha was brought into court at Coppermine for the murder of her husband, Ayalik, on Richardson Island, where they were wintering. She shot him while he was asleep, but didn't quite kill him, so she grabbed a net twine, made a tourniquet and strangled the poor fellow to death.

"It came out at the inquest that Mapha's lover, Aogak, was hunting nearby when Ayalik was murdered. This provided the motive. A few days later Aogak killed his wife Kuptana, and went to live with Mapha.

"Our headquarters at Coppermine got wind of this affair and Constable 'Frenchy' Chartrand was sent to Richardson Island to investigate. He found Aogak, the wife slayer, stretched out in his sleeping bag, his brains blown out. Aogak had apparently seen the Police team coming and shot himself through the ear by pressing the trigger with his toe.

"Mapha was escorted back to Coppermine for the trial. Since she had three small children and the evidence against her was circumstantial, she was acquitted. How do you like that for a surprise ending, Father?"

"Purely from an Eskimo point of view, I'd say chances are that even if she had been found guilty, she wouldn't have understood why she was punished, anyway," I rationalized. "She may still think that the White Man is stupid and should mind his own business. After all, that was a lovers' affair, between two couples. It wasn't anybody else's concern—least of all any White Man's, even in a Police uniform," I said facetiously. When neither Scott nor Reggie rose for the bait, I asked Scott if he'd ever heard of a man called Okrenak and the circumstances that landed him in jail.

"Never heard of him, Father. Must have been before my time."

"I believe you're right, because I first learned of Okrenak from Father Delalande. He told me Okrenak helped him on his trips inland. Subsequently Okrenak visited our Mission a few

163

times, and that's when Father Delalande mentioned that Okrenak had killed two young men.

"What happened was that Okrenak was chosen by the elders at Kraomavaktok to permanently remove a pair of troublemaking young hunters menacing the camp, especially the women. At any rate, the local *angakuk*, or medicine man, and the group's elders chose Okrenak for the job. The reason they picked him was that Okrenak was training to become a medicine man and was therefore expected to take orders from the older *angakuk*.

"On the evening of the 'execution' day, the two trouble-makers were invited into an igloo for a meal of caribou and broth. While they were eating, Okrenak hid in the recess of the snow porch. One of the doomed young men chose not to linger over his food, and as he came out of the igloo, Okrenak shot him in the head. On hearing the shot, the other guest ran out to see what had triggered it. In the darkness he tripped over the body of his friend, and Okrenak gave him a full charge in the back of the head.

"Okrenak received a two-year jail term at Herschel Island in the Western Arctic for what the White Man considered a double murder, but what the Eskimos thought was a rational way of ridding the community of undesirable characters. "I imagine you Mounties must have quite a time solving native murders nowadays. Over the years the Eskimos have learned to fear the Police, and now tend to keep their secrets as far as possible from you. Isn't that so?"

"That's largely true," Scott concurred. "And the Eskimos aren't making it any easier for us by doing their dirty work in more isolated hunting grounds. By the time word reaches us that a good hunter died returning from the tree line, or was killed stalking caribou or disappeared in the sea on a bright, calm day, nothing is left of the body and the survivors have their stories well-rehearsed."

Years later I would remember Scott's stories of policing difficulties and the "logical" Eskimo explanations. That future occasion involved Okrenak and an older hunter named Tamarnek. Though short, Tamarnek was not only proportioned like a professional wrestler, but had the power and agility of one. His sole physical weakness was his degenerating eyesight. He had cataracts in his eyes which were so advanced, his pupils were almost white. With his wife Anangayak and their son Hikhinuak, Tamarnek chose in the late fall to move to Hiorkretak, Gordon Bay.

In early June, just before the ice break up, Anangayak and

her son Hikhinuak came by dog team to our Mission at Burnside. I was glad to see them, as I would need help in this busy period to prepare new supplies of dried fish and dried caribou meat for future winter travels. Noting that Tamarnek was not with them, I asked Anangayak of her husband's whereabouts.

She answered with a nervous giggle. "He lost his breath, he wanted to die." She appeared energetic, high-strung. Her face, with its protruding cheekbones, was tattooed, like most Inuit women's (given by sorcerers, tattoos were considered a beauty treatment). Her son Hikhinuak, whose looks strikingly resembled his mother's, added, "We shall stay here for the summer and we will help you." They pitched their tent beside the Mission and came into the living room for tea.

Two days later another dog sled arrived. On it was Okrenak, the one who had earlier killed the two young troublemakers at Kraomavaktok and had long-since served his jail sentence. With him was his only son, his wife having died the previous year of flu. "I have come to stay with Anangayak," Okrenak declared. "She has no husband and I have no wife."

That evening Anangayak and Okrenak came into my living room. They seemed upset so I tried to make them comfortable at the kitchen table. While they were drinking tea, Okrenak spoke up, coming straight to the point, "*Fala*, you baptized us. Now marry us, like White Men do!"

As requested, I married them in our little chapel the following day. They both giggled when they took their vows, not understanding the fuss made for such a common ritual. There were no wedding rings, and, because the Vital Statistics bureaucrats had not yet reached out that far into the Barren Land, no papers to sign. I simply made an entry in the Mission's register, recording their names and the date of their marriage.

Ordinarily a quiet, shy man, Okrenak seemed very happy. Through the years he became my constant guide and companion to the distant camps scattered in the barrens. I can still visualize his dark complexion, penetrating black eyes, and black mustache, uncommon to most Eskimos.

Toward the end of July when I was getting ready to visit my fishing nets, a small schooner anchored in the channel below the Mission. There were two men aboard, an Eskimo and a White Man. When the White Man approached me, he introduced himself as Constable Levins of Cambridge Bay R.C.M.P. Detachment, and I invited him up to our Mission. "I'll have coffee ready and you can tell me what brought you so far on your patrol."

Over coffee, Constable Levins said, "Father, we heard rumors at Cambridge Bay of Tamarnek's death and we are curious about the accompanying circumstances. Do you personally know anything about the case?"

"Only that his wife Anangayak and their son Hikhinuak are here. They arrived a month ago. They told me Tamarnek died, but they didn't elaborate."

We looked up Hikhinuak and asked him to guide us to the spot where he had laid his father's body in the early spring. He did so readily. Among the scattered bits of bones we found an old .30-30 rifle, a tobacco tin containing needles, caribou sinew, some fine-cut tobacco, and matches, all left by his family for his soul's use in the afterlife.

The young Mountie was visibly disappointed. "Let's go back, Father. I'll never get anything from this."

"Wait a minute, Constable! There's an important part of the body missing—the skull. Neither wolves, foxes, nor wolverines can break it, so chances are they wouldn't bother to haul it very far. Why don't we look for it?" He hesitated before replying, "You're right, Father. Let's do that."

In a patch of dwarf willows at the bottom of a small creek I spotted the skull. "Look, here it is! Pretty badly cracked, too." I held up the cranium for the policeman to see. It still had a tuft of hair on the ridge of the parietal bone.

"Oh, that's the work of a wolf, Father!"

"I'm not so sure about that. A wolf can't break a human skull because it's too large for its jaws."

His confidence slightly shaken, Constable Levins examined our find more carefully. We both observed a small hole in the occipital part of the skull and several cracks extending in all directions in the shape of a star.

"Guess I'd better send it onto our experts in Ottawa," he remarked tersely.

The report from the R.C.M.P. crime labs in Canada's capital came back the following winter. A .25-20 slug was lodged inside the frontal bone of the skull. Anangayak was tried and got a fifteen-month sentence. Yet, according to her son Hikhinuak, she merely did her husband's bidding. And, while Eskimos generally disapprove of deliberate murder or manslaughter, mercy killings are practised and condoned by the family concerned, as well as by the community at large. Here, I thought, lay yet another unbridgeable gap between the Inuit and the *Kablunaks*.

Late that afternoon I reminded Reggie Goodie that it was time for me to return to my shack "before the curfew-law took effect." Both Constables laughed, then Reggie said, "Here's hoping that one of these days we'll have a curfew for the Bad Spirits of this God-forsaken land!" And Scott added, "In the meantime I have another idea. Why don't we walk you to your cabin and continue our chat?" There were no vocal objections. While the coffee pot perked gently on my kitchen stove, I went out to feed my dogs. Scott and Reggie made themselves comfortable on the caribou skins stretched out on the floor.

Relaxing with a cigarette and coffee, I told my friends of my trip to Nokadlak's place, the birth of Naoyak, and the hunter's decision to keep her. Then I asked, "What is your position when you hear about the murder of a baby girl?"

"There isn't much we can do, Father," answered Scott. "We don't know what actually goes on in an Eskimo camp and, when we later question them, the Eskimos don't tell us anything that might incriminate them. Of course, we hear that baby girls are killed here and there, but obtaining positive proof is another story. On our patrols we keep warning people that killing a baby girl is wrong. However, our interpreter must make some kind of a joke about that when he translates our reminder because he gets a laugh out of them almost every time."

"When you really think about infanticide," Reggie joined in, "it's not much worse than an abortion. The main difference is that the baby is already out of the womb."

"Eskimos kill not only girls, but sometimes even boys who have no fathers, if they become burdensome to the family group," I added. "The father may have died or he may have been just a visitor, and the woman is left alone to feed the child. And what about their old people? They are told to get lost—literally—or else they are abandoned on the trail. Less frequently they are pushed over a cliff or are helped to strangle themselves. I suppose there isn't much you can do about it. Theirs is an extremely tough existence, at best. What do you say, Scott?"

"Obviously, they don't look upon murder or manslaughter the same way we do. I'd say that, in general—purely self-preservation—the welfare of their group precedes all other considerations. Private killing is a personal affair only if it does not weaken the group as a whole. It will take time—a long time—to bring the Eskimos up to our Christian moral standards, including respect for the value of human life. After all, they've lived that way for thousands of years."

"On the other hand, we still have a great deal to learn about the Eskimos," I suggested. "And that, too, will take a long, long time."

After exchanging their perspectives, Scott and Reggie decided to return to their barracks. I thanked them for their kindness and the good time we had together. At the door, Reggie's parting words were, "A philosopher once said that when God measures a man, he puts the tape around his heart, and not his head."

"I heartily agree, Reggie! That's what we should all try to do. Only it's much easier said than done, my friend."

7

Jigging Through Ice

"How long do you plan to stay in Cambridge Bay this time around?" Constable Alexander inquired.

"You know me by now, Scott. I'd like to visit the different camps in this area as soon as possible. There's one snag, though—my dog food is running low. I think I'll go up the Ikalututiak Lake and try my luck at jigging."

"Tell you what, *mon vieux*. I'll lend you enough rice to keep your dogs happy while you are fishing, and you can save everything you catch for your travel. I'll send my man Karlik over to you tomorrow. How does that suit you?"

It was a thoughtful gesture, typical of the experienced Arctic traveler that Scott certainly was.

"Many thanks, Scott! That's a deal. And, by the way, is there anyone here you'd recommend as a fishing partner?"

"Let's see. . . .I think your best bet would be Kunak, if he's still in camp. He belongs to the Ikalututiarmeun group and really knows the ropes."

It was comforting to know that Ikalututiarmeun is Eskimo for the People of the Rich Fishing Grounds, and that my guide Kunak was an old acquaintance.

Early next morning Scott's interpreter and helper came by dog team and delivered a fifty-pound bag of coarse rice. Kunak was with him. He was a young man in his early twenties, short like me, but with an unusually broad face.

The "nearby" lake was a good four miles north of Cambridge Bay. Approximately four miles long and three miles wide, it drained into the Bay when it wasn't frozen, as it was now in December. As soon as we reached it by dogsled, Kunak said, "First we have to find the right depth." To do so, he removed the thin layer of snow with his knife, knelt down and peered through the thick, clear ice, his hands shading his eyes and nose against the frozen surface. Unsatisfied, he repeated this procedure in several locations until he found a spot with about six feet of water under the ice.

"This is just fine! Now let's bring the dogs closer."

Using a long-handled ice chisel and scoop, we took turns at digging a hole through the ten feet of ice. The work was so warm we took off our outer parkas, although the temperature was easily 30° below, with a light, ground wind. Half an hour later, we finally struck water. It gurgled over the rim of the foot-wide opening, sounding like air forced from a kitchen tap.

Twenty-five feet from the first hole, we dug another so we could both fish at the same time. Part-way around each hole we built a wall of snow blocks to protect us from the freezing breeze, then spread caribou skin over a block of snow to sit on.

Our fishing gear was used by the Krangmalit everywhere. Our twine line was wound around a curved caribou antler; our copper hooks were homemade, Kunak's riveted to a bear's tooth and mine to a polished fragment of ivory. It likely came from one of the mammoths that once roamed the Far North. These scattered bones are preserved in sandy ice on riverbanks in the western Arctic. For bait we cut strips from the white belly of a lake trout, about the size of a little finger.

Slowly we lowered our lines into the watery holes until the hooks were a few feet form the lake bottom. Then we began jigging the line—up, down, up, down—with pendulum precision. Otherwise motionless lest we frighten the fish, we continued this rhythmic toil for hours without a single bite.

I was cold, restless, cramped, and miserable. Almost flat, monotonously white, devoid of vitality and silent except for a rustling round wind, the cruel landscape filled me with desolation. To make it worse, fifty feet away was a bleached skull leaning sideways on the shore gravel. Partly out of curiosity and partly for a break, I left my jigging line, rose stiffly, and trudged toward it. Crushed bones and the unbroken pelvic girdle of a young woman lay near the skull. I lifted the skull to show Kunak and asked loudly, "Who's that?"

"That's Avinak," he replied without hesitation. "She died last summer."

I returned the skull to its resting place and resumed my jigging, wondering who Avinak was. Poor thing, I thought, she probably died of the flu.

The only natural relief in the surrounding flatness was a hill to the east of the lake called Mount Pelly or *Uvayok* by the Eskimos because it looked like the belly of a pregnant woman. Its top rose to the unglamorous height of 690 feet above sea level. And the only man-made landmarks visible from where I sat were rocks arranged in narrow ovals between which the Eskimos laid their dead.

Some earthly possessions of the departed were still discernible through the light snow covering: parts of shattered sleds, tea kettles, tobacco tins, harpoons, and sundry implements. Looking at the human remains surrounded by the rusting contrivances, I said to myself, How lucky you are! Now you have an answer to afterlife, my friends.

A primitive hunter and fisherman born to the Barren Land, Kunak did not show the slightest discomfort. I asked him if he was tired. "I'm not tired," he smiled back, instinctively returning his attention to the water-filled hole before him. He jigged the line with one hand while holding a *kakivok,* or trident, in the other, like a winter-clad Neptune. His trident differed from the sea god's because it was made of two caribou antlers with a steel spike between them, set on the end of a long pole.

Kunak seemed to be dreaming, and at times I felt sure he was. Yet no fish passed by or nestled in the weeds and gravel below without his jigging harder and cheerfully mumbling, "Fish, great fish, where are you going? Come here, I'll take care of you, and your flesh will make me strong." At the same time, with the hand that held the *kakivok,* he kept touching an ivory harpoon's head hanging on his right sleeve, as if it, too, had magical powers.

We fished right through until the early darkness of the afternoon, interrupting our vigil only to stretch our knotted muscles and warm ourselves with jogging (as opposed to jigging), mouthfuls of dried caribou meat, and tea from my thermos.

Perhaps the day was too bright and visibility too good because despite Kunak's repeated appeals to the fish and his superstitious reliance on the harpoon's head, we returned to Cambridge Bay empty-handed.

So oppressed was my body with the unremitting cold, and so depressed my mind en route to the Mission post, I could not bear the thought of repeating that fruitless experience the next day. Yet, when Kunak asked me if I wanted to fish again, I acquiesced, "Yes, I'd like to go back with you tomorrow morning." What choice was there?

I was glad that Aniliak and Tuktuknak, both native sons of

Cambridge Bay, and their families chose that evening to drop in and renew our previous year's acquaintance. They had heard I had been to the lake with Kunak and were curious to know how I was doing in general.

Aniliak was blind in his left eye, while Tuktuknak had lost the small finger of his right hand. They told me both disfigurements were caused by circumstances considered natural in the Barren Land.

"When I was a boy," recalled Aniliak, "I bit into a chunk of caribou meat that I held with my left hand. I was about to slice it off at the mouth with a knife in my right hand when my young brother accidentally pushed my right elbow from behind. The blade pierced my eye and since then I have never been able to see properly."

"Yes, yes, it couldn't be helped!" Tuktuknak commiserated. Then the latter asked me, "Do you know, Fala, how ill luck crossed my path?" Correctly assuming that I didn't know, he continued, "One day I went out on the sea ice to look for the seals' breathing holes. I found one, then speared a seal, not realizing it was *ugiuk,* a very large bearded seal. Stung by the spear in its neck, the *ugiuk,* used its powerful square flippers to drive itself down its breathing hole. He did it so fast, I had no time to wind the harpoon cord around my waist and brace my body against the pull. I had scarcely secured it around my hand when the heavy *ugiuk* gave a sudden mighty pull. The cord ripped through my little finger, leaving only the stump you see now."

Over the loud crunching of hardtack and slurping of tea, my guests and I exchanged information about people we had seen since our last meeting here at the post. I noticed that one of the women sitting across the room kept looking at my slippers with bewilderment.

"Do you like my caribou slippers?" I finally asked her. Wrinkling her nose, an expression of the Eskimo negative, she said, "No. I am looking at your feet. Yesterday our Minister told us in his church, that you, the Long Robe, have feet like the cloven hoofs of a caribou. He urged us not to pray in your house."

That was news to me. I first met the Reverend Nicholson at Scotty Gall's place. He was standoffish and never smiled. but Scotty had warned me earlier, "Don't mind the Anglican minister. He was gassed in the Great War and is still in a daze. For some unknown reason he doesn't like Papists."

Two years later I was to meet Mr. Nicholson again on the Hudson's Bay ship, the *Fort James.* I was returning to Bathurst with my dog team, courtesy of the Hudson's Bay Company. The

172

cargo boat was to unload winter supplies at Perry River, 200 miles east of Cambridge Bay, and at the same time deliver the bride of Angus Gavin, the H.B.C. trader there. The Reverend Nicholson had been asked to perform the wedding on the deck of the ship. After the ceremony an elaborate banquet was held in its commodious galley.

The local acting Anglican minister, an Eskimo named Angulalik, well-known in this part of the Arctic, was invited. I was not. From the galley a platter of food was brought to me on the deck. One had to be content with small mercies. After all, I was merely a Papist.

"Shorty" Sommers, the skipper, and the rest of his five-man crew, who were to become my friends through the coming years, were embarrassed over the glaring discrimination and apologized to me later, although it wasn't their doing. The order had come from the Reverend Nicholson and trader Angus Gavin, the groom.

I took off my caribou slippers and displayed my bare feet to the curious woman and my other visitors. "No kidding, his feet are shaped just like ours!" They rejoined gleefully, breaking out in Homeric laughter. When the strange subject of Fala's feet was exhausted and accompanying guffaws had subsided, we heard noises on the porch. People were knocking the snow off their boots, blowing their noses, and spitting the cold mucus out of their lungs. A woman was hushing her crying child; others were laughing.

Suddenly, without so much as a knock on the door, they were all in the kitchen. Paoktok, Amiraernek, their wives and children, and Otokreak entered noisily, smiling widely, muttering customary admiration like, "It's very beautiful here," and wiping their runny noses with the backs of their hands and sleeves at the sudden increase in temperature and decrease in humidity.

"It's really warm! It's beautiful indeed!" they enthused over what to them were the almost unbelievable comforts of the White Man. They walked around, examined our religious pictures and questioned me about our various kitchen utensils with child-like wonder. When the kettle's shrill whistle announced the water was boiling, one of the older children smartly interpreted the signal, "The kettle is calling for tea!" And again everybody laughed happily.

Their curiosity largely satisfied, my guests grouped themselves on the benches around the walls while I passed around a tin of tobacco and cigarette papers, realizing that smoking was one the rare pleasures of the Inuit. The women rolled their own

173

as expertly as the men, and soon the place was so warm and thick with smoke that I was obliged by their hints to open the door. The cold air rushed in, almost blowing out the gasoline lantern hanging from the ceiling.

Merriment continued when I told the gathering about fishing on Lake Ikalututiak—the one with a name which promised great fishing—and returning empty-handed. Many were the helpful suggestions:

"Maybe you cut the hole too far from shore, *Fala.*"

"Did you go early enough? The fish bite better then."

"It was too bright today the fish saw you were a Kablunak!"

"They could see your feet and got scared. They took you for *Tupilak* (the Devil!)"

At this point the suggestions became obscene and the guffaws grew louder. There was nothing to do but join in the gaiety and then redirect the conversation. "Just as you came in," I said, "I was going to ask Aniliak and Tuktuknak about the *iluvit* (graves) on the lakeshore. Who is buried in them?"

Amiraernek took the bait. "I well remember Pigadlak, an old woman who was left there. She belonged to the Coppermine Falls People. One day she left with her husband and three other families who went seal hunting on one of the small islands in Coronation Gulf. They killed many seals and were enjoying themselves so much that they did not notice the ice breakup. When they discovered that the northwest winds and currents had broken the ice between their small island and the mainland, it was too late.

"They did not bring their kayaks on their sleds and had no way of crossing the water. They had spears and rifles, but could not reach the seals without kayaks and there was no game to be found on the rocky island. All they had for themselves and their dogs was a large number of seals. After eating the seals, they fed on the dogs. Some of the people got sick and died; the others lived for awhile on the bodies of the dead. In the end, only Pigadlak remained in the camp."

"How did she manage to survive?"

"By feeding on the scraps of the corpses. The buttocks and thighs had already been eaten. They are the best parts. She also fed on the eggs of migratory birds, and by jigging for tom-cod off the rocks. Pigadlak was almost dying of starvation and sickness when the Good Spirits froze the sea again. A hunter came across her and took her to Nagiuktok Island."

"What happened to her there?"

"She lived with some friends and got well. Then she found a husband. They had children and moved to Cambridge Bay. She was an old woman when she died there in her *Krepik* (sleeping bag). When word got around about the many deaths on that island, people called it Graveyard Island."

"Yes, indeed it was hopeless," added Malrukhak, Amiraernek's wife, as she nursed her newborn son. "Some of our people also ate human flesh when they were starving because fish and game were scarce. They had to. There was no choice. Starvation maddens the mind, like a terrible disease."

"But why did Hinnihiak and Ulukhak kill Fathers Rouviers and Le Roux? They weren't starving, yet they ate their victims' hearts and livers."

Again Amiraernek was straightforward. "I was only a young man when that happened at Coppermine River. The *angakuk* (shaman) told Hinnihiak and Ulukhak that by killing the two Long Robes they would possess their powers because the Falain (Fathers) were also shamans in the land of the kablunak (White Man). That's the way it is, although you may find it difficult to understand why our people act that way."

"Yes, yes," Malrukhak backed him up. "But we do not judge our people. Life is uncertain in our land. The spirits make us do things we don't like. Sometimes they mislead us. Like my brother-in-law, Mitkroernek. You remember?" she put the question to her husband, but before Amiraernek could reply, she told us of Mitkroernek's sad ending.

"When his family's food supply began to run low at Starvation Cove, Mitkroernek went hunting ptarmigan, or Arctic grouse, up the Ikaluktok River. He had good success and was about to return home when he was overtaken by a *pirtok*. He weathered it that night in a makeshift igloo, but driven by his impatience to bring food to his family, ventured out the next day. He had not gone far when he was forced to make himself another small igloo. But the wind was so strong, he couldn't put the snow blocks together. Leaving his hunting bag (full of ptarmigans) behind, Mitkroernek—now lost and panic stricken—pushed blindly on. He was ultimately found in a tiny shelter, his strength spent in fighting icy blasts and swirling snow, his frigid body huddled in a vain effort of self-preservation. It was strictly a case of *ayornaronarevok illa,* as Arnaluk put it; that is, there was certainly nothing one could do about it."

As informally as they came, my visitors rose to leave. I told them they were welcome to come the following evening to my midnight service when I would talk to them. "Now you know that I'm not *Tupilak,* the Devil, with the hoofs of a caribou!" They were still chuckling when they filed out.

Outside, the moon was wreathed in a huge halo, the usual

precursor of an imminent storm. "The big circle is showing," remarked a youngster, causing others to crane at the phenomenon. I, too, knew a drastic change in the weather was coming. My warning was a terrific headache. I hurried to bed.

In the morning a bitter wind howled from the northeast, reducing visibility to a few feet. Late in the afternoon the winds reached gale force. Although the storm abated somewhat with the onset of night, I did not expect anyone to attend my Midnight Mass. To my surprise and delight, Scott Alexander, Hikhik and his family showed up around ten o'clock. "We could see the light in your window," explained the Constable, "and I asked Hikhik if he would like to come along." Both men carried storm lanterns. Behind them were Kommek and Arluk, Hikhik's wives, with their two boys. "The wind is not so bad at present," observed Hikhik. "We had no difficulty finding your place."

To my further astonishment, Otokreak, Paoktok, Amiraernek, and Makara arrived shortly thereafter with their families. My hut was full.

At midnight, with Scott serving, I said Mass. I talked to them about God, the Good Spirit, Who took care of them and loved them. After Mass, Scott and I made big pots of tea and opened up a case of pilote bread and jam cans to mark the advent of Christmas.

We had no musical instruments, record player, or radio to bring additional warmth and joy for this occasion, but at least the driven snow provided a fitting adornment.

Scott, the only other Kablunak present, remained subdued, probably thinking of his Christmas Eves with his family in Canada. Before leaving, he said to me, "Father, I almost forgot to pass on Scotty Gall's invitation to his Christmas dinner. Reggie and I will gladly pick you up on our way to the trading post." He hesitated momentarily, then added, "I don't know if Mr. Nicholson will come or not. He may have his church service at that time."

On his way out, Hikhik—always the perfect gentleman—smiled and said, "Stop for tea when you return from jigging, Fala. Arluk and Kommek like you."

Before heading for bed, I stepped outside to look at my dog team. Surrounded by snowdrifts, the huskies were all curled up like women's fur muffs. The sky had cleared and the Northern Lights were flickering and dancing, weaving their ethereal patterns across the heavens. My migraine gone, I felt at peace with the world at large and my immediate environment.

Just before noon Scott and Reggie knocked on my door. They came in and we exchanged Christmas greetings. "And now let's go to the Trading Post and have a good time with the Galls!"

proposed Reggie.

Scotty Gall was at the door, waiting for us with a welcoming grin. "Merry Christmas to you all!" was his cheerful Santa Claus greeting. "Come in and let's be happy together."

His wife Isabelle must have heard the commotion, for she came out of the kitchen with a big smile on her gentle face. She shook hands with the two Constables and they exchanged seasonal greetings. Then, turning towards me, she impulsively grasped my arms and asked Scotty, "Darling, you won't mind if I kiss Father?" She gave me a warm hug and kissed me. The last woman to do that was my mother upon our parting in Paris, and it felt good to have a woman's arms around me again. "We're truly sorry about last night, Father. Scotty and I were hoping to attend your Midnight Mass, but Scotty thought we shouldn't chance it in the storm."

The festive dinner included roast caribou meat and gravy, mashed potatoes, peas, carrots, and a lemon pie for dessert. Scotty had just opened a bottle of French wine, "courtesy of the Hudson's Bay Company," when a stranger appeared from a bedroom. "Gentlemen," said Scotty with unusual formality, "let me introduce you to our future dinner guest, Charley." Hearing his name, Charley nodded right and left. He looked so forlorn and emaciated that Isabelle decided to distract our attention from him by showing us a skinny plucked bird and saying, "Here is the rooster we were supposed to have on the table today— again courtesy of the Hudson's Bay Company. But since Mr. Rooster arrived last autumn, he could not get used to the cold and loneliness. He had two hens with him, but a loose dog got to them before we did. Our friend Charley never recovered from their loss." As we all laughed, Reggie couldn't resist the temptation: "You see, Father," he quipped, "even roosters can't stand celibacy!"

After the enjoyable meal, we moved from the kitchen to the living room where Scotty produced a bottle of Canadian rye whisky while Isabelle served coffee. The inevitable topic of casual discussion was, naturally, our common friend, the Eskimo. Our host opened the subject by telling us he had just finished reading an article on the Arctic explorer Vilhjalmur Stefansson and his discovery of the blond Eskimo. "So far as I'm concerned," he continued, "that's plainly not true. I've spent many years in the Arctic as a trader and I've seen countless Eskimos during that time. Of the few who inherited some white men's features, a mere handful were the offspring of lonely traders, Mounties, or missionaries. What would you say to that, Father?"

"I'd say that among the entire Eskimo population at Bathurst

Inlet I met a nice-looking girl about twelve years old who resembled a white trapper in Arctic Sound. But I certainly have never heard of a blond Eskimo. How about you, Reggie?"

For some unknown reason Constable Goodie appeared embarrassed by my innocuous question, and even more so when Scott, his comrade, teased him with "Come on, you old rogue, what do you have to say?" Isabelle wasted no time defending Reggie. "Leave him alone! He knows what you are talking about, and he has lost his tongue."

Sucking contentedly on his pipe, Scotty resumed his appraisal of the article on blond Eskimos. "Stefansson reportedly met some Eskimos of Victoria Land who had gray eyes and fair hair and claimed they were descendants of Norsemen from Greenland. But anyone living in the Western Arctic will tell you that those Eskimos are the half-breeds who came from Alaska and are living around Banksland and Victoria Land. As for our eastern part of the land, the blond-type Eskimo is not confined to Victoria or Banksland. Remember there have been several Arctic expeditions in the past century! The Franklin expedition was one of them, for example. So it's no wonder that some brownish hair and blue-eyed Eskimos are found here and there—such as the one Father mentioned at Bathurst, or the few still around Perry River and King William Land."

For the next two weeks, except when it was too stormy for comfort, Kunak and I fished in the same holes in the lake ice. After the first fruitless day, our luck wavered between good and indifferent. Our biggest catch for one day was twenty trout for Kunak and sixteen for me, ranging in weight between three and twenty-five pounds each. These delectable fish still had lots of fat on their bodies, but would lose most of it before the ice break-up in June.

Each time Kunak pulled out a fish, he promptly clubbed its head. I simply threw those I caught on the ice, where they froze in a couple of minutes. Whenever I fished from a boat, I usually clubbed the larger fish caught in the nets to make sure they would not escape, as well as to shorten their misery. Curious about Kunak's reasons for doing so, I asked him: "Why do you hit the fish over the head with your stick? Are you afraid they might fall back into the hole?"

"Because they die more quickly."

Superficially this coincided with one of my reasons, except for one consideration: Eskimos have no feeling or pity for animals, birds or fish. Kunak was holding back the real reason, and I wanted to know what it was.

The next time Hikhik dropped in to see me at the Mission

with his two wives and two sons, I asked him in front of his family. This time he didn't hedge. "Fish have souls like all living beings, *Fala*. They have to be killed in a certain way, and they have to be killed at once, or they will speak evil words to the hunter. You see, Little Man, we fear the souls of the dead—human or animal, bird or fish—for they may bring starvation, sickness and suffering. That's why we must obey the rules of taboo."

I felt privileged to be told the truth in such a straightforward manner, since the Eskimo characteristically mistrusts the Kablunak. Seeing or sensing that the White Man does not share his beliefs, he guards them jealously to avoid ridicule.

Additionally I learned that the Eskimo's reticence on supernatural concepts frequently reflects that he is too preoccupied to think in the abstract. His thought patterns stem from his own life and from the experiences of those around him. Through generations, his ancestors collected the anxiety and terror of the Barren Land—the great burdens of the long winter nights, the dread of sudden storms, the hazards and disappointments of the hunt, the pains of slow starvation, the horrors of being lost and freezing to death. Consequently his attention is inevitably focused on things material or bodily comforts that he can see, feel, and comprehend.

Finally, the Eskimo has been suddenly subjected to the White Man's civilization by explorers, missionaries, police, traders, and other trespassers on his primitive habitat, who worry about the past as well as the future. Such anxieties are at once the White Man's greatest strength and greatest weakness as he searches for happiness. The Eskimo, on the other hand, simply accepts things as they are, and lets them go at that. When they do not work out for him, he will dismiss misfortune with one word: *ayornartok*, meaning there isn't anything one can do about it— that's destiny, that's life.

8

Spring Madness

The mouth of the Kunayuk or Ellice River lay a hundred miles to the southeast. I avoided the rough ice we had encountered on the way to Cambridge Bay by following the shoreline to Anderson Bay, then cutting across Queen Maud Gulf past the eastern tip of Melbourne Island. Here my compass went berserk, although the island was two hundred and fifty miles from the north magnetic pole on Boothia Peninsula to the northeast. Because of our proximity to the pole, the force directing my compass needle was weak, and on that day, owing to additional magnetic disturbance, the instrument was useless. I therefore resorted to nature's best guide, routinely used by the Eskimos—the sun—and reached Campbell Bay without incident on the third day.

Ten miles off the mainland I saw thousands of dark dots moving towards me. The dogs recognized them for what they were long before I did. They were migrating lemmings which had completed their life-cycle and were heading instinctively for the sea. Light gray with beige bellies, the small Arctic rodents averaged five to six inches in length and were easily distinguished from their rat and mouse cousins by their short three-quarter-inch tails. They appeared bent on committing mass suicide by drowning perhaps because of an adrenal-gland disorder that reduces their capacity to cope with such adverse conditions as heat, cold, or food shortages.

Although they broke ranks as we neared them, some lemmings did not dodge my dogs' paths fast enough and were promptly eaten by the hungry huskies. But even if I'd had a hundred teams of starving canines, they would have hardly made a dent on this vast host of rodents. Eventually they swarmed all around us as far as we could see, stampeding for the mouth of the river.

It was evening, but the sun kept shining in the early May sky as we traveled eight miles up river to the rapids where some Ahiarmeun, People of the Berries, had their camp. I counted at least fifteen families there, some still living in igloos with their snow roofs replaced by caribou skins. A few of the more optimistic were housed in caribou and canvas tents. For the first time in months, spring's advent was evident.

Reawakened hope and good cheer pervaded the little community as its reception committee—nearly everyone in camp—greeted me with cries of "How are you, Kablunanuak, Little White Man? You've come at a very good time. The weather is beautiful. The land is stirring!"

It was easy to understand their infectious enthusiasm. As they greet each new spring, the sunlit hills and lowlands are softly bathed with mauve; never has the sky been so blue, so clear, so filled with the cry of life. And after months of semi-darkness, freezing on the trail, near starvation—all combining to lull them into mental torpor—never has there been such joy of living.

The sun transforms the dreary stretches of snow, ice, and rocks in a silvery landscape deserving an artist's canvas. Even the cold becomes exhilarating. Instinct tells the People of the Berries that life has meaning. Every passing day becomes more precious as light and warmth permeate nature. The mysterious Power of the universe gives tangible evidence of His friendliness, gradually assuring them protection from the dangers of the polar night and the *pirtok*.

There was another reason for levity in the camp. The seal hunting had been good for the past few weeks in the Gulf, and now, as they awaited the coming of the caribou from the tree line, the hunters and their families were going to have some fellowship with their friends, most of whom they had not seen all winter.

Anticipating other arrivals from every direction, the men had just finished building a *kalgik,* or large community igloo, on a deep snowdrift along the riverbank. Everyone would attend a dance there that night.

In the tent of the host Krilalugak, who was one of the best hunters in the camp, the *kattuk* or big drum, was being readied with the help of three musically-talented neighbors. While they held the frame, Krilalugak secured the stretched and scraped caribou skin around the wooden hoop using braided caribou sinew. I was standing at the door of the tent when Krilalugak's wife, Uhuk, welcomed me with "Come in, Little Man, and join us." It seemed incongruous that this gentle woman was burdened with an Eskimo name meaning penis, but I overlooked that, realizing that others are even smuttier.

I sat down silently with several onlookers on a low matting of dwarf willows covered with caribou fur. They were sipping tea and exchanging news about their newcomers to camp.

"Krirpak arrived yesterday," Uhuk was saying. "He has only one eye now. He told me he went hunting ptarmigans with his young son. Krirpak was crawling in the willows along the riverbank when his son shot at a ptarmigan with his bow and arrow. He missed the bird and the arrow hit Krirpak in the eye. Krirpak said he pulled out the arrow with a piece of his eye on it. "It's too bad."

The grisly subject was promptly changed by a young woman named Ivarlo. "Two of my friends, Naneroak and Unipkhak, came here on foot from Kidlinek, looking for me. They had walked many days. But I am married now, so they traveled in vain," she laughed gaily. Kidlinek, or Kent Peninsula, is at least a hundred miles west of Ellice River. That is a long walk to look for a woman, I thought, particularly for one no longer available.

Krilalugak's assistants had tightened the drum in the mean-time and returned it to him for critical testing with a stick the size and shape of a policeman's truncheon. Holding the flat drum by its handle in his left hand, he beat a brief tattoo. "That's not right yet!" was the prompt consensus, so Krilalugak handed the instrument back to the trio. Satisfied that it was sufficiently retightened and wetted for extra tautness, he gave it impulsively to me, saying "Fala, why don't you try the kattuk?" to the delight of everyone present.

The large drum was heavy and cumbersome but for a novice I managed a fair imitation of a native drummer. "That sounds better," judged the experts, while the rest laughed and teased me. Kuhuk did neither. Instead she said pleasantly, "Fala, we would like you to sing for us."

To please the hostess, I tried to recall a song I'd heard at Burnside:

"Mane, nunakhamne. . .Here on my land,
Aya-aya-ya-a-aaa
I saw a great herd of caribou,
Wagging their small tails in the wind
And feeding happily in the low land
Where juicy grass grows in the summer,

And I ran towards them with my bow and arrow,
Aya-aya-ya-a-aaa. . .

While I was singing and beating the drum, two young
women stood up facing each other, waving their arms like birds
flapping their wings, and repeating the refrain "*Aya-aya-ya-a-
aaa.*" Soon everyone else joined them in a spirit of almost
tangible gladness and friendliness.

Obviously the drum was ready. Nothing more held up the
communal dance. Gaily we trooped over to the spacious *kalgik*
where we were soon joined by others in the camp. The dancing
began at once. Nerlak, one of Krilalugak's young helpers, took
the drum, wiggling and nodding solemnly to the assembly as if
inviting appreciation for his offer. He began beating the drum
slowly, his feet immobile, but his body shaking up and down and
sideways by fits and starts, like a dog just out of water. Warmed
up, Nerlak beat the drum louder and faster as he jerked and
leaped around the circle of standing spectators.

Encouraged by all, including nearby dog teams which
howled mournfully in unison, he added a song to his gyrations:

"*Ubluk taman, unnuk taman*
All day, all night, *a-ee-ay*
I searched across the land for a woman,
For a young woman to sleep in my arms,
A-ee-ay-a-ee-ya-ya
For a woman to keep my igloo warm
And sew my clothes when I hunt, *a-ee-ay*
For I am a good hunter,
For I am a good lover, *a-ee-ay-a-ee-ya-ya*

As he sang, Nerlak became more and more hysterical,
increasing his frenzied tempo and emphasizing the rhythm of
the song by hops and jumps, perspiration pouring down his
strong face.

Fascinated by the deep reverberations of the *kattuk*, the
solemn-faced spectators wailed the endless refrain, *a-ee-ay* as
the dancer kept quickening his pace until he was virtually in a
trance. Lost in a magic dream, he was evoking the innermost
secrets of his soul. Each time he beat the drum he spun around,
finally bending forward as if to leap like a fox. Then, soaked in
sweat and groaning with near exhaustion, his voice hoarse and
his mouth overflowing with saliva, Nerlak passed the *kattuk* to
the nearest woman, muttering, "Here, take it and dance!"

She took the *kattuk* and moved gracefully to the middle of
the snow floor, her long parka covering her legs halfway. She
spun around a few times, tapping a cadence on the *kattuk*—
"Boom! boom! boom!" The onlookers seemed mesmerized,

for she was a good-looking girl, with piercing dark eyes, a slender body, and bulging breasts barely modified by her parka. Her song's sensuality could not fail to generate response:

"*Kuviahupagluta atauthikun*...Let's be happy ee-ya
The sun is melting the snow on the land
And breaking the ice on the sea...
Let's be happy together...
I am eager to meet my lover,
Share his igloo and share his *iglek*,
And I will take care of his needs...
Let's be happy together, ee-ya..."

All the adults in the communal igloo eagerly repeated the refrain, "Let's be happy together, ee-ya-ee-ya-a-aaaa..." With heightened sexuality, they began to circulate and whisper to each other, as they chose their partners for the night, while the girl with the *kattuk* writhed and twisted in exultation, continuing to sing in her seductive voice, "Let's be happy together, ee-ya."

Outside the sky began to darken, leaving only a mauve glow on the western horizon. To counteract the failing light, small blubber lamps were lit and placed in large recesses of the dance igloo's snow walls. The resultant light cast strange silhouettes against the shimmering snow crystals all around us. While I absorbed this arresting effect, three older couples arrived on the scene, all of them dressed in ancestral gala costumes. The women wore short bolero-type vests, with large round *amaon*, or hoods, and long sleeves pointed at the shoulders. The vests, I noticed, were made of the finest caribou fur with black and white patterns. And one of the women had her vest V-shaped in front, from the shoulders to the waist. They all favored the same kind of breeches that tapered below the knees to the top of their boots. The men also sported bolero vests, but with long flaps that covered their buttocks and thighs. Their sleeves were rounded at the shoulders, while their hoods were pointed like the prow of a kayak. Embroidered with strips of white caribou fur and ermine, their *karlik* or short pants partly covered their breeches.

Since no one was using the drum at the moment, the apparent leader of the sextet, a tall man with a face burnt black by the sun, picked up the *kattuk* and began dancing to a slow beat, conjuring the Spirits of the Land:

"*Ya-ya-ya-a-aaaa, kraiguit, kraiguit*...come, come,
Spirit of the Wind,
Come soon, come fast,
The shaman, is calling you. *Ya-ee-ya-ya*
He is calling you now
To take away the misfortune

That awaits all of us, ya-ya-ee-ya, ee-ya-ya. . ."

The incongruous mood of the shaman's lament had no visible effect on the gathering's behavior. Spring was in the air and so were sensual pleasures—at the moment nothing else mattered. Actually, the shaman's ill-timed foreboding was wholly wasted on the smaller children and the teenagers who kept coming and going as they pleased with their playmates and sweethearts, capitalizing on the freedom enjoyed by Eskimo youngsters. Some of the boys invited their betrothed girls into the empty igloos and tents; others ran off with them into the snow in the dusk now settling over the camp. Having observed their parents through all stages of lovemaking, they let the excitement of the spring reunion run its natural course, as instinct taught them the facts of life. It was the season of rut for all living creatures, an almost insatiable drive for old and young alike, day and night.

Normally little Eskimo girls are first shown by their parents how to submit sexually to those little boys to whom they have been promised and to whom they will be married at puberty or sooner. If the young females do not yield their bodies to the advances of their affianced, or if they prove unreceptive, the adults will urge them on with words of encouragement and by suggestive movements. Or else they will poke fun at the beginners and tease them, all the while roaring with laughter. Most children were introduced to such sexual games when they were still taking milk from their mothers' breasts. Their parents and neighbors had manipulated their intimate parts as far back as they could remember. It was nothing new to them, and they seemed to enjoy these experiments.

Visiting their young friends was another opportune occasion for the children to fondle one another, to excite their sexual desires, and to caricature the physical raptures of their parents with cries of "It's wonderful!"

Now here again was an opportunity to toy amorously with their new-found playmates, and the youngsters were not going to waste precious moments idly on the sidelines, passively watching the oldsters dance and sing. They left to make their own fun. But tragedy struck them dramatically that night during their sexually oriented hanging game. By no means the children's most popular pastime—that honor went to blind man's bluff—the hanging game was usually played by thrill-seeking youngsters during the Eskimos' great spring assemblies, or at other large gatherings of several families. To my knowledge, adult Eskimos did not indulge in it.

The boys had placed a piece of driftwood atop an igloo's

dome, tied a sealskin thong around the wood, lowered the other end of the narrow strip of skin through a small hole in the snow roof, and made a lasso at its dangling end.

On this occasion a tall, slim 12-year-old boy named Attiguyok used a block of fresh snow underfoot to allow him to reach up and place the sealskin loop around his neck. With his hands tied, he then pressed his feet down against the snowy support until the leather noose tightened about his neck. This maneuver decreased the flow of oxygen to his brain, and heightened his sexual arousal as he was masturbated by some of the young spectators near him.

Unfortunately at that moment, word came from beyond the igloos confines that a dog team was approaching the camp. Ever-curious, the children scrambled outside to have a look at the latest arrivals, leaving a helpless, struggling Attiguyok alone to his fate. The partly flattened block of fresh snow, which had supported him, gradually gave way under his feet and he choked to death.

By the time his playmates finished welcoming the newcomers to their campsite and returned to their unfinished hanging game, Attiguyok was dead. The children's agonizing cries for help then reached the adults who were blithely singing and dancing in the big igloo.

Two male dancers, whom I recognized as Immerak from Hanimok River and Aliknak from Perry River, responded immediately and I followed them. Groups of youngsters milled around the entrance to the fateful igloo, excitedly muttering misgivings such as "Attiguyok is dead! He's hanging in the igloo!"

We crept through the narrow passage of the igloo to be confronted with the motionless body of the thin-faced, stubby-nosed, open-mouthed lad. His feet barely touched the crumbled block of snow, while his breeches were pulled down to this knees, exposing his genitals.

Immerak and Aliknak pulled up the boy's pants to his waist and lowered his body on to the snow floor. I tried my best to revive Attiguyok, but it was too late.

Sorrowful wails now emanated from the big igloo as its adult occupants ran toward us with shouts of "It's too bad, too bad! The little man is dead!" Particularly pathetic were the mournful outcries of Attiguyok's parents who had come for the Celebration of Spring from a little place called Kilinguyak on Kent Peninsula.

Attiguyok's body was taken to his family's tent where it was placed in a *krepik* (sleeping bag) in the customary reclining position with the legs bent, and secured like a bundle of furs—ironically—with sealskin thongs. Traditionally, too, the body was placed behind the tent where it would remain for the next three days.

Although Attiguyok's death understandably put a damper on their festivities, it was temporary and the adults returned to the *kalgik* to continue dancing and singing throughout the night.

The children, too, resumed their frolic as if nothing untoward had happened. But they did not go back to their hanging game.

(Upon my eventual return to Cambridge Bay, I would tell my R.C.M.P. friend, Scott Alexander, about the fatal accident. The understanding policeman would sympathize with Attiguyok's family, but frankly acknowledge that there was really nothing he could do about it.)

Back in the *kalgik*, by the flickering light of the blubber lamps, a tall, slim woman called Tupertak gyrated and chanted:

"How is it, how is it
That Kakit is so happy
And his voice so hoarse when singing? A-ee-ay-ae. . .
I have never seen anyone like him anywhere.
His wife is an old woman
Whose breasts cannot drip milk anymore,
A-ee-ay-ee-ay. . .
He came to me, Tupertak,
The name my mother gave me,
And he sat on the *iglek*. A-ee. . .
'I am a good hunter,' he said,
'But my wife no more creates in her body,
And I am still a young man.' A-ee. . .
When I looked at Kakit
Staring into the gloom,
I saw a powerful man, A-ee. . .
I am not ashamed that I submitted to him,
For a man must bring forth fruit. A-ee-ay-ae-ee-ay. . .

Tupertak danced as though possessed, but her singing was more impetuous, more sensuous, and more exciting than any of the singers' contributions before her. Having turned the drum by its short handle attached to her wrist by a wide string, she beat it sporadically to accentuate the swaying of her body right and left, back and forth, her legs hardly moving.

Those who stood around her were truly entranced. Eyes half-closed, their faces impassive, they chanted the same refrain, building up inside themselves the joyous promises of spring while blotting out the dark and dreaded memories of the long winter.

No one appeared to follow Tupertak's voluptuous move-ments with more delight than chubby Iharoitok who squatted on the snow floor beside his decrepit, wizened old wife. A lascivious grin dented Iharoitok's jolly moon-shaped face, belying the startling fact that both of his legs were cut off at the ankles. This handicap did not prevent him from traveling widely by sled, and only slightly limited his reputation as a good hunter. I had met him several times on his trips to the trading post at Burnside where, in the comfort of the Mission living room, he told me about the misfortune that beset him at Gordon Bay.

"I was visiting my trap line, when the *uyaluk*—the all-powerful storm—struck. I didn't have time to build an igloo. I quickly buried myself in the snow with all my dogs around me. The *uyaluk* lasted three days, but I didn't want to wait it out. I was young and strong then; also foolish and impatient. So with my dogs I left our shelter on the second day and returned to my camp where I had left my wife. As soon as I entered my igloo, I could not feel my feet anymore. They were hard like soapstone and just as lifeless. I asked my wife to cut off my toes. She did. They fell like chips of dry wood. My feet were so badly frozen, I had to let her continue. So she cut to the heels. When the blood began to trickle, I started to yell because it hurt so much."

"But how did she stop the blood from running out?" I asked Iharoitok.

"She tied the vessels with caribou sinew and wrapped the stumps in small fur bags. She bound them very tight. It was all very painful. And for a long time I lay uselessly on the *iglek*—I, who had once been a great hunter!"

"Can you show me where she cut off your feet?"

"I'll take off my boots, *Fala*, while you fill my cup with tea," he chuckled. From the bench he sat on, he lowered himself to the floor, then slipped off his boots and fur socks. Both the boots and the socks were shaped like tubes and each was sewn at the bottom like sausage ends. While the feet had been removed neatly at the tibia and fibula, both ends of the bones were exposed with the surrounding skin and muscles shrunk flat against the sides. It wasn't pretty.

Though Iharoitok couldn't dance, he joined in the spirit. His voice often rose above the rest at each refrain. His frail wife, nearly blind and partly deaf, huddled close to him, trying to sing in a thin, off-key wail. She rocked slightly back and forth, eyes closed, her mind probably recalling dances of her spent youth.

Despite his handicap, Iharoitok retained his sense of humor and his fondness for fun. His name, translated literally, means "He has no wings" and Itigaitok (his wife's name) means "She has no feet." Expectedly, he made fun of their irony, just as he joked about the idiosyncrasy of some of his friends.

Drenched with perspiration, tired *kattuk*-beating dancers staggered out of their circle, breathing fast and stertorous, with their tongues hanging out. Other aspirants eagerly took over. Some, following Tupertak's example, revealed their loves; others sang of scandalous incidents in their drab lives, or personal faults of their rivals, male or female. Most of them resorted to songs passed from one generation to another, recalling the golden age when game was plentiful and the land was inhabited by giants and kindly spirits. Hunting songs were popular choices, and so were melancholy laments like the one sung by an old woman from Melville Sound:

> I am afraid when I see winter
> Swallowing the no-man land.
> I am afraid when my eyes follow the moon,
> On its old, old trail, A-ee-ay-ee-ay-ee-ay
> I am afraid when I hear
> The wail of the wind and the murmur of the snow
> Passing over the land;
> And when in the dark, distant sky
> The stars move on their nightly trail, A-ee-ay
> But now I am filled with joy,
> As I see the sun rising in the heavens.
> And warming up the land and the sea,
> Driving away the long winter nights
> To the land of the dead, A-ee-ay-ee-ay-ee-ay

Outside, the inevitable call for tea emanated from a tent, and the great community of dogs, disturbed in their sleep, began their own melancholy wail.

Early in the morning, despite frequent excursions to their igloos and tents for tea and sustenance, the last of the singers and dancers was spent. Some drifted back to their own abodes, others exchanged their mates, and several unmarried young girls went off to bed with their boyfriends.

I returned alone to my tent, pitched conveniently only fifty yards away from the *kalgik*. Upon opening the tent flaps, I received the shock of my life. There, sitting on my sleeping bag, was the young girl who had performed so spectacularly on the dance floor. Confounded, all I managed to ask was a feeble "Who are you?"

"I'm Pokiak." Then, with a radiant smile, she added without guile, "I want to sleep with you in your *krepik*."

Considering the attraction an Eskimo generally has for a White Man I should have expected the offer. Its timing caught me off guard. Even being tired from the trail and protracted proceedings in the big igloo, could not subdue my sexual arousal. Pokiak was extremely desirable with her long, black hair partially covering her eyes and face down to her rounded bust. My composure deserted me as I sought an appropriate response to her undisguised invitation. So I stalled. "You may sleep in my *krepik*, Pokiak, but I have to step outside just now. I'll be back in a while." I wheeled around and exited before she could change my vacillating mind.

Agitated I walked slowly and almost reluctantly to the dog line. Although my dogs appeared tired, they stood up expectantly, not knowing whether they would have to pull the sled, be examined for possible injuries, or be offered a surprise extra ration. I stroked each one leisurely, took more time than usual to examine their legs and paws, and subsequently procured small extra snacks for them from the sled.

My heart was no longer pounding when I reentered my tent. A quick glance told me Pokiak had removed all her clothes and was sound asleep in my bag. Heaving a sigh of relief, I spread a few caribou skins on the snow floor beside her and literally fell on them, travel attire and all, exhaustion finally overcoming my emotional excitement. I didn't even repeat my evening prayers. I merely cried out my frustration, "My God, sometimes it's tough to be a priest!"

The last sounds I heard before dozing off came from my neighbors. They were gay and jubilant. Winter held no more fears for anyone at Ellice River. Spring, with its exploding, passionate madness had taken over. . .

I slept late that morning. Pokiak had already left when I at last awakened. As I emerged from the tent, my eyes blinking in the bright sun, only one person was evident. Iharoitok, the irrepressible amputee, was readying his sled for a trip.

"Come and have tea with me!" I hailed him. With a smile splitting his face, he hobbled over on his knees.

"Are you going hunting today?" I asked.

"Yes, *Fala*, for small game. And maybe also to look from the hills for signs of caribou."

"I saw you at the dance last night. Did you and your wife have a good time?"

"Most certainly! Only it's too bad that my stumps and my wife's age did not let us dance. A long time ago I was one of the best dancers among my people. My wife was pretty good, too."

"After the dance I noticed some of the men exchange wives. Why do they do that?"

"Among our people a man can dispose of his wife as he pleases. He can lie with a woman as often as he gets a chance."

"Even if he is fond of his wife?"

"Sometimes a man's wife is not responsive. Maybe she has a lover, then he gets another woman. Or a man gets tired of his own wife, so he changes wives with a friend for a while. It is a good feeling to have a change from the same thing day after day. It makes the men better friends. Better partners in hunting."

"Doesn't it make them jealous?"

"Why, *Fala*? The wives do not wear out, like a bitch that loses its urge after being in heat. They come back to us happy and as good as ever," he smiled confidently.

"Then why does a hunter go after the man who stays with his wife while he is away hunting?"

"That's not the same thing. If a man doesn't ask the husband's permission, he may get killed, and the wife will be beaten. Her husband alone has the right to share her with others."

"Have your people similar customs for girls who are not married? Last night I didn't see the boys ask anyone's permission to take them. Even Pokiak came to my tent and asked to sleep with me."

Iharoitok grinned knowingly. "Women like White Men! And unmarried girls can do what they want. They have no husbands to ask."

"I know they cannot ask their husbands because they don't have any, but what about the girls' parents?"

"They don't care. Why should they, *Fala*? Every girl has to learn, and she has to find that right mate. If she and the boy enjoy each other's company, they will live together. If my wife and I had not liked sleeping together when we were married, we would have parted company after a while. My people think that is the right way."

Accompanying a series of cock-like crowings of "Come and have tea!" the camp began to rouse itself to life in the noon-day sun. When Iharoitok left, I circulated among the igloos and tents, curious to learn about the "morning after."

Answering the call for tea, a woman came out carrying a baby in her hood. It took me a moment to recognize her as one of the earliest dancers, the one who had sung about her lover Kakit.

"You danced very well last night, Tupertak," I complimented her.

She giggled with proper modesty, patting her baby's bottom behind her back while her torso shook in gentle, sympathetic rhythm.

"How is your child? Is it a boy or girl?"

"Indeed it is a Little Man!" she sang out with pride, lowering her parka's hood a bit to show off the naked child.

"Shake hands!" she added to the baby.

"He is certainly a nice looking Little Man," I said, holding his tiny hand. I judged him to be about a year old. Set in a round head, his slanted eyes matched his straight hair for blackness. His brown skin toned down his rosy lips. His nose was running. For a soother he sucked on a lump of blubber held across his mouth by a five-inch bone. He looked healthy and alert, but did not resemble his mother. When Tupertak's husband approached us, it was evident that her son didn't look like him either. To ask them if the Little Man was the image of Kakit didn't seem appropriate under the circumstances.

Of medium height and wiry build, Tupertak's mate looked ascetic as his wide cheekbones and jaws tapered sharply to a small chin. His parka hood was down, revealing thick black hair short on top but long to the back of his neck. We shook hands and, following a respectable silence, I said, "I saw many men dancing last night, but I do not remember seeing you dance."

"I did not dance, but I will tonight."

"I forgot your name."

"I'm Krilugok."

Formal introductions over, I told him I was starting my visiting rounds. "So are we, *Fala.*" It was a sufficient invitation to follow the couple into the nearest tent. The place was already crowded with callers, some of whom were sitting on the fur-covered *iglek,* and others standing around. Everyone was either eating, drinking tea, or talking about the dance and the newest arrivals in camp. I squeezed past and sat by Krilugok and Tupertak. "Whose tent is this?" I asked them quietly.

"It belongs to the family of Pangun," answered Krilugok, inclining his head in the host's direction.

"Which one is his wife?"

"There she is." His eyes directed me to a large, broad-shouldered woman with eyes so slanted they seemed closed. She was pouring tea, a fixed smile on her fat, red face.

"Father," our hostess said to an old woman next to her, handing her a filled cup. The latter did not rise, but passed it along to an elderly hunter who, in turn, gave it to a young couple, so that it eventually reached me.

"Krilugok, do you know everyone in this tent?"

"Yes, Father." He proceeded to tell me their names and I wrote them down in my diary. Intrigued by my preoccupation some of the older people crowded around me, poking their faces into my little black book.

"Looks like lemmings' droppings," one of them observed,

and everybody within sight roared.

"There's a long string of them," pointed out another amid renewed laughter.

"Maybe they have diarrhea!" diagnosed a third. The joke had endless possibilities and they played with it till it died.

But when Krilugok included Unipkhak in his list of names, the guffaws started afresh. "Why is everybody laughing?" I asked, bewildered.

"Because that is a nickname. His real name is Nerlak. But we call him Unipkhak, the Storyteller. He likes to tell stories." All eyes were now on Nerlak, the same hunter who could not wait to open the dance the night before.

"How about telling a story for *Fala?*" Pangun, our host, urged him. And even the youngsters who had been running in and out of the tent paused in anticipation.

Pleased by the attention, especially in front of a *Kablunak*, Nerlak was non-committal, expecting further inducement. When the increased clamor suggested Nerlak was not up to telling stories after the dance, he yielded to the challenge. In a voice still hoarse from the night before, he began, "When I was a young man I had a friend whose name was Kahak. One winter when he was hunting near Cambridge Bay he met a hunter called Alikamek and his wife Ikalupiak. Kahak was not married, and when Alikamek went hunting, he stayed with Ikalupiak. She liked my friend, so he ran off with her to Ungevik or Wilmot Island."

"Everything went well for Kahak until one day a red-headed policeman found him and took him back to Cambridge Bay where he locked him up in jail. Kahak was about to go to sleep that night when the *Amakro* (or R.C.M.P. "Wolf") opened the jail door and said, 'Here is a big kettle of hot tea for you. And here is an empty tobacco tin, your *korvik* for the night. Drink all the tea you want, but if you spill any urine on the floor, I will hang you in the morning!'

"It was cold in the little jail, so to keep warm Kahak drained the tea kettle. After a while he filled the *korvik* and fell asleep. He woke up during the night because his bladder was full again. He reached for the tin, but it was full. Although he was sleepy, he remembered what the policeman had told him and was afraid. His belly became bloated like a bag full of blubber and he could not sleep anymore.

"The *Amakro* returned in the morning. He looked in the kettle and found it empty. He looked at the tobacco tin full to the brim and noticed the floor was dry. He looked at Kahak and saw him squatting on the sleeping bag, his arms around his belly, a pained expression on his sleepy face. The *Amakro* began to laugh. When he had finished laughing, he said to Kahak: 'You can go now, but don't ever steal your neighbor's wife again!'

"Kahak left the jail like a *pirtok*, drenching his trousers as he flew out of the Police Station."

Under the cover of laughter that followed Nerlak's story, I escaped from what I knew would develop into a dirty storytelling contest and went over to Iharoitok's igloo. He wasn't there, but his wife was. When my eyes adjusted to the dim light, I saw two men squatting at the far end of the *iglek*. They had tied strips of caribou skins around their heads to cure their headaches and, as they wiped away their tears, they moaned in unison, "It's painful. It hurts."

"Why are they crying so?" I asked the white-haired old woman.

"It's too bad. They are my sons and they have been snow-blinded." She sat hunched over the blubber lamp and kept pushing bits of blubber closer to the flame, licking the fat off her fingers with a loud smacking of her shriveled, colorless lips.

"How did it happen?"

"My boys came here yesterday with their families from Lake Garry. They had been traveling over hilly country for many days. It was hard going. They were hot so they removed their wooden snow goggles. They came in after the dance because it is not so bright here. But there is nothing I can do to help them," she concluded resignedly.

"I have something here that should relieve their pain," I offered. When she did not object, I took a couple of salt tablets from my first-aid kit and, after dissolving them in cold water, squirted the solution into the men's inflamed eyes with an eye-dropper. Then I applied soothing ophthalmic ointment just inside the corners of their eyes. As I did so, I noticed that the skin at the corners had recently been incised.

"Why did you cut your eyes at the corners?" I asked one of them.

"There was too much blood in my eyes and it was burning them. I sliced the skin to let the blood out." I had heard of this native remedy before, but had never come across an actual case. I knew, too, that instead of blood letting, some of the few White Men I met in the Arctic used drops of kerosene or tobacco juice. As for me, whenever I had symptoms of snow blindness, I simply washed my eyes with salted water and avoided the snow's glare.

"Do your eyes feel any better now?" I asked the suffering brothers.

"They are getting better, thank you, *Fala*," one of them

194

replied.

"Where are your families? Are they together?"

"Yes, in the big tent behind here on the deep snow of the riverbank."

"I am going to look them up."

Several young children were sleighing on the riverbank's slope. They had harnessed playful pups to their little sleds and guided them after the manner of their fathers. To the right! To the left! They directed their "teams," pretending to beat them with little whips when the pups refused to obey.

Nearby a group of older boys and girls were playing *taptaoyak*, an advanced version of blindman's bluff. A blind-folded boy had just caught hold of a girl who was doing her best to stiffle her giggles, so as not to aid her captor who now had to identify her. Ignoring his playmates' attempts to tease and distract him with whimsical noises, the boy felt methodically over the girl's face and body. He was enjoying himself and took his time. Disguising her voice, she wriggled and squirmed, but made no attempt to escape.

Finally he shouted a girl's name and, hearing his playmates applaud, untied the calico blindfold and fastened it around the girl's head. Now it was her turn to catch and identify her quarry. I decided to go to the large rectangular tent.

The two wives of the snow-blinded brothers were mending clothes as they glanced at a young woman being tattooed. The "artist" was a long-haired, bearded man who resembled a Chinese mandarin. His beady eyes were focused on the sharp point of a long copper needle which he kept jabbing into her chin. Her eyes closed, the girl recoiled almost imperceptibly at each stab of the needle as it drew drops of blood curving in vertical lines below her mouth. The girl's husband sat on the low *iglek* close by with his boots and socks off, showing no emotion. He barely looked at me when I came in. He was far too engrossed in his own pedicure to be concerned. Wielding a pocketknife with practised skill, he cut back his toenails, scraped the accumulations between his toes and, cleaned the blade with his lips.

Finishing the line of bleeding dots on the young woman's chin, the tattooer picked up a wooden needle and dipped it into a gray-blue powder finely scraped from soapstone and the soot of blubber lamps. This he pushed into the skin perforations to complete the procedure. Customarily, five lines were tattooed on the chin of a Krangmalek woman—three horizontal lines over each cheekbone, and three vertical lines in the center of her forehead. It took hours of silent suffering to be branded for life with the mark of the People Beyond.

"I just saw your husbands and put a few drops of salted water in their eyes. It made them feel better," I told the older women.

"Thank you very much, Father!" they responded with open friendliness, and offered me tea and lengths of boiled seal entrails resembling thick macaroni about the diameter of a little finger. Their rubbery texture made easy chewing and I liked the sweet-and-sour taste.

After learning my hostesses' names, I asked them where they had spent the winter.

"During the early winter we camped on the Haningayok River or Back River. Then we moved to Imeriuak (the Great Water or Lake Garry) where fish are plentiful."

"Are any families living there now?"

"Yes, *Fala*, five families."

"Can you give me their names?"

Possibly because they were grateful for the aid I had given their husbands, they told me not only the names of the hunters, their wives and children, but also those of their relatives and their last-known whereabouts.

Outside, the playful screams of children suddenly changed into a delighted chorus of "Travelers! Many travelers!" Their happy outburst rivaled that of the dogs and the adults who rushed out to greet the latest arrivals. Among them was Igutak, his pretty wife Oviluk, and their little girl, who had followed me to Cambridge Bay from Taherkapfaluk, the Big Lake.

More people in camp, more news to learn, more food to share, more stories and songs to hear, more dances to enjoy, more women to choose from! Life was wonderful at that moment, the long, harsh winter forgotten.

Once again it was the effervescent Nerlak, the storyteller, who opened the dance that night. His lithe, long frame and the wild, faraway look in his dark eyes blended perfectly into the eerie setting, and fascinated the younger women in the dance circle. Characteristically jealous of one another's looks, personality, and sewing skills, the women folk mentally compared their husbands with the other men in camp including Nerlak.

"Who is Nerlak's wife?" I asked Iharoitok, my amputee friend, who sat with his spouse in their customary corner.

The old man laughed. "Nerlak has no wife!"

"Why not? He is tall, and young, and happy."

"No women wants to depend on a simple-minded, irresponsible man. He may be a good dancer and storyteller, but he is a poor hunter, *Fala*."

In the noisy *kalgik*, I noticed that at least one woman did not

196

agree with Iharoitok's summation of Nerlak. She was Oviluk, Igutak's wife. Her sparkling eyes, radiant face and general excitement betrayed deep admiration for the dashing young man with the *kattuk*. And, poor hunter or not, Nerlak noticed the pretty newcomer's obvious interest. A natural show-off, he now danced faster and more sensually until his exhausted body refused to continue. Wild-eyed, with his long black hair ringing wet, he still managed a triumphant grin as he staggered towards Oviluk and silently, but meaningfully, handed her the drum.

At dawn, when the dance began to break up, Igutak and Oviluk finally wended their weary way to their tent. No one was surprised that Nerlak tagged along and remained their guest for the next few days and nights. Nor were they surprised that Igutak, as host, gave his guest permission to sleep with Oviluk. Krangmalit hospitality demanded it.

By the end of the week, however, Igutak's usual smile and friendliness were gone, preempted by jealousy, hate, and helplessness.

9

Caribou Hunt

Several hunters had reported the arrival of scattered caribou herds a day's trip beyond the hills to the southeast. On hearing the good news, men, women, and children could be heard shouting happily in every corner of the camp, "Caribou have arrived! Caribou have arrived!"

They were the advance guard of pregnant cows. The bulls, following far behind, trotted like pacing horses with their heads up and long legs beating the tundra surface. Their groups numbered from a few score to several hundred stopping here and there to graze or rest, their mouths open to cool their lungs in the sun's heat.

An innate impulse drove the caribou to the sea and its islands, where they could escape the summer's brief but torrid heat and the clouds of mosquitoes and flies accompanying it. Others headed for the windswept hills, also to avoid the armies of insects that would normally cover the lowlands in early July.

No one—not even the finest Inuit hunter—can predict with certainty exactly when and where the caribou will arrive. For years they may follow the same route on well-worn paths, meandering between eroded mountains and hills. Suddenly, however, they may shift their march by one or two hundred miles, forcing the Eskimos to move their camps or face starvation. Sometimes a river's early overflow or premature break up might cause these detours and delays. Or a herd may be trapped by wolves, their natural enemies, in a narrow mountain pass. In the resulting panic and stampede many caribou are crushed, or

198

break their legs on rocks, while others scatter and gallop many miles off their customary course.

Eagerly awaited by hunters, the appearance of the huge intact herd was another reason for jubilation in the camp. When the peacefully grazing caribou drew nearer, only a few women with small children remained in the camp. Everyone else, including children as young as six years old set out joyfully for the hunt.

I had been following Krilugok's dog team and pulled up when he stopped. He was accompanied by his wife Tupertak and their little boy, who was asleep in her parka hood. "The dogs are getting jumpy, *Fala*. Better to leave them here so they cannot see, hear, or smell the caribou in the valley beyond," Krilugok suggested.

We took our rifles and climbed the hill. The expanse was unforgettable. The warm sun had created a delicate haze over the snow covered tundra dominated by the majestic caribou. They flowed from every gully, pass, and ravine by the thousands. Their endless streams fanned out into the broad valley, as they paused to graze and then slowly push on towards the glittering island-studded sea.

Nimbly and silently we moved down the slope nearer the endless herds. Some of the caribou closest to us scented an unfamiliar presence and raised their heads, pricking up their ears at the faint sounds from the sleeping land. Seemingly reassured, they continued to graze and scrape the hard surface snow with their wide, round cloven hoofs for the lichen and moss below.

A series of sharp rifle reports shattered the silence. The hunt was on! Krilugok and I took cover behind some rocks and began firing at passing caribou. Like the other hunters, we avoided shooting the cows, as only they could replenish the depleted caribou ranks. Nevertheless some of the cows and startled bulls started to gallop aimlessly only to stop and survey the ground. Bewildered, the great herds milled about in the valley while the hunters picked off the caribou at will. Eventually, taking their cue from the leaders, the animals resolved to scatter out of this valley of death as best they could.

By now most of the hunters had all the meat they wanted—some thirty or forty carcasses per family. This was what they had dreamed about all winter: fresh meat in abundance.

As the herds dispersed, Krilugok, his eyes sparkling with satisfaction, said, "We have done well! Let us go and get our teams." Reaching the crest of the hill, we saw Krilugok's sled and dog team, but mine was nowhere in sight. His wife Tupertak laughed as she later explained the mystery, "*Fala*, your dogs heard the shots in the valley. They pulled hard and took off after the caribou. You had not anchored your sled well enough!" We followed my sled tracks in the snow, and soon detected my dogs resting in the distance. As we walked in their direction, I tried to memorize where I'd shot my caribou. Krilugok, too, was singling out his carcasses on the hillside and valley below. Abruptly he stopped short by a boulder and yelled, "Come quickly!"

Face down in the bloodstained snow, with a gaping bullet hole in his right temple, lay inert Igutak. The other side of his head was blown out, leaving open what was left of the brain. There was no sign that anyone else was near him. Igutak might have been the victim of a hunting accident, but I wasn't surprised when Krilugok said reflectively, "I wonder where Nerlak was shooting from."

We did not have to sound another alarm. While I ran to retrieve my dog team, other hunters—suspecting something was wrong—came over and crowded around Igutak's body.

My sled had got stuck in an outcrop of rocks, but I had no trouble extricating it and returning to the place of the fatal shooting. The gathered hunters seemed mildly excited and I overheard repeated expressions of "It's too bad! Igutak was a kind man and a good hunter. Ah! It cannot be helped!"

No accusations were made, but the air was full of silent suspicion. No hunter would have mistaken a man for a caribou in broad sunlight. I offered to take Igutak's stocky body on my sled, while a young hunter volunteered to drive his team back to camp. Krilugok joined me with his team. All the rest went back to their slaughtered caribou. After all, Igutak's untimely end was none of their business. It was a private matter.

Back in camp Igutak's wife Oviluk did not seem unduly surprised at the sight of her husband's corpse, but for a few minutes she wept and moaned according to the Krangmalit custom. It was a long, pitiful cry of grief, a high-pitched wail that provoked all the dogs to join her lament. Composing herself, she brought Igutak's sleeping bag out of the tent and we placed his stiffened body in it, bending her husband's knees into the traditional sitting position. We tied the bag with strips of caribou skin, leaving a part of Igutak's face uncovered which, according to custom, would enable his soul or breath to come and go at will. Krilugok wrapped additional skins around the *krepik* as a temporary protection against marauding foxes, and we secured the entire bundle with more caribou strings.

Neighbors gathered round ceremonially, howled mournfully, and one of their number began a song of the dead:

Where is he gone?. . . *Aye, aye. . .*
He is gone to the Land of the Dead,
Where summer is endless, Where the sun
Always roams in the heavens, Chasing away
The great Spirit Storm. *Aye, aye, aye, ye. . .*
We moved Igutak's bundled body behind his tent. There it would rest for the next two or three days so that according to custom, his soul would still be close to the family and not turn angrily against them because they isolated it. His remains could not be left inside the tent because the place would become taboo. Its occupants could do no work, not even hunting, while it was there. With the body out of sight, however, and evidently out of mind, the hunters and their families resumed their normal occupations as if nothing had happened. After all, they reasoned, what is more natural or more inevitable than death? And what more important than life?

Just as Krilugok and I were leaving the camp to pick up our caribou prizes, we saw Nerlak pull in with a similar load, some of them doubtlessly shot down by Igutak. Nerlak drove past his own igloo and made for Oviluk's tent. He was now her provider and, hence, her husband.

I diarized the day, approximate time, locale, and circumstances of Igutak's death for my Mountie friends at Cambridge Bay, wondering how they would reconcile the "accident."

Rejoining other hunters still in the valley, Krilugok and I moved among the caribou we had shot. We killed the wounded ones by driving a hunting knife in the base of each animal's skull where the vertebrae end, piercing its brain. Whenever this merciful act was necessary, I used an old Corsican dagger, a family relic that my father gave me when I left home.

Hot and flushed, Krilugok pulled off his parka. His torso glistened with sweat in the bright sunshine. He grinned happily as he worked, singing in a low monotone:
"*Tuktuk, tuktuk,* caribou, caribou, come to me!
I'll make boots with the skin of thy legs;
Stay, stay with me, o creature of the land,
Roamer of the valleys, wanderer of the mountains;
Fear me not, and let me catch thee,
Eyaya, eya, eya, eyaya, ya, ya."
He incised each caribou leg from hoof to abdomen, then slit the carcass from head to tail along the center of the belly. Thrusting his fist under the skin, he tugged at it with his hands and teeth until it came off. Deftly he cut the paunch and plunged his arms inside to the elbows, hooked his forefingers behind the kidneys and pulled out the entrails. Blood trickled over his

cupped hands as he brought them to his mouth and eagerly drank the thick red fluid. "It's very good!" he said, noticing that I was watching him. "*Tuktuk* blood is wholesome for man. It makes my own blood bubble with life. Try some, *Fala!*" Rather than hurt his feelings, I scooped some blood with my hands from the cavity left by the guts and took a quick sip. It was warm and sticky. "It is good," I said politely. Fortunately, I was prepared for his next offer.

In the spring, caribou, like musk-oxen, are infested with the larvae of the warble fly, a wasp-like insect that follows migrating caribou in the summer months and lays its eggs in the animal's rump. When the eggs hatch, the larvae work their way up the caribou's back, hollowing out sockets in the victim's underskin where they stay and feed during the winter months. By May they look like hazel nuts covered with gray, fuzzy, raspberry-like skin and contain a sweetish yellow juice. At about that time they begin to emerge and fall on the ground to pupate. Left behind are round holes on the caribou's hide that must be patched when the skin is used for making clothes.

These larvae, or *komak*, are considered a great delicacy by the Eskimos. Krilugok picked them off one by one, placing some into an empty tobacco can for storage and periodically pressing one into his mouth. Like a child sucking a grape and spitting out the empty skin, he said contentedly, "*Komak* are the best! They make a man hungry for fresh meat. Eat your fill, *Fala!*" My stomach turned over. As nonchalantly as I could, I wiped my mouth with my hand in a gesture of "I am now too full," and went to attending my caribou. While removing their tongues, I noticed that several caribou were infested with tapeworms lodged around their throats and inside their snouts. I wondered how they got there. Perhaps they had come from the grass where foxes, dogs, or wolves had left their droppings.

Other hunters and their families hustled about noisily, skinning the carcasses, discarding the skins (useless because the caribou were molting), and loading their sleds with fresh meat. Children were cutting off and chewing pieces of cartilage from the muzzles and jaws. They also removed the animals' eyes from their sockets, pierced them with a bone, and sucked them like oranges, ostensibly to prevent the dead *tuktuk* from warning their survivors against the hunters.

Because hearts and livers were taboo, the hunters tossed them to their dogs, and left the rest of the entrails and hides on the frozen white floor. This was their offering to Nuliayuk, the Spirit Mother of Beasts, who had brought the caribou their way, as well as to the wandering souls of dead hunters.

Before loading the carcasses, Krilugok cut off their legs at the knee joints and stacked them separately on the sled. He could not resist the temptation to pick out three or four shin bones and crack them by tapping along them with a rock. He pulled out the marrow with his fingers and devoured it as one might a thin, long sausage. Since the marrow had not had sufficient time to freeze, Krilugok promptly regretted his impatience. He vomited again and again. It was far too rich for a stomach accustomed for so many months to a diet of frozen meat or fish, or dry meat and fish.

"I could not wait," he admitted lamely.

"You have killed a lot of *tuktuk*. How many trips will you make to the camp to take all the carcasses?"

"It is not far, *Fala*. I can make three trips before dark."

Although I had brought down fifteen caribou, and had only five dogs hitched to the sled, I was able to take them in two trips. The industry that greeted me when I arrived in camp with my first load was a rare sight. Everybody who could wield the fan-shaped *ulon*, or any other suitable knife, was busily carving the carcasses or skinning those *tuktuk* that had been brought in with their skins intact by hurried hunters.

Squatting with her baby on her upper back, Krilugok's wife Tupertak sliced the caribou flesh into strips of varying lengths and shapes, depending on its location. Then she hung them over strong seal ropes suspended between the tall handles of the scoops, ice chisels, and tent poles. Chewing on parts of the ears and other gristle, she sang old hunting songs, such as this one:

> "*Attorniartunga*. . .I will sing a song,
> A little song, about the white caribou
> Perhaps it was a big bull, *eyaya, eya,*
> Running the plains of the earth,
> *Eyaya, eya, ya, a.* . . ."

When the sun sank toward the reddened horizon, and Krilugok arrived with his last load, I asked him if he and Tupertak were planning to complete their cutting chores that evening.

"Definitely not *Fala!* Everybody is full of fresh meat. Everyone is happy. Now we shall dance more than before! Tomorrow we'll hang up the *tuktuk* meat to dry."

Even as he spoke, the sounds of testing the *kattuk* in Krilalugak's tent reverberated through the camp. Somehow the great drum sounded louder than ever.

Though Igutak was dead, he was still part of the communal life as he lay behind his wife's tent. That was too bad, but it could not be helped. Life was for the living, and one took it as it came. Nerlak and Oviluk danced, sang, and laughed far into the night. The wild spring continued its reign over the People Beyond.

On the third day, under a bright morning sun, Nerlak and Oviluk loaded Igutak's body on his sled with seven dogs harnessed to it. I went along with Krilugok and his wife Tupertak. Our small cortege headed for the same lookout on the hill from which we had observed the great herds of caribou. They were still coming, but in smaller bands. We could also see wolves at the far end of the valley. They were trotting without haste, like sheepdogs guarding their flock, but with opposite intentions.

Krilugok helped Nerlak unload his sled, placing Igutak's body on an elevation with a perfect view of the valley below. It lay there facing the sun, the source of life. Oviluk knelt close to the opening of the bundle where Igutak's face could be seen. She leaned forward and breathed around his face, simultaneously touching his nostrils and mouth as she murmured and called his soul to come forth, "Come, oh come! And go up into the mountains until your name is given to a newborn. Go down into the valley and follow the roaming caribou until your name rests with the newborn."

Symbolically she placed the beak of a falcon on her deceased husband's mouth to give his soul the bird's power to fly at will to the hills or the lowlands.

Around Igutak's frozen body the two men placed a ring of stones to guard it against roaming spirits, always on the prowl in the Barren Land. As he helped complete the stone circle, Krilugok said the magic words, "Troublesome Spirits of the Air and Land, turn away, turn away and return to the dark."

Oviluk then laid down an old hunting rifle, a tin of tobacco, a bow, some arrows, and a copper hook with its fishing line, inside the ring of stones. They were among Igutak's most valued possessions, and they would help him on his final journey. On our own departure from his open grave, Oviluk and Tupertak began to cry out their sorrow. Down the valley the caribou looked up, suspicious of the strange noises emanating from the hills. The sad duet was short-lived, and the caribou resumed their relatively peaceful march to the sea.

Every passing day the sun warmed the land, while a gentle breeze from the south helped it melt the snow. More slain caribou were brought into our camp from the hills. In the afternoons the men would drive their dogselds to the sea and hunt seals until late in the evening. Eventually, one after another, the families began to drift away to their inland summer camps—west towards Kent Peninsula, southeast to the inland lakes. It was time for me, too, to move before the snow disappeared.

On my last evening at Ellice River, I visited the few remaining families in the camp. When I returned to my tent, I was in for another surprise. Pokiak, the attractive young dancer, was there—all by her lovely, lonesome self.

"I am leaving tomorrow," she said sadly. Then she put her hands on my shoulders and rubbed her nose sensually against mine. I hugged her in return, my feelings in a jumble. Though sorely tempted once again, the Oblate in me told her gently with little conviction, "Now you go, Pokiak. I'll see you again. . . ."

10

Arctic Summer

For the rest of May and into early June the sun kept softening the snow until the strong and warm southern winds arrived. In a few days the snow was gone, exposing the nude Arctic barrens. Although criss-crossed with rivulets, the land was far from inspiring. Eroded by endless frost and winds the barren floor looked ploughed up by a careless giant who forgot to harrow. Its countless clods were appropriately called by the People Beyond the *angiptain* or the *niapkrotain*, meaning human skulls. Elsewhere the retreating glacial ice had left behind an incredible variety of broken limestone and sharp shale, split like dirt in the giant's plow.

Unsorted boulders of various sizes dotted the surrounding hills and valleys. Amid this vast confusion of rocks, gravel, sand, and "plowed" fields, only the hundreds of small, shallow, gem-like lakes salvaged the beauty. Not a single tree marked the landscape—only scraggy birch and willow bushes hiding in depressions and creek beds, ancient dwarf willows snaking several feet, and frequent clusters of moss, lichen, and grass hugging the ground. The rest was muskeg and stone.

I had stayed at Ellice River longer than I intended, so I began to wend my way back to my Mission at Cambridge Bay. Because the Ellice River and sea were still frozen, I could travel by sled all the way. Following their extended rest and ample doses of fresh caribou meat, my dogs were in top shape and made the tip of Melbourne Island—a good fifty miles from the camp at Ellice River—the first day.

I was greeted there by my friends who had accompanied me from Taherkapfaluk, the Big Lake, to Cambridge Bay. They had left Cambridge Bay a few days after me when Hikhik decided to spend some time seal hunting before returning to the Big Lake. Now they were about to leave Melbourne Island to take advantage of the cool evenings and travel as far as possible during the night. But the men lingered to help me pitch my tent, while the women brought us tea, meat, and fish.

I told them about the coming of the great caribou herd and the death of Igutak. When Hikhik asked me about Igutak's widow, Oviluk, I replied, "Nerlak has moved in with her." The response was general laughter and a comment from Kommek, Hikhik's older wife, "We all know Nerlak. We call him Unipkhak, the storyteller. Oviluk has made a poor choice. Igutak was a good hunter." Her words abashed Amiraernek and his wife Malrukhak, who had given birth to a child on the trail. Feeling sorry for Igutak, they began to cry. Their emotional reaction prompted everyone to lament the great hunter's tragic end.

Consoled, they shook hands with me and wished me a safe return to Cambridge Bay with words like, "See you some day, Little Man, maybe in the fall." Grandmother Itireitok looked genuinely sad on parting, saying, "Come back soon to Taherkapfaluk, *Fala*. I will tell you many more stories about the Spirits of the Land." I didn't know then that that was the last time I would ever see Hikhik, his younger wife Arluk, and Anerodluk, Hikhik's son by his first wife, Kommek.

I left the Melbourne Island camp early the following morning. Although the temperature dropped to the freezing point morning and evening, my light fawn parka felt comfortably warm for the rest of the trip "home." By noon the sea ice was covered with melting snow, giving the impression that this slush and water were floating. But my dogs didn't mind, for it was easier to pull the great sled, now shod only with steel runners to minimize friction. With the nightmare of winter winds and compacted snow long past, I couldn't help but agree with my friends at Ellice River that the long-awaited summer was indeed close at hand.

Only the howling dogs at the Police Barracks saluted my return to the adjacent Cambridge Bay Mission Post late in the evening. Not unexpectedly, my Mountie neighbors, Scott Alexander and Reggie Goodie, climbed the slope to my shack the next morning. They were followed by a young Caucasian couple. Scott greeted me with his usual warmth, "Welcome home, *mon vieux!* You look pretty good and well-rested." Reggie handed me a freshly baked cake wrapped in foil. "I thought you might welcome a little change from your daily fish and meat, Father." I expressed my thanks, adding, "I didn't forget you, either. I have brought you gentlemen a load of caribou meat."

"Father," said Scott, "I'd like you to meet Mr. and Mrs. Lincoln and Tahoe Washburn. They arrived yesterday by plane from New Hampshire." We shook hands and I invited them all into my humble abode.

The Washburns were the first Americans I met in the Arctic—a striking pair for whom I felt immediate affinity. Linc, as the well-built young man preferred to be called, stood about 5'10", moved deliberately and—as I learned subsequently—was meticulous in everything he did. He had fine features and his thick dark hair made the skin on his shaven face appear lighter than it actually was. Little wonder he wooed and won such a beautiful young lady. Slightly taller than her handsome husband, Tahoe had a perfect complexion, long black hair, and animated smile, and a gentle voice. The Arctic setting merely emphasized her loveliness.

Over coffee the Washburns explained that they intended to stay in Cambridge Bay until the end of August. As geologists, they had come to study the sedimentary and trap rock formation of Mount Pelly, eight miles northeast of Cambridge Bay.

At the first opportunity, Scott asked me if I had compiled a list of the Eskimos I had met at Ellice River. "I'll have a copy for you in a few days," I assured him.

Still envisioning the caribou migration I broached the subject, "You won't believe it until you see it with your own eyes! The incredible sight of thousands of caribou invading the land. And to make the scene even more memorable, while we were hunting them, an Eskimo by the name of Igutak was shot in the head—another of those strange accidents."

"Why strange, Father?" Scott asked intuitively. When I related the circumstances, he responded tersely with "Quite convenient for Nerlak and Oviluk." Then he added as an afterthought, "Father, do you think those people might still be around if I were to go there in the next few days?"

"I doubt very much you'd find anyone at Ellice River. Most of the Eskimos had already left when I pulled out; and the rest were ready to leave for their usual camps far inland. As for Igutak's body, in all probability you'll find only few broken bones and his skull with a bullet hole in it. You know how fast and thoroughly the foxes and wolves can dispose of a corpse."

While Linc and Tahoe listened to our discourse with apparent interest, they obviously had a difficult time under standing my poor English pronunciation, often asking Scott or Reggie to interpret what I had said. At one such moment Reggie encouraged them with "If you stay long enough around Father, you may acquire a French accent." Turning to me, he said, "By the way, Linc and Tahoe told me they'd like to try living in an igloo for a few days. Do you think you could build them one close to your shack, Father?"

"I'll be delighted to, although I'm not certain the snow is firm enough this time of the year."

"Would you have time to give it a try tomorrow morning?" Tahoe asked me sweetly. "I'd sure like to take some pictures of an authentic Arctic igloo so I could show them to my family and friends back home."

"Tomorrow's fine with me. I'll try to build you a nice one and furnish it with caribou skins."

On this promissory note, Scott said, "Father, we are going to the trading post to see Scotty and Isabelle. Would like to join us?"

"I certainly would—I promised I would visit them this morning."

We walked together to the sea floor and the Hudson's Bay Company buildings. Isabelle came out to greet us with her warm smile. "Come in, come in! Grand to see you again, Father. A real honor to have you all in our house!"

Moments later Scotty appeared from the warehouse. Holding his ubiquitous tobacco pipe he grinned in welcome, "Why, isn't this a wonderful surprise! Let's open a bottle of Scotch and celebrate!"

We trooped into their kitchen and sat down around its table, while our hosts prepared the drinks. It was a wonderful feeling to be reunited with such congenial people. We talked until late in the afternoon before leaving for our respective dwellings.

Early next morning Linc and Tahoe drove up to my place with Kunak, my former helper. "We've hired Kunak for a few days," Linc said, "and thought you could use him to build us an igloo. We also brought our gear Father. If you don't mind and have the space, we'd like to leave some in your house."

I helped them to unload the sled and asked them to come in for coffee. Then Kunak and I went out to look for a deep snow drift. We found a spot about a hundred feet from my shack. At noon the igloo was finished, but we knew it would last only a few days under the warm sun. I was happy to see Linc and Tahoe so excited with their new toy. Kunak returned to his tent near the R.C.M.P. buildings. He would return the following morning to drive the young geologists to Mount Pelly where they would be doing their research.

I didn't see much of them for the next two weeks. They left early each morning and stayed out late, taking advantage of the little remaining snow to drive back and forth with Kunak. Then one morning a Norseman aircraft landed on the iced bay to pick them up. Before they boarded, Linc and Tahoe came to say goodbye and repeat their thanks for my igloo effort.

"Father, we've decided to fly across Victoria Land to Prince Albert sound and study its geological features," Linc explained. "The pilot, Al Caywood, will drop us off there, then go back to Yellowknife until July."

I learned subsequently it was during their crossing of the immense island (named after Britain's Queen Victoria) that Al Caywood mapped two large lakes, both draining into Prince Albert Sound, and named them Washburn Lake and Tahoe Lake in honor of his passengers.

The snow was gone. Here and there under the bright sun vibrant color patterns broke the gray monotony of the barrens. Although the Central Arctic plants and flowers are puny at best, they did reassure me of their link with the rest of the world. Primroses, bluebells, goldenrods, catspaws, poppies, and rock-loving purple saxifrages, as well as a great variety of berries and other cosmopolitan flora like ferns and heather gradually appeared to the delight of the Kablunak and Inuit. Bees and butterflies also joined the summer floral scene.

This season included bird migration, which added succulent ducks and geese to our menu. For nearly two weeks they passed over us in an almost continuous northward stream enroute to their breeding grounds—the hundreds of Arctic Ocean islands and the countless inland lakes. There they could raise their young out of the reach of foxes and wolves and stop to rest on some of the many lakes fringing Cambridge Bay.

Kunak showed me the best approaches to Ikalututiak Lake, which always got its share of the winged visitors. He knew all the rocks and boulders that would provide the best screens and, using them we crept unobserved toward the lakeshore where the migrant wildfowl were feeding in the marshes and meadows.

Among them we saw king eiders (source of the prized duck family, eiderdown), the aptly named Arctic snow geese (their dazzling white plumage contrasting with their black-tipped wings), the hefty, predominantly gray-feathered Canada geese, as well as the majestic snow-white swans and the dark, diving loons—a veritable hunters' paradise!

On the tundra the energetic smaller birds wheeled about, clamoring and chasing each other. Long-legged wading plovers, amphibious phalaropes, snow buntings, larks, and sandpipers were some of the species I was able to identify. Though they appeared content and secure in their environment, they had to be alert for they never knew when those consummate hunters, the falcon or the gull family's long-tailed jaeger—so graceful in flight—would suddenly drop out of the sky for an impromptu meal.

Our own arsenal included .30-30 rifles, .25-25 carbines, and shotguns, but we favored our .22s because they created a minimum of noise and disturbance. The way the ducks and geese reacted to our shooting reminded me of the recent caribou hunt. When one of their kind fell, the nearest birds would glance casually at their luckless neighbor as if to say "Poor guy! He must be dead tired," and turn their attention back to feeding.

After a couple of hours' rest, the leader would rise and the flock would follow suit into the sky beyond. If no other birds descended close to our hiding place, we waded out in our waterproof seal boots to collect the ducks and geese we had shot. Then we hid in ambush again and waited for the next flight.

On one such occasion Kunak said, "*Fala*, listen to the story of the Loon and the Raven. I was told it when I was a child. *Aypago*, in the olden days, all birds' feathers were snow white. Then one day the Loon asked the Raven to draw black lines on her white feathers. The Raven poked a stick into the soot of a blubber lamp and made all sorts of dark lines on the Loon's white feathers. The Loon was so displeased with the result that she blew soot all over the Raven. This got the Raven so mad, he beat the Loon's legs with a stick, until she could barely walk. That's why today all Ravens are black, and all Loons have a hard time walking on land."

Our silent vigil was broken one afternoon by a whirring noise in the sky, so loud that at first I thought aircraft were approaching. When the noise became visible, Kunak didn't have to tell me that the "planes" were giant white swans. Fortunately, Kunak had packed his .30-30 rifle that day, and with it took a quick pot-shot at the high-flying birds. He laughed when he missed, then automatically reloaded his rifle and handed it to me. "Here, *Fala*, you shoot the Kablunak's *tigmialuk!*" (the big bird, meaning the flying machine.)

About twenty swans were flying at a fast clip some six hundred feet above us. The chances of my hitting one of them with a single shot were small indeed. But, to please my companion, I drew a fast bead on the receding flock and fired. The impossible happened.

211

"You hit one!" Kunak was just as flabbergasted as I.

Like a disabled plane, one of the swans began to fall crazily, favoring first one wing, then the other, finally crashing with a thud a hundred yards away.

As the ducks and geese in the lake had taken off with Kunak's earlier rifle report, we had nothing to lose by scrambling as fast as we could over the rocky ground to retrieve the swan. Although both its wings were broken and its breast badly bruised by the fall, it was easily the biggest, most beautiful bird I had ever bagged.

When I walked proudly over to the R.C.M.P. barracks that evening with my prize, I intended to impress the two Constables with my extraordinary shooting skill, but instead was startled by the dismay on Scott Alexander's face, which accompanied his pregnant question, "Didn't you know, Father, that it's forbidden to kill swans?"

"Surely you're not serious, Scott," I countered feebly. "I've seen many Eskimos shooting at swans. And, besides, nobody ever said anything to me about a law against taking a rifle shot at a flock of high-flying swans."

"Well, there is one. If you don't believe me, ask Reggie."

Constable Goodie nodded solemnly. "Unless there are extenuating circumstances, such as starvation, the penalty for killing a swan is jail."

"There you have it, *mon vieux!* Will you come quietly or shall I slap on the handcuffs?" Scott chuckled.

The upshot was that we took my unlawful kill to the Hudson's Bay trading post where the five of us enjoyed a rare feast prepared by Isabelle Gall. Her husband, Scotty, gallantly proposed two toasts befitting the Swan's Song. One was to Isabelle, the chef, who outdid herself in the kitchen. The other was to "the man the Mounties did *not* get!"

It was on such occasions like this—in the security, warmth, and plenty of the Kablunak—that the perpetual struggle of the People Beyond for meagre existence stood out in stark contrast to the world's peoples.

The week I returned from Ellice River, all the Inuit (with the exception of the native families attached to the H.B.C. trading post and the R.C.M.P. barracks, and my helper Kunak) left Cambridge Bay. They would not risk being caught by the sea's break up in early July. They headed for various mainland points to hunt caribou and set nets in the rivers to stock up on dry meat and fish for their winter traveling. There they would await the caribou's southward trek in September. In the spring the *tuktuk's* fur is almost worthless but its early fall coat and the fat

212

game of bridge. Scotty partnered Mr. Nicholson against Isabelle and me. She was watching me and at the same time trying hard to bring a smile to Mr. Nicholson's face with such remarks as "You are so bright and exciting!" to no one in particular. Scotty sensed his wife's intentions and, puffing on his pipe, grinned and rejoined with "Isabelle, when I do exciting or crazy things, you tell me how wonderful I am. Why don't you tell our guests how exciting and lively they are?" Some playful spirit of the Far North, likely assisted by Scotty's bottled variety, prompted me to laugh and say, "Maybe I should show the Reverend Nicholson my cloven feet. . . ." And that did it!

At this unexpected suggestion Reverend Nicholson's face flushed, then softened to a gently amused expression as he spoke to me, "I did not say that, Father. My interpreter chooses his own translations, and likes to make fun of anybody who is not an Anglican."

With Mr. Nicholson's cards finally on the table, so to speak, each of us relaxed. What's more, following our card game, Mr. Nicholson told us of many sad incidents he experienced as a chaplain during the First Great War, and I came to admire him as a man truly dedicated to his work.

We left the Galls' party together that night and on the way to our respective abodes I asked Mr. Nicholson to visit me whenever he was so inclined. But I never saw him again. My Mountie friends told me that he went to another Anglican Mission post located in a more salubrious climate.

Having no such option, I felt privileged to have good friends at the trading post and the R.C.M.P. barracks with whom I could occasionally dine, converse, and otherwise relax in comfort and safety. These enjoyable get-togethers helped us retain our sanity during the endless storms. Our relative isolation was especially hard on Isabelle, the only white woman at Cambridge Bay, and between us men we tried to alleviate her loneliness by pretending cheerfulness.

Reggie Goodie introduced a pleasant and practical diversion when he asked me to help him learn the Eskimo language. Because of my Corsican birth I had grown up speaking both Italian and French. Perhaps it was this bilingualism that had made it easier for me to acquire a working knowledge of everyday Eskimo by the end of my first year in the Land Beyond. Reggie's interests were evidently other than linguistic, and he freely admitted he had difficulty remembering Inuit words and their meanings, let alone twisting his tongue around them. His comrade, Scott Alexander, took part in our "lessons," too, but he frequently went off on short sorties to outlying camps to allay his boredom at the Police Station.

One evening our language studies were interrupted by the arrival of an Eskimo family. Having built their igloo, they trooped into the R.C.M.P. barracks to greet us. The hunter, Nerreok, was tall with broad shoulders and sombre looking. His closely clipped hair gave his round head the appearance of being almost flat on top. His receding forehead was deeply furrowed, and a flat, wide nose separated his narrow slitted eyes. He had a straight mouth with a prominent lower lip and thin upper lip above which a moustache spread in a wide crescent, curving down to a generous chin. His face was expressionless, except for his dancing eyes. They seemed permanently amused at everything. It was this peculiarity, rather than his countenance or his name, that enabled me to recognize Nerreok as the the lone-wolf hunter I had met two springs ago at Burnside. He had just strung his six-foot bow prior to our first acquaintance and, noting my curiosity, handed it to me with an invitation to try it out. I huffed and puffed with all my might, but I could not draw it to its full. Although he said nothing, his eyes laughed at me.

"Will you trade your bow?" I asked him in partial self defense.

"Certainly not. This one was made for my strength only."

At that moment I thought he was boasting, but during the next few days I discovered that no one at the trading post could do any better than I. His trading done, Nerreok departed as inconspicuously as he had come, and I did not see him again until now. But I never forgot his eyes. In the meantime I learned from others that, while he was generally acknowledged as one of the most powerful of all Krangmalit hunters, Nerreok could not bear keen rivals and habitually hunted and lived with his family at Hope Bay in Melville Sound, isolated from other camps.

A true Krangmalek, he brimmed with energy and vitality. In many ways he was the image of my friend Kakagun, whose sister he had taken as a wife. The Krangmalit people from Umikmatok and Kiluitok of Bathurst Inlet used to say of Nerreok, "He is very smart, very capable." He had acquired the reputation of a tireless wolf hunter. He knew their ways and peculiarities, their trails across the hills, their dens in the rocky mountains, their howling cries when calling each other. And he had the infinite patience of a great hunter. Scotty Gall told me Nerreok always amazed him when he came to trade at his H.B.C. post. "I can't figure out that guy, Father. Every time he comes, he's got a load of wolf skins. Unlike everyone else, he brings in more wolf skins than foxes. Incredible! But it's also smart, because he gets a bounty of fifty dollars for each wolf, besides the value of its skin."

218

"What is the value of a wolf skin now in 1941, Scotty?"

"The fur of a gray wolf will bring up to thirty dollars or so. You know, of course, that each animal's fur varies in size and color. The huge gray wolf is the most common. The white may have a value of up to fifty dollars. The black, with a delicate blue tinge—the one the Eskimos call *arluk*—could easily be worth seventy-five dollars."

On my many trips to Cambridge Bay from Burnside I made a point of stopping for a day at Nerreok's camp. Invariably our conversations would gravitate to his favorite topic—wolves. The previous time I visited him, Nerreok said, "Come outside and see my young wolves. I took them from their dens, after shooting their parents." Four of them were attached to the dog line along with his sled dogs.

"What are you doing with them?" I asked.

"I'm breeding them to one of my bitches. The bitch does not like them too much. But she has no choice. She has to take at least one of them. When the wolves are old enough, I shoot them for their skins and bounty."

Other hunters had told me that dogs born from such crossbreeding don't make the best pullers in a team. Their chests are too narrow, their legs too long, and because of their extreme timidity they are victimized by the other dogs. However, crossbreeds have a reputation for toughness on long trips. Avoiding this controversy, I asked Nerreok if he had ever been attacked by wolves. He laughed in response. "The wolf does not like the scent of man, *Fala*. Even when he is starving, he won't come close enough to a camp to attack anyone."

Nerreok's wife was a small, thin woman who had borne him two boys and a girl. Her name was Talareak, and she was the best seamstress I ever met at Bathurst. At the moment, though, she, Nerreok, and their children were shuffling about shyly in the Constables' kitchen, uncomfortably warm after the cold trail. Scott invited me to act as his interpreter.

"Did you come from Aivartok?" (Aivartok is the Krangmalit name for Hope Bay. It means "He got a whale.")

"Yes, *Fala*."

"What brings you here this time, Nerreok? Isn't the hunting good at Aivartok?"

"There is plenty of game to trap, seal to hunt, and fish to jig. But we ran out of tea and some other things we need from the trading post."

"Have you been down to Burnside recently?"

"I went down at the start of the trapping season to get more traps and ammunition."

"Did you take the Kattimanek Portage?"

"Yes *Fala*. I had a cache of seal at the Kattimanek Sound."

"Did you meet Nokadlak at the Portage?"

"I saw him. He is getting a lot of foxes."

"Is all his family well?"

"His wife Angivrana and their son Kudnanak are fine, but old Grandmother Manerathiak is not well."

"What about Nokadlak's baby daughter, Naoyak?" I asked as casually as I could, fearing the worst.

Nerreok shrugged his shoulders and the usual twinkle left his eyes. With impatient indifference he replied, "Maybe she is all right." After all, she was only a little girl. Nonetheless, I was relieved. If anything untoward had happened, Nerreok would have treated the subject differently.

Bored with the White Man's small talk, he turned to more significant news. Eyes shining, he declared, "Nokadlak told me he had heard from other travelers that Hikhik had died at Taherkapfaluk!"

"You don't mean Hikhik, the great hunter, who had two wives?" I said incredulously.

Nerreok leered back, "Yes, certainly." He had always been jealous of Hikhik's fame as a great hunter and of his ability to keep two wives. Now his greatest rival was gone. Unmistakable jubilation lighted his eyes.

"I'll be darned!" exclaimed Scott. "It wasn't so long ago that we saw him here."

"There wasn't anything wrong with Hikhik when I traveled with him all the way from Taherkapfaluk," I blurted. "He was in perfect shape, better than the rest of us. I saw him again last spring at Melbourne Island on his way back inland. He seemed happy and, as usual, was full of vitality." I was completely baffled.

Seeing our dismay, and without waiting for more questions, Nerreok went on, "Hikhik died. His younger wife Arluk and his older son Anerodluk are also dead. Hikhik's older wife Kommek took the baby boy and went off with Kivgalo." He paused to enjoy our reaction.

"They sure disappear fast in this country!" commented Reggie grimly.

I wasn't thinking about that, but rather about the unusual look on Kommek's face when, some six months earlier, I had told Hikhik and his family of meeting the widower Kivgalo. Then in a mental haze I heard Scott say, "Please ask him if he knows exactly what happened, Father."

At first Nerreok hedged. "I don't know. Nokadlak just said

Hikhik, Arluk, Anerodluk all lost their breath." We didn't press him, but let him take his time. Eventually he let it out. "One morning—it was late spring—Kommek made tea while they were still in bed. Then she went out and fetched a large can with fish in it. She gave them all some fish to eat. After a while they got sick—so sick they did not leave the *iglek* alive. Only the baby boy remained well. Kommek did not feed him any fish. After they died, she dragged their bodies to the lakeshore. Then, with her little one, she drove Hikhik's dog team with his possessions to Kivgalo's tent nearby, on the Angimayok River. . . ."

"Who's this Kivgalo, Father?"

He is the man we met when we were getting close to Taherkapfaluk, the Big Lake. He was heading for Burnside. He told us his wife had just died and that he was going to the trading post. I thought Kommek looked pleased when I relayed this news to Hikhik. And I remembered Hikhik quietly telling me, 'Kommek is my first wife. She is getting on in years. In the *krepik* she is often cold. Now I also have Arluk. She is tall and young and warm. It's too bad you don't want to sleep with her, Little Man. She likes you. I took Arluk from her husband Naogalluak who was sick. Later he cut his own throat with a knife.' "

"Did Hikhik tell you anything else?"

"He didn't have to, Scott. It was fairly obvious that Kommek resented Arluk, and it was just as clear that there was only one woman Hikhik wanted. He slept with Arluk when I stayed in his igloo. Kommek slept with her child."

"I bet this would have been quite a case, *mon vieux*, but what's the use of speculating about it now? Sure, Reggie and I could go and take this woman to her former camp to show us where their igloo was located, and to explain what happened. And what would we find? Nothing would be left of the corpses, and—knowing the Inuit—we wouldn't get anything helpful out of them. They would all cling to the same story and laugh behind our backs."

"I'm afraid you're right, Scott, when you say you wouldn't get very far interrogating the Inuit. Even though they may be jealous of one another, they will not betray their fellow men to the Kablunak. Remember you are the *Amakro*, the Wolf, to them. True, you might have found some additional evidence a few days after their deaths, but the fall and winter have swept over their bones since as well as countless foxes, wolves, and wolverines."

The untimely deaths of Hikhik, his wife, and son really bothered me. I thought about it often and, two years later in the spring, I actually visited Hikhik's camp with Okrenak, who had become my regular helper. We knew that Hikhik's last earthly abode at the time of the tragedy was on the western shore of Lake Krimakton, which we found completely deserted. With Okrenak, I walked all over the place, looking for even the slightest clue. Expectedly, we found solid evidence of habitation—broken caribou bones, a few empty coal-oil cans, bits of rope, and other old remnants. Nowhere, though, did we find a trace of human bones or skulls.

Thinking back, I recalled Nerreok saying, "Kommek dragged the bodies to the lakeshore." That was a strange statement, I thought. We had searched the shoreline, but found no evidence of skulls or stone rings not to mention the customary objects to be placed inside them. I studied the surroundings and asked myself, Is it possible that the answer lay on the bottom of the lake? Kommek could conceivably have sunk the bodies into the water. But there was no way to determine that now. The lake was frozen solid. . . .

Restless Nerreok stayed at Cambridge Bay only a couple of days. Once he had acquired all the tea and other supplies he needed from Scotty Gall, he could not wait to return to Melville Sound and his active life among his traps and wolves. Yet, when I asked him why he was in such a hurry he gave another reason, "It's too cold, too windy, and too damp here, *Fala.* The weather's better in my camp. Nobody would come to Cambridge Bay if it did not have such good trapping grounds nearby."

Nerreok was correct in his assessment. Those of us head-quartered here were perfectly aware of the damp-fog drawback that rolled in too often from the open waters of McClintock Channel. But he might have added its advantage—a harbor that is undeniably the best on the south coast of Victoria Land.

12

Through The Islands

When the next spring had erased the black memories of the Arctic night, Kunak and I ventured out toward Jenny Lind Island, presumably named for the renowned Swedish opera singer who toured the United States under P. T. Barnum's auspices prior to her death in England in 1887.

At the end of our first day out of Cambridge Bay we reached the two igloos at Sturt Point, some fifty miles distant on the southeast coast of Victoria Land. We were greeted by everyone except Piruana. She was a woman of twenty-five winters, who was dying of scurvy—a disease usually caused by a deficiency of vitamin C. While Kunak and I put our tent and took care of the dog team, the sufferer's husband, Irkrarek, asked me if I would try to help her.

Poor Piruana lay moaning in her *krepik*. Her face, grayish blue and so horribly swollen that she could barely open her eyes, told me that she was beyond human help. Braving the stench of her breath, I drew closer and asked her how she felt. For what seemed like several minutes, Piruana stared at me through the slits in the monstrous ball of bluish flesh. Finally she managed to whisper, "There's no hope for me, the end has come."

Her mouth was a mass of sores, her spongy gums swollen and inflamed. She was in nightmarish agony. Yet her mind remained clear, for when I asked "Where does it hurt you most?" She forced herself to expose her abdomen, murmuring "Here." Tucked under her buttocks was the bloodied fur of an Arctic hare. I surmised that she was suffering from excessive blood loss due to intestinal hemorrhaging. At best Piruana's hours were numbered.

Outside his igloo I asked Irkrarek what had brought on her disease. "We were starving before spring came," he replied. "I had no foxes to trade for food. She got sick."

Fresh meat from seals, caribou, or even ptarmigans or fish would have saved Piruana, for they all contain the vitamin C required to avoid scurvy.

Irkrarek didn't look well himself, while his sled team was reduced to five emaciated dogs whom he kept alive with infrequent feedings of tomcod, a fish with little nutritive value.

As an afterthought, Irkrarek told me, "I'm going to call Anilianaher in again to help my wife." Not until then did I know that the other hunter in camp was a sorcerer. I had heard that Anilianaher of Ellice River was a close friend of the helpful spirits who could accomplish wondrous things with the sick, as well as bring good luck to the hunter. Now I was curious to see him at work.

Anilianaher did not seem to mind my presence. He squatted on the snow floor, resting his hands on his knees, his eyes closed. Observing his starved face with its protruding cheekbones accentuated by his shoulder-length hair, I couldn't help thinking that he had certainly been shortchanged by his spirit masters that winter.

Perseveringly, Anilianaher began invoking the spirits of the recent dead. Several names he called out sounded familiar— Ataatakhak, Kuerkrun, Aviuyak. All had died the previous year.

Pitifully, like a sorely ailing child, Piruana cried out, "I am sick, I am sick!" Without paying any apparent attention to her pathetic wail, the sorcerer chanted away, as if in a trance, "Who are you? Who is that, anyway? Where are you? Do you hear me? Come here, come now!" He kept invoking the spirits until his voice grew hoarse.

His persistent pleading must have been heard by some benevolent spirits, because he stood up and walked over to the dying woman. He tied a string to her ankle and began pulling on it, all the while commanding the *tupilain* (the evil spirits) to leave her. But Anilianaher did not win this psychic tug-of-war with his invisible foes. Hysterically the condemned young woman gasped, "I'm truly without hope. I want to die!"

As the sorcerer chanted hoarsely on, the merciful spirits must have pitied Piruana. Although her husband tried to forestall the inevitable by pulling on her tongue "to bring back her breath," she died that night.

I helped Irkrarek prepare his wife for burial. Her legs were

224

so puffed that we could not flex them according to custom. But we did manage to bend her body forward a little and place her hands on her abdomen. In this image of a fetus in the mother's womb she could be reborn to a new life. We then carried her out through a special opening Irkrarek had cut in the side of his igloo to conform to yet another Krangmalit belief that her soul must enter a new life through a door unsullied by man. As also customary, we left her body beside the igloo for a few days. But we hadn't counted on the next morning's warm sun which caused the corpse to stink beyond human endurance. Irkrarek needed only a suggestion to move the remains away.

"Where are you going to take Piruana?" I asked him when we placed the heavy caribou-wrapped body on his sled.

"Just close by," he replied.

Irkrarek was true to his word as he and Anilianaher walked ahead of the dog team for just a short distance to a little knoll overlooking the gulf. They lowered the body to the ground facing it east so that the next morning it would greet the protective sun, source of all life and strength in the Land Beyond.

Somehow it seemed appropriate that after wandering so much and so far during their lives, the Krangmalit invariably took their shortest journey after death. And it was usually to a height of land commanding a pleasant view where the open grave would be easily noticed by passing wolves and foxes.

From a little bag Irkrarek took out Piruana's few personal belongings and arranged them near her. Before we left the *iluvek* (burial ground), he performed the final rite. Through the opening in the wrapping over Piruana's face—affording free passage for her soul—he gently touched her mouth, nose and ears to secure their friendship and good fortune on the other side of life. Then, with real grief and loud cries, he looked for the last time upon his dead companion.

Back in camp her death and burial were promptly forgotten. Everyday work had to be done, for the struggle to exist was never ending. From my tent I could see Piruana's body on the little hill. In a few days it would be reduced to scattered bits of bones and a grim weather-bleached skull. A passing hunter would glance at them and say matter-of-factly, "This used to be one of us. . ."

From Sturt Point, Kunak and I pushed on directly to Jenny Lind Island, or Krikitariuak, some thirty miles to the east in windy Victoria Strait. Despite its atypical name, I found little to distinguish it from dozens of similar islands—such as the Royal Geographical Society Islands—with similar rock formations, rolling hills and sparse tundra vegetation. It is exceptional only in that it is completely surrounded by relatively shallow, clear water, making it a favorite sealing ground in the summer.

Although it was late April and the sun was in the sky around the clock, daytime temperatures ranged from -15° to -20°—too cold for the seals to crawl out through their breathing holes in the ice and sun themselves on it. Nevertheless we were accorded a warm and joyful reception by the local men, women, and children, who willingly helped us pitch our tent and bank it halfway up with snow to cut off the ground wind. That evening, as I visited the families camped there, I told them of Piruana's death. They cried loudly, repeating, "It's certainly hopeless! It was a bad winter for us all."

Upon return to our own tent, Kunak suggested, "Why not go to Taylor Island, *Fala*, and hunt bear with Tulugak, Ablurek, and Nuvuligak?" These three hunters and their families had wintered on Lind Island, and were planning to soon go to Taylor, fifty miles to the north and six miles off the coast of Victoria Land.

I fell in readily with Kunak's proposal, especially as I had heard that other families were on that island whose particulars I could use in my survey. We spent two days preparing for the trip. While the women mended the caribou tents for the hunt, we men patched up our sled runners with thawed peat and strengthened the crossbars with additional lashes. Then we carefully checked our dog harnesses and towlines, tools and implements, fishing and hunting gear, including the all-important firearms. These we took apart and degreased to avoid congealing in the intense cold which would block their mechanisms.

Ablurek, who spoke indistinctly (as a youth he had bitten his tongue in a wrestling match), was the most enthusiastic of all. He carried out his preparations with such infinite care that Tulugak nudged Nuvuligak and said, laughing, "Ablurek is like a young lover grooming himself to sleep with his woman!"

"I am sure the beautiful big white bear is not bothering as much with his preparations!" contributed Nuvuligak.

"You can joke as much as you like," Ablurek shot back in his thick, halting speech, "but I'm tired of this place, of the same food. Seal, seal, nothing but seal all winter, except the odd hare." I want to travel and find some different meat."

Three topless igloos gaped at the blue morning sky after the hunters removed the caribou skins they had used for overhead protection instead of the usual snow-blocked roofs which would have melted much faster in the warm sun than the snow walls beneath them. Eagerly we left the camp and headed in the direction of Taylor Island.

On the whole, the going was fairly good. Only occasionally did we encounter the heavy ridges of ice that Eskimos aptly call the

226

koglunek, or fearsome thing. These frightening natural obstacles are caused by cracks in the ice which, in expanding, are thrust upwards by violent shifts in the icepack, building up huge mounds of sharp ice, like the teeth of a gigantic saw. Terrifying, too, was the everpresent danger that as the ice moved with the constant undercurrents of the sea and the winds, wide lanes or leads of open water would form without warning to isolate the unwary traveler.

Incidentally this perpetual motion of the polar ice cap has made it practically impossible for any Arctic explorer, traveling solely by dog team or on foot—that is, without any aircraft support whatsoever—to reach the elusive North Pole. In the particular cases of the Pole's two "discoverers," Dr. Frederick A. Cook and Rear Admiral Robert E. Peary, anyone thoroughly acquainted with the actual Arctic travel hazards finds it difficult to accept their respective claims. I will tell you why.

Dr. Cook, a surgeon who had participated in an earlier Arctic expedition led by Peary, left Axel Heiberg Island (adjacent to Ellesmere Island) on March 18, 1908. Accompanied by two Eskimos, twenty-six dogs and two sleds, he allegedly accomplished his 575-mile (strictly as the proverbial crow flies) trek to the Pole over the shifting ocean ice in thirty-five days, arriving at his destination on April 21, 1908. The world did not learn of Dr. Cook's historic feat until he announced it a year later, just a week prior to Peary's return to the United States following claimed conquest of the North Pole on April 6, 1909.

Peary, a civil engineer in the U.S. Navy, reported that he had left Cape Columbia "atop" Ellesmere Island with his large expeditionary force of twenty-four men, 133 dogs, and nineteen sleds on February 22, 1909. For his final dash to the top of the world he was accompanied only by his chief assistant Mathew Henson and four Eskimos. In all, it took Peary's expedition forty-four days to traverse the circa 455 "crow-flight" miles from Cape Columbia to the Pole.

When Peary learned of his former colleague's claim, he promptly and angrily denounced it as a lie, thereby starting the famous dispute which remains unresolved to date, despite an endorsement of Peary's feat by the National Geographic Society and a subsequent Congressional bill crediting him with discovering the North Pole and retiring him from the Navy with the rank of Rear Admiral.

My own unconcealed skepticism is largely based on personal observations and travel experiences during my twelve consecutive years in the Arctic. I learned the hard way that under the very best, most favorable natural conditions—among them being such rarities as flat, even, unbroken ice underfoot—a team of dogs can pull a loaded sled approximately 35 miles a day in a seven-hour run. Dogs can maintain that daily distance up to about a week. Then they'll require at least three days' rest and extra food rations. And that, remember, would be predicated on ideal sledding conditions. Facing adverse circumstances, the dogs progress might well be reduced to an average of some five miles a day. What's more, after struggling for three or four consecutive days in truly rough ice, the men and their canines would, in effect, become total wrecks. And, in either event, direct-line distances between any two map points and the actual zig-zagging, up-and-down-and-around land measurements on rough ice are extremely divergent.

Bearing all this in mind, I find it most significant that many of the photographs taken by Peary expeditionists show mountains of broken ice—the fearsome things described above—which confronted them in the frozen Arctic Ocean. Such common obstacles alone would have prevented both the Admiral and Doctor from attaining their mutual goal within their professed time frames.

Tulugak and Ablurek chose to walk along the leads of open water ahead of the four teams, looking for narrow passages that could be crossed with safety. Whenever they found a suitable crossing, they would wave and call us to join them, "Come, come! Let's cross before it gets too wide!"

With a light, nimble jump, Ablurek jumped over the crack and directed his leading dog to follow him. Used to this method of traffic flow, the rest of the team hopped unhesitatingly over the gap and the long sled spanned it easily with the women and children aboard clinging to the ropes around the heavy load.

The only casualty during such a crossing happened to be Sultan, one of my wheel dogs. He slipped and fell into the freezing water with his companion; and while they were scrambling up the other side of the lead, the sled ran over his left hind leg and broke it. I unharnessed the luckless husky and tried to make him walk, but Sultan limped so badly that there was only one recourse. I took him on his leash behind an icy boulder. He sank down to my side, whimpering like a hurt child, looking up at me with his big, sad eyes. Unseen by the other dogs, I caressed Sultan for the last time.

"Here's something for you, my old friend!" I put a piece of fish on the snow before him and, as he sniffed it, I shot him through the head.

228

In the afternoon Taylor Island rose in the haze ahead. It seemed to have no foundation, no anchor; it simply floated like a mirage.

"I have friends there, *Fala*. One of them is Kivgayuk." Kunak's tone gave the impression that something about him was special. I tucked Kivgayuk's name away in my memory for future reference.

Moments later the dogs smelled a foreign presence and Ablurek, standing on his sled, pointed to a black spot on the ice about a mile away, "That's a seal there!"

The dogs broke into a run—they wanted to be in on the kill. When we were close to the lost, forlorn seal, the men told their women to hold back the dogs while they approached the frightened animal. The poor creature must have crawled up on the ice through his breathing hole, to sun himself in the spring sun, and fallen asleep. Meanwhile the drifting snow had probably covered up the watery opening and sealed it frozen. On awakening, the seal could not find his escape hatch, got helplessly lost, and became easy prey for a polar bear, wolf, or passing hunter.

Kunak chuckled at this unexpected find. "Killing the seal will be as simple as slipping on lake glare ice. Watch Tulugak!"

He grabbed the seal by the flippers, turned the victim on his back, deliberately sat him up partway, and then with a quick forward jerk broke the doomed animal's neck. Although Tulugak did not hurry, the entire operation lasted less than ten seconds and, more importantly, required no ammunition. Pulling him by a flipper to his sled, Tulugak hoisted the hundred-pound seal on his sled like a sack of coal and said, grinning, "We'll all eat him tonight!" The implied invitation brought only abject disgust to Ablurek's expressive face.

The camp on Taylor Island was located on a promontory jutting into Victoria Strait, some five miles up the eastern coast of the mushroom-shaped island. Far to the north, the snowy banks of Driftwood Point glittered in the evening sun, beckoning us to Admiralty Island. Several Eskimos came forward to greet us. Their children were highly excited at the sight of such an expedition. Poorly dressed in mangy caribou skins, their noses running freely, they gathered noisily around my dog team, making me the uncomfortable centre of attention.

"Who can this one be, a White Man, eh!" a couple of the older boys shouted.

"I am indeed a White Man," I humored them, pulling the silliest grimace I could muster on such short notice. This frank admission in their own tongue and the accompanying histrionic

229

display seemed at once to amuse and satisfy them. Laughing and chattering they ran back to their elders to describe the strange little man with white skin and dark whiskers and eyebrows who could speak their language and make funny faces.

When I had a chance, I asked Kunak which of the hunters was Kivgayuk. He nodded his head in the direction of a medium-sized young man whose long black hair, carelessly parted down the middle, made him almost indistinguishable from a woman. His features were regular enough, except for a prominent hooked nose and a lower lip so full it drooped under its own weight.

"Kivgayuk is a Natchilik of Orhoktok," Kunak volunteered, meaning that he belonged to the Seal People from the Blubber Grounds of King William Island. It seemed unusual for a Natchilik to be living with members of the Kivalereit group who normally dwelt north of Cambridge Bay on Victoria Land, so I asked Kunak for an explanation.

"He ran away from the Natchilit because he killed a man, *Fala*."

"Where was that?"

"At Orhoktok. He was crossing the big bay with his friends Pangun and Ugiuk. They were hunting together. A storm came. They built an igloo in the lee of a boulder of ice. The wind grew worse and worse. On the third day it ripped off a block of snow from the top of the igloo. Pangun, Uguik, and Kivgayuk were eating at the time. Pangun said, 'We must patch the roof.' Ugiuk said, 'I'll do it.'

"He was a short man, but very fat and strong. He put on his parka, took his snow knife, and went out. Pangun and Kivgayuk ate their frozen meat and listened to Ugiuk scrape and cut the snow above them. Then Pangun bent back his head and through the hole in the roof saw his friend's naked belly protruding under his parka. Pangun silently continued his meal.

" 'Pangun,' whispered Kivgayuk, 'Look up again! Ugiuk's belly is as big as a pregnant woman's!' 'Yes,' said Pangun, 'his belly is white like a seal's.' Quietly but quickly Kivgayuk picked up his snow knife, stood up on the *iglek*, and plunged the blade into Ugiuk's belly."

"Why did Kivgayuk kill his friend?" I asked in amazement.

"I don't know, *Fala*. It wasn't a kind thing to do to Ugiuk, but he had such a nice big belly!"

Since Kivgayuk was a native of King William Island, I was anxious to ask him if he had ever heard anything from his parents or other older people about the disastrous John Franklin expedition of a century ago. Most Eskimos have long memories, and facts such as the greatest tragedy in the history of Arctic exploration must have been transmitted from generation to generation.

Sir John Franklin left England in 1845 with two ships, the *Erebus* and the *Terror*. They were bark-rigged vessels of well under four hundred tons and both were fitted with old railway engines driving screw propellers. Their combined crews totalled 129 officers and men. The captains' instructions were to sail north of the American continent in search of a passage to the west. At that time everything north of about latitude 70° and west of longitude 95° was unexplored. Neither the captains, nor their respective crews were ever seen again.

Subsequent expeditions were sent and in 1857 Lady Franklin, Sir John's wife, commissioned the *Fox* under Leopold McClintock, who had already been in the Arctic under James Ross in search of the Franklin Expedition, to seek additional evidence of her husband's fate. McClintock brought back a torn piece of paper from Point Victory, on the western coast of King William Land, which told the little we know of Franklin's tragedy. More information was obtained later from the Orhotormeun, the island's Blubber Eating people themselves.

In my tent I offered Kivgayuk abundant amounts of tea, dry meat, and caribou fat. As he warmed up, I questioned him leisurely, "Kivgayuk, do you come from Orhoktok?"

"Yes, White Man, I come from Orhoktok, on the side of the island whence the dark of the evening comes." He obviously meant the isle's west coast.

"Did your relatives ever tell you about the *umiarpak,* the great ships, that came long ago and were left on the west coast of Orhoktok?"

"Yes, yes, but they said there were no men alive. They found many dead men inside the boat."

"Was there only one boat?"

"Yes, only one. It was far from shore. It was early spring and the hunters walked on the ice to the boat. But in the late spring some men were hunting caribou where the sun is at noon (That is, south of the island). They saw a boat in Kagneriuak, or Terror Bay. In it, too, many men were dead."

"Do you know what happened to the boats?"

"No, I don't know. I heard some men made holes in the sides of the boats because they could not see while they were inside. When the ice melted, the water rushed in and the boats sank."

"Did your people find any bones of the White Men inland?"

"Yes, when I was at Orhoktok I saw some places where bones can still be found. They are mostly on the mainland, going towards the Hanimor River, where my people hunt caribou in the spring. Even now hunters are using knives and pieces of iron from guns lying around the graves."

"Did your people say why the White Men died?"

"Some said they starved to death. Others said they were sick and died."

The search for Franklin's lost expedition dragged on for about ten years. The first clues to its fate were brought back by Sir John Ross. Finds of open graves on the frozen tundra, pieces of clothing, empty tins, all indicated that the survivors of the *Erebus* and *Terror* headed south to the mainland across Adelaide Peninsula toward the Back River, over a stretch of about one hundred miles.

Ironically, I thought in retrospect, the two barks were aptly named. In Greek mythology Erebus represents the place of darkness between Earth and its Lower World, or Hell, abode of the departed souls. And Terror, of course, speaks volumes.

After a day of exchanging visits with the four families on the promontory (which they picturesquely called big forefinger), we headed northeast towards the middle of Victoria Strait for the realm of *nanuk*, the polar bear, king of the Land Beyond.

13

Nanuk, The Polar Bear

Our destination lay only twenty miles to the northeast, but rough ice and frequent lanes of open water stretched it into a tiring all-day trip. The water made the going hazardous, but it was reassuring at the same time because polar bears feed entirely on seals when far away from land. Otherwise they will eat anything—grasses, roots, seaweeds, fish, and crustaceans—making their haunts unpredictable. Their favorite foods, however, are seals in the Central Arctic, and walruses in the waters of the Eastern Arctic. They naturally find it easier to catch seals by diving after them in the open water lanes than by stalking their breathing holes in the ice.

That night, as we rested in our tent, Kunak reminisced, "When I was a boy, my father took me hunting on the sea ice with other men. They said *nanuk*, the bear, prowled near the lanes of open water and the seals' blowholes. *Nanuk* waited patiently for the seals to come up, just like the Krangmalit hunters. As the men caught sight of *nanuk*, they used their dogs to attack him first. In those days it was always a great fight to watch."

"The dogs circled *nanuk* and jumped on his back. They tried to tear him apart. But they couldn't. *Nanuk* has such tough skin. Then the men rushed in with their long spears and plunged them into *nanuk's* sides near the ribs. Many dogs were usually wounded or killed during these battles. It was dangerous for the men, too. Some of them were badly hurt. A few were killed. But the old way was much more exciting. Although, even now, nobody can predict what a wounded bear might do. *Nanuk* can lope as fast as a dog and easily overtake a running man."

I had never been on an organized polar bear hunt, but I had naturally heard other native hunters' stories about the unpredictable white giant of the Arctic wastes. Kakagun, for instance, always claimed that *nanuk* was a playful creature: "If *nanuk* finds an empty barrel near a trading post or mission, he will take it up a hill and roll it down like a little boy. When he gets tired of the game, he flattens it with a blow of his powerful paw. *Nanuk* likes to play with trap lines, too. He will drag the snares across the ice and fling them around like a fox playing with a lemming. But if a fox who follows him gets caught in a trap, *nanuk* will tear it to pieces."

When Tulugak and Ablurek dropped in for tea, *nanuk* was on their minds, too. "He is good-tempered when he is full of seal blubber, but I don't trust him," said Tulugak.

"That's right," agreed Ablurek. "When *nanuk* is hungry, he will eat all the blubber on a seal. Even the whole seal. And anything else he can kill. I have seen a starving *nanuk* attack my dogs on the dog line. I shot him, and when I removed his skin, I found his stomach was full of blubber. *Nanuk* will fill his belly until he can hardly stand up. Sometimes he will even go after a dog team on the trail."

"Did a bear ever attack you, Ablurek, when you were traveling?"

"Yes, *Fala*. One evening my friend Okpinuak and I were returning to camp from our trap lines. We were smoking rolled cigarettes and anticipating the warm tea and the companionship of our families. Presently our dogs sensed something. First my leader, then the other dogs, glanced back and broke into a gallop. I turned to look behind us. So did Okpinuak. Sure enough, we were being chased by a *nanuk!* Suddenly I remembered that when we packed up after visiting the trap lines, we wrapped everything, including our rifles, in caribou skins.

"You should have seen us trying to get our rifles out while the dogs tore as fast as they could for camp! Okpinuak's team was faster than mine. And *nanuk* was faster, too. He was getting closer and closer, but still I could not get my .30-30 (Dirty-Dirty, Okpinuak pronounced it) unpacked. At last I got it! But I could not shoot from my bouncing sled. So I jumped off. *Nanuk* was very close now. I knelt down and fired. That was my only round. The rest of the ammunition was still packed away in the sled. *Nanuk* bounded a few more leaps towards me and fell. I was certainly lucky. We had a good feed in camp that night. And everybody said I was a good hunter."

With these hunting stories still fresh in my mind, we left the women and children in camp the following morning and began our search for bear tracks. They crisscrossed here and there, but the trick was to pick out and follow the most recent ones. From the tops of intervening ice ridges the four Inuit hunters and I surveyed the surrounding ice fields for signs of *nanuk*. At best he was difficult to spot against the white background. For, although the polar bear's fur has a yellowish tinge, it is white enough to blend effectively into the Arctic landscape. But the men I accompanied would not to be deceived or denied indefinitely.

"There's a bear!" Kunak whispered excitedly. I trained my telescope on his discovery. At first I could not make it out at all. Then the rare sight took shape. Yes, it was a bear, reared on his hind legs, motionless, like a grotesque snowman.

"Why is he standing like that, Kunak?"

"He is not standing, *Fala*. He has already scraped the ice around it and covered it with a little snow. Watch! He does not move, but his left paw is ready to strike the seal's head when he comes up to breathe. *Nanuk* will get him. He never misses."

"But each seal has several breathing holes. He may not use this one at all."

"The bear is clever. He is almost a man. He finds the other holes and covers them with snow. Then the snow freezes, the seal has no choice. He has to use the remaining one that has but a thick film of snow over it. Keep watching! Maybe you will be lucky enough to see him in action."

Ablurek, Nuvuligak, and Tulugak also sat glued to their telescopes (obtained from the H.B.C. trading post). They were all of one mind—to let the bear have his fun with the seal and then to take him. Minutes passed. The bear was still as immobile as a marble statue. Suddenly it happened. In a flash the statue crumpled, its powerful left paw crushing the seal's head and its right paw scooping the seal up on the ice almost in one movement.

We watched silently as the bear had his meal of fresh seal blubber. The hunters knew that the more *nanuk* ate, the less dangerous he would be. They were content to wait until he had his fill. When that time came, each of us unharnessed a dog or two and led them to the bear's tracks. Then we let them loose, and with loud, excited yelps they hurled themselves across the snow. We followed them with our sleds until we were about a hundred yards from where the huskies held their quarry at bay. *Nanuk*, however, knew exactly how to handle the pesky canines. Sometimes standing up, sometimes almost sitting down, he swatted at them as if they were a swarm of hornets. So quick were his movements and so well did his heavy, coarse mantle shield him, that no dog actually got its teeth into him.

Kunak and I anchored our sleds as we continued to watch the developing scuffle. Ablurek, Tulugak, and Nuvuligak walked towards the battlefield. When they were about halfway between us and the bear, they sat down a few yards apart, crossing their legs in the usual shooting position. Their actions were unhurried, deliberate, and methodical.

Instinctively the bear recognized his real enemies. He kept beating off the snarling dogs routinely but now turned his attention to the strange two-legged creatures who did not seem to fear him.

The three hunters raised their rifles, elbows steady on their knees. Nuvuligak, who was in the middle, glanced at his companions and pointed at his chest and then at the bear to let them know he intended to shoot first. His signal was respected in silence. Deliberately he waited until he could zero in on *nanuk's* shoulder. When his mark was exposed, minus the intrusion of dogs, Nuvuligak pressed the trigger.

With a loud roar of pain the bear bit the wound and sprawled on his belly. The dogs pounced on him with glee, but their joy was short-lived. In a moment the bewildered bear was fighting back, now mad with rage. One venturesome dog connected with his wild swings and was torn wide open, its guts flying through the air. The rest attacked with renewed fury, heightened by the sight and smell of *nanuk's* blood. But they were still no match for him. He ploughed on, despite them, towards the hunters.

Two more rifle shots, fired almost simultaneously by Ablurek and Tulugak, stopped his progress. Then all three hunters fired once more to make sure. The bear was in his final convulsions when they closed in on him. Then he lay still and, as if by command, the dogs stopped yapping and began licking the bear's blood and their own wounds. As an ultimate precaution, Nuvuligak kicked the seven-foot carcass a couple of times, then poked it with the butt of his rifle. There was no response. *Nanuk*, the king of the ice, or the sailor of the floe (as the Norsemen of old called him) was truly dead.

With his long-bladed hunting knife Nuvuligak ripped out the bear's liver, walked over to a crack in the ice, and dumped it.

"Why did he throw away the liver, Kunak?"

"So that the dogs would not get it, *Fala*. If a dog eats *nanuk's* liver, it will get very sick. It may even lose its hair."

"Is it safe for a man to eat it?"

"Certainly not."

"Why not?"

"Man will vomit. And he will have sores on his skin."

Kunak's straightforward answers weren't based on superstition, I learned later. The polar bear's liver is toxic, possibly—as some studies show—because of its extremely high content of vitamin A.

All five of us were needed to roll the 1,000-pound carcass onto Nuvuligak's sled, but the task of unloading it in camp was lightened by many willing and expectant hands. With the prospect of feasting on *nanuk's* sweet pink meat and the seal it had eaten, the women eagerly stripped the bear's hide and divided the carcass among the families. They laughed gaily as they toiled, full of fun and joy, heedless of the ever-present dangers surrounding them on the ice pack. One young woman expressed some of her feelings in this song:

> "Ye, ye, ya, ya, ye
> When I was a young girl, living on the seashore,
> Playing with my friends, hiding in the broken ice,
> I was the first to see the great *Nanuk. Ye, ye, ya, ya*
> He was standing, his white fur shining in the sun,
> He came toward me, his rear end swaying,
> His head and long neck stretching and snarling,
> He was ready to eat me. *Ye, ye, ya, ya, ye, ye* "

The men joined in the refrain, their voices mixing pleasantly with the women's higher tones.

Each family packed off its share of the bear. They all helped fill a big cauldron with its meat, fat, and bones, and waited patiently for the blubber lamp to cook it.

Ablurek's wife was the first to call out, "Come and have bear meat!"

Although Ablurek's tent was crowded when I got there, he made room for me on the *iglek* while his wife brought me a slice of bear meat weighing about a pound. It was half-boiled and still bleeding. I found it tough to eat. Its taste reminded me of a certain brand of toothpaste I used when I was in boarding school. But the hunters and their family members swallowed large chunks of the stringy, pinkish flesh, barely chewing it. Despite our lack of polite table manners, it was a happy, almost dignified assembly.

I was wrestling with a bone when Ablurek smiled and said in everyone's hearing, "*Fala*, why don't you eat the marrow? It's even better than the caribou's!" All eyes were on me; their owners were grinning and I didn't know why.

"Give *Fala* an axe!" someone suggested.

Afraid to shatter the bone with the axe's sharp edges, I hit it with the flat side. The bone held together. Everyone giggled.

237

Again and again I struck the obstinate object, but succeeded only in augmenting their laughter.

At last Ablurek took pity on me, "There's no marrow in *nanuk's* leg bone. It's made strong like a stone!"

I also had to discover for myself—as did the Danish expedition team led by Knud Rasmussen in the early 1920s—that a polar bear's limb bones are very porous and contain palatable fatty oils. This characteristic explained why my Eskimo companions persisted in chewing or sucking the bear's bones. "Live and learn, Raymond!" I comforted myself.

The feasters moved on from Ablurek's tent to Nuvuligak's, then to Tulugak's, winding up the night with an outdoor dance in a beautifully bizarre Arctic setting. Looming large and crimson near the western horizon, the sun had turned the snow into shimmering pink and so grotesquely lengthened all shadows as to make the entire scene fantastic.

When I retired to my tent, Kunak was already there. "I ate too much meat. Now I feel sick," he complained. Then added, "Tulugak wants you to sleep with his wife, Aligunek. I heard them talking about it. And as I was leaving their tent, Tulugak said, 'Tell the Little *Kablunak* he can have my wife for the night.'"

"That was very kind of him," I smiled back. "However, I'm too tired, and—like you—I also ate too much." My reasons being more than plausible, Kunak pressed no more.

As I knelt at the side of my *krepik* before drifting to sleep, I added this silent plea to my prayers, "You know, God, what I have to say. Please help me be a good priest!"

Everyone in camp—even those who had not overestimated their stomachs' capacity and paid for their folly with sickness—loafed in the spring sun next day. But early on the third day, with the bear meat almost gone and the hunters restless once again, we went after more *nanuk* tracks. Our luck held. In a broad lane of open water a female bear was giving swimming lessons to her cubs. Two balls of fluff, with black eyes and noses, they crouched hesitantly at the water's edge. Their mother signaled them to come in. They refused, almost crying. She climbed upon the ice, went behind them, and gently pushed them with her snout into the cold, dark-blue water. Automatically the cubs began to dog paddle, keeping their sharp-nosed heads above the surface. Their mother dove in and gave them a piggyback ride to the ice.

While the swimming instruction continued, the hunters crept as close as they dared, hiding behind ridges of ice. Once again the she-bear plunged into the water and invited the cubs to join her. Again they hedged. But before she had time to return and push them in once more, four shots rang out in rapid succession. The frightened cubs threw themselves into the water to seek her protection. Valiantly the wounded bear struggled to swim to them, but before she reached them, a second round finished off all three bears.

"We were fortunate to find *nanuk* in the water," remarked Kunak. "On land she would fight more fiercely than the cubs' father. And if one of her cubs was killed or wounded first, nothing would stop her from attacking the hunters."

When the wind did not bring the floating bears to the icy shore fast enough to suit him, Tulugak tossed his harpoon and we all helped pull them in. As we did so, he said, "Now our women can make some warm breeches and heavy mitts from the young bear skins for next winter. And, if there is anything left over, we'll have soft sled runners for hunting seals." His prediction sounded reasonable, but in reality most Eskimo hunters exchanged white bear skins at the trading post for much needed ammunition, tea, fishing nets, tobacco, and other White Man merchandise. At that time, an adult bearskin was worth about two hundred dollars, far outweighing the value of ornamental knee-length pants with fur out, worn over the trousers with the fur against one's body.

Our subsequent hunting trips were often interrupted by high winds, snowstorms, and occasionally by *taktuk* (fog), which followed unusually warm days and forced all hunters to remain in camp. During the long hours of waiting for the depressing fog to lift, everyone in camp participated in indoor pastimes.

One of the most popular games, especially with children, was *Taptaoyak*, a word derived from *taptiitok*, meaning "he who cannot see." A modified version of our blindman's bluff, it required a blindfolded participant to catch someone in the group, then guess that person's name by touching his or her face and body.

The adults preferred the game of *Akhak*, the Barren Grounds grizzly. As one player pretended to be the bear, everybody danced around him or her, teasing and baiting the "animal." The *akhak* crawled about, charging here and there in bear fashion, finally bringing down the chosen victim to the floor and tickling the latter until the "prey" succumbed to laughter.

Late in the evening the favorite pastime was *Ayarak*, the original version of our cat's cradle game. Using wild animal sinew instead of string with practised dexterity and incredible speed, the participants would manipulate the "strings" into a variety of shapes—such as a caribou, a fox running, people dancing, and so on. Passing the sinew figures around from hand to hand, they would entreat each other to twist or change the various figures. Inevitably, they ended in the portrayal of the intimate parts of the human body and suggestive sexual couplings. Yet the lively game was played with good humor, for to the Inuit, such sport is extremely natural and neither lewd nor obscene. As such, the presence and participation of their children who laughed and played the game among themselves was encouraged until everyone—young and old—called it quits early the next morning.

When we had been away from Taylor Island for two weeks, a terrific storm blew in from the southeast, marooning us for three days.

"That rumbling does not sound like thunder, Kunak. What is it?" I asked at the height of the storm.

"That's ice breaking in the sea. The smaller floes are driven by the currents against the large ice fields. When they crash and the ice piles up in ridges, you hear this loud noise."

"I'd like to see how much ice has been broken."

"We can do that when the storm blows over, *Fala*," he agreed and tacitly I thought I detected a sense of anticipation in his voice.

Every adult in our camp must have been stung with much the same curiosity when the wind subsided causing the bitter cold to give way to warmer temperatures. But curiosity wasn't their only reason for looking at the broken ice. A tinge of fear and foreboding was in everyone's heart. Taylor Island was now miles away and wide lanes of open water could have formed behind us. Looking at the broken ice would tell us about how fast the main great mass of ice was disintegrating. So as soon as their sleds and supplies were ready, the hunters took their wives and children for the day's outing.

"*Fala*, you heard the big noise during the storm?" Ablurek asked.

"Yes," Kunak answered for me. "I told *Fala* it was ice breaking up."

"That's right. Now there will be more open water and we might need a kayak. My sled is loaded with the family. Can you take my kayak for me?"

I was glad to oblige Ablurek. The precautionary measure seemed well-advised, and I could easily handle another seventy or eighty pounds on my sled.

We all traveled together for nearly ten miles. Then the dog teams began to fan out as the hunters followed the bear tracks of their choice. Only Tulugak's sled continued straight ahead. Kunak and I inclined a little to the left when he picked out a fairly fresh set of tracks. From the top of a hummock we checked the surroundings for *nanuk* and the progress of the other hunters.

There were no visible signs of polar bears, nor did any hunter wave his arms as a sign that he had spotted one and needed help.

I noted that Tulugak had stopped his sled by a long lane of open water and was sizing up its extent before venturing across. Apparently satisfied that the crack was not endless and that the ice ahead was connected to the main field of ice, he took his team over the narrowest part and proceeded to the outer fringe a couple of miles beyond.

When I surveyed the scene again with my telescope a little later, Tulugak had anchored his team and was now sitting at the water's edge, his rifle at the ready for appropriate action against any seal that might bob up for air. Beside him sat his wife Aligunek and their young daughter. They made an appealing picture of Inuit family life. Involuntarily my thoughts flew back to the lush, semi-tropical valleys of Corsica and its maquis, or evergreen shrubs, covering the mountain flanks where my father took me on hunting forays after wild boars and goats. The spirit of the hunt was the same, but what a stark contrast in context.

My momentary abstraction ended abruptly when, without warning, a thunderous cracking noise filled the air. Tulugak had been tricked by *Agiortok*, one of the evil spirits who caused the great floe—on which the hunter tred—to split and break away from the main frozen mass. I saw Tulugak pick up his little girl and dash for the sled, his portly wife hurrying behind. With every passing moment the chasm of deep open water widened perceptibly, inexorably. By the time they reached the near edge of the drifting floe, they stood no chance of bridging the gap.

The closest hunters sped towards their friends. Seeing Ablurek among them, I remembered his kayak on my sled. I ran to my team with Kunak, picked up the anchor, and headed for the meeting point. Nuvuligak, the first to reach the edge of the main ice, wasted no time trying to throw a contact line to the marooned family. He kept flinging his spear, to which was attached a cord of caribou strips, but his best efforts fell short.

"My *nikhik* will be better!" shouted Ablurek as he unpacked a four-pronged hook resembling a miniature anchor weighted with scrap metal. A long twine, gathered around a stick, was tied to the *nikhik*. Ablurek wound up like a softball pitcher and let the *nikhik* fly with an underhand throw. It was a long, straight pitch—the kind hunters use in retrieving a shot seal. But it was not quite far enough, either.

"There's only the kayak to save them, *Fala*," he told me. "Let's get it into the water!"

We placed the long, slender craft in the water alongside the ice. While Nuvuligak, Kunak, and I held the kayak steady,

Ablurek stepped into it carefully and sat down, stretching his legs in front of him. I handed him his double-bladed paddle. He found his balance with it and pushed off. It looked deceptively easy.

"Get your *krammotik* ready for crossing!" Nuvuligak yelled across the widening water. Despite the crosswind, or perhaps having himself guessed Ablurek's plan, Tulugak began taking his rifles, ammunition, and knives off his sled. Meanwhile Aligunek anxiously awaiting the approaching kayak, her little daughter clinging to her.

"I'll take the girl inside the kayak, Tulugak. Aligunek can stretch out on top. You push the dogs in. I will come back for you next trip."

The little girl wormed her way into the belly of the kayak and lay snugly on the bear skin covering the bottom amidships. Ablurek took up his place in the oval hole, which resembled in miniature a conning tower I once saw on a submarine in the Mediterranean. He spread his legs so that the girl's head rested between his knees, steadied the kayak, and asked Aligunek to get aboard behind him.

Although it was about fifteen feet long and extremely buoyant, the kayak dipped appreciably when Aligunek climbed cautiously on it. It took all of Ablurek's abundant skill to prevent it from rolling and tipping while she first squatted, then followed his curt orders. Without once turning around to look at her, he was balancing the kayak with the paddle like a tightrope walker using a long pole and saying, "Hold on to my parka. Now get down on your knees. Easy, easy. Stretch your legs back slowly. Right out. Stay flat and be sure to hang on. Are you all set?"

"Yes, I'm ready," she giggled back, as if all danger had long since passed away.

"Let's go back!" commanded Ablurek. And the kayak moved off.

Tulugak had brought his lead dog to the edge of the floe. Now he pushed it into the water while all the dogs yapped in protest. Ablurek called to the lead dog and it responded by swimming for the kayak. One after another the dogs—and finally the sled—were pushed off the ice by Tulugak, who remained cheerfully behind, confident of rescue.

The strange convoy ploughed on tediously through the rippling waters, its speed controlled by the slowest dog. My sympathy went out to Aligunek, who was straining to remain motionless in the cold breeze.

Ablurek successfully brought the kayak to our waiting hands. Aligunek alighted stiffly, but her round face was beaming.

"How is my daughter?" she inquired.

"She is fine," replied Ablurek, vacating his seat to let the child out.

Presently the dogs were scrambling on the ice. Freed from their harnesses, they were booted and whipped into motion to keep them from cowering and freezing. They ran off, stopping only to shake themselves, then rolled in the snow to dry themselves further.

Ablurek did not wait while we pulled up the sled. He was off to pick up his friend whose silhouette was receding into the sun. The immense floe was picking up speed in the strong currents.

No trace of apprehension remained in the group. Gathered around the rotund Aligunek and her little girl, they laughed gaily at the near disaster. When Ablurek and Tulugak landed safely, Tulugak and his wife rewarded Ablurek with a big thank you for all of us. In addition, Aligunek told her daughter, "Say thanks." This brief formality, which Ablurek did not acknowledge verbally (since the Eskimo language has no formula for it) was the only break in their chain of gaiety.

To me it was incomprehensible that any normal person could remain unperturbed and smiling no matter what misfortune befell him. Yet this resigned acceptance is perhaps the Eskimo's finest defensive weapon. His relatives might perish in a storm; his family may be starving or freezing; death in many guises may brush past him, but he will give the evil spirits no satisfaction. He will conceal his emotions. He will grin and say, "Indeed, there is nothing one can do about it. That's life!" Any deviation from this behavior would be construed as weakness. And weakness has no place in the Land Beyond.

Much more demonstrative than their masters were the hunters' dogs. Still licking the salty water off their shaggy hair, they were obviously unnerved by their compulsory swim and even more so by the distant rumbling of breaking ice.

"The dogs are listening and they are afraid," Kunak declared. "Let's help Tulugak harness them and then move closer to the solid land."

14

Natherk, The Seal

After a dinner of seal meat that evening, our conversation unavoidably turned to the dangers of broken ice. Tulugak's wife Aligunek summed up everyone's fears. "Arnakapfaluk, the great woman Spirit of the Sea, has been good to us. But we don't know how long she will be pleased with us. We don't have Anilianaher, the shaman, to tell us if we have disobeyed any rules. Misfortune may come to any one of us at any time."

It was agreed that the day's experience was a warning to move closer to land, so the hunters decided to set out the next day to look for their friends on Admiralty Island, twenty miles to the north. We were surprised to find that Driftwood Point, protruding into the sea like a pedagogue's forefinger, was deserted. We did find caches of winter implements, some wrapped in sealskins and others in bearskins, stored safely atop steep boulders away from roaming animals. But those were the only signs of order. In characteristic Eskimo style, the rest of the campsite was littered with messy bits of caribou and sealskins, ptarmigan feathers, bones, lumps of frozen peat, and dog droppings. Dirty patches of snow marked several spots where the tents had been pitched, while table-high blocks of snow indicated where the hunters had hoisted their sleds to repair them.

Ablurek and Tulugak searched the ground for the freshest sled tracks and promptly decided which way their friends had gone.

"What sealing grounds lie in that direction?" I asked Ablurek.

"Uyaraguit Bay, *Fala*. Good hunting there in the spring. And land is very close." It was a fair description of Albert Edward Bay. The sun was bright in a clear sky the next morning when we started along the northern coast of Admiralty Island. Hardly any pressure ridges were there; it was mostly smooth sea ice, allowing us to cover the thirty miles to Prince Edward Bay in seven hours. Kunak and I were well ahead of the other teams (my dogs were a superior breed, and were regularly well fed) when we spotted some stark objects in the distance.

"Those are tents, *Fala*. We'll see new people and have a good time!" my companion explained.

Sure enough, we were welcomed with usual Eskimo hospitality by the entire population of the five-tent community. Then we watched the lagging teams pull in. Decked out in their best parkas (they had changed a few miles out of camp for the occasion), the three hunters and their wives screamed at their dogs to show them off. But their huskies were tired and paid little heed. Nevertheless, our friends' efforts weren't entirely wasted, for their display of importance was succeeding magnificiently before a gathered crowd of admiring men, women, and children, as well as howling dogs.

Their ostentation indulged, they climbed off their sleds and walked about, shaking hands silently with the camp's twenty inhabitants. Among them I was glad to see my young friend Otokreak. We exchanged greetings, and he added, "You seem to be visiting a lot, *Fala!*"

"Yes, I like to visit as many people as I can. And what about you? Have you found yourself a wife yet?"

"I found one, and I am trying her out now. She is a little old, but she sews well and takes good care of me," he beamed with pride.

"Last winter I saw Nerreok in Cambridge Bay and he told me that he'd heard about your father. He said Kakagun was inland at Taheriuak where he was getting lots of foxes. Nerreok also said that Kakagun had adopted a little girl, Naoyak, who is promised to your half-brother Naodluak. Did you know that?"

"I have not seen anybody from Burnside, *Fala*. Who is this girl Naoyak?"

"She is the daughter of Nokadlak and Angivrana. She was born almost four years ago when I was visiting his camp at Portage Bay."

Otokreak showed no further interest either in his young half-brother, or in his wife-to-be. He was more curious to know when I might be returning to Burnside.

"I expect to go back next winter or next spring. Then I think I will give distant traveling a rest and stay one or two seasons with the people there. Why did you ask?"

"Because I may go with you. The land here is too cold. Hunting is often poor during the winter. Caribou are few inland and they are very small. We nearly starved last winter. Some friends came from the far end of Uyaraguit Bay to stay with us. For a long time they had nothing to eat except tomcods and, once in a while, ptarmigans and hares. Things got so bad they lost most of their dogs. We gave them some blubber for their lamps, but we were short ourselves. So we had to spend many days on the sea ice hunting seals at their *aglus* (breathing holes) to provide for everybody. Even then we got just enough to avoid starvation."

"Did you get many seals lately?"

"No, *Fala*. We arrived only two days ago. But tomorrow we are all going after *nathek* (seals). The sun is warm and they are beginning to come out of their *aglus* on the ice."

Leaving Otokreak, I wandered from tent to tent, chatting with the occupants and jotting down their names and other particulars. One name, Akraliak, I had heard before. Eskimos at Cambridge Bay had often mentioned his peculiar legs—so short that they seemed to have been amputated—and his long, ape-like arms. He reminded me of the legendary French painter Toulouse Lautrec. His wide face was a labyrinth of concentric wrinkles arranged around a large flat nose, and his shifty eyes were almost crescent-shaped.

I had heard his story, too. His wife had been taken away by his elder brother, and Akraliak allowed his anger to stew until it boiled over. He drove about a mile to his brother's camp, and walked stealthily into his igloo wherein the couple slept. Akraliak crept up close and blew his brother's head to pieces with his rifle. He dragged the naked body out of the sleeping bag and into the cold Arctic night. Then he crawled in with the woman and told her he would adopt his brother's frightened son.

My census notes showed that Akraliak had kept his promise; also that his wife had since borne him a boy and a girl. Mittek, the adopted boy, was now old enough to hunt with the men. This must have made Akraliak apprehensive because of the Krangmalit tradition of ultimate revenge. A hunter can kill his neighbor without fear of being punished by other Eskimos, who consider it his own business so long as it does not injure their community as a whole.

But with relatives of the victim, it's another matter altogether. Custom behooves them to destroy the murderer. This is a purist's vendetta, executed without anger, without passion, just like killing caribou or any other game. And patient stalking and waiting for the opportunity is an essential component of such a manhunt.

Amazingly, the murderer may know that an avenger has been chosen and that he is a doomed man, but he'll do nothing about it. In fact, he might even raise the children of the man he has killed, knowing that one of them will ultimately murder him. Meantime the executioner and everyone else, treats the murderer as if nothing had happened. But everyone knows that sooner or later, even if it takes years, the avenger will strike him down.

I discussed retributive Eskimo justice some time later with Scott Alexander at the R.C.M.P. post and made him aware that some of the murders he might have to deal with, having no apparent motives, could be the result of blood feud.

"Isn't it somewhat similar to the vendetta of your native Corsica, in which the relatives of a murdered person try to kill the murderer or members of his family?" he asked.

"Not exactly, Scott. Here the murderer alone will be killed and he'll do nothing special to prevent the revenge."

In the morning all the men fanned out across the sea "floor" while the women remained in camp to carry on their favorite occupations—scraping caribou hides, sewing, and gossiping with newcomers.

Kunak wasn't enthusiastic about this seal hunt. "I'm kind of crazy," he said with a lustful leer, "leaving all those women alone in the camp!" But when I insisted that I needed his help, he consoled himself, "I'll have time to enjoy myself at tonight's dance. Meantime I'll show you how good a seal hunter I am!"

To double my chances of seeing true experts in action, I chose to stay close to Otokreak and Tulugak. Just as Kunak and I were about to leave, Akraliak, teamed with Mittek, pulled alongside my sled and asked Kunak, "Are you and *Fala* going by yourselves?"

"No, *Fala* and I are joining Otokreak and Tulugak."

A fleeting shadow passed over Akraliak's face, but he answered cheerfully, "We'll meet you later at the dance! Don't eat too much fresh seal liver today!"

We traveled north on the bleak frozen surface of the sea. I turned to Kunak, who was unusually silent, "Did you ever meet Mittek before?"

He thought for a while before answering, "Yes, I knew him when we were boys. He was younger than I, but we used to trap weasels together near the camp. Then his father was killed and Mittek went away with Akraliak."

"Is this the first time you've seen him since?"

247

"No, *Fala*. I've seen him several times. Mostly at the trading post in Cambridge Bay."

"Is he a good hunter?"

"He's quite a good shot," Kunak replied condescendingly. Behind us Otokreak was having trouble with his dog team. I knew his dogs had diarrhea because their droppings were mostly masses of tapeworms, but this fact alone could not account for his falling so far back. I asked Kunak what was the matter.

"It's his sled. It's too heavy for the dogs. Otokreak traded his good sled for a new rifle when he got himself a woman. He built a sled with runners of willows wrapped in caribou skin and sealed in ice. Now his team crawls like a worm on a piece of dry meat. Tulugak has to stop and wait for him to catch up."

"Don't you think we should be seeing seals soon, Kunak?"

"Let's turn up to this ridge and look around," he proposed.

From the mount of pressure ice, we scanned the frozen sea. Snowdrifts lay like downy pillows on the lee sides of the ridges of rough ice. But where the ice was smooth, the snow covering was thinly spread. Kunak pointed to some distant flecks on this silvery expanse. "Those faraway seals look like lemmings, *Fala*. Watch and you will see them shifting, swaying, and turning in the sun."

"I can see some of them moving. But many seem to be quite still. Are they asleep?"

"Not for very long. They put their heads down to doze, then raise them to look around. Keep looking at only one *nathek* and see what he does."

I picked one out and watched through my telescope. Kunak was right. In a few seconds the seal stirred, looked warily about, and resumed his catnap. I timed his waking intervals—about forty seconds apart. He was almost clock-accurate.

"Why is he so afraid, Kunak? I can't see anything else around except seals."

"*Nathek* knows he is not the only living creature on ice. His main enemy *nanuk*, the bear, may be prowling about. Or there might be other strange, dangerous shapes that he should shun, like us and our dogs," he laughed.

"Tell me, just how does a big fat seal climb on the ice?"

Kunak chuckled at my ignorance. "First of all *nathek* sticks his head out of his *aglu* (breathing hole). If he sees nothing to fear, he places both fore-flippers on the edge of the *aglu* and with a push of his rear-flippers flops out onto the ice. He stays there, always close to the edge of the *aglu* so he can plunge back into it at the first sign of danger."

"Does every seal use his own *aglu*?"

"An older *nathek* always does. But two or three young ones might share the same *aglu*. Sometimes they get playful and overconfident. They crawl away and, if it is a little foggy, they lose their way. Then they might crawl toward the shore because it looks to them like a stretch of open water."

When Otokreak and Tulugak caught up to us, Kunak said to them, "*Fala* is watching the seals over there." They studied the sealing ground as a field commander might the disposition of enemy troops, before Tulugak pointed to a restless seal. "There's a wary one. He is all alone and unhappy in his sleep, like an old woman with bad dreams."

"A hunter must use all his cunning to get a vigilant *nathek* like that," added Otokreak for my benefit. Kunak agreed. "*Nathek* is aware of his usual enemies and of his friends basking in the sun. But he is not so sure of other moving objects. A hunter must try to look like a seal and act like one. Or else he must not be seen by *nathek* at all. The only way to do that is to advance when his head drops for a few moments of sleep. That's what we should do now."

Otokreak and Tulugak descended to their sleds and took off. In high spirits they kept running back and forth alongside their sleds, not only to keep warm, but also to exercise their bodies. Periodically they paused to glance at the occasional openings in the network of ridges. Recalling what Otokreak had told me of the previous winter's hardships, it wasn't difficult to imagine that they were feeling the exuberance of life, now that the Barren Land promised them warmth and food aplenty after so many months of struggling for meager existence.

To give Otokreak, Tulugak, and ourselves ample elbow-room, Kunak and I proceeded in the opposite direction. We stopped a few hundred yards from a couple of seals and hid my team out of sight and sound behind a mass of rough ice. The dogs sprawled on the snowy bed, glad for the opportunity to rest and cool off.

"Now, *Fala*," said a smiling and confident Kunak, "I'll show you that an Inuk is more capable than a Kablunak!"

From the sled he picked a parka and a pair of overpants, both made of sealskin. He spoke as he changed his parka, "We picked the right couple. They are mating. Look at them! They are too busy to notice us."

"Seals certainly mate soon after having their young," I aired my thoughts. "It wasn't so long ago we killed a pup, you remember. He was lying in his little igloo under the snow on top of the ice, close to his breathing hole. You speared his mother as she came up to breathe and feed him. While you were pulling her out, I noticed the pup, with its beautiful white fur."

"Yes, *Fala*, I remember. We even drank the milk from the dead mother. You said it was very thick and sweet. It doesn't take long for a pup to grow with this kind of milk. Now the mother is ready to mate again. She will have a pup, maybe two, early next spring. Seals are not like wolves or caribou. Female seals mate again shortly after the birth of their pups."

So saying, Kunak stepped into his *karlik*, or outer pants, with their seal fur exposed to view below his knees.

"I'll stay close to the dogs," I told him, "to keep them quiet and see they don't run off somewhere. I'll be able to watch you at the same time."

Exuberantly he disappeared between the ridges. Now I could see him at the edge of the rough ice. Only two hundred yards separated him from the affectionate seals, alternatley nuzzling each other and catching a few winks of sleep. Kunak moved toward them with cat-like furtiveness.

When the seals lowered their heads, he stepped out of his hiding place and ran for a few seconds toward them, falling prone to anticipate their reawakening. Even then, his presence did not entirely escape suspicion. The seals raised their heads and stared at him. But the intruder's actions were normal. He lifted his head, shifted, and wriggled his seal-garmented body as if to make himself more comfortable beside his *aglu*.

In starts and stops, regulated by the seals themselves, Kunak kept gaining yards. But why doesn't he shoot? I wondered. He can't be more than fifty yards away from them now. Yet he kept on inching towards his quarry.

Suddenly he leapt up like an Arctic hare and was on top of the seals in a flash. He clubbed them right and left with the butt of his rifle as if possessed. But he wasn't fast enough to handle them both. Stunned though it must have been by his blows, one of the seals managed to scramble to the *aglu* and dive out of sight.

My dogs sensed the mortal battle. Yapping away, they would have galloped off had I not been able to grab the sled in time and quiet them.

Kunak was waiting for me, leaning on his rifle and beaming all over. "I'm pretty good, eh, *Fala?*"

"You definitely are! Any woman would be proud to have you as a husband."

"I have been thinking about that. But where shall I find a wife?"

He cut open the seal's belly and pulled out the steaming, bloody liver. To drain its excess blood, he dropped it in the snow and waited for a few moments. Then he sliced off several portions and threw one to Arnakapfaluk, the Spirit of the Sea, as a token of goodwill. Finally, motioning me to help myself, he plunged in with gusto.

"Eat, *Fala*. This is good even for a Kablunak!"

Kunak had flung the glove of challenge, or so he thought. He didn't know that his compatriots had fed me raw seal liver on numerous occasions. I felt I had to show him that a White Man could do as well as an Eskimo, at least when it came to eating wild game. I pretended to be disgusted, exclaiming "It's no good!"

Mockingly he blurted, "The White Man is really good for nothing!"

And then, to his astonishment, I consumed most of the liver.

We loaded the seal aboard the sled and looked around for Otokreak and Tulugak. We could just discern them heading north toward a lead of open water.

"The seals must be crowding along the crack like mosquitoes on a child. Let's go there too!" Kunak said impulsively.

"What's wrong with the *nathek* on our left? He should not be too hard to get. There are plenty of spots where you can take cover and shoot from close range."

"Yes, there are shadows. Wait for me. I'm going to get him!"

In the same manner as before, Kunak advanced towards his goal, but he appeared puzzled (like I was) because the seal did not move.

"Must have made a pig of himself at supper and now he's sleeping it off," I surmised.

Within easy range, Kunak fired. Still his quarry did not move. He shot again and then ran towards the motionless prey. Excited by the rifle shots, my dogs raced to Kunak's side, hoping to be in on the kill.

Even before I reached Kunak, I realized it was my turn to chuckle at his expense. For a moment he was speechless with embarrassment. Then, grinning sheepishly, he said lamely, "One of the hunters had to get rid of his sick dog. I thought it was a seal, but I wasn't really sure."

"I'll have a good story to tell in camp tonight! The women are bound to enjoy it," I teased him.

"Perhaps they will, *Fala*," he said, recovering his confident manner. "But they will like me all the more."

I was still trying to fathom his logic when we joined Otokreak and Tulugak who had halted in the lee of a hummock near the open crack in the ice floor.

"Where did you shoot *nathek*?" Tulugak asked, eyeing my sled.

"Kunak didn't shoot it. He clubbed it," I answered for him.

"But we heard rifle shots."

"Oh! That was when Kunak mistook a dead dog for a sleeping seal!"

Tulugak and Otokreak roared with laughter at my cocky friend.

"I am going to make tea," said Kunak, openly peeved.

"Let me know when it's ready!" Otokreak was still laughing, but his mind was once more on live seals. "I'm going to have a try at those *nathek* by the open water," he apprised us as he strolled off, his rifle dangling in his right hand.

"The best Otokreak can do is kill one *nathek*," said Kunak. "They may be excited at meeting so many friends, but there are always some of them on the lookout for enemies. If he shoots at one, the rest will plunge to safety."

None of us spoke while we watched Otokreak alternately crawl forward to take cover behind the snowdrifts. He had one decided advantage: he was advancing into the wind. Over the silent frozen sea, the same wind brought us the characteristic noises of playful seals, something between the snorting of an impatient horse and the friendly grunts of a well-fed hog.

Otokreak had apparently gone as far as he could go without scaring off the school. He raised himself slightly off the snow, aimed and fired. The frightened seals, their flippers pounding on the ice, slithered off into their watery refuge.

"He killed one!" exclaimed Tulugak. "He is a good hunter."

In a matter of seconds Otokreak was at the smitten seal's side. He bent over to rip open the belly, pulled something out, and began to pace around it.

Mystified, I turned to Tulugak, "What is he doing?"

"He's marking the snow with *nathek's* guts."

"Why?"

"To show other hunters it belongs to him."

"Does he have a special mark?"

"No, *Fala*."

"Then how will they know it was Otokreak's seal—not Kunak's, for instance?"

"They won't."

"I don't understand."

"If Otokreak leaves the seal where it is and others find it, they will know by the snow marks that someone shot it. They will not take it. It is Otokreak's."

"I see. But does this also mean that if a seal is wounded and crawls away to die and no one leaves any markings around him, then whoever finds him can keep him for his own?"

"Certainly, *Fala*."

On top of the ridge Kunak was waving his arms, motioning Otokreak to join us for tea. It was steaming and we sipped it cheerfully. Before long Otokreak brought his contribution—the seal's warm liver.

"My belly's full," Tulugak spoke for the rest of us, too, when the liver was gone. I passed around a tin of tobacco and we relaxed on the sleds.

Suddenly a muffled shot rang out.

"That might be Akraliak," suggested Kunak. "I think he is the only one who was going to hunt in this direction." True to his restless, boastful self, he looked out at the lane of open water and teased me with *"Fala*, you are a Kablunak. Where should we go now?"

"Perhaps it might be better if I followed you, Inuk. You must surely know where to go and what to do."

He accepted my sarcasm as a compliment, saying, "Let's go to the open water."

Our little tea party over, I set course for the open lane. Once again Otokreak and Tulugak drove off in the opposite direction. The crack was about twenty-five yards wide for the most part, narrowing to ten or fifteen feet in places and stretching as far as Kunak and I could see.

"I'm going to get off her, *Fala*, and wait for a while," he said. "Maybe *nathek* will pop up."

I continued alone. It was an exceptionally bright day, warm and languorous. The dogs weren't in a mood to pull my sled, and I couldn't blame them. We were barely moving. I watched the water for something to do. In contrast to the glittering white surroundings, it looked almost black.

Unexpectedly, out of this dull blackness rose the shiny dark head of a seal. I don't know which one of us was more surprised. I only know that while *nathek* stared at me with his big glassy eyes, my hand automatically reached for the rifle and I shot at him. There was a loud splash as he disappeared. Blood marked the spot, but the seal was nowhere to be seen. I waited for a while, but without success so I urged my dogs to move along.

About an hour later, when I had turned around to rejoin Kunak, my lead dog noticed something unusual lying on the ice ahead. The whole team joined Bobby in a race for what soon became the outline of a seal. I stopped the dogs just before Bobby reached it. It was the *nathek* I had previously shot!

Expecting little resistance, I grabbed the seal by the back flippers to pull him away from the water. But I had under-estimated the big fellow. Instead I was drawn to the edge of the ice against which he anchored his fore-flippers. The poor fellow's breathing was wheezy; he was almost gasping. At first I thought that was caused by fear or the strain of our tug-of-war. But then I saw a trickle of blood on his short, thick neck and realized I had shot him through the gullet.

Strained by the seal's supreme effort to free himself, the ice suddenly cracked and I lay prostrate with my legs still on the ice floor and torso on the broken chunk of ice nearly two feet lower. The seal had accomplished his purpose. I let him go and hung on for dear life like a bridge between the main ice and the little floe. If I slipped any more, it meant a watery grave. I could not turn or move without risk. I yelled for all I was worth, hoping that Kunak would hear me, "I'm drowning! Help me!"

Two minutes passed—the longest two minutes I think I've ever counted before Kunak came to my rescue. He was about a quarter of a mile away when he heard my call and was panting from the unexpected run. Wasting no words, he grabbed my feet and pulled me back onto the ice floor.

"Thanks a lot! You came just in time, Kunak! The water is too cold for bathing, and the ice bank would have been too high for me to scramble up."

He hardly listened. He was shaking his head and laughing as he let me have it with both barrels, "Kablunak may be capable of doing many things. But in the Land Beyond he is always like a useless old woman!"

I was in no position to take offense. It was the way of the land to laugh at danger. Unlike me, true Eskimos remain cool in the face of imminent danger.

Meanwhile, the wounded seal had apparently found it even harder to breathe in the water. He had crossed the narrow lane of open water and had climbed up on the ice, snorting in pain. I quickly put him out of further misery with a shot through the head. Kunak fetched his *nikhik* from his sled, threw the four-pronged hook past the dead *nathek*, and brought him through the water as the hook caught the seal's side.

We hoisted *nathek* aboard the sled and sat down to wait for Otokreak and Tulugak. Rifles made ready, we kept our eyes on the water.

Tulugak, who was now only fifty yards away, took from his sealskin bag a small harmonica he had traded at the store, and began playing it.

"Seals like this kind of sound, *Fala*, so watch the water, Kunak advised me. He was soon proved right as several inquisitive seals rose to the surface. Within the hour, a quartet of more serious music lovers were unlucky enough to raise their heads not far from us. They did not get a chance to stare at us for long. We shot them with our .22 caliber long rifles, which made less noise than the "dirty-dirties." All other seals within earshot dived below. It was late afternoon now and they had had enough warm sun for one day anyhow.

Ototkreak and Tulugak sat proudly on their seals' bellies as they drove up. "We had good hunting today, but it should be better still in the next few days when more seals will be coming from the north along the leads of water," Tulugak said brightly.

"You should have come with us for a good laugh," smiled Kunak. "*Fala* was going to have a swim with *nathek*. Then he changed his mind."

They both relished Kunak's embroidered description of the incident, and it was a happy foursome of hunters that headed for camp into the red sunset.

On the trail our dogs did not share our lightheartedness. Some of them were limping, and blood was spotting the snow.

"We should put their boots on next trip, *Fala*. The snow has been thawing and freezing. It makes icy needles. Some of the dogs are not tough enough yet. Especially those who were born last year." Kunak was wise after the damage had been done. And I was partly to blame, too, as I had left the dogs' boots behind, not expecting to need them on a single day's trip.

"Something is wrong," Kunak said apprehensively as we pulled into camp. "Those three teams are leaving."

He hailed the nearest driver, "Where are you going?"

"Mittek came back with the news that his father Akraliak had fallen into open water and disappeared. Mittek is going to show us where it happened."

As the sleds glided by, I saw young Mittek sitting on one of them. I turned to Kunak, "Why are they going after Adraliak? If he drowned, as Mittek says, nobody can help him."

"It's not good to leave a body alone. His soul stays with the body for a while. We must try to find the corpse or it will cause the wrath of evil spirits to descend upon the whole camp. They are going to fish Akraliak's body out of the water and bring it back to his wife."

Some evil spirits appeared to exhibit their displeasure even as Kunak spoke. Chased by a northeaster, heavy clouds raced in our direction. Under our feet the loose snow, hardened by the alternate thaw and frost, screeched like sand against rock in a wind storm. "Looks like bad weather again," Kunak said resignedly. He was grateful for the few days of fine weather and he knew it could not last.

We could barely make out the three teams now in the distance. They disappeared at times behind curtains of drifting snow. I wondered if the storm would preclude them from locating the exact spot where Akraliak went down.

Our tents were flapping furiously in the stormy evening, but they were well banked with snow and could not be blown away. When the searchers returned, some of the men and women gathered around them to see if they had been successful. Save for the drivers themselves, the sleds were empty.

The hunter who had spoken with Kunak on departure reported, "We found the lane and the place where Akraliak plunged to his death. But we saw nothing of him. Not even a sign that he had been there."

Tulugak's wife Aligunek said, groaning, "It's too bad. I hope the spirits will not be displeased with us."

One could almost sense the dread descending upon the camp.

In Akraliak's tent the widow was brewing tea for the company. Nothing in her expression or manner indicated her inner state as everyone milled around, repeating their hollow sympathy, "It's really too bad."

Her repeated reply was equally traditional, "Yes it's too bad, but it cannot be helped."

No tears, no lamentations. Everyone had howled according to custom for a couple of minutes on first hearing about the tragedy from Mittek. Now all eyes were dry but all ears were eager for details.

After devouring a chunk of seal meat and washing it down with a mug of tea, Mittek obliged, "Akraliak and I reached the crack in the ice and stopped to eat the liver of one of the seals we had killed at midday. We made tea and rested for a while. Then my father told me he would walk along the edge and watch for seals. I took over the dogs and drove in the opposite direction.

"I was going to shoot a seal swimming ahead of me when I heard the report of a rifle. I looked back and saw Akraliak unwinding his *nikhik*. He threw it and brought *nathek* to the edge of the ice. He bent over *nathek* to pull him out of the water by the back flippers, but the animal escaped his grasp and plunged down. Akraliak lost his balance and fell headlong into the water.

"I swung the sled around, whipped the dogs, and raced to help him. But when I got there, it was too late. The seal left a circle of blood where he dived, but the only sign of my father was the rifle he had dropped on the snow."

Mittek spoke slowly, but smoothly, as if he had rehearsed his speech. His listeners were most attentive, yet their faces were skeptical. Plainly they did not believe his story. More likely their thoughts paralleled mine: The boy had accomplished his duty imposed by Krangmalit tradition.

In our tent that evening I asked Kunak what he thought of the explanation offered by Mittek. "You are only a Kablunak," he replied derisively. "You don't understand the ways of our people."

An eiderdown of fleecy wool covered the sky for days as the storm's aftermath. A subdued white light was diffused everywhere with nary a shadow. It was impossible to tell the lay of the land even in front of your feet. Elevations and depressions, snowdrifts and rough ice, all lost their normal contours. We stumbled about, unable to guage the snow underfoot or the distances ahead.

Everything wore deceptive disproportion. The most familiar signs, such as our dogs curled up in the snow a few yards away, looked like remote hills. At closer range the same dogs seemed to be sinking in holes.

On some days, mostly in the afternoons, great distances were visible—we could see for miles. Yet it was practically impossible to tell what lay close at hand. At first I was inclined to think that either my eyes were failing or that my glasses were. But Kunak reassured me, "There are no shadows, *Fala*. It is a moonless night. Man and dog stumble because they cannot see properly. It will pass." He recognized the phenomenon for what it was—a natural Arctic white-out which occurs mostly in the spring as steam and clouds create a uniform condition over the land, blotting out normal perspective.

"When the good weather returns, Kunak, I think we should go back to Cambridge Bay. We have been away long enough and I have to get ready to return to Kringaun, the nose-shaped hill close to my Mission at Burnside."

He shrugged his shoulders. It was immaterial to him.

As the weather continued to improve, some of the hunters made short sorties to the sea floor, returning with various numbers of seals. One day held great surprise. The hunters brought back two walruses on their sleds. I understood that these amphibious long-tusked mammals weren't andemic to this particular area, so I asked Kunak if he'd heard of walruses being killed here before.

"Certainly, *Fala*. *Arverk*, the walrus, lives in open water or follows the leads in the ice at this time of the year. In summertime, when the ice is gone, he will venture to Cape Barrow and even Coppermine."

As I had never seen a walrus before, I watched the men skin them while the women cut off great chunks of meat and blubber

257

for each family. Each walrus must have weighed a good 1,500 pounds and averaged about ten feet long. Their carcasses would provide food for many days. Even the dogs received large portions of their entrails and blubber.

The hairless walrus skins, all wrinkled and warty, were promptly stretched out on the snow to dry in the sun. Later they would be used to make kayaks. "Waste not, want not" seemed to be a tacit tenet of Arctic subsistence.

The hoopla of the walrus hunt did not last any longer than that of the recent seal hunt, of which only one aspect remained unchanged: Kunak was still the favorite target for the women's jests. It was typifid by such queries as, "What were you going to do with that dog you shot? Make a seal parka out of its skin and give it to some girl, eh?"

Delighted to be singled out, especially by women, Kunak would shoot back saucily with a significant wink, "Maybe. But I know a good skin when I see it!" Like a spoiled child, he craved and thrived on any attention.

The women scraped and sewed skins, rolled and smoked cigarettes, continuing their banter and gossip until the nightly dance. Aligunek, Tulugak's wife, was urged by one of the men to sing a song. Before complying, she said coyly, "Why do you ask me? I'm only a woman." But she was obviously flattered by the request and didn't hesitate to sing her walrus song with everyone repeating the refrain:

> "Where have you been?" Aye aye. . .
> Aye, ye, ye, ye. . .
> "I went down to the bottom of the sea
> To eat clams and shellfishes."
> "Where have you been?" Aye, aye. . .
> "I went down to the bottom of the sea
> Looking for my lost calf."
> "Where have you been?" Aye, aye. . .
> "I went down to the bottom of the sea,
> Searching for Nuliayuk, Mother of Beasts."
> Aye, aye. . .

After her song, the men talked about their dogs, their hunting, and what they would bargain for at the trading post. My own thoughts wandered through a maze of blurred images of these people whom I might never see again, and my friends at Cambridge Bay and the Mission at Bathurst Inlet. For some unknown reason my most recurrent thoughts were of Nokadlak's family and, in particular, of his baby daughter Naoyak, the Seagull, my little godchild.

15

Goodbye To Cambridge Bay

Two weeks after my return to Cambridge Bay in July, I invited Scotty and Isabelle Gall to dinner in my Mission shack. It was the least I could do to show my appreciation for their kindness while I recuperated from my travels. Always concerned about my welfare—just like his wife—Scotty asked if I had enough dog food to last until the ice break up.

"Thanks, Scotty, I think I'll manage. But I will have to do something about finding a rowboat. Since this place is considered as only a *pied-a-terre* by my superiors, my supplies did not include a boat of any kind."

"If you'd like to, you are welcome to use my jolly boat for a while, Father. It's the only one I have, though. I may need it periodically to look after my nets and to visit our friends at the R.C.M.P. Station across the Bay."

"Many thanks for your generous offer, but I have something else in mind that just might solve my problem. I may have enough lumber here to build a skiff. Although I've never built one before, I'd certainly like to take a crack at it."

"I wish you lots of luck. And remember, if you need anything, please let me know. I'll be only too glad to help."

I knew Scotty meant what he said, but I was determined neither to borrow nor to scrounge anything from this magnanimous friend.

The lumber I found consisted of old planking that served as shelving in my fish house. I removed the dozen bundles of dried char and lake trout from the shelves and stacked them on the floor. Each bundle contained about a hundred fish and weighed a good twenty-five pounds. I took out the boards. They were ten inches wide and fifteen feet long, running the length of the storage room. With a handsaw I ripped some of them into three equal strips and used these for framing a fourteen-foot flat-bottomed craft. All went swimmingly until the bow needed shaping. Then I realized there was no way of steaming the planks so as to bend them without breaking.

Kunak, who still helped me on a part-time basis, offered his contribution with characteristic style, "Fala, what's the matter with you? A Kablunak is not always so smart, after all! I'll show you what to do."

His ego indulged, he sawed halfway through the bow end of the one-inch planks at intervals of two inches. The job was slow and laborious, but it did the trick. We were now able to shape the planks at will and, as we did so, the cracks contracted, seized, and held as if the boards were whole.

"You see, Fala, that's what we Krangmalit do sometimes when we build kayaks and cannot bend the main frame."

"You are very smart, Kunak," I acknowledged his practical know-how. "But I still can't figure out why you cannot find yourself a wife. Any girl would be glad to have such a clever husband!"

Pleased no end, he laughed and shrugged his shoulders as if to say he'd answer that when the right time came.

I had traded an animal pelt for nails, caulking, and paint at Scotty's H.B.C. Post. He seemed genuinely interested in the progress of my first boat-building effort, as were our mutual Mountie friends Scott Alexander and Reggie Goodie, who often came over for coffee and lingered to watch me sweat and toil. Thus, with my labor thrown in, the total cost of the good skiff Santa Maria equaled the price of a fox skin. The name became prophetic because she definitely needed divine intervention to keep her from capsizing. I discovered this unsettling character-istic the first time I floated her with Kunak's help while Constable Goodie, Scotty and his helper looked on with frank amusement.

Only the well-balanced oars I had painstakingly whittled from two-by-fours saved the launching ceremony as I rowed uncertainly into the bay accompanied by my friends' shore-based exhortations. With total approbation Reggie yelled above the rest, "Hey, Father, now I can see that a man of God is still a man!"

Speckled with ice floes, the water was so calm and inviting that I kept rowing toward the bay opening. Suddenly the bow of a low, slender craft rounded the rocky point and Constable Scott

Alexander waved to me from his canoe. An Eskimo was reclining behind Scott. He held no paddle and seemed to be resting.

"Hello, old friend," Scott hailed me as we drew closer together. When his craft came alongside mine, I hardly recognized his helper, Karlik. Deathly pale, the poor fellow sat propped up by his sleeping bags, his face thin and immobile, his eyes dull, and apparently unseeing.

"How are you, Scott?" I greeted him. "Looks as if you had a tough trip," I added, noting that his face and nose sported large, raw blisters while his cheeks were sunken, visible evidence of hardship on the trail. "And what is wrong with Karlik? He looks like a ghost."

"He cut his hand opening a seal, and blood poisoning set in. Just look at it!"

Karlik's arm was an awful sight. We hurried him to shore, took him to his shack, and left him with his wife and children. Reggie heated some water and I prepared to incise the wound. As Scott shed his parka and outer breeches in favor of his uniform, I got another shock. He had lost so much weight that his sunburned skin hung on his tall, bony frame like a wet raincoat on a hanger. Even his blond hair had turned almost white.

"Scott," I said, managing a weak smile, "how did you pick up the clerical look?"

"It was easy, Father. I've been in frozen hell."

"Where exactly is that?"

"I went to Perry River and met some natives from MacAlpine Lake who told me that a man had been shot at their main camp. So I decided to go there with them, to investigate. As luck would have it, we hit soft snow all the way, plus terrific weather. Snow, wind, bitter cold, more snow—you know, the whole works. It was so bad that I had to walk ahead of the dogs, wallowing at times in the mushy snow, for about eighty miles."

Scott paused to sip some hot tea laced with whisky and take a bite of buttered bread (that Reggie had prepared for him) before resuming his narrative. "The fellow I was after had supposedly shot his father in the early spring because (as Karlik, my interpreter, said) he found him beating his mother. By the time we reached the lake camp the suspect was gone, of course, and nobody could tell me where. I had no time to waste. The snow was melting fast on the land. I hurried back to the coast to survey the camps of Sherman Inlet. It wasn't long before I regretted this move. I hadn't brought all my winter clothes along and now I paid for my optimism. Snow fell and drifted day after day. Even with my primus stove going, it was freezing in the tent.

"When the weather cleared for a few days I surveyed a good part of the inlet. There were thousands of caribou. Seals were few, but Karlik managed to shoot some. That was when he cut his hand. The infection spread to his elbow, then to his shoulder. I had to take care of everything for us. A southeaster came along, melting the snow on the land and on the ice, too. We were in cold water up to our knees. Two of my dogs died from continuous soaking. That was the kind of luck that followed me all the way. I left the rest of my team and most of my equipment at Stuart Point with a couple of Eskimos. I'll get it all with the patrol boat after the breakup."

"Let's at least be thankful, Scott, that you made it back all in one piece! I remember when you started out you intended to go as far as Back River and then inland to Bathurst. And you wanted me to travel with you. Under the conditions you've described it's likely that no one would have found our bones!"

"I realize it sounds crazy now, Father, but at the time I felt so tired of this place, my mind was ready to snap. I really didn't care where or how far I went; but I knew I had to get away for a while."

"Pardon me for changing the subject, but I see my scalpel's been in your boiling water long enough. I only hope that Karlik can stand the pain."

"After what he's been through this should be only a relief to him. Let's go, Doctor."

Surrounded by his wife and their three children, Karlik was moaning dreadfully. We asked his frightened spouse to send the youngsters out to play. Scott stood by with a basin of hot water and soap.

"What are you going to do with me, *Fala?*" Karlik muttered defensively as I approached.

"I'd like to help you. Let me wash your hand and take care of the wound. You'll soon feel better."

"Father will empty the bad stuff you have in your arm," Scott explained.

"I want to die!" Karlik cried out. "I want to drown in the river! I want to sink to the bottom and lie dead! Can't you see I am ready to die?"

"You are not going to die!" Scott countered with conviction, emphasizing the "not." "Father will relieve your pain and you will be well again."

I asked Scott to put the basin on the floor and to hold the patient down by his shoulders. Then, ignoring Karlik's protests, I washed the week-old grime off his hand and arm. Although he kept mumbling, "Let me slip into the water and drown; I want to die!" he did not jerk them away. With mercurochrome from my scanty Mission medical kit I swabbed the dirty gray wound in the palm of his hand. I was all set now. "The scalpel, please, Scott!"

The sharp instrument sank like a stick in deep mud. The pus poured out of the neglected wound, repulsively thick. Then dark blood followed. I cleaned the cut with soap and boiled water. Karlik didn't even wince. He groaned only when I applied pressure along his arm to help drain the purulent discharge.

"Pass the gauze, please. I'll pack a drainage in the cut."

Over the gauze I placed a pad of cotton wool and bandaged the hand. Karlik was quiet now. I was hoping he would doze off. I gave him a couple of aspirin tablets.

As Scott and I were leaving Karlik's hut, I whispered to his wife, "Let him sleep and rest all he wants to, and give him tea often."

"Thanks, thanks very much," she replied, putting on a brave front.

A week passed before Karlik began to show signs of improvement. His wife continued to fuss over him and did not rush him. In turn, he no longer asked to be allowed to die. I visited him daily to check and change his dressing and give him further encouragement. His progress gave me a good feeling inside, a reason I surmised why some people decide to become doctors.

One fine day, as I was getting ready to row over to Karlik's shack, I was startled to hear the unmistakable drone of an airplane engine. I dashed outside and watched a seaplane land gracefully in the bay, then taxi toward the Mission. I ran down to the water's edge and was soon able to discern Bishop Gabriel Breynat—more formally known as the Vicar Apostolic and Archbishop of the Mackenzie Vicariate in the Central Arctic who resided in Fort Smith, N.W.T.—waving to me from the plane's open door.

The pilot, Louis Bisson, a French-Canadian from Hull, Quebec, did not want to take a chance on damaging the pontoons, so he stopped the plane a little offshore. I rowed out to it in my skiff.

A tall, corpulent, dignified man, the Bishop climbed out of the plane onto the pontoon, then stepped jauntily into the skiff. No respecter of persons my temperamental craft dipped crazily, the Bishop tottered momentarily, and I had a lightning vision of us floundering in the cold bay waters. Providentially I managed to grab the pontoon with one hand and pull my eminent guest down with the other. The *Santa Maria* steadied.

"You were wise to choose such a good name for your fickle

boat, Father!" His Excellency said, quickly regaining his composure.

Still ruffled, I tried to cover my embarrassment with an excuse, "My apologies, Monseigneur! I should have warned you to be careful. I made the skiff only to mind my needs. I never expected the honor of carrying such a distinguished guest."

He grinned back to put me at ease, "I can see you made it for a light-footed tightrope walker, not for an elephant like me! I hope you will have less trouble with the pilot when you go back to pick him up."

Bishop Breynat's hope was promptly upheld by the heavens. I had not the slightest trouble ferrying Louis Bisson to shore.

As the three of us walked up to my shack, the Bishop said, "I can stay here only a few hours. I dropped in just to look over this place and see how you are doing. Also to tell you that I'll have to move you back to Bathurst as soon as possible. As you know, Father Delalande is currently at Coppermine, but Father Adam, who replaced him at Burnside, is in poor shape. So I'd like you to take over the Bathurst Mission."

"What is wrong with Father Adam, Monseigneur?"

"I believe he froze his lungs last winter during a difficult inland trip. But I suspect there is more to it. I want him to see a doctor this coming fall and let him have a good rest."

"What should I do with all my equipment and supplies?"

"Dispose of them as best you can. I have other plans for the opening of a new Mission in this territory."

I warmed at the prospect of returning to Bathurst, for I was tired of the endless cold wind, the unvarying landscape, and the daily struggle for dog food at Cambridge Bay. I looked forward to the relative comforts of the Mission I had helped build and to seeing some of my old friends like Nokadlak and his family. But I also had many friends at Cambridge Bay, so my feelings were mixed.

Prior to boarding his plane, a beautiful Waco that could use pontoons or skis, the Bishop gave me his final instructions for the coming year, "I don't know much about the Barren Land, Father, yet the merest glance is enough to convince me of its harshness. Try to learn all you can about the Eskimos at Bathurst and the other groups not yet contacted inland. But be careful not to undertake any long trips unless you find it absolutely necessary. This land is big and cruel, and priests like you are few and far between."

It had been a treat to see him again—a man I deeply respected for his kindness and understanding. He had been raised in the elegant surroundings of French nobility and still carried with him the refined and tactful touch of a grand seigneur. Yet his missionary life in the Northwest Territories had been tough and demanding from the day he landed at Fort Chipewyan. He was a man of action as well as vision and when he became Archbishop of the Mackenzie District, his vast vicariate—the world's largest—boomed with new hospitals and schools along the entire Mackenzie River basin to the Arctic coast. More than anyone else alive he was a true spiritual Father to all the Far North missionaries like me.

By the time the Hudson's Bay Company's boat arrived two weeks later, I had sold several bags of dried beans, rice, cornmeal, and two tons of coal to Scotty Gall to clean out the Mission's inventory. I had also packed my few personal belongings, and was ready to leave Cambridge Bay.

"What about your skiff, Father?" Scotty asked when I went over to the Trading Post to say good-bye to the Galls.

"I'd be grateful if you could handle it for me."

"I know my helper wouldn't mind buying it, but you'd have to wait till next winter for his payment."

"I'll be satisfied with five foxes."

"That's a fair price, Father. Your skiff is certainly worth it."

The *Margaret A.* was a flat-bottomed vessel of about one hundred tons, originally built for the shallow waters of the Mackenzie River. When the *Fort James* was crushed by ice in August 1937, that same month she was pressed into service on the thousand-mile run between the Mackenzie Delta, Tuktuyaktuk, and Perry River, moving supplies and personnel between the H.B.C. trading posts on the way. Somehow or other she always managed to escape the iron grip of the free-floating fields of ice, or pack ice, and was known far and wide as a lucky ship.

A year after the *Fort James'* disaster, the *Fort Ross* took over the runs along the Arctic Coast. Now in the summer of 1944, the *Margaret A.* was back again, the *Fort Ross* having been sent back to Vancouver, B.C., for repairs and refitting.

I was glad to see the old *Margaret A.* again, but my main concern at the moment was to persuade her skipper to transport my team of nine dogs. I asked Scotty if he could put in a good word for me with Captain "Shorty " Summers. "Sure," he replied, "let's go aboard and look for him."

We found "Shorty" in his cabin drinking coffee and checking the bills of lading. A native of North Vancouver, he was a small man, even shorter than I, redheaded with a ruddy complexion. I would soon learn that his temper was as fiery as his hair.

"Have a nice trip, Captain?" I asked him innocently.

"A nice trip? Huh! It was one hell of a trip on that sabot of a boat! We got stuck in the ice; we got lashed by hailstorms and snow squalls. In the open sea it was even worse. Wind day and night. Huge waves over the starboard bow. And, to top it all, that crazy pilot of mine gets drunk and falls into the forehold, damaging his precious ribs. Now the bastard's not fit to take me down to Bathurst; and if he was, I'm not so sure I'd trust him in those treacherous waters anyway."

The skipper swore a lurid oath, his reddish face turning purple. But I suspected—and Scotty knew—that he was putting on a show for my benefit. Thus, while I was still recoiling from the captain's language, Scotty found his opening: "Captain, Father here came to ask you for passage to his Mission at Bathurst. And I wouldn't be surprised if he could take over as your pilot."

"Shorty" Summers looked me over carefully with mounting interest. His color receded to normal, his voice leveled. "Now you tell me, Scotty! Of course, I remember Father Raymond. He was on the *Fort Ross* when we sailed to Perry River for the wedding of Angus Gavin. Sorry I didn't recognize you, Father! With your parka on, you look like an Eskimo. What do you know about Bathurst Inlet?"

"I've been up and down that stretch a dozen times, Skipper—both in my whaleboat visiting the camps, and by dog team in the winter. I think I know my way around the inlet as well as any White Man."

"You sound pretty sure of yourself. I like that. Tell you what. I'll take you free of charge, courtesy of the Hudson's Bay Company. How's that? Agreed?"

"Certainly, Captain! Only I must tell you that I'm not alone. I have nine dogs with me."

"That puts a different slant on it, Father. You see, there's not much room on deck and there aren't any spare hands to look after the cleaning."

"Oh, I can take care of the cleaning myself. I'm quite used to that. Besides, the dogs could be tied anywhere along the railing. I'll guarantee they won't damage a thing."

"I just hope you're right. But you should know that I am not heading directly for Bathurst. I have to take on some supplies at Read Island, and I shall probably call on Coppermine. So you'd better take along a load of dog food for at least a week. We ought to be finished unloading tomorrow. Bring your dogs aboard in the afternoon."

While I muttered my thanks, the Captain turned on Scotty, "Get the hell outa here, you scheming old rascal, before I lose my temper!"

"Okay, Skipper," Scotty laughed back, "but remember to

come to our party tonight. We've got a few bottles of whisky and rum to assault and the best company in the world!"

"God help you if you don't make it wonderful for me. I'll tear the hide off you!"

Scotty was still chuckling as we went ashore to help with the unloading, " 'Shorty' isn't such a bad egg, after all. He blows up like cream-puff cloud just to let off steam."

Kunak and Scotty's helper were working like proverbial Canadian beavers, carrying sacks of coal, lumber, and crates of merchandise aboard the *Margaret A.* In fact, their indefatigable industry amazed the crew.

We had a cheerful farewell party that night. Feeling no pain, "Shorty" Summers cornered me with an unexpected admission, "Father Raymond, it wasn't smart of us to keep you out of Angus Gavin's wedding reception at Perry River. Good manners should override religious persuasion. I apologize on behalf of my crew and the Hudson's Bay Company."

Astonished and gratified, I answered him automatically, "No need to, Skipper. That's all past and buried. Let's get on with the party and have ourselves a good time!"

At sailing time next day, however, I couldn't escape a melancholy parting as Isabelle Gall wrapped her arms around me, saying, "Please remember, Father, if you ever come back this way, we are your friends and will always be glad to have you with us."

In my mind's eye I can still picture her and Scotty, as well as Constables Scott Alexander and Reggie Goodie, standing on the improvised jetty, superimposed on empty oil barrels, trying to look cheerful as we pulled away.

How different it was with my helper Kunak, Scotty's assistant Karlik (now fully recovered) and their families. In their practicality, the Kablunak had somewhere to go and that was that. No regrets, not even a good-bye. The People Beyond are too tough for sentimentality.

16

Naoyak Again

Separating the mainland and Victoria Land, Dease Strait and Coronation Gulf were not yet free of ice even though it was August. In addition, strong currents and the prevailing north-wester were dead against us. Nevertheless, the *Margaret A.* plowed grimly on between tedious miles of flat ice floes, driven by her dependable diesels and twin screws.

In the morning of the following day we passed Richardson Island, the home of the People of the Caribou Antlers. And late that evening we entered Dolphin the Union Straits where skipper "Shorty" Summers decided to take refuge for the rest of the night in the lee of Lady Franklin Point, while the midnight sun still shone above the horizon, casting long golden shadows among the fast-moving ice floes.

When the regular pilot, a tall, gaunt Scandinavian, appeared on deck for the first time in mid-morning, the captain introduced us. "Ole Johnson, here's our new pilot, Father Raymond. He will be taking us to Bathurst, so you can rest your broken bones."

Limping badly, Ole came closer and regarded me with a transparent mixture of fear and disgust. "Another preacher, eh? How do you expect us to have any luck on this tub, Skipper? Remember what happened to me when we took on that Anglican Bishop Flemming a couple of weeks ago? I twisted my ribs, nearly killed myself falling on the railings. And what kind of weather did we get? Snow, wind, and drifting ice all the way!"

"You didn't even know what hit you!" Summers retorted scornfully. "You were so full of booze, you can't remember where or when you fell. But you can bet your boots I won't take a chance on you any more!"

Ole's towering shoulders drooped as he slunk below. "He knows exactly where he stands with me now," confirmed the Captain. "And don't worry, he won't bother you none. He drinks more than he can handle on occasion, but he's not really a bad guy at heart."

The *Margaret A.* anchored at Read Island late in the afternoon. The unloading of supplies began without delay-- men, women, and children all pitching in. By midnight the last load had been taken to the warehouse. We had dinner in the galley and soon after left for the mainland. In the morning barrels of oil and several crates of essential supplies were unloaded at Cape Krusenstern for a trapper. That same day the *Margaret A.* anchored at Coppermine.

In front of the H.B.C. Trading Post, Father Louis Le Mer stood waiting on its dock. *"Bonjour, mon vieux!"* he hailed me. "You're certainly taking the long way home! Did you know our schooner was here a few days ago and should be at Burnside by now? She had a rough time in the ice fields around Baillie Island. Now let's go over to the Mission and have a long-overdue chat."

"Where's Father Delalande?" I inquired en route.

"He's been fishing at Bloody Falls, a few miles up the Coppermine River, and should be back in a couple of days. You know he doesn't like to stay put, especially when we have guests in the house."

"Oh, who are they this time?"

"One is our new Bishop, Joseph Trocellier. The other is a visitor from Rome, Father Desnoyers."

"What happened to Bishop Breynat? He came to Cambridge Bay just a few weeks ago."

"Haven't you heard? He retired unexpectedly. He was simply worn out," my colleague said sorrowfully.

"That's terrible news!" I burst out in disbelief. Then, recovering, I lamely inquired what the new Bishop was like.

Father Le Mer frowned and scratched his black whiskers. "I'm not really sure. He's obviously different from Bishop Breynat. But you'll, no doubt, figure that out for yourself." Because he seemed embarrassed by his own answer, I dropped the subject.

At the Mission two large men strode back and forth in the living room, like two black crows in a cage. Both wore white plastic Roman collars and dark business suits. Their outfits seemed completely incongruous.

Father Le Mer presented me to Bishop Trocellier, whose

outstanding features were an extraordinary large face and a florid complexion. "Ah, here you are, Father Raymond de Coccola!" he said condescendingly. "I hear you're being moved to Burnside. In that case I'll probably see you again next fall when *Our Lady of Lourdes* brings you supplies." As the Bishop spoke, he kept picking his teeth and sizing me up with ostensibly unblinking eyes.

I cannot honestly declare that Father Desnoyers, though also tall and well fed, impressed me either. He was reputedly a stickler for antiquated regulations and was visiting the Arctic Coast missions to enforce the Catholic Church canon law, as well as the rules of conduct imposed by the Oblate Order.

I went into the kitchen to help Father Le Mer prepare supper. He was dressed in the same practical clothes as I—a plaid shirt, caribou knickers, and boots. Our parkas were hanging in the porch. As he cut up a big chunk of caribou meat for the stew, a broad, mischievous smile accompanied his whispered questions, "What do you think of our city birds? Glad you met them?"

"Actually I'm sorry for you, being stuck here with them. And I certainly don't blame Father Delalande for absenting himself. I think our new boss is a boor. As for the other one, he would look good as an official for the thirteenth-century Inquisition."

Later, resting reflectively on my bunk as the *Margaret A.* pushed on toward Burnside, still some three hundred miles away, I knew intuitively that the new Bishop was no friend of mine. When he addressed me formally as Raymond *de* Coccola, accenting the "de", I sensed his contempt. "De" (meaning "from") is the preposition used before surnames by French nobility and passed on from generation to generation like any other family name. But, having been born a French peasant, my new superior was clearly prejudiced against anyone higher on the social ladder, especially a subordinate.

The *Margaret A.* was taking the heavy seas in her stride. Only a few small fields of drifting ice remained. She was now zigzagging between several islets and dangerous reefs. I was finally in familiar waters and gave directions to the helmsman without hesitation. After passing Cape Barrow, we entered calmer waters, threading our way between the Chapman Islands and Galena Point, all the way down the inlet. The Skipper seemed content, and even Ole had apparently forgotten his misgivings. "You are different from those dung peddlers in your trade I've met," he confided to me in the pilothouse when we were plotting the ship's course through the islands.

"Wait and see, Ole. We haven't berthed yet."

As we neared Burnside Harbor at noon on the second day,

violent westerly gales whipped up mountainous waves that cascaded over the deck, fore and aft, drenching my dogs and tossing them about. I felt sorry for them, but could not leave the pilothouse.

At the height of the storm we finally gained entrance to Burnside. A mere three miles now separated us from its trading post and Mission buildings, but the Skipper wisely chose to delay a landing attempt. Instead he ordered the anchor dropped in the lee of Koagiuk Island.

During the next three days we rode at anchor while I listened to an indignant monologue from "Shorty" Summers. Condensed and expurgated, it went something like this: "It's depressing here beyond human endurance! It's still August, but look at that dark sky, the snow, the freezing temperature, and that unearthly wind! How can you stand it, Father? Everything here seems empty, ugly, disgusting to me. Do you think the wind will ever stop? I certainly don't want to be stranded in this godforsaken place the whole winter. I'd go crazy!"

No one could blame the Captain. Ahead of him lay a thousand miles through Coronation Gulf and Amundsen Gulf, and it was getting late in the Arctic season. Lakes and rivers already donned thin coats of ice during the night, and fields of pack ice, blown by stiff, icy westerly winds, would drift towards him from the Beaufort Sea.

I tried to cheer him up. "Such hellish weather doesn't last long, Skipper. Before you know it, you'll be back to the warmth of your family in Vancouver. Imagine the stories you'll be able to tell them and your friends about all the crazy characters you ran into up North, and you'll soon wish you were back on the Arctic Coast for more! For instance, do you know that this Bathurst Inlet is rich in copper all along the Banks Peninsula and the Arctic Sound? I've picked up chunks of almost pure copper to use as sinkers for my nets. And you remember Galena Point we passed on our way down the Inlet? You'll find lead and silver right there!

"If you come back someday with your wife on a second honeymoon, I'll gladly show you the beauty of Bathurst Inlet with its great herds of caribou flowing down to the sea like living rivers, the musk-oxen along the Hood River, the incredible amount of fish in the rivers and lakes, and the ever-friendly Eskimos."

Instead of blowing up, as I expected he might,"Shorty" Summers laughed amiably, "You must forgive me for my bitchy moods, Father. Maybe you should have a word with Ole, too. Who knows, he just might change his stupid attitude toward preachers."

"Will he mind?"

"Mind? Does a polar bear mind snow? You can try."

Towards noon on the third day the gale abated and the Skipper brightened accordingly. "The wind is still strong, but I'm itching to take a chance. Do you think we can reach the post without drifting on the sandbar?"

"That will depend on your speed, Captain. You'll have the shoreline and shallow water to port, and the wind and waves to drive you ashore to starboard. If you can maintain your speed, you should make it. The only other thing to keep in mind is the narrow channel near the post, with a sandbar on either side."

"Can you find the channel?"

"Yes, but then you'll have to slow her down."

The Skipper considered the dilemma at length before snapping his order. "Let's go! And if anything goes wrong, I'll drop anchor."

Almost immediately everything went awry. The wind kept pushing the *Margaret A.* to shore, so the Skipper rang for more speed. She payed out beautifully, but it was too fast for me. I could not locate the deep waters of the narrow channel with the sounder (a cord marked by knots for each fathom, with a five-pound weight at its end). From my starboard location I kept throwing the sounder and calling the changing depths of the water: "Only two fathoms!" I yelled to the Captain.

"Don't you see," he roared back, "if I slow down, we won't make it!"

"Well, keep going, Skipper. I'll try my best."

I did try, but it was hopeless. We struck the sandy bottom portside and stuck fast in less than a fathom. Summers left the wheel and rushed out as if possessed by all the evil spirits of the Barren Land. "By heaven, Father, where do you think you're taking us? To hell? What if it takes me the whole winter to dig her out of this blasted sandbar?"

Ole Johnson followed suit by reviving his favorite superstition. "I told you, Old Man, these spellbinders with reverse collars bring nothing but bad luck to a ship. The devil haunts them wherever they go. I say toss him overboard to the devil and be done with him!"

"My oh my don't we have a short temper!" I mocked Ole.

The Skipper, who had been briefly speechless with rage, told Ole to clam up, and ordered fore and aft anchors dropped. Then he resumed his own blasphemous tirade. Fortunately, most of it was wasted on me, for I was watching a whaleboat heading in our direction from the post. She rose and dipped, disappearing from sight altogether in the troughs of the rolling waves, then climbing to the crests, and falling again. I could not recognize her two oarsmen, but the bearded helmsman was unmistakably Father Adam.

"There's your rescuer, Skipper!" I said hopefully, pointing to the approaching craft.

"Not another preacher by any chance?" put in Ole sarcastically, completely unaware of his accurate prediction.

Once aboard the *Margaret A.*, Father Adam took charge of our deteriorating predicament. "Skipper, send two men in my whaleboat to drop a spare anchor fifty yards aft of your ship and attach a cable to the winch. The tide is still in and that's the time to get her off."

Unable to fault that reasoning, Summers complied. He had both anchors hauled up and the winch put into action. With surprising ease the *Margaret A.* slid off the sand and was afloat again. Nonchalantly, as if accustomed to rescuing distressed vessels, Father Adam led the way through the channel in his whaleboat. We dropped anchor by the Hudson's Bay Company's pontoon wharf, and I was home.

Gathering my dogs, I thanked "Shorty" Summers for the free passage. "I'm sorry, Skipper, that I let you down in the home stretch."

But the Skipper had already recovered. "It was partly my fault, Father. One must learn to take adversity in one's stride in the Arctic. And it is I who should thank you, anyway."

Father Adam and I hardly had a minute together aboard the *Margaret A.* But in the bright, warm kitchen of the Mission we made up for lost time during the past two years over cups of coffee. I learned that, besides chilling his lungs while climbing and maneuvering the sled on an extremely rough trail, he was sure he had contracted some kind of lung disease from a young Eskimo girl named Katuktuk whom he had nursed in her parents' igloo the winter before.

He also told me that Nokadlak and Kakagun were in the neighborhood, and that Nokadlak's little daughter Naoyak (the Seagull) was now living with Kakagun and his wife Kablunak, the baby's prospective in-laws, and their son Naodluak, to whom she was promised.

In the evening Father Adam embarked on the *Margaret A.* despite shocked protests of one, Ole Johnson. As she headed out toward the islands of Bathurst Inlet, I turned to go back to the Mission. I had taken only a few steps when I heard the voice of Billy Joss, the H.B.C. trader, who emerged from a pile of freight he had been examining.

"How would you like to come over to my place, Father?" he

said affably. "We need a good drink after all this excitment!" He didn't have to twist my arm.

Billy had originally come to the Eastern Arctic as a lad of eighteen from Scotland apprenticing with a Hudson's Bay Company's trader. For the next twenty years he moved from one H.B.C. post to another until he found himself a wife among the People of the Falls at Coppermine and settled down at Burnside a year ago. Billy seemed happy with his wife and boasted that he didn't know of any white girl who could stand the loneliness and harshness of the Barren Land as she could.

While Billy was stationed at Coppermine, Father Adam saved her life when she gave birth to her first child. A small amount of placental tissue was retained in the womb, causing serious hemorrhage. Father Adam capably performed the required cleaning. Since then Billy Joss remained his close friend and that bond transferred to other local missionaries, including me.

My first job at Burnside was to prepare my quarters for the rigorous months ahead. I put up the storm windows and caulked every joint as best I could. From the shore I brought up all the supplies left there by *Our Lady of Lourdes* a few days earlier, stacking them in the little storehouse. The ground was barely covered with snow, so my dogs had a hard time dragging the sled up the slope. Their harnesses and towlines were so torn, it took me literally hours to mend them.

Then there was the problem of fresh-water supply. The choice lay between the Burnside River and several tiny lakes across the channel. It was a good two miles by boat to the mouth of the river and about half a mile to the nearest lake. The choice seemed obvious, but the little lakes were already frozen and that meant cutting blocks of ice with a saw. I was filing the long crosscut saw in preparation when Kakagun and Nokadlak rowed up in one of the Mission skiffs.

"*Fala*," said Kakagun, "fish are starting up the lakes. We have brought you many fish for your dogs."

This was payment for using some Mission nets. I was not surprised that the "many" fish turned out to be about fifty Arctic char, lake trout, and white, totaling about one hundred fifty pounds—a mere handful from their week's catch. It would suffice to feed my dogs for a week, but no more. Yet the entire winter—all nine months of it— was staring me in the face, and I did not want to narrow my perspective to the day by day existence of the improvident People Beyond.

As we sipped tea in the Mission, I told my two friends, "I need ice for the winter. Will one of you help me cut it? I'll give you tobacco, tea, and ammunition for your work."

'I'll help," Nokadlak said without hesitation.

"*Fala*, I have to return to my camp and take care of the nets," Kakagun explained. "But when I visit you again I'll bring you a load of ice on my sled."

After the great hunter rowed off to Net-Fishing Bay, some five miles distant, Nokadlak and I crossed the channel in my jolly boat and walked the remaining fifty yards to a small frozen lake, carrying the necessary tools—an axe, ice tongs, and a crosscut saw. It was only mid-September, but pure glare ice already covered the lake to a depth of six or seven inches. So transparent was it that we could clearly see the sandy bottom a dozen feet below. Nokadlak took the axe, walked a few yards offshore, and chipped a hole in the ice. "Here, it's finished. You can start cutting!"

I stuck the end of the long saw into the hole and cut two lines at right angles, like the baselines of a baseball diamond, each twenty feet long. Two feet away from the home plate, along the fourth baseline, Nokadlak made another hole, and I sawed a line parallel to the first baseline. Nokadlak followed behind, chipping two-foot square blocks between the two parallel lines and picking them up with the ice tongs. This maneuver cleared a lane two feet wide, enabling me to saw a grid of lines parallel to the fourth baseline at two-foot intervals. With a knock of the axe Nokadlak freed the squares, took them out and piled them up on shore. He seemed to be amused by what he was doing, so I asked him if he was enjoying himself.

He grinned back, "Little Man, you could have built your house at the edge of the lake. Then you would have had water winter and summer. We never cut ice blocks. We make a hole in the ice, so we always have water."

"Sure, Nokadlak, but it's handy being close to the seashore where the big boat can unload my winter supplies."

Six hours of steady, unhurried work later, enough ice blocks were stocked on shore to last me the winter, especially as I generally used melted snow for washing. We carried several ice blocks to my boat and rowed back to the post. The remainder would wait until I was ready to fetch them by dog team.

"You should stay with me tonight, Nokadlak. Tomorrow I'll go with you to Net-Fishing Bay and set up more nets."

"Yes, I'll eat and sleep here, I'm too tired to return to camp now."

After we had eaten abundant portions of caribou meat cooked with rice, and between cups of tea, I asked Nokadlak about his family. Full of food and unaccustomed to the warmth of my small kitchen, he became languid and not particularly interested in my questions. Still, he answered almost automatically, "They are fine. All in good health. Even Grandmother Manerathiak still eats and sleeps like a young woman."

He was muttering something about his son Kudnanak having grown into a good hunter when his head dropped on his chest and he dozed off. I laid caribou skins on the floor of the living room, shook him to awareness, and asked him to sleep there for the night. Then I left him to his dreams and his snores and went over to the trading post.

In the dim light of a Coleman lamp Billy Joss was restocking the shelves with newly-arrived merchandise. I told him what I had in mind. "Sure, Father, I'll be glad to look after your dogs while you're gone. You just fish as long as you need to and don't give them a thought."

"Thanks, Billy! I knew I could count on you to help me out. And now I'm going to bed before I fall asleep on my feet."

Early next morning in a flurry of snow Nokadlak helped me pack my tent, sleeping bags, food, ammunition, rifles, and fishing nets. The sky was almost dark and the damp cold made me wish I had stayed in my *Krepik*.

Two hours of rowing later, forlorn bluffs, worn by centuries of erosion, rose steeply before us to a tableland several hundred feet high, creating the illusion that the channel ended right there. But as soon as we passed the point, we turned into a large bay. On its southwest shore, sandwiched between huge boulders that screened them from the wind, stood my friends' tents.

A howl rose from the resting dogs. Three women, a youth, and a tiny girl walked to the water to greet us. Nokadlak's wife Angivrana and her ancient mother Manerathiak smiled their welcome as we shook hands. "You must be Kablunak, wife of Kakagun," I said to the other young woman, extending my hand to her.

"Indeed I'm Kablunak," she smiled at my recognition, then bent down to the little child nudging her side, "and this is Naoyak, my adopted daughter."

"Naoyak, the Seagull! Last time I saw her was at her birth!"

I picked her up and gently rubbed my nose with hers, vividly recalling that memorable event of two years ago. She looked up at me, her small mouth pursed as if to say "I don't remember you."

"You are beautiful, Naoyak!" I said softly.

"Naoyak had been sick lately, but I gave her milk from my breast and now she is better," Kablunak informed me. "She follows me around as a fawn does the caribou doe." Her genuine fondness for the child was apparent from the way her eyes watched Naoyak's every move. The latter's natural mother, Angivrana, and grandmother Manerathiak stood close by, their smiling faces indicating how happy they were that the little Seagull had found a nest of love.

I had initially met Kablunak the first winter I came to the Central Arctic at a camp on the shores of Lake Kiluitok at the far end of Bathurst Inlet, south of Burnside. I remembered her as a slim, strongly built, striking young woman with an extremely delicate face of light complexion and pronounced eyebrows, most unusual for an Eskimo girl. That was the obvious reason her parents had named her Kablunak, or White Woman.

She then had two husbands. One of them, of course, was my friend Kakagun, the big, dark, restless man of about thirty years, at once hawk-nosed and hawk-eyed, befitting his enviable reputation as the best hunter among the Krangmalit.

The other was Nivikhana, a tall, effervescent young man with a babyface whose protruding cheek bones were covered with a skin so red that I sometimes wondered if he used rouge.

The two men appeared to be good friends. There was no overt strife between them, not even a harsh word. They had apparently reached a perfect understanding and were quite content to share Kablunak on an equal basis.

Several weeks elapsed before I saw Kakagun and Kablunak for the second time. "Where is Nivikhana?" I asked conversationally.

"He died. Something happened to him inland," Kakagun answered in his usual deep, dull voice.

The news caught me by surprise. "That's too bad. Navikhana seemed well the last time I saw him here in my house. Some kind of illness must have killed him in short time."

Kakagun's piercing eyes narrowed and he laughed uneasily, "I don't know. Who knows what it might have been?" It was the polite Eskimo way of suggesting I should mind my own business.

During a subsequent coffee break I repeated to Father Delande what Kakagun had said about Nivikhana's death.

"Even though you're a relative newcomer to the Arctic, you can probably guess what happened," he said thoughtfully. "No Eskimo is normally richer than his neighbor, except in his ability to hunt and to survive. What he has, he readily shares, but there's a limit—that's the continued sharing of one woman on an equal basis. Eskimos naturally have the same feelings we do. But the more civilized measures used in our society to settle disputes don't necessarily suit the People Beyond. For them an easy, expedient remedy is frequently murder."

Pensively he finished his coffee, then gave me a knowing

wink along with his funny crooked smile, "Don't be offended, *mon vieux*, but having observed Kablunak, I'd say that she is definitely attracted to you."

"Under normal circumstances I'd feel flattered, not offended. But now I'm terrified!" I laughed back. "Besides, my vices— for the time being, at any rate—are strictly spiritual."

I had not seen Kablunak since that day. Outwardly she had not changed in the two intervening years. Still stately, she was attractively dressed in a long parka adorned with white and tawny trimmings around the wrists and the bottom hem. The fur, lining her hood, was blue wolf and wolverine.

As we walked up to the tents, I asked her about Kakagun. "He is visiting the nets with my son Naodluak. They will be back soon. Come in and have tea." Little Naoyak followed Kablunak into Kakagun's tent. Accompanied by Angivrana, Manerathiak, and young Kudnanak, Nokadlak meantime disappeared into his own tent.

Caribou skins served as walls and even the floor of the tent, providing an intimate cozy atmosphere. The air was fragrant with burning dwarf willow and brush wood branches glowing in a ten-gallon oil drum through whose top Kakagun had attached a rusty stovepipe he picked up at the trading post. I squatted on the furs while Kablunak put some ice in the kettle and placed it on the improvised stove. Before long, perhaps sensing the boiling kettle, in walked Kakagun and his son Naodluak.

"How's the fishing?" I inquired.

"The water is cold, but the fish are coming in great numbers," Kakagun said, shivering involuntarily.

Naodluak studied me for a moment, then turned to his father, "That's a White Man!" Kakagun agreed and smiled.

There was no mistaking the six-year-olds origin. With his long black hair still in bangs and his finely etched features, he looked strikingly like his mother. But the red cheeks were indubitably Nivikhana's. I wondered if Kakagun cared. Predictably, though, if he did kill Nivikhana, the youngster would eventually present a potential danger for him. Even though single paternity for all one's children wasn't considered all-important, traditionally Naodluak would be expected to avenge his natural father's murder. Meanwhile the family's unity had to be preserved.

Young Naodluak came over and sat down beside me like an old friend. Kablunak poured us tea and when she sat down Naoyak went to her and asked for her breast. As she sucked contentedly, Naodluak pointed to the baby, "That's Naoyak."

"Yes, I know, Naodluak. Do you play with her?"

"No!" He wrinkled his nose in scornful Eskimo style. "She is too small. She is like a newborn pup." Naoyak gave no hint that she overheard, understood, or resented the mockery. She was too busy enjoying her drink.

"I could catch more fish if the nets were not so full of driftmoss." Kakagun told me. "They should be taken ashore and cleaned."

"Don't worry; I brought along some new ones. I'll ask Nokadlak to help me set them, and then you can pull up the old nets."

When I called on Nokadlak, he and his son Kudnanak had just taken apart a .30-30 rifle and were cleaning it assiduously. Nokadlak's wife Angivrana was stirring a boiling cauldron of fish heads, while her aged mother Manerathiak kept scraping a caribou skin, her face expressionless, her lips moving automatically in a monotone song. So intent were they on their respective jobs that none of them noticed my entry. "How are you?" I greeted them.

Slightly startled, but smiling broadly, Angivrana spoke for the family: "We are all fine, *Fala.*"

To avoid wasting their time, I approached Nokadlak, "When you finish cleaning your gun, would you set up my nets?"

"Kudnanak can help you, *Fala.* And while you are gone I will pitch your tent."

"Have some fish heads! It will be cold on the water. Eat and warm up your blood before you go," Angivrana suggested thoughtfully. She dished up a pan of char heads and placed it on the floor in the center within everyone's reach.

Kudnanak got off the raised *iglek,* went to the door, and called out to Kakagun's family, "Come and eat heads!"

From a youngster of twelve when I last saw him two and a half years ago, he had grown rapidly into a tall youth. His face was burned dark brown by outdoor exposure, yet retained a constant smile, as if he enjoyed everything he did. Proud of the man-sized assignment his father had entrusted to him, Kudnanak quickly changed into his sealskin garment and followed me to the boat. We left my tent and grub boxes ashore and pushed off. Kudnanak leaned over the bow while I used the oars to propel the heavy craft towards the head of the bay.

"There are fish here," he speculated as his eyes searched the dark blue waters. Then excitedly, "All kinds of them!"

I feathered the oars and looked over the gunwale. Myriads of fish were heading in our same direction—towards the creek: white fish, huge lake trout, Arctic char, all with lots of fat, ready for the long winter under the ice. It was difficult to reconcile this profusion of sea life with the privation of the surrounding Barren Land

I remembered how, after my first Arctic winter, I thought that most aquatic creatures would be destroyed. Yet, as I browsed through the meagre library at the trading post, I learned that explorers like Nansen and Sverdrup had discovered living creatures or plant organisms at various depths in the polar basin. By dragging nets along the ocean floor as deep as two thousand feet, or sinking them under the ice, they often hauled up infinite varieties of small crustaceans, plankton, and worms. Moved at random by the strong polar currents, they provided an inexhaustible supply of food for seals and fish—far greater than inland lake and stream supplies.

A sampling of these riches now swarmed below us. As I watched them with unrepressed fascination, I could not help wondering how the People Beyond could ever starve in the midst of such plenty. The obvious answer was the paralysis of the cold.

"Kudnanak, which do you prefer—fish or caribou meat?"

He took his eyes off the water and stared at me in astonishment. "Caribou, of course!"

"Why?"

"Why? Because fish is a woman's game!"

It was as abbreviated a synopsis of the Krangmalek paradox as I ever received. Fishing was recreational, not to be taken seriously by a manly hunter. Inuk (an Eskimo) fished only to supplement his meat reserves—just in case caribou hunting did not meet his expectations. Even at summer's height when fish left the lakes for the sea, he often ignored them. He greatly preferred to stalk the caribou. His woman, however, sometimes took advantage of this two-week river and creek breakup. She either dried the fish she caught in the sun and wind or froze them for winter traveling.

Now that the summer was virtually over, the fish were mustering their legions around the sandbars, fjords, and channels to launch their all-out migratory advance. How incredible that the Eskimos paid little heed to the inexhausible food supply swimming literally under their noses. Like young Kudnanak, they watched and laughed at the finny hordes driven by timeless instinct to peaceful inland lake spawning grounds before the inevitable freezeup.

I asked Kudnanak what kind of fish he preferred. He hesitated for a moment, then said candidly with a bright smile, "I like the *ikalupik* and *ivitaruk* (both Arctic char). They are big and fat. But I soon get tired of eating them."

We beached the boat near the creek's mouth. I tied one end of our net to a boulder close to the lapping waves. The tides would not submerge it because the highest tides in this part of the Arctic rarely reach four feet. As I rowed slowly away from shore, Kudnanak unwound the net and let it drop overboard. Weighted with small half-pound stones every five feet, it sank until the floats I had made from salvaged freight crates and attached to the main twine buoyed it up. When the net ran out fifty feet, Kudnanak tied the free end to a large rock he had picked up on the beach and dumped it in as an anchor.

At intervals of about one hundred yards, we set up three more nets in the same fashion, grading the mesh from six to three and a half inches in that order. Following the shoreline in search of creeks, some fish were bound to snag their gills in a mesh their size. This would allow the small fry less than three inches in circumference, which we didn't want to escape.

Eagerly we rowed back to camp to warm ourselves, eat, and rest. Leaning on a willow stick, Grandmother Manerathiak was waiting for us by the tent, and urged us to go inside. "Let me help you remove your parka, Little Man. It's all wet at the sleeves. I'll put it on the rack to dry."

Angivrana had a kettle of water boiling on the stove and a large cauldron full of caribou tongues. Nokadlak, sitting in a corner, said, "I have put up your tent. You'll sleep well tonight."

"Thank you, Nokadlak."

Kablunak came in with Naoyak and sat on the caribou skins, urging her to sit by my side with, "*Fala* will give you pieces of tongue to eat." The little Seagull came and laid her head against my duffle shirt, all the while studying me with her dark eyes. Apparently satisfied, she made herself more comfortable by anticipating a tasty snack.

Kakagun and his son Naodluak didn't show up. Kablunak explained that they had gone into the hills to look for caribou now returning to the tree line.

Even though they had been cooked without salt (Eskimos didn't use salt until the coming of the White Man. Still, they seldom used it), the caribou tongues and their broth proved a real treat. I sometimes wondered if the lack of salt and iodine in the Eskimos' diet had affected their fertility. Although birth control was unknown among the People Beyond, the average birthrate per family was only three children. It seemed to me like a challenging subject for genetic research.

Appearing content and happy in the secure warmth of the tent, Manerathiak was humming a song in her corner:

"Little girl, little girl. . .Aya, ya, ya. . .
I knew a little girl who brought me a cup of berries
She had picked in the lowland. . .Aya, ya, ya. . .
She was a beautiful little girl with shining eyes

And a smiling face,
All red with berry juice. . .*Aya, ya, ya*. . .
She came to me and climbed on my lap, saying,
'These berries are for you, Grandmother!'
Then she ran off to play
With her friends. . .*Aya, ya, ya, ya."*

Three hours later we returned to the nets. Starting at the shore end of each net, Kudnanak and I took turns at the bow, lifting the net from the water and extracting the fish.

The air was damp and cold, the water icy. My back ached from continual bending, my fingers were numbed from repeated immersions. Handling the dripping nets and the slippery, cold fish offered little relief. I was almost ready to reveal my misery, but it was the end of the net and Kudnanak's turn at the next one. He took the ordeal stoically, without a word, without a whimper. He was a true hunter now, and hunters don't wince under such ordinary inconveniences—not even when the fish weighed thirty pounds and he had to haul it up along with the soggy net, club the squirming catch then hold its slippery bulk between his seal-clad legs, free it from the mesh and toss it into the boat.

Not all the fish we caught were as big as that, of course, nor were they all the same variety. Along with the Arctic char and lake trout came fat *pikuktok* or hunchbacks, for instance. Covered with large silvery scales, some were so plump that their fifteen pounds took the shape of oversized footballs. Common were the tomcod, possibly relatives of the cod but not nearly as nutritious. They were not the best marine food, but they can be caught through the ice all winter and constitute the last resort of starving Eskimos. Most plentiful were the *kapielik*, a white small-scaled fish rich in oil, which literally went to the dogs because most harbored ribbon-like tapeworms that often infested Eskimos and their canines. So sturdy were these parasites that they remained active even while frozen.

The bay also abounded with schools of herring and when some got caught in the nets by the mouth, they would contort and create intricate knots. The same thing happened with Arctic halibut, plentiful in the waters of Bathurst Inlet. Flat and large, they were always difficult to unhook from the nets. But the extra effort was certainly worth it when it came to mealtime.

"Here's another whitefish, Kudnanak. What do you think of it?"

"It's good and full of oil."

"And what's this big red one with the white belly?"

"That's one of those I like, *Fala*! It's *ivitaruk* (a species of salmon). In some lakes they get so big that there's enough meat in one of them to feed three families. This is not a big one."

"Why do you like to eat *ivitaruk?*"

"Because its red meat is tasty and full of oil. You will like it, too, when my mother cooks it. But we like it best when it has ripened after being buried many days in the gravel."

Right now I could really go for a juicy sirloin steak, young fellow, I thought silently. Aloud I said, "Let's finish this net then, and return to camp so your mother can do that fish justice!"

17

Talking Fish

Perched on a big flat boulder, her face partly concealed by her furry hood and her old eyes half-closed, Manerathiak watched us bring in the fish. Holding her mitted hands partway up a walking stick and resting her chin on her right arm, she muttered unintelligibly. At the risk of frightening the spirits with whom she was conversing, I shouted, "Manerathiak, look at all the fish we caught!"

"I can see, Little Man," she answered in her worn, flat, lifeless voice not looking up. You really know how to catch fish! You're not so stupid at sea as I thought you would be."

"It's easy with nets," I brushed aside her left-handed compliment.

"Yes, yes, I know. When I was a young woman, I used to help my mother make the *kubiak* (fish-net) with caribou and musk-ox sinew. The net was no more than three or four times the length of my outstretched arms and only one arm deep. But it took us many days to make it. We used to set the net at the spillway of a creek we had dammed with rocks. Now Nokadlak can get a White Man's *kubiak* at the trading post all ready for fishing!"

"Without nets I could not feed my dogs. Unlike *Inuk*, I cannot fish or hunt much in the winter. I have to travel, see the People Beyond, talk to them about the Good Spirit Who is *Atanek*, the Chief of all Spirits, and help them."

"Do you fish like a *Kablunak* or an *Inuk*?"

"What do you mean?"

"When you take the fish out of the water, do you kill it with the *anaotak* (stick or club)?"

"No, I just throw it into the boat. But if the fish is big and still full of fight, then I kill it."

"Kudnanak, what do you do to all the fish as you catch them?" she asked her grandson.

"I hit them over the head with the *anaotak*."

"You see what I mean, *Fala*? Kudnanak fishes like Inuk. He knows that the Spirits of the Land speak through the mouths of the fish. They often speak evil, and they wish evil on those who hear them."

"I have yet to hear a fish speak to me, Manaerathiak. Perhaps I don't know how to listen or else it's afraid to talk to me. But, now that you've told me, I'll club every one I catch if it's still alive."

"Good! If you stay long enough with us, Little Man I'll tell you more things you don't know. And you can talk to me about the *Atanek*, the Master of all Spirits."

Old grandmother Manerathiak slid off the rock slowly, stood up creakily, painfully, and shuffled off, saying, "Come, young men! One is hungry for fish."

As we began to unload my boat, Kablunak appeared at the tent door summoning us and everyone around with a more direct invitation, "Come and eat cooked meat!"

After Kudnanak and I had spread out our catch on the frozen ground and changed clothes in his tent, I answered Kablunak's call to dinner. In the tent, little Naoyak was whimpering in Kakagun's husky arms.

"What's the matter, Little One?" I asked her as she sobbed softly.

"She has a stomachache," Kablunak replied for her.

"Did she eat too much today?"

"No, she has not eaten since last night. She won't eat even when I offer her my breast."

"When did her stomachache start?"

"Last night she did not sleep well, *Fala*. She had foam in her mouth. When you came this morning she was fine. After you went to the nets, she had pains."

"Does she have diarrhea?"

"No, she hasn't had a bowel movement for three days."

I touched little Naoyak's head. Expectantly, it felt hot. "I'll be back soon," I said as I headed for my tent which Nokadlak had pitched close to a large boulder about twenty paces away. I returned with my compact medicine kit and placed the thermometer in Naoyak's mouth, while I looked her over. Her tummy was slightly swollen, but she had no other symptoms. Although

285

the mercury reading confirmed that her temperature had risen, it was not necessarily abnormal under the present circumstances. Taking a small can of powdered milk from my kit, I asked Kablunak to give me a cup of hot water. I poured some powder into it and set it down on the *iglek*. From my medicine bag I took a bottle of castor oil, some sugar, and a teaspoon.

"Give this drink to Naoyak, Kakagun," I said, handing him a spoonful. "That's good. Now another one. Fine! Naoyak is a good little girl. Now she can have some of this warm, sweet milk."

Poor Naoyak! I sympathized silently. "Her body is already suffering from her deficient diet consisting mainly of meat, mother's milk, and fish without the benefits of cereals, fresh vegetables, fruit, or their juices enjoyed by most other people. Deprivation from what "civilized" white men consider essential food for a balanced diet was part of the price the People Beyond paid for their almost-unlimited freedoms in the Barren Land."

Kakagun didn't seem impressed with my internal medicine nor outward confidence. He remained silent, a worried look on his face. To distract him I told him that while I had caught lots of fish that day, I would still need many, many more to feed my dogs during the imminent long winter when I'd have to travel.

"How many more fish do you want, *Fala?*"

I figured I'd need several thousand, but I didn't know how I could communicate such a large number to him because the Eskimos' counting method then was vague—to say the least—beyond one hundred. The obvious reason for the limitation was that the nomadic People Beyond had so few material possessions to enumerate.

They did, however, have a name for each number up to five: *atahuek* meant one, *malruk*—two, *pignaun*—three, *ittaman*—four, and *telaman*—five. These accounted for a person's five fingers. Six was expressed by *taleman atahueklu*, the *lu* suffix meaning "and." Seven—just as logically—became *taleman malruklu*, and so on to the count of nine. The fingers on both hands obviously added up to ten or *kollit*. The further addition of ten toes produced twenty or *Inuk*, the total man. It followed, that the equivalent of eleven was *kollit atahueklu* (i.e. ten and one); twenty-eight comprised *Inuk (a man—20)*, *taleman* (5 fingers), *pignaunlu* (and 3 fingers); and ninety-nine was *Inuk ittaman* (20 x 4) *kollinitlu* (and 10), *taleman* (5), *ittamanlu* (and 4). Because of the progressively more confusing combinations to denote numbers beyond 100—*Inuk taleman* (20 x 5)—most Eskimos I met simply resorted to the loose *amigaitun* expression, which meant "There are many." It was apparently sufficient for their everyday needs.

Incidentally, Eskimo hunters who sought .30-30 ammunition for their rifles at the H.B.C. Trading Posts realized that White traders might not understand *"Inuk kollitlu-Inuk kollitlu"* and so attempted to say "thirty-thirty" instead. But since they had difficulty pronouncing the "th" sound (as do other language groups), they settled for "dirty-dirty," and got the "ammo" they wanted just the same!

At any rate, I thought I'd try a different tack. "Kakagun, do you know how many pebbles you can put into your hunting bag?"

He relaxed somewhat as he answered with *"Amiumik,"* another word for "many."

"How many is that?"

"Inuk kollinit (man ten times, or 200) and many more times."

Feeling that was as close as I could get to the thousands of fish I'd require I dropped the subject and made for the door. Just before I stepped outside, I said to his wife, "Kablunak, let me know if Naoyak has a bowel movement during the night. Right now she should sleep."

The evening air was cold and damp. It began to snow. Rather than sit alone in my unheated tent, I walked over to Nokadlak's dimly-lit one. There, too, the silence hung unbroken, as if everyone was oppressed with thoughts of winter's inexorable approach. Only grandmother Manerathiak's scraping of a caribou skin gave life to the gloomy scene. In her customary corner the old woman squatted on a well-worn parka, puffing over her bone scraper.

Wondering if a little controversy would enliven them, I said casually to Nokadlak, "I was telling Manerathiak that I never heard a fish speak to me. Now I'm not too sure than a fish can talk to any man or woman."

"Our forefathers certainly believed this to be true. And so do we," he responded.

"White People know only one Spirit, and He does not talk to men through fish. He is always good and He never wishes evil to anyone."

"May be, *Fala*. But our land is full of evil spirits. Summer and winter they are always around us. On land and at sea. At night they whisper in the sky. Sometimes they show their displeasure. They mislead us when we travel. They chase away our game. They starve and freeze our bodies. Whatever you may say, we have many, many evil spirits with us."

"Your Land Beyond is different from my native land, Nokadlak. There it's always warm. No snow lies on the land, no ice covers the sea. Dark days are unknown, and so is hunger—

287

there's food for all."

"If your land is so warm, so beautiful, and so plentiful, why did you come here?"

"To tell you, your family, and your friends about *Atanek*, the Almighty Good Spirit, Who makes all those good things possible."

Manerathiak could contain her thoughts no longer. "What does the Little White Man say? What is his talk about? I should indeed be ashamed to lie here, old and useless, weak as a child. I will laugh no more, for my father and mother and many of my old friends are gone to the Land of the Dead with plenty to eat. But a strange fear has come upon me. Don't you know my grandchild is sick? The evil spirits are rushing across the land and they are after Naoyak because the Little White Man has listened to the fish."

Her ominous words roused Angivrana, who spoke with maternal anxiety, "Kakagun should fetch the *Tunrak*, the shaman, from Kiluitok Lake, which is not far from here. I am sure he has the power to cure. When Kudnanak was a little boy, he became very sick. He was shaking. His eyes were rolling. He could not part his teeth. We had to pry his mouth open with a flat piece of wood and feed him broth with a spoon. Nokadlak called the *Tunrak*. He came and lay close to my child. In his sleep he went down to the Mother of the Sea and came back in the morning with her good wish. Since then, Kudnanak has always been able to eat."

"There you are, Little Man! What did I tell you?" Manerathiak chimed triumphantly.

Having stirred my friends into consciousness, I let them converse while I relaxed and listened. Our spiritual beliefs were worlds apart, and it seemed they would so remain indefinitely. Their groping for an answer to life and death mysteries would continue somehow, they would experience the mystery of God as did their fellows in other great cultures.

Kudnanak was getting restless. He turned to Nokadlak, "Father, let's play *ayarak*, cat's cradle, with strings! I want to learn more ways to make figures."

"Why don't you ask Grandmother Manerathiak to be your partner? She knows many more ways than I do." Nokadlak knew she would refuse because of her failing eyesight, and it would then please him to display his skill before us all.

He took a two-foot long piece of net twine, tied both ends and stretched the twine between his thumbs and the small fingers of both hands. With the remaining fingers he began to make all kinds of patterns. It didn't take much imagination to recognize a trotting caribou, a seal basking in the sun, an Arctic hare running away from a fox, a man and woman embracing, and male and female genitals. At each figure, he would pause and ask Kudnanak or me to identify them. And all would laugh like children amused by a toy, especially when we hesitated. Even Manerathiak seemed to wake up from her torpor and chuckle a whit, temporarily forgetting about Naoyak's illness and her own suffering.

Encouraged by his father's nimble exhibition, Kudnanak proceeded to make himself an *ayarak*, string. He, too, was adept at the game, twisting his own figures and asking his parents to name them—a weasel caught in a trap, a fish, children dancing. Then father and son would deftly transfer the figures to each other's fingers, skilfully converting them into various shapes.

Going back to my tent, I listened to the silent night for any cry of pain from Kakagun's tent, but heard none. I assumed Naoyak was sleeping, at least for the time being.

Early the following morning I called on my little patient. Naoyak was about the same, but she reportedly had a good night's sleep. I gave her another teaspoon of castor oil and asked Kablunak to make her drink some broth.

Noting that Kakagun was not there, I asked Kablunak his whereabouts. He's gone to Kiluitok, *Fala*. He left on foot at daybreak." She did not have to add that he would be back with the sorcerer.

The sun rose over the headland when Kudnanak and I rowed out to the nets. It brought cheer to my young fishing partner and gave voice to the song in his heart:

Fish, fish! Am I such a fool
To let you talk to me? *Aya, ya, ya, a*
You come from the bottom of the sea
To tell evil things to young and old,
Children, men, and women, *Aya, ya, ya, a*
I'll not let you speak to me,
For I am but a young man still
Who does not have a woman. *Aya, ya, ya, a*

The plaintive melody echoed through the closest cliffs as we tackled the nets, now heavy with a sizable overnight catch. When my turn came to empty a net, Kudnanak looked on, his hands buried in caribou fur mittens. "I'm glad to see that you knock out the fish now, *Fala!*" he observed. (I did this in deference to their beliefs.) "You are quickly learning the ways of my people."

"I am trying to," I replied, as we both noticed an owl flying past the eroded bluffs of Kringaun, southwest of Burnside Harbor.

Still keeping his eyes on the nocturnal bird, Kudnanak asked me if I'd like to hear a story about *Orkpik,* the owl, and *Aangnek,* the little old-squaw duck. I knew how to distinguish the latter by its short beak, white head and neck, black-brown chest and back, as well as by its distinctive cry that resembled a choleric old nag which earned the bird its less-than-flattering name. But I hadn't heard any stories about it, so I replied, "If you can tell stories as well as you play the string game, I'm all ears." And my young companion proceeded to tell his tale.

"On a lakeshore was an *Aangnek* crying '*A-an-gnek, a-an-gnek, a-an-gnek*' because her husband had been killed. A big, fat *Orkpik,* who was flying by, heard the little duck crying, so he asked her, 'Why are you crying for your stupid, skinny husband? You should be glad he is dead. Now I'll be your husband!'

"*Aangnek* was angered. 'You think I'll take you as my husband? You're crazy! You're too fat. Your eyes are too big. Your small, crooked beak looks funny on your sleepy face. Your legs are too short. And you eat nothing but lemmings!'

"Hearing that, *Orkpik* lost his temper, swooped down on the little duck, and struck her on the head. *Aangnek* cried in pain, '*A-an-gnek, a-an-gnek, a-an-gnek,*' and pleaded with the Owl to stop hurting her.

"'Ah! Now I see you for what you really are!' *Orkpik* mocked her. 'You're nothing but a stupid woman who can feel pain and have a sharp tongue at the same time!'"

I laughed politely. "Who told you this story?"

"Grandmother Manerathiak. She knows many stories. You should ask her to tell you some when you come visiting. She likes you."

Upon our return to camp, we found Nokadlak readying his dog team. "It's such a nice day! I'm going to hunt bear in the mountains along Burnside River," he informed us. "Want to come with me, *Fala?* It's not far, and we'll return before dark."

"I'd like to, but Naoyak is not very well. I'll wait till she gets better."

"Then Kudnanak will come with me. Can you visit the nets alone while we're away?"

"Sure! There's no wind. I'll take my time."

The women appeared glad to see their men disappear among the boulders that dotted the Burnside River valley. Their absence meant more time to themselves. Angivrana and Manerathiak wasted none. They trooped over to Kablunak's tent, taking their sewing with them. Kablunak looked out and saw me gazing up the valley to the west. *Fala,* you should have gone with Nokadlak," she said considerately.

"There will be another bear hunt. Meantime I'd like to help

Naoyak, if I can. Besides, I have to look after my nets."

"Come in, then! I'll make tea and we'll have dry fish," she smiled.

I could see part of Naoyak's little head in Kablunak's hood, but there wasn't a sound from her.

"How is she?" I inquired.

"She is asleep. But her body is very hot."

"Naoyak is sick because the Little White Man listened to the fish," Manerathiak mumbled into her wrinkled chin.

I sat down by the stove and pretended not to hear.

With her sharp-edged *ulon* (half-moon-shaped knife), Angivrana was cutting caribou-fur trim on a small box shook. She fashioned squares, triangles, and circles from white belly fur, contrasting them with similar geometric designs of black summer fur. I was curious, "Are you making trimmings for Nokadlak's parka?"

She giggled. "No. Such pieces are cut for a woman's parka! I'm making one for myself."

Manerathiak cackled gleefully: "The Little Man is like a child! He has to learn our ways by asking silly questions." The old woman's wide grin exposed her yellow teeth, worn down to the gums. They were perfect for the job at hand—chewing the soft, thin, delicate skins of caribou fawns to make them still more supple for the little girl's clothing.

"*Fala* belongs to another land where they have different parkas," Kablunak rationalized. With rare skill, characteristic of the Kiluitomeun group, she was making herself a pair of caribou slippers. Small wonder the group got its name from *Kiluitok*, which means "to sew in small stitches." Like Angivrana, she had cut small pieces of black and white fur and was sewing them in a predetermined pattern that occasionally called for the insertion of red strips of scraped caribou skin.

"Kablunak, how did you tint the skin red?" I was not going to let Manerathiak's taunts prevent me from satisfying my curiosity.

"With soft pebbles I found on the beach. I crushed them and mixed them in seal oil. I also used the juice of *paunrain*, the berries of the tundra. When the juice has dried out on the caribou skin, I rub in some blubber oil to protect it."

Noting the boiling kettle, Kablunak stood up and went to the stove. "Let's have tea," she said. Just as she started filling the enamel cups and passing them around, Little Naoyak woke up crying. "I want tea!" she whimpered.

"Give her some, Kablunak. It'll do her good," I suggested. Obediently she lifted the naked child from her hood, cradled her fondly in her arms, and brought the cup to her mouth. Naoyak barely touched it. "It's bad!" she cried.

Unperturbed and with consummate patience, Kablunak held the little girl with her right arm as she lowered the front of her parka with her left hand and eased out her bulging breast. "Come, drink from it," she coaxed, gently pushing the teat between Naoyak's unwilling lips. But the sick child was not to be so easily pacified. She closed her eyes and cried again.

"Give her to me. I'll put her to sleep," said Grandmother Manerathiak. Tenderly she drew Naoyak close to her, rocking her, and muttering the while, "I'm busy, you know. What a nuisance you are. Don't you see I'm a very old woman, weak and stiff like a worn boot sole? My breasts are now shriveled up and useless. I can't give you milk. You ought to have been a boy—but I care for you just the same."

Having secured the child's attention, Manerathiak began to chant in her toneless voice:

"In our land, *ahe, ahe, ee, ee, iee*. . .
The wind has wings, winter and summer.
It comes by night and it comes by day,
And children must fear it. *Ahe, ahe, ee, ee, iee*. . .
In our land the nights are long
And the spirits like to roam in the dark.
I've seen their faces; I've seen their eyes.
They are like ravens, hovering over the dead,
Their dark wings forming long shadows,
And children must fear them. *Ahe, ahe, ee, ee, iee*. . .

In our land, *eeya, eeya, yea, ya, a, a*. . .
The great winds blow the snow across the frozen earth,
Chasing away all living creatures,
And children must fear them.
Eeya, eeya, yea, yea, a, a. . .
In the Land Beyond the days are long,
The sun warms up the land night and day,
And the Good Spirits descend from the sky,
Bringing to the People Beyond joy and food,
And children must love them.
Eeya, eeya, ya, ya, a, a. . ."

Naoyak had stopped crying and seemed to have been lulled to sleep again. There was nothing I could do to help her, and the old woman's laments depressed me. I finished my tea and rose to leave. Kablunak must have sensed my dispirited mood. "Little

Man, bring your *krepik* to my tent tonight. It's too cold to sleep alone." I thanked Kablunak for her considerate invitation, but made no commitment.

My tent was cold and uninviting. I lit the Primus stove and sat on my sleeping bag with my notebook, but could not concentrate on writing for long. Instead, I donned my fishing clothes and spent the rest of the afternoon around the nets. They were full of fish, and among them I found many blue herrings of the species common to both the Atlantic and Pacific Oceans. I was so lonely that to me they loomed more important than all the other catch. At least, they provided a tangible link with the civilized world.

18

Kirluayok The Sorcerer

Nokadlak's dogs were howling and Kudnanak was impatiently signaling for me to hurry as I approached the camp. I sensed that something was wrong.

"What is it?" I yelled to the youngster as I hit the beach.

"*Akhak,* the grizzly bear, has wounded my father. His head and face are covered with blood!"

I ran towards Nokadlak's tent. His dogs were still harnessed, and the carcass of a good-sized grizzly lay roped to the sled. Most of the dogs were yelping, still excited by the hunt and the smell emanating from the bear's carcass. Some were licking their battle wounds. The Barren Land bear must have given them a memorable fight.

Nokadlak was sitting on the edge of the *iglek,* the raised resting platform, with his bleeding head bent over a hot water basin held by Kakagun's wife, Kablunak. With a stained calico rag Angivrana was trying to keep the blood from running down her husband's face and neck. In her usual corner Grandmother Manerathiak was sedulously scraping a fawn's skin. Naoyak was asleep in Kablunak's hood.

Apart from snorting through nostrils caked with blood, Nokadlak sat quietly, holding his head stoically over the reddened water. His scalp had been badly scratched, and several red furrows revealed the skull bones beneath.

"How did you let the grizzly get so close to you?" I asked him.

Keeping his eyes closed against the dripping blood and

sniffing deeply, Nokadlak replied, "I'm like a clumsy old woman. I forgot to load my rifle! *Akhak* was feeding on some berries when we saw her. Kudnanak took care of the dogs. Using large rocks for cover, I got close to the bear. I shot, but my aim was off. The bullet grazed her neck. I pressed the trigger, but my chamber was empty. *Akhak* heard me, saw me, and rushed at me. There was no time to load. I tried to ward her off with the butt of my rifle. But *akhak* was too angry. I went down. She tore my parka. The only reason I didn't get killed was that I played dead, burying my face in the snow. She began to claw my head. She certainly had a bad temper, that one!"

"And that's when I shot her with my .22," Kudnanak finished the account for his father. "I fired at *akhak* many times while four of my dogs I had let loose kept attacking her."

"Kudnanak is a good hunter," Nokadlak conceded, and the young fellow beamed proudly.

I clipped Nokadlak's extraneous hair with my scissors, then bathed and dressed his wound as well as I knew how. Finding no needles or catgut in my medicine bag, I put the torn pieces still attached to the scalp where they originally belonged. The multiple lacerations gave the impression of severe injury, but fortunately the damage was superficial. I was about to bandage his head when Angivrana interrupted me, "*Fala*, put this hare skin on first. The wound will heal faster."

I didn't take the silky fur from her, but suggested that she could do that herself. This she did skillfully, and I applied the bandage.

"Are you hurt anywhere else, Nokadlak?" I inquired.

"Yes, here," he said, placing his hand on his crotch. "My penis is sore."

"Take your belt off. I will have a look."

There was no outward sign of injury, but a strong smell and pus exuded from his penis. I knew the reason for the problem—a fairly common one with the People Beyond, married or single. Since they wore no undergarments, caribou hair tended to get under the skin covering the glans, causing irritation and infection. I told Nokadlak what to do and he washed the offending organ with hot water. "Lie down and rest now," I added. "Kudnanak and I will take care of *akhak* and your dogs."

Although the grizzly was a young female, she was no lightweight—a few hundred pounds or more. When the lad and I got the bear off the sled, Angivrana and Kablunak came out to skin it. The hide was thick with a sliver-tipped brown coat that turned to gold in certain light. "She is fat," observed Angivrana, throwing chunks of the rich meat into a cauldron. She went about her job casually, betraying no emotion toward the animal that had nearly killed her husband only hours earlier.

Also squatting by *akhak's* remains, Kablunak cut open the bear's stomach. It was full of various Arctic berries and the white roots of the parsnip-shaped *maho* shrub which grows only a few inches above the ground in the Central Arctic. With dexterity, she stuffed these into the bear's bladder whose contents she had squeezed out earlier.

The stooped old Manerathiak emerged from the tent's small frame door carrying pan and her *ulon* (fan-shaped knife). She hobbled over to the carcass and began scraping bits of fat into the pan. Her baked-apple face softened. She sounded extremely pleased, "Now we'll have brighter light in the tent!"

Nokadlak appeared tired and depressed but, for a casualty, he consumed an enormous amount of boiled bear meat that evening without ill effect. I found the meat to my taste, too, but balked as diplomatically as I could at the vegetables a la bladder. Having witnessed their preparation, I was quite happy to take Kablunak's word for their goodness.

Grandmother Manerathiak, however, more than made up for my small appetite. As a result of her gorging, she was in difficulty. So much had her stomach expanded that she was unable to loosen her belt of braided caribou sinew. "Woe is me!" she groaned. "Like a wolf I have gulped too much. My belly's bloated like that of a pregnant caribou cow. Now this belt is choking me." The old woman cringed while Angivrana smilingly tugged at the loop and the semi-circular ivory bone inserted into it. Finally she managed the unfastening.

"Thanks!" Manerathiak said sighing with relief. "I feel as if I'm going to give birth to a fawn!"

Beside her on the *iglek* lay the bear's small tail, ears, and some claws. Pointing to the trophies, I asked, "Are you going to use these to make a toy?" The ancient woman laughed. "No. I'll clean them, sew them into a satchel, and hang it around Naoyak's neck."

"What for?"

"You want to know so many things, Little Man! You see, *akhak* the grizzly bear is strong and her soul will be pleased that parts of her body are used to give strength and good health to Naoyak."

"What do you call these things that will help the little girl?"

Her lips moved without uttering a word, and her eyes hardened.

"Dumb of me to ask you such silly questions," I said deferentially.

"You are only a *Kablunak,* a White Man, but I will tell you because you are like a child who is willing to learn. We call these things amulets. To their wearer they will bring good fortune and protection against the bad spirits of our land. I shall teach Naoyak to say the magic words that go with this amulet: 'Roamer of the plains, roamer of the hills, rush out across the land and the frozen sea, ride with the wind, and help me!' "

As if on cue, Naoyak began to cry and complain of an aching tummy. "I want to relieve nature!" Hurriedly Kablunak carried the child outside the tent.

When they returned, I felt Naoyak's head. It was still hot. "Has she eaten anything at all today?" I asked.

"*Immana.* No, she has refused everything."

"Keep trying to feed her some broth. She'll feel better for it."

"I'll try again, *Fala.*"

Before we dispersed to our tents for the night, I asked Kablunak when she expected Kakagun to return to camp. "He should be back tomorrow—unless the *Tunrak* (sorcerer) is so busy he cannot come right away." Again she invited me to remain in her tent for the night so as to be close to Naoyak. Knowing better, I declined with thanks and a lame excuse, "You are a nice woman, but I have so many things I want to do before going to sleep."

There was no sign of human life when I poked my face out of the small frame door early next morning. No smoke rose from the stovepipes above the other two tents. Even the dogs were still asleep, curled up in the snow.

The weather was raw, cold, and sleeting. I made myself some coffee and breakfasted on oats and cornmeal cooked in powdered milk. Then I dressed warmly for visiting the fish nets. Two seagulls were picking at the fish I had laid out in the snow to freeze. The birds' days were numbered. They were too old to fly south. If they weren't caught in the trap lines, they would freeze to death before the height of winter. I left them to their fate and rowed to the head of the bay.

Upon my return Kudnanak met me at the landing, but now—by contrast—the camp was very much alive. "Did you get many fish, *Fala?*"

"Yes, Kudnanak. However, a lot of spiny-headed sculpin also got caught in the nets. Taking them out I scratched my hands and nearly froze them in the bargain."

My young friend smiled, "A big wind must be coming. That's why they're seeking shelter in the bay. They're certainly small, but their large heads are so prickly and so ugly, we call them

Tupilak, the Devil."

Looking pleased, as if he had just been to a party, Kakagun strode up to take a look at my catch. I asked the great hunter when he got back.

"During the night. Kirluayok also came."

"Who is he?"

"He is the sorcerer. In springtime he moved from Hanimok River to Kiluitok. That's where I found him."

I was anxious to see the sorcerer, but the fish came first. Kakagun and Kudnanak helped me unload them and then we walked to the tents together.

"Come with us, *Fala*. We'll eat presently," said Kakagun.

A middle-aged man squatted on the *iglek*, swaying and humming a doleful tune. His long black hair, with a few white streaks at the temples, fell to his shoulders, almost covering the hood of his parka. It was the first time I ever saw an Eskimo with some white hair. He had a slightly hooked nose, and his long whiskers covered his upper lip, the side of his cheekbones, and chin. He was a handsome man, who looked more Indian than Krangmalit. Indubitably his most striking feature was his eyes. They were set widely apart, like two slits. When he glanced up at me, they were alert and suspicious, showing cold-gray pupils, unusual for an Eskimo. As we shook hands, he smiled and said with unconcealed mockery, "Are you the Long Robe?"

"*Illa*, yes, I am such a man—like those killed by the People of the Falls."

Hinnikhiak and Ulukhak, who killed the Long Robes, were two young fools. But they would have died all the same because the *Tunrak* had placed a curse on the Long Robes."

Kakagun and Kablunak, who sat apart with Naoyak in her arms, recoiled at this talk. It frightened them even more than the powerful natural forces which undergirded their whole belief system. They knew, for instance, how to guard against the icy will of Hilla, the Evil Spirit of great snowstorms and winds. But the storied powers of sorcerers were beyond their comprehension and, therefore, far more awesome.

At the risk of damaging our relationship, I reminded Kirluayok that the two Catholic priests were murdered by order of the the sorcerer at Coppermine when he discovered that they possessed far greater power over evil spirits than he did.

"Who knows about that?" was his non-commital answer. "The Long Robe may be all-powerful in his own land, but not here. In the Land Beyond the sorcerer is supreme."

"If that is so, then why did Hinnihkhiak and Ulukhak eat the hearts and livers of Fala Rouviere and Fala Le Roux after shooting them? I'll tell you why. Because by doing so they hoped to gain greater powers than those of the sorcerer!"

"May be. But they were two young fools anyhow. They did not use those powers. Soon after the policeman released them from jail in his land, they died here."

"They were young men, as you say—not old or sick enough to die. Yet Hinnikhak drowned at Imaernek Lake, and Ulukhak died in his tent shortly after returning to the People Beyond. What do you think of that?" I said guardedly. "What have you heard?"

"Nobody hurt them, *Fala*. Nonetheless the power of the *Tunrak* is great. He can cure the sick and he can cast spells on those who go against his wishes."

I was fairly certain that Kirluayok knew more than he let on, as he must have been about fifteen years old when Fathers Rouviere, then 28, and Le Roux, 25, were murdered. Both came from France. Le Roux made his initial contact with Eskimos at Imaernek Lake, since renamed Lake Rouviere in his honor. In the summer of 1911 he left his Mission at Good Hope on the Mackenzie River, paddled across Great Bear Lake, and then covered the remaining two hundred and fifty miles to the Eskimo camp on foot. He built a log cabin on the shore of Imaernek Lake where he was joined a year later by Father Le Roux.

Nothing was heard from them or about them until three years later in 1914 when an explorer met some Eskimos in the vicinity of Coppermine. He later reported to Bishop Breynat that he had seen local natives wearing Mass vestments. The following year the R.C.M.P. sent a patrol to Coppermine to investigate. The Mounties found Father Rouviere's prayer book and diary in the possession of an Eskimo family, and subsequently reconstructed the dastardly crime.

Both priests were apparently ill when they decided to return by dog team to their log house at Imaernek Lake. At Bloody Falls on the Coppermine River they were wantonly murdered by Hinnikhak and Ulukhak, who then extracted their victims' hearts and livers and ate them. Hinnikhak and Ulukhak were found guilty and sentenced to death. But Bishop Breynat compassionately obtained their freedom on the ground that they had merely obeyed a command of the sorcerer at Coppermine. Bloody Falls, incidentally, had been so named to commemorate the massacre of local Eskimos by Indians traveling with Samuel Hearne, a Hudson's Bay Company explorer, back in 1771.

"If you are a capable *Tunrak*, Kirluayok, why don't you cure little Naoyak?" I challenged. "You might make her feel better with your good-luck charms than I with my medicine."

"She will be cured. As soon as I came in I put Manerathiak's amulet on her." Even as he spoke, I noticed that Kablunak's eyes dropped to the satchel and the few bear-claws dangling on a string from Naoyak's neck.

"What will those claws do for the child?" I questioned the sorcerer.

"They will give her strength," he replied with self-assurance.

I was on the verge of asking him about his next move when Manerathiak's doubled-up shape eased itself into the tent amid muttered complaints of her ancient aches. She straightened part way, as far as her stiff old frame would allow and grinned at the sorcerer as if he were a long-lost relative. Then, after a perceptible shiver, she announced to no one in particular, "I feel like having some tea. It's so cold in Nokadlak's tent!"

Having helped herself to a cup of tea, she gave me a side glance and said to Kirluayok, "The Little Man, doesn't understand. I told him he made Naoyak sick by listening to fish talk."

"She is sick indeed," agreed the sorcerer. "Everyone—even *Kablunak*, the White Man—must observe the rules of the spirits. Now I may have to call on them if the amulet does not ward off her illness."

"Even with my misty old eyes I can see that the *Tunrak* has given poor little Naoyak some fine charms. What are they, Little White Man?"

"They're the ones you made from the bear's claws, Manerathiak. And the *Tunrak* has attached two owl's claws to them."

"Yes, yes, owl's claws," the Grandmother echoed. She closed her eyes and delved into her ancient memories, "Orkpik, the owl, flies silently, even during the still winter nights. No one can hear it. It is all white then, and nobody can see it against the snow. Only when the moon shines during the long winter night can his shadow be seen on the earth's white layer. *Orkpik* talks and listens to the good spirits of the land. Its claws bring the friendly spirits closer to us when we need them."

"Manerathiak," I interjected, "you are getting old and weak. Why don't you use some of Kirluayok's charms while he is here? Surely they can give you youth and good health."

"I have some of my own!" She lowered her parka for visual proof. Between two desiccated breasts which hung down to her belly, dangled a small dirty bag of caribou skin. She held it up for all to see. "I put a caribou ear into the satchel because I cannot hear well what people say. There are also strips of wolverine skin to help me keep my wits together. And other charms to protect me from danger and sickness."

Kirluayok accompanied Manerathiak's disclosure with

approving nods. "Manerathiak speaks wisely. Amulets inter-vene for us with the good spirits. Sometimes they give the wearer the cunning of the animals they represent. When Kakagun was a young man I gave him the teeth of a caribou to carry inside his parka. Now he is the best caribou hunter in the Land Beyond! I gave Kablunak the dried skin of an Arctic char, showing its small scales. Today she is one of the best seamstresses among the Lake Kiluitok People at the end of Bathurst Inlet. Her stitches are so small and so tightly sewn, one can barely see them. And some day I'll give Naoyak the beak of the great white swan to help her have male children. But one has to wear the amulets for a long time to get real help and protection."

"If your amulets are so wonderful and the *Tunrak* so powerful why don't you help Naoyak recover?" I repeated.

From time to time the spell is broken, Little Man. Perhaps it is because you are here with us!" His beady, glowing eyes attempted to drill right through me as he asked, "Are you an *Ilihitok* in your faraway land?"

The sorcerer had flung his sharp, double-edged challenge. I knew that literally *ilihitok* meant "the clever one." But I was also well aware that Eskimos used this word to describe the *Tunrak's* adversary. His foreign incantations and evil eye were supposed to bring disaster upon his enemies including the *Tunrak*. Under-standably then, the *Tunrak* was justified in summoning the protective spirits to his side and, on their advice, order the death of the *Ilihitok*.

I stared squarely at the sorcerer's cold, gray, eyes and said steadily, "I left my country and came here to help the Krangmalit, the People Beyond, in their sickness and trouble. But I don't use amulets to cure sickness. I use medicines taken from plants or made by the *Kablunak*. They do not dispel the evil spirits or summon the good ones. They simply clean the blood and mend the wounds."

He grinned eloquently as if to say, "And who, do you think, believes you? Words, nothing but words!" Then he went into action. He rubbed his stubby hands on his fur britches, beat a tattoo on his chest with his fingers, and stetched his arms out in supplication, "Now the feeling is coming back to me. I hear the spirits whispering outside. Listen!"

Their faces intent, Kakagun, Kablunak, and Manerathiak sat straining their ears. Miraculously, there were voices outside! For the moment it was hard to tell which one of us was most surprised. Then, unceremoniously—yet with a diffidence I had not noticed in them before—Angivrana, Nokadlak, Kudnanak, and Naodluak trooped into the tent. Nokadlak's face was ashen

301

gray and his white bandage seemed comically incongruous.

The transitory spell dissolved as my hosts realized it was their visitors' voices they had almost accepted as supernatural. But Kirluayok was not one to give up easily. Paying no attention to the intruders, he stared ahead, his eyes unblinking, as in a trance, invoking the ghosts of long-gone relatives who could presumably help him cure Naoyak. He must have succeeded in contacting the spirits again, for now he fervently, repetitively pleaded for their advice, "What do you wish me to do? What do you wish me to do?"

I don't know what the spirits suggested he should do, but he did begin to move among us, staring sedulously at everyone in turn, calling the names of the dead and asking his audience, "Do you remember our friends, our relatives? Their spirits are here now." And all but Naoyak and I would chorus in response: "Yes, yes, we remember them. They went to the Land of the Day."

Simultaneously the dogs began to howl outside without special cause, while a strong breeze blew in suddenly from the bay, rustling around the tent. Coincidentally, too, the waning rays of the autumn sun hardly penetrated the tent through the stretched gut inserted in the caribou skins as a skylight. Combining these normal phenomena, it took little imagination to create an atmosphere of eeriness in our midst, and the sorcerer added his masterful contribution. He doffed his parka, revealing a powerful torso and two old wounds below his right shoulder. He moved closer to Kablunak, in whose arms poor little Naoyak lay shivering and sobbing. Around the child's head he tied a band of caribou sinew intertwined with musk-ox *kiviut* (silky wool) and wolf hair. Attached to the band were assorted animal teeth and claws, as well as beaks of wild birds.

Then, as all but Kablunak backed away from him in accordance with custom, Kirluayok began to sway in front of the child like a cobra before the charmer's flute. His eyes were fixed on her navel while he rocked back and forth, periodically pinching his nipples and entreating the little girl to do his bidding, "You are hungry, you are hungry. The spirits are whispering: 'You must eat to feel strong again.' "

After a spell of swaying and invoking the spirits concerned, he raised his arms dramatically, demanding, "Give me the drum!"

Among the sorcerer's belongings deposited at the far end of the tent in a sealskin haversack, Kakagun found a small drum and a short narrow bone that was once a seal's rib. Solemnly, silently he handed them to Kirluayok. Using the bone as a drumstick, the sorcerer began a light stacatto beat as if to sound out his

302

audience's reaction. Satisfied that he held our rapt attention, he started to chant in his dull, quavery voice. Although it grew stronger and less tremulous as he went on, I could not make out all the words. Some of them were, no doubt, long-abandoned phrases retained by tradition and passed on to him by other sorcerers. Yet the antagonist in his song was easily identified—it was Hilla, the malevolent spirit, who created the frightening winter storms:

"But we are mere shadows
Lost shadows of the People Beyond,
Lost amid the awesome forces of earth and sky.
Ehye. . .ehye. . .ye. . .ye. . .eh. . .eh. . .
We are but restless shadows, lost shadows
When the sun lies dead, the moon is veiled with mist,
And Hilla prowls in the night through snow and wind.
Ehye. . .ehye. . .ye. . .ye. . .eh. . .eh. . .
We are the lost shadows that Hilla haunts
With rain and thunder, death and hunger,
Mere shadows, fleeing the unrelenting
Forces of the land.
Ehye. . .ehye. . .ye. . .ye. . .eh. . .eh. . .
So come to our aid, good spirits,
To the side of the helpless shadows
To save us frightened, sick little shadows!
Ehye. . .ehye. . .ye. . .ye. . .eh. . .eh. . . ."

Drenched in sweat, frothing at the mouth, Kirluayok stopped before the crying Naoyak just long enough to remove the band from her head. Then he collapsed on the *iglek*. His half-naked form heaving from the ritual dance, he panted for several minutes while none of us stirred, and dread seemed to encompass my friends. Eventually Kirluayok rolled on his side, opened his wild eyes, and sought me out. When he did, a triumphant sneer betrayed the thought behind it as if to ask, "Can you do better, *Kablunak*, White Man?"

Kakagun rowed in silence all the way to my nets. He was visibly moved by the sorcerer's performance, and I did not wish to interrupt his thoughts with mundane talk. Besides, I was busy with my own: "My friends see forces in and behind things which they personify as Spirits. They believe God or Supreme Beings dwell in the tangible world rather than the cathedrals of White Men. They try to influence the higher world by magical rites. One should be tolerant enough not to ridicule their beliefs. I believe it will take a long time for the concept of a loving God to penetrate their minds and souls."

Naoyak's condition remained unchanged. Nevertheless it was clear that Kirluayok was vastly superior to Napayok, the sorcerer I had once encountered at Kraomavaktok, southwest of Bathurst Inlet. He was a regular rogue. Like a wily old hound, he would insinuate himself into the confidence of the native people, especially women. Endowed with a crow's profile and slack jaws, his face was far from handsome. His half-shaved head was not flattering. In fact, some Eskimos referred to him as the Raven. Despite his unattractive appearance, he was a clever healer by Krangmalit standards, but a poor hunter by any measure. He found hunting more demanding and less profitable than traveling from camp to camp and taking full advantage of the people's unreserved hospitality. In fairness one must add that he would repay his hosts in part with his advice and remedies, as well as bring them news and gossip from other camps. On balance, though, Napayok was a lazy bum, an adulterer, and—according to veiled innuendos circulating in the camps—even an expert murderer.

Napayok's antagonist—his *Ilihitok*—was a wiry, determined fellow named Kaodluak. He and some of his friends had grown tired of Napayok's lawlessness and decided to get rid of the scoundrel. On at least three separate occasions Napayok was given up for dead after he had been either shot, stabbed, or strangled by Kaodluak and his accomplices. Yet in each case he was revived by his wife Alinak, taught by Napayok how to stop his bleeding and bring him out of unconsciousness.

When Kaodluak discovered this, he contrived to have the skilful Alinak eliminated first so that no one remained to deny her husband justice. To all concerned she simply vanished into the Arctic air while visiting a small trap line along the Hanimok River. Napayok was probably dispatched the same day, as he slept. A sealskin thong had been secured around his neck, cutting deep into the skin. This time he was garrotted for good.

So far as sorcerers went, then, Kirluayok was a far cry from Napayok. At worst, he was a more acceptable social parasite. Like Napayok and other Central Arctic sorcerers whose paths occasionally crossed mine, Kirluayok hunted little and fished less, depending for the most part on the People Beyond to feed, clothe, and lodge him in exchange for his magical services and advice. Unlike his late colleague, however, Kirluayok had no wife, only a male friend called Aitok, who lived with him and shared a mutual happiness. Kirluayok was said to lead an exemplary life, minding his own business, and protecting his followers from their supernatural foes.

It wasn't altogether surprising that Kakagun appeared to

have great confidence in him. Possibly no other place on earth, with the exception of the Antarctic, makes such exacting demands on a man's body and soul as the Barren Land. And no matter how capable or inventive an outstanding hunter like Kakagun may be, he can never consider himself the complete master of his surroundings. Time after time he finds himself thwarted by mysterious powers of the land, sea, and air— insurmountable ice conditions, unbearably cold temperatures, sudden snowstorms, devastating famine and disease. They hold his destiny in bondage, leaving him utterly helpless. When the evil spirits thus conspire against him, no one can help except the good spirits or a *Tunrak*. And of these two choices the *Tunrak* is more tangible and more often available than the ethereal souls of the departed.

To confirm my reflections, I questioned Kakagun as he rowed evenly, without haste, scanning the landscape for signs of wildlife. "Tell me, when your people are starving, do they call on anyone in particular for help?"

He mulled over my question momentarily and gave me his answer with unmasked suspicion. "Yes, *Fala*. We usually call on *Munarhie*, the Guardian Spirit. Why do you ask?"

"I was wondering if you called on *Munarhie* when Naoyak became ill."

"No. When my people feel sick, we call on the *Tunrak*. He intervenes with the spirits for us."

"I'm rather curious to know why you don't use medicine as do the Indians and the White Men. They make them from plants that grow on the land and even from animals that inhabit it."

"We follow the ways of our ancestors. Maybe they didn't know about such things. They always turned to the good spirits for every undertaking and difficulty."

"Do you mean that in everything you do, you aim to please or pacify some spirits?"

"Yes. We must choose the hunting season and the method of hunting according to the spirits' wishes. And animals must be killed, cut, and eaten in such a way that we do not displease them."

"What about making clothes, or building an igloo?"

Kakagun displayed his growing impatience by ignoring my question. His behavior was typical of every Eskimo I questioned on spiritual matters. Whenever I tried to penetrate beyond the sphere of tangible reality, they became reticent and almost sullenly non-communicative. Like other people, they struggled with the ultimate philosophical question which was always beyond their understanding: "What is it all about?" They found

305

their universe and the mysteries of life and earth unnerving, and bewildering to say the least, and downright terrifying.

The afternoon was waning when we returned to our camp with a large load of fish. Thinly coated with freshly fallen snow, the barrens around us seemed vaster and more rugged than ever. From the eroded peaks to the deep valleys, the land would soon be in the throes of bitter winds and snowstorms heralding another Arctic winter's tyrannical reign of misery.

Carrying Naoyak in her hood, Kablunak came down to the beach to watch us land. She smiled at the large catch: "Fish are still plentiful, *Fala*. But winter is close at hand. How much longer will you be visiting your nets?"

"Until I get enough for the whole winter."

She gave me a searching, incredulous look. Obviously no Eskimo she knew was ever that provident.

"How is the little girl now?" I changed the subject.

"Again she would not eat today. But Kirluayok, the *Tunrak*, said she will live to make a good wife for Naodluak."

"I'll see what I can do for her tonight."

Late that evening Kakagun woke me up in my tent with an invitation to have tea with him. I had dozed off after the tiring job of unloading the boat and spreading the fish on the beach. As we walked between the tents in the stillness of the clear, cold night, Kakagun said, "Listen to the Ayapapartovik River. The ice is making a lot of noise. Soon the bay will start freezing, too. In a few days we must take out the nets. Then we'll fish under the ice. Everyone will be setting nets under the ice because no one shot many caribou this fall."

In her tent Kablunak was vainly trying to get Naoyak to take her breast, while near them on the *iglek* Kirluayok was mumbling something below his breath. I felt little Seagull's forehead. The fever hadn't left her. It had been *three* days.

"I gave her a little broth a while ago, just as you told me to, *Fala*, and she took it," Kablunak informed me.

Hearing this, the sorcerer grinned derisively in my direction, "I'd like to hear your words of wisdom, Little Man. What do you think of her illness?"

"Despite all the noise you made this morning, Naoyak will be all right," I smiled back optimistically.

"And do you know why she will be all right, Little Man? Because the good spirits have listened to me. They always do."

Kablunak stood up, went over to the stove and filled the cups with steaming tea. Then she opened the door and called out, "Come for tea!"

Answering the call with surprising alacrity, old Manerathiak sat down creakily by my side. "It's cold outside," she complained. "I'm always cold nowadays." Politely she blew her nose into her cupped hands and licked them clean.

With the arrival of Nokadlak, Angivrana, and their son Kudnanak, the tent was filled again, but deferring to the sorcerer, no one spoke up as they drank. This gave me an opportunity to quiz Kirluayok a little further, "You've told me that the *Munarhie*, the good spirits, are your friends. Would you say, too, that they are more powerful than Agiortok and Tupilak, the evil spirits?"

"They certainly are! When someone disobeys the *Munarhie*, dreadful things befall that person or his family. The guidance of these good spirits must then be sought so that misfortune can be avoided. But the calamity itself would be the work of an evil spirit, and the *Tunrak* can destroy him by recourse to the good spirits."

"How do you call upon the good spirits?"

"You should know by now, *Fala*. You saw me do it."

"How did you become a *Tunrak*?" I asked just as abruptly, fully expecting to be told to mind my own business. But Kirluayok must have felt flattered by my public display of interest in his career, for he responded directly, "When I was a young man I often had dreams. In them I saw strange things. Big birds flying high in the sun. Naked men and women leaping and embracing each other in the snow. Caribou running and vanishing in deep holes. I did not know how to interpret such visions, so I asked a *Tunrak*. He told me I was predestined to become a *Tunrak* too, and he took me under his wing. He taught me much of what I know today. Eventually he appointed me to take messages from the good spirits and help my people."

Manerathiak was drinking in the sorcerer's every word and now her memories returned to her lips, "I had a son who was a great *Tunrak*. He is dead now. His wife strangled him in his sleep because he beat her every time he had a vision. When he was chosen as a *Tunrak*, the hunters built an igloo around him. Every third day they gave him a piece of meat from different animals and birds. Then the camp's established *Tunrak* took him into his igloo. After tying down my son on the *iglek* (raised platform for sleeping), he invoked the good spirits saying, 'Come and stand before me in the calm of the morning. Come and stand before me under the midday sun and speak to the young *Tunrak*.'

"The Spirits made my son a great *Tunrak*. Once, when I was sick, I was spitting blood. My son commanded all the women in the camp to drive their family sleds around the nearby lake in the moonlight. With five teams they circled it several times while my

307

son appealed to the good spirits on my behalf, and hurled challenges at the evil ones. Each time the sleds went around the lake, the moon got brighter. That's why the lake was named the Big Bright Light. Three old dogs died that night, but I did not die!" Manerathiak concluded triumphantly.

When no one else spoke, I threw another question at Kirluayok: "Who is the most powerful of all the good spirits?" Taken back by this unexpected query, he replied non-committally, "They are all powerful, Little Man. Some are stronger than others, of course. But each one of them is a mighty spirit."

"What about the evil spirits?"

"They are powerful, too. And some—like Hilla—must be feared even more than the others."

"Why is that?"

"Because Hilla's approach can be subtle and deceptive. He manifests himself in the stillness of the land and in the peaceful quiet of the mountains. He might whisper tenderly and softly to children to lead them astray. Or he may bring dreadful tidings to the hunter or his wife on the wings of the breeze."

"Is Hilla always bad?"

"No, *Fala*. He is definitely malevolent to those who violate taboos. But he is merciful to his followers."

"What must a hunter do to please Hilla, then?"

"He must observe the rules imposed by the sorcerer."

"What rules for instance?"

"At Kiluitok the people have been told by me not to eat caribou meat until the sea freezes. That is the rule they must obey. They cannot kill or touch either the skin or any meat of a newly killed caribou. If they do, the soul of the land animal will call Hilla and bring a curse upon the camp."

Kakagun cleared his throat before restating the rules of taboo for my benefit in his own words, "A man can eat anything he wants to in our land, *Fala*, if it is not forbidden by the sorcerer."

I took this to mean that there were no perpetual "sacred cows" in the Barren Land. With food ever scarce, the Eskimos simply could not afford such a luxury. But they were prepared to abstain temporarily from certain animals at the sorcerer's bidding, and then go back to eating them when the taboo was lifted.

Kablunak's excited whisper interrupted my thoughts. "Look, *Fala*, she is taking milk!"

I offered a silent prayer as again I felt Naoyak's head. Her fever was finally breaking! I could feel Kirluayok's fathomless eyes dogging my every move. Disregarding him, I said to Kablunak: "Naoyak should be well by tomorrow. But to make her sleep better tonight, give her this before you go to bed." As I put an aspirin tablet into her palm, she studied it curiously, no doubt wondering how such a tiny white object could possibly have an effect on anyone's sleep, let alone a sick child. "Crush this little medicine in your cup and add a bit of warm water or tea to it. Naoyak will take it that way," I assured her.

Slowly but surely the sorcerer began to relax. His gray eyes took on a soft expression I had not seen before. He gave me a friendly grin, and when he addressed me I could hardly believe what I heard, "At first I didn't like you, *Fala*. I thought you worked against my people. But now I see you are helping me take care of them. You are a good Little White Man!"

I remained speechless as old Manerathiak made my day complete. "*Fala* has always helped us," she said smiling. "If only he could follow the customs of the People Beyond, he would be one of us."

It was getting chilly in the tent, but I was aglow with this unexpected turn of events. The eerie atmosphere evaporated with the sorcerer's voluntary appreciation, replaced by a mutual respect and kindliness I had not experienced for some time.

Kablunak handed Naoyak to the baby's Grandmother and went outside. In a few moments she was back with an armful of dwarf willows for the stove. She broke the longer ones over her knee and shoved them through the little door. They crackled noisily, cheerfully, like pine boughs. She made two additional trips to the willow pile, returning with loaded arms each time. No man offered to help her. Traditionally it was a woman's duty to keep the home fires burning.

With the grandchild in her arms, Manerathiak was humming a canticle she had heard from Father Delalande at the Burnside Mission:

> "Good God, do bless this new winter
> And make us and our relatives happy.
> You have given us our time on earth,
> Asking us to prepare for Your Heaven."

19

Lake Kiluitok

Overnight a sheet of ice covered the bay. The air was calm in the early morning and the sky clear. With no time to lose, I asked Nokadlak if he could help me take in the nets.

"I thought you were going with us to visit our friends at Kiluitok today, *Fala*. But that can wait. There'll be time to go later if we help you now," he answered.

Kakagun and his son Naodluak joined us on the beach and helped us break enough thin ice to float the boat. "Would you like me to come with you, *Fala*?" Kakagun offered. "I can break the ice as we go."

"Thanks, Kakagun. I'm sure we'll need your help. With you it won't take us so long to get the nets, and then we can all go and see the people at Kiluitok."

With Kakagun and Nokadlak breaking the ice from the bow of the boat, I did not find the rowing too tiring. Methodically we emptied the nets of their substantial catch, pulled them ashore, cleaned them of seaweed, and stretched them out in the snow. They would be ready for use under the ice shortly, once the bay was frozen.

My hands were red and numb from the ice-cold water, but I dared not slacken the pace set by Kakagun and Nokadlak. They didn't seem to mind the cold. Their small hands and stubby fingers were used to it. I was playing with professionals and I didn't want to remind them that I was an amateur *Kablunak* (White Man). As a result, the job was done in record time and we set our homeward course along the narrow channel we had created earlier. The ice was a mere half-inch thick, but the ways the temperature kept dropping, it would be only a matter of days before we could walk on it with comparative safety.

After emptying the boat of fish, we took time out for a cup of tea, then returned to the bay to pick up Kakagun's and Nokadlak's nets. They had set only a half-dozen nets between them and all had three-inch meshes.

After I thanked my friends for their help, Nokadlak asked, "May I take some of your Arctic char, *Fala?*"

"Certainly but what are you going to do with them? You have fish of your own."

"Yours are bigger than mine, *Fala*. I'll dig a hole in the gravel, bury them wrapped in sealskin and covered with peat and sand."

"Why will you do that?"

"To give the fish a strong flavor. The taste will be different from the fresh fish we've been eating all summer."

"In that case, take all the big Arctic char you want, Nokadlak. And if you'd like to bury some for me, I'll feed visitors to my house this winter."

From Kakagun's tent his wife Kablunak announced that a meal was ready for us all. "Come and eat frozen meat!"

The tent was comfortably warm from her cooking efforts. Large chunks of caribou meat were piled in a tin basin, but they were not entirely frozen evident by the blood oozing from them. Mugs of steaming tea were passed around. As an added attraction, Kablunak offered us bannocks of unleavened white flour dough which she had cooked in a pan containing caribou fat. She called them *"bannik."* Flat and round, they were heavy and compact for lack of baking powder, but nonetheless a welcome change from the staple Inuit diet.

While we were eating, I mulled over Nokadlak's underground method of adding flavor to his fish, and decided to sound out my friends on a similar mode of food preservation on a year-round basis. So I aired my thoughts to test their reaction, "Next summer I'm going to build an icehouse to keep my meat and fish frozen and safe until I need it."

"We know what that is, *Fala*. But we have never made one. We move around too much," Kakagun responded defensively.

"Just the same, Kakagun, you could have an icehouse in your main camp, as well as one here. Then your fish and meat would never spoil and wild animals couldn't take them away."

"How would you build it, *Fala?*" Nokadlak inquired noncommitally.

I based my information largely on that of other White Men in settlements like Coppermine, Holman Island, Burnside, and Cambridge Bay, where various types of icehouses had been erected. Without doubt one of the best icehouses in the Central Arctic was built by Father Roger Buliard and friends at Holman Island off the west coast of Victoria Land. I can vouch for it because I found it most satisfactory when I used it during my stay there.

With the willing aid of several Eskimos, Fala Buliard dug out an eight-foot by twelve-foot pit to a depth of fifteen feet in light gravel at a conveniently short distance from the Mission. He chose the porous gravel bed not only because it wouldn't retain water and thus freeze like ordinary soil or clay, but also because it was comparatively easy to dig with a shovel. The shaft was framed with 2" by 4" lumber and planks, then covered with heavy timbers and several layers of sod. All the lumber was shipped in from Fort Smith on Alberta's northeast border to the Arctic Missions for house building and other needs. The entrance to this outdoor "fridge" was from the top. Measuring about four feet square, the trapdoor also provided adequate ventilation for the freezer. A ladder gave access to the chamber bottom. Permafrost sides of the pit assured constant, even, freezing temperatures, winter and summer. In fact, the maximum depth of summer thaw would hardly exceed a foot.

As I expected, however, my Eskimo hosts seemed more interested in the imaginative icehouse devised by the Oblate Fathers at Gjoa Haven, on the east coast of King William Land. Their gravel shaft was lined with igloo-type ice blocks and its "roof" resembled an igloo's dome. They proudly considered it to be a superior year-round outdoor freezer for their particular needs.

Although they dug out the shaft during the summer, they delayed lining it with ice blocks until the fall when the lake ice was about ten inches thick. Wisely, they never used sea ice since its salt content caused it to melt too fast. After putting the ice blocks into place, they sealed them together with slush which froze and effectively bonded them. For the entrance at the top, they installed a 45-gallon drum with both ends removed. The ice dome was then banked with clay, sand, and sod. On the permanently frozen floor of the ice-coated shaft they placed an adequate number of empty oil barrels (obtained from the trading posts or Missions)—one for each settlement family to cache their food supplies. Eventually, with the exception of a small access area (about 3' X 3') in the chamber center to accommodate the entrance and ladder, the icehouse would be filled with ducks, caribou, fish, and other meat like stacks of confined firewood.

I had hoped that my icehouse, with its dome-shape top and igloo-style ice blocks, might encourage my Eskimo friends to build similar structures in some of their camps to compensate for their leaner fishing and hunting periods. But that proved to be mere wishful thinking. The reality was that, during my protracted sojourn among them, I never saw an Eskimo build an icehouse for his own use. The People Beyond considered their *torho* (porch) the most convenient storage area, and even circumvented it in the fall by piling the slain caribou near the place they were shot and covering them with peat moss. The storage method for seal carcasses was simpler yet—they merely leaned them against each other like rifles.

When, with the help of their sons, Kakagun and Nokadlak had harnessed their dog teams, the women emerged from their tents with caribou furs for the sleds and sleeping bags. Kablunak's hood was bulging as she approached me in a pigeon-toed, bouncing gait, characteristic of female Eskimos.

"Is Naoyak asleep?" I inquired, hearing no childish cries in the hood.

"Yes, *Fala*. She slept quietly last night. She took milk this morning. Then she went back to sleep. She is much better!"

With lighter hearts we sat down on Kakagun's sled and were presently joined by the tall hunter himself and his son. As we drove, Kakagun and Nokadlak expedited our progress by traversing the ice on the many small lakes. The rolling tundras clad only in its thin mantle of snow, impeded us and we had to lighten the load by walking beside our straining dogs.

Eight miles from Kubiortorvik, the camp at Lake Kiluitok lay in a saucer-like depression sheltered on all sides by rocky hills. The lake itself was ten miles long and a mile across. As we descended, we could see the local residents watching us outside their two tents and three fur-covered huts strung along the lake's eastern shore. The huts looked unfamiliar to me. "Kakagun," I said pointing to them, "what kind of igloos are those?"

"They are made of peat and covered with caribou skins."

"Why don't your friends live in tents, like everybody else?"

"They walked here with their dogs last summer from their winter camp at Taheriuak. They left their sleds and belongings behind. They will live in these peat shelters until some of their relatives bring their teams. Then they will all go back to Taheriuak together."

Poorly dressed in old caribou parkas and breeches, the campers greeted us with joyful shouts of "A lot of people, it's wonderful!" Then donning their gladdest smiles, they shook hands with us all. Since I had met them previously at Burnside, introductions were unnecessary.

A simple reason explained their shabby clothing. It had not been very cold until the last few days, and the women were still preparing their new winter wardrobes. "Now that it's getting colder, the women will work faster," my informant told me. He was Imerak who, despite his advancing years, was still a fine hunter. Like old Manerathiak, he seemed toothless when he smiled; and, like her, he was shriveled-up, his face burnt and wrinkled by the elements, giving him an ancient look despite his abundant black hair. I had heard that Imerak was one of the Eskimos involved in the murder of two American explorers, Radford and Street, in 1913. Since he was now in his mid-forties, Imerak must have been about twenty at the time. Radford and Street had made their way by dog team across the Barren Land, probably from Fort Reliance at the eastern tip of Great Slave Lake, a good four hundred miles south of the end of Bathurst Inlet. I didn't know the details of the crime, but I hoped to find out from Imerak's friend and accomplice, a small, thin, Asian-looking hunter named Haala, whose wife Kuptana was now inviting me into their hut for tea.

To the northeast the crumbled bluffs of Burnside were painted a rich yellow by the setting sun. It was an oasis of beauty in the ugly frozen desert. Seemingly plated in gold, the snow-veiled rocks were built on a scale without regard to puny man. It was how God had created them and a world of ice and snow, dreaming the aeons away under the Arctic sky. Regretfully, I turned my back on this grandeur and faced a primitive people bound in the squalor. Disheveled dogs lay in trampled, wet snow, their droppings blemishing the dogs lines; caribou car-casses were stacked in array around the peat huts and tents; gutted Arctic char hung on ropes, drying in the wind.

"I'm coming Kuptana!" I answered the call of Haala's wife, a sickly-looking young woman I had treated on several occasions at the Burnside Mission, as she tried to get my attention. Little in Haala's hut gave comfort to a man's mind or body. Roughly oval in shape, it was a narrow abode with a fur ceiling so low that even I had to stoop a bit to avoid brushing against it. The gravel floor was covered with caribou skins and a stone oil lamp served as a cooking area. The usual smells of caribou fur, rancid seal oil, and plain humanity were augmented by the reeking dampness of the peat walls. None of the smells could escape, save through the occasional opening of the fur-hung door. Oppressed by the stench and the semi-darkness, I felt like I was locked in a medieval dungeon.

Haala ended my reverie by beckoning me to squat near him,

and telling me that his wife had a sore on the side of her head. "Kirluayok, the *Tunrak* (sorcerer), cannot cure it, *Fala*," he added. A hole festered behind Kuptana's right ear, and I could see pieces of decayed flesh attached to her jaw. It was an advanced abscess that had deepened and was matted over with hair and dirt. Worse than that, I could see lice crawling in the periphery of the wound. Unfortunately I had brought along nothing with which I could help the poor woman. The best I could do under the circumstances was to cut her hair around the ear with her *ulon*, the half-moon-shaped knife used by Eskimo women, and wash the sore with hot water. She winced from the pain, but neither cried nor shrank away. "I've done what I can," I said to Haala. "But you should take your wife to the trading post and tell the *Kablunak* (White Man) there that I sent you. He will know what to do for her."

As I spoke, Kakagun came in and squatted at the entrance. Silently he watched me mop up, then said, "*Fala*, we are not going back to our camp today. The dogs are tired and it's too late. We'll go tomorrow."

"You can stay with us, *Fala*," offered Haala.

His invitation was thoughtful but hardly appealing even though I'd have little choice since the other dwellings would likely be fully occupied. Still, I was determined to stay out of Haala's hut. "I'm going to visit the other families," I said, rising.

"I'll do some visiting, too," echoed Haala, unceremoniously leaving his wife with her troubles.

Pleasing amounts of meat, fish, and tea were available to everyone in the camp, while for dessert and entertainment the people enjoyed Kirluayok's description of his and my own activities at Kubiartorvik. An excellent storyteller, the Sorcerer held their interest far into the night with a variety of Eskimo legends. His ample repertoire embraced the tale of *Tiriginiak* and *Amakro*, the White Fox and the Wolf (the animal, not a policeman this time), a myth that children sometimes told each other.

"A fox and a wolf," Kirluayok began, "were searching for food along the shore of Lake Kraomavaktok. When they chanced to meet, the fox held a fish in his mouth which he had caught moments earlier. The wolf, who had had no such luck, complained to the Fox, 'I'm hungry and I would certainly like to catch a fish, too. How can I do that?'

" 'It's easy,' replied the Fox. 'Come here when the moon is shining and look for a crack in the ice. When you find one, put your tail through it into the water, then look at the moon, and say many times: 'Fish, fish, come and bite my tail!' The fish will come, and—as soon as he bites it—pull up your tail and the fish with it, too.'

"So the wolf returned to the frozen lake the following night. In the bright moonlight he had no trouble finding a crack in the ice. 'This is going to be quick and easy!' he told himself as he lowered his tail into the freezing water, gazed at the moon, and uttered the magic words many times: 'Fish, fish, come and bite my tail!' When no fish apparently heard him, he kept repeating his invitation until the moon disappeared and he decided to give up his vigil. But now his tail was firmly frozen in the ice! He simply couldn't budge it out of the crack. Still he strained with all his might until finally most of his tail broke off, leaving only a stump on his behind. The wolf was livid and went looking for the tracks of the wily fox. Eventually he came across a fox who was holding a willow twig over his eyes. The wolf asked, 'Have you seen the fox that made me lose my tail?'

" 'No, how could I when I'm snow-blind,' replied the fox. 'Look at my eyes; they are almost closed.'

"The wolf took him at his word and trotted off in search of the fox who had made him lose his tail."

I was surprised that this simple folktale produced so much laughter from all its hearers. But then I remembered that familiar fairy tales retold to us children countless times also seemed to improve with each repetition. After all, I thought, unsophisticated minds are much the same the world over.

The sorcerer reacted to the favorable response by telling us about a legendary character named Kiviuk who wasn't trying to right all the wrongs of mankind, but nevertheless got into all kinds of adventures and comical situations in pseudo-Don Quixote style as he roamed the Land Beyond. "One day Kiviuk came to Imeriuak Lake, the big lake that lies far from here where the sun rises. There he found a man who was carving a piece of driftwood with a knife.

" 'Who are you?' Kiviuk asked the stranger.

" 'My name is Ikalupik. I produce the *ivitaruk* (Arctic char) that live in lakes faraway from the sea.'

"As Ikalupik continued cutting the driftwood, its chips fell in the water and each one turned miraculously into an *ivitaruk*. Kiviuk also noticed that Ikalupik had a large hole in the back of his neck through which he (Kiviuk) could see the other man's mouth as he talked.

"As if reading Kiviuk's thoughts, Ikalupik asked him, 'Did you come from the front or the back of me?'

" 'I came from the front.'

" 'Good! I don't like people who come from the back and

316

can see through my mouth.'

" 'Actually I'm seeking a goose and her little ones. Have you seen them around here?'

" 'Yes, I have. They flew across the lake, towards the rising sun.'

" 'But how am I going to cross the lake?'

" 'Just wait; I'll call the Great *Ivitaruk*.'

"In no time a huge *ivitaruk*, as big as a man, swam ashore and Ikalupik said to Kiviuk, 'Sit on his back and hold on to his fin. He will take you across the lake. When you get close to its other side, be sure to wade ashore in shallow water.'

"Then Ikalupik, the Father of all *Ivitaruk*, commanded the giant fish to ferry Kiviuk across the lake. That is the way, it is said, that Kiviuk came to the Land of the Geese. There, not far from the shore, were many huts and tents where these geese live in human form. Some of these people ran toward the shore to meet Kiviuk. But when they saw him and recognized him, they ran back to their mother crying, *Apaput,* our father, has returned!'

"But their mother—who was now married to another man—disagreed, 'Your father lives in a distant land, far across and beyond Lake Imeriuak. It can't be him you saw!'

"Overhearing their conversation, her new husband—who had changed from a goose into a man and had filled his stomach with various tools so as to transport them more conveniently—warned her, 'Don't go near Kiviuk! He will kill you!'

"As Kiviuk approached their tent, the new husband tried to run away. But he tumbled to the ground because his stomach was too heavy and couldn't get up again. Seeing what happened, the wife sat down on the *iglek* and sobbed happily, 'At last my real husband has come!'

"That was how Kiviuk found his wife and their children and took them all back with him."

When I saw the oriental-looking Haala heading for his hut, I followed him. The short-statured hunter was yawning from drowsiness largely brought on by stuffy huts, but otherwise he seemed to be in a cheerful mood. His wife Kuptana was still up, but their two children, a boy and a girl, were already asleep. As soon as she saw us enter her abode, Kuptana put another kettle above the stone lamp.

Sitting on the *iglek* of willow stems and fur, I began to wonder if I should ask my host about the murder of the Americans in the vicinity of Burnside. Seeing him so self-satisfied and so mellow, I thought this might be as good time as any. "Haala, I learned from some people that two *Kablunan* (White Men) came to Burnside in the spring a long time ago from the

317

land of the White Man far, far away. Did you see them?"

"Yes, *Fala*, I did," he answered matter-of-factly, as he bent forward to take off his boots.

"Is it true that while they were crossing the ice at Koagiuk Island, somebody killed them?"

Contrary to my expectations, Haala neither denied knowledge of the incident, nor evaded the question. Still tugging at one of his stubborn boots, he said firmly, "Imerak and I were there when the Kablunan were killed. Our friends Araliuk and Kraniak killed them. We had to kill them."

"Why do you say you *had* to kill them?"

"Because they were angry with us and we were afraid of them."

"What made them angry? Did you hurt them in any way?"

"No, They came by dog team from where the trees grow. When they reached our camp at the head of the inlet, at a place we call Aniarhiurvik, they made signs to us. They pointed with their hands to the entrance of the inlet. We did not understand what they meant or wanted. Then one of them grabbed me and pushed me toward his sled. We understood this to mean they wanted one of us to take them toward the entrance of the inlet. But we were afraid to go with strangers who had guns and could not speak the language of the People Beyond. So we pretended not to understand their signs. They seemed confused and frightened. They began to argue angrily between themselves. They didn't know what to do next.

"Finally, Araliuk, Kraniak, Imerak and I decided to go with them. Their dogs were a poor lot; very tired from too many days of traveling. The *Kablunan* made us walk all the time. When we reached Koagiuk, we were worn-out from trudging in the soft spring snow. We stopped to rest on the sea ice and Araliuk said to us, 'The *Kablunan* can't go on like this for very long. They are going crazy! Before they go mad and turn on us, we'd better kill them.'

"I was much younger then and I was scared to try that. We were all scared. But Araliuk and Kraniak kept saying it was the only way we could save ourselves.

"In the end, Araliuk said to Kraniak, 'When the *Kublunan* start eating, take your harpoon and spear the tall one. I'll take care of the other one.' And to Imerak and me he said, 'Walk ahead of us and stay close to the dogs.'

"When the taller *Kablunak* bent over his Primus stove, Kraniak plunged the harpoon below his left shoulder. He shrieked, stood up grasping his chest, and fell dead on the ice. The other *Kablunak* jumped up, but Araliuk was too quick for

318

him. Seizing an axe off the sled, he split his skull. Then, to make sure, he did the same to the taller Kablunak. We left their bodies on the ice and covered them with snow. The next day we returned to our camp at Aniarhiurvik."

Haala sipped his tea with audible contentment before concluding his narrative, "Araliuk and Kraniak left soon after with their wives and children for the Land of the Nathilit. They took with them everything that belonged to the *Kablunan*. They were afraid that some day the Police would come from Coppermine."

Haala did not ask for my approval or criticism of his story, so I made no comment. But, out of curiosity, the following summer I surveyed on foot the eastern shores of Koagiuk Island and the mainland, hoping to come across pieces of clothing or even some bones of the two murdered Americans, Radford and Street. I found nothing. Whatever the foxes and wolves may have left of their bodies must have drifted away with the ice at the summer breakup. Under the circumstances I felt the least I could do to honor their memory was to erect a small cross with loose stones on the south promontory of Koagiuk Island.

On the surface, Haala's story rang true enough and it remained consistent with that of other Eskimos I interrogated. In a weakened condition, Radford and Street might easily have lost their "cool" amid the natives and provoked them to the breaking point. Nonetheless, knowing something of the Eskimo mentality, I still entertained doubts about Haala's version of the crime. That's because most of the murders among the People Beyond were irrational and not premeditated. They killed for the sake of killing, for the thrill of the hunt. It was one of the few excitements afforded by their dreary land. From early childhood they learned to kill every form of animal, bird, and fish for personal survival. The habit of taking others' lives was as strong in them as their everlasting struggle with the elements and nature's uneven odds.

If so inclined, one Inuit hunter would stalk and kill another one without reason or remorse. Why should he, therefore, have any special respect for the life of a complete stranger? What's more, such feelings can also be subconsciously developed to an extent by a White Man, missionary or trapper, who stays long enough in the Arctic and hunts for all his daily needs. In the long run he simply becomes immune to pity or compassion toward any animal or human life.

My scepticism had other grounds as well. In their everyday occupations of hunting and fishing the Eskimos rely on inbred cunning to achieve success, and this native chicanery carries over into their dealings with one another. To be raised in such an environment and forever exposed to its modus operandi could subconsciously make a habitual liar out of anyone. This, too, was something to consider about the People of the Land Beyond.

Oblivious to my speculations, Haala continued to undress. His wife turned his fur socks inside out and placed them on the drying rack above the lamp next to the two children's pairs. Still wearing his breeches, he crawled into the family *krepik* (bag) with the sleeping youngsters and removed his final garment. Noting that I had brought along my own sleeping bag, Haala said considerately, "There are enough caribou skins on the *iglek*. Make yourself comfortable. Have a good rest!"

Before undressing, I asked Kuptana if she wanted me to wash her sore again, but she said she was fine and I could do that in the morning. I took off my clothes and Kuptana placed them on the rack. I folded my parka to use it as a pillow.

Kuptana lingered by the blubber lamp, lowering its flame for the night. After placing a *korvik*—an empty can to be used as a chamberpot—within her husband's reach, she undressed and crept beside her husband into the family's sleeping bag.

For a short while I slept as soundly as my hosts. But before very long I was awakened by intense itching all over my body. I started to scratch myself by reflex action, but found, to my complete dismay, that I could stop scratching only at the risk of being eaten alive by lice. I was even more concerned that besides the common lice, their cousins the crablice could have been patrolling my pubic area.

Involuntarily my thoughts flew back to my arrival at Aklavik. After disembarking from the supply barge and while we were having dinner at the local Mission, I mentioned that I couldn't stop scratching at night aboard the craft because of constant itching in the lower parts of my body. Everyone around the table laughed and Father Biname, who was then the skipper of the Missions' schooner *Our Lady of Lourdes*, asked me, "Do you know what crablice are?"

"Sure," I answered. "I was in the Army and after each furlough we had to pass inspection for crablice and venereal disease."

"Well, you probably got a load of those little critters aboard the barge! We frequently transport Indians to our schools and hospitals, and some of these people are covered with crablice. But don't worry. After dinner go and see one of the Sisters in the Mission Hospital. She may have a good laugh at your expense, but I'm sure she'll give you the stuff that'll enable you to get rid of of the lice and their itch."

Contrary to his kidding, the Sister I talked to was understanding and helpful. "Poor little Father," she sympathized, "didn't they tell you not to sleep in bunks used by Indians? Do you know why the Eskimos call them *Itkrelereit?* That's their word for lice!"

"Nobody thought to warn me, Sister. We were very crowded, so I put my sleeping bag down on the first unoccupied bunk I could find."

"That's only logical. And you, no doubt, know what a crablouse is—a tiny, transparent parasitic insect that looks like a miniature crab. Now take this bottle, please, mix its contents with water, and apply the liquid to your lower parts before going to bed. Do that several times, Father. Meanwhile hang all your clothes and sleeping bag out in the sun."

I thanked the Sister and went back to the Mission post. Later in the day, after we unloaded the barge, Father Biname asked me if I had obtained the necessary medication. When I answered in the affirmative, he said, "You are lucky that our Hospital carries the right stuff! I remember at Tuktuyaktuk the mate on the Hudson's Bay Company's boat, the *Fort James,* was so loaded with crablice that he nearly went out of his mind! To get rid of them, the Skipper ordered one of the kerosene barrels to be opened, then suggested the Mate take off his clothes and soak his body in the kerosene. Of course, all the crewmen surrounded the poor fellow, laughing their heads off and teasing him with such observations as 'You old rogue! You should know better and leave the squaws alone!' "

So accustomed to lice bites were Haala, Kuptana, and their children that they scratched themselves periodically throughout the night without awakening until morning. With them it had indeed become a conditioned nocturnal response. In my case the nightmare did not end until the howling dogs mercifully announced the break of day. Haala stretched, yawned, and greeted me with the customary "Did you have a good sleep?"

"No, I scratched all night!"

"Since we built this hut we have been troubled with lice. We don't like them; but they like us. We can sleep now, though. They are well fed!" His giggle was tempered by his understanding.

"I think my lice were starved!" I managed a sick smile.

Kuptana's day started before the rest of us got up. She took our parkas outside and beat them with a stick, knowing that in the cold of the morning the lice would shrink just enough to lose their grip on the fur and drop off to oblivion. Replacing the *anoraks,* or parkas, on the *iglek* where we rested, she went out with a kettle to get water from a hole in the frozen lake. By the time she returned, we were all up. Kuptana increased the flame in the stone lamp and put the kettle on. Then she sat down on the *iglek*, took her daughter in her lap, and began to hunt for the little parasites on the youngster's body. Her son reciprocated in kind by searching for them in her thick hair and around the sore behind her ear. Haala meantime went methodically through his breeches. Their preoccupation reminded me of monkeys in a zoo. When Haala found a louse, he would hold it between the tips of his fingers, bite it with obvious satisfaction, and pass an earthy remark. And they would all titter, looking sideways at me, pretending to be embarrassed.

At one point Kuptana protested her son's overzealous pursuit of the tiny invaders in her hair with "Take it easy, Little Man! After all, they belong to me. I fed them!"

Their morning exercises over, everyone downed some frozen fish and meat along with tea, and the children ran off to play.

"Would you like me to clean your sore now?" I asked Kuptana.

"Yes, *Fala*. It hurts a little when I move my jaw."

As I washed her deep sore with hot water, I silently deplored my poor, almost non-existent training in practical medicine during the six years I spent at the Seminary. Too much of our time was wasted on the useless debates of uninspired teachers under the yoke of old church disciplinarians who seldom made any clear-cut judgments. With their heavy-handed ecclesiastical power they left us in a kind of theological limbo, forgetting that our Lord was a down-to-earth Man, always ready to cure the sick.

We did not tarry in the camp that day. The sky was clear, the air cold and bracing. Sitting next to Kablunak on the sled, I inquired after Naoyak. "She slept all night. And she ate like a weasel," she told me happily.

Running alongside, her husband Kakagun said to me, "It's much colder today. We can set the nets under the ice tomorrow."

Abruptly the weather worsened that evening. A snorting northwester roared through the silence of the Barren Land, carrying a cloud of snow in its path. It hit the bay with such force that the thin ice began to break and pile up on the seething shore.

Inside the tents it was almost impossible to keep warm, and ancient Manerathiak was suffering more than the rest of us. Bundled up in her long parka on the *iglek*, her hands deep in her sleeves, she kept repeating the obvious, "It's cold, cold! It's freezing!"

Even little Naoyak, resting in the arms of Kablunak, winced at times as particles of ice fell on her face from the top of the tent. Shivering, she too complaining, "It's cold! It's cold!"

Next day the wind and cold increased their onslaught on our little corner of the Arctic. Combining their forces, they penetrated everything, including the water in the bay, lowering its temperature and serrating its surface like it was gelatine. The men and the boys ventured out long enough to pile up snow around the tents for a measure of insulation against the bitter wind. The womenfolk remained inside, except to fetch some willows for the stove.

Towards nightfall the wind dropped and by morning the bay was covered with smooth, glossy ice. A mile or so offshore, the sea remained open. Thus was the stage set for a titanic struggle between these powerful natural forces. Although the outcome was a foregone conclusion, the sea could be counted on to carry the fight into November, when it would succumb to the temporarily superior strength of the Arctic freeze. From now on, Hilla—the great malevolent Spirit of the Air—would reign supreme, blowing his fury from the massive frozen plateaus of far-off Greenland.

On the third day after our return to camp, Kakagun and Nokadlak walked out on the frozen bay, periodically punching holes in the ice to test its thickness. As soon as they had ascertained that it was uniformly thick, they began preparations for setting their nets below it. Their two boys, Naodluak and Kudnanak, helped me with mine. Every three paces I chopped holes through the ice, large enough for the lads to pass twine through them by means of a pole provided with a hook for the purpose. The line was lowered into the first hole, picked up under the ice from the second hole with the pole, brought to the surface and held there until hooked from the third hole, and so on. With all the twine except its ends under the ice, I fastened the net at one end and drew it down into the watery hole while Naodluak pulled at the other end. Kudnanak, meantime, watched to make sure that the sinkers and floats remained in place to keep the net upright in the water. To prevent it from being seized in the ice floor, which would thicken by the day, I used willow stems to maintain both ends of the net a couple of feet below the ice.

By noon we had set eight nets between us, spaced every hundred feet, and were ready for rest and food. While we filled ourselves with boiled caribou meat and tea, Angivrana proposed that we spend the afternoon at the creek. "The water is still open in some places and we should catch plenty of fish at the old dam," she said.

Kakagun did not need further coaxing, and we jumped into the shallow basin, *kakivoks* poised for the unwary fish. *Ikalupik*, Arctic char, and *kapielik*, brilliant elongated whitefish, were still running. Meanwhile Kablunak and Angivrana had climbed up on the rocks and were spearing the fish right and left. We stood our ground in midstream, thrusting our harpoon-like spears into the clear water each time a fish swam by. Loud cheers went up on all sides whenever anyone's *kakivok* found its mark. Even Manerathiak and her little granddaughter Naoyak joined in, yelling excitedly from the sidelines.

Unfortunately, I had neither skill nor luck at the sport. Worse, I was shivering so much, my aim with the *kakivok* was consistently inaccurate. The water was so cold that it seemed to penetrate right through my sealskin boots. Unable to take it any more, I scrambled ashore, gasping, almost numb, and thoroughly miserable.

"*Fala*, come back and help us!" the men joked.

"I'm freezing! Let me run around and get warm. I'll help you bring the fish ashore," was all I was able to tell them through my chattering teeth.

Jogging upstream and down, flinging my arms across my body to speed up the circulation, I continued to marvel how my friends could endure the cramping cold for so long. Judging by their shouting and laughter, they were wholly unconcerned about their numbed limbs. Undoubtedly they were blessed with a tremendous release of stored energy within their bodies resulting from their constant diet of fatty meats.

Seeing me run like a madman, the women screamed with delight, and Kablunak called out, "Little Father, why don't you come in my arms and hug me? I'll warm you in no time!"

I must confess that it took most of my courage to reenter the icy water, even though the running exercises had warmed me considerably. Kakagun handed me his catch, which he had hung on his belt with twine, and I carried the struggling fish to the shore. Somehow I managed to complete several such return trips, stacking the fish in separate piles for the two families.

When they were satisfied that most of the bigger fish were taken out of the pool, Kakagun and Nokadlak called a halt to the fishing. Upon replacing the welcome parkas over our chilled, damp bodies, each of us filled a caribou or seal bag with a dozen fish of various sizes. The men took about fifty pounds of theirs, the youths and women proportionately less. I picked up my bag and slung it over my shoulder. Not so the others. They had a tumpline sewn on the top of their carrying bags which fit around their heads so that the bags hung down their backs, allowing

them free use of their hands. Only old Manerathiak was spared the packing chore. Instead, she was given Naoyak to carry in her hood.

By the time we returned to camp we were too tired and too cold to check the nets in the bay. So we changed into dry caribou clothes and the menfolk stretched out on the *iglek* in Kakagun's tent. The youths followed their fathers' example, but there was no immediate rest for Kablunak and Angivrana. Without uttering a word, their respective husbands handed them their damp fishing garments and waited for tea to be served.

I had expected the brawny Kakagun and Nokadlak to assist their wives in drying the heavy, wet parkas and breeches, so I said gallantly to the hunters, "I'm going to help Kablunak and Angivrana."

Kakagun's scornful answer stopped me short, "You don't know our ways, *Fala!* You must understand that they are only women. And *Arnak* (Woman) is meant to take care of *Inuk* (Man)." By choosing the term *Arnak* he made his meaning doubly uncomplimentary, for the People Beyond apply the same word to a she-wolf or a bitch—that is, creatures deserving no special consideration. As well, the same word can denote animal or human excrements. Actually to them a woman's status rated just a notch above that of animals. Trained from childhood to do all manner of menial tasks, the Eskimo woman is accustomed to enduring the weaknesses and appetites of men. Although cognizant of that, I still couldn't get used to what appeared to be a master-and-slave relationship between a hunter and his wife.

My feelings must have shown through, because Kakagun turned to Nokadlak and said for my benefit, "If *Fala* had a wife, he would be too good to her! He doesn't know that women should be given little attention or they become spoiled. They are made to bear children and work for men. Who could hold them in check otherwise?"

Kablunak and Angivrana grinned in mild amusement at Kakagun's degrading remarks. They could afford to, for they knew that Eskimo women potentially held the trump cards. Since females are considerably outnumbered by males in the Land Beyond, they had a vast choice of partners. They could simply move in with other single hunters. Married men, on the other hand, would be absolutely terrified by such a calamity. So let the men brag of their superiority. The women realized they held the axe handle. True, to them belonged the serving, cooking, child rearing, and all the menial tasks of the household. They didn't mind that at all, so long as their men took care of all the other vital necessities, including hunting, fishing, building igloos, looking after the dogsleds, the boats, the firearms, the fish nets and other implements. Otherwise the menfolk could find themselves living alone or even end up murdered.

Apparently quite well again, little Naoyak approached and perched on my knee. The wolverine trimmings around her hood and sleeves were the nearest things to toys in that plain shelter and she tugged at them playfully. To amuse her I told her about some White Men who had built a boat much bigger than the tent we were in, which could travel under water like whales in the sea. I wasn't sure she understood what I meant when I added that the sea fish were smart enough not to take the giant boat for a huge whale, although it certainly looked like one, but swam right up to its windows and peered through them at the strange people inside. Suffice to say that she laughed spontaneously and encouraged me to continue with, "More, more!"

By the time I finished embroidering a tale about three polar bears and a little dark-haired girl who got lost in the tundra, then stumbled into their igloo, she was fast asleep in my lap. Without waking her, I handed Naoyak gently to Kablunak, bid good-bye to my hosts, and went to my tent.

Next morning, with Grandmother Manerathiak and Naoyak for an audience, the camp's male population went to work on the nets. Emulating Kakagun and Nokadlak, I chiseled the ice at both ends of the submerged net. Kneeling on the ice, Naodluak attached a long twine to one end of the net by which we would later be able to pull the net back into place under water.

With Kudnanak's help, I dragged out the net. Many a whitefish, the last of the fish to run for the lakes, floundered in my gill net. There were Arctic char, too, and trout, and the odd tomcod—in all, a pleasing catch. Getting the nearly frozen fish off the net with bare hands, however, was anything but pleasant. Painfully we freed them from their entanglement and tossed them onto the ice, where they froze in a very short time.

Manerathiak, the inflexible soul, made absolutely sure the fish held their peace by clouting them over their heads with a suitable stick to the tune of an old fisherman's song:

> O, fish, where have you been?
> I know where you have roamed
> In the darkness of the sea,
> In the depths of the inland lakes,
> Aya, ya, ya, ya. . .
>
> Fish, where have you been hiding?
> I know one place you have visited:

326

The distant abode of Nuliayuk,
The mighty Spirit of the Sea. *Aya, ya, ya, ya. . .*

Fish, to Nuliayuk you have gone,
To the lost Spirit of the Sea,
To the Land of the Day.
But do not tell me what you heard,
For I shall die and be eaten by worms.
Aya, ya, ya, ya. . .

Suddenly Manerathiak stopped singing and groaned, "Soon
I'll be leaving this life. My soul is drained. I'm too old."
Nokadlak heard her, shrugged his shoulders with apparent
indifference, and observed, "Perhaps it's time for you to go,
Manerathiak. A long winter is settling on the land. Food will be
scarce. You will do what you must do. Your dead relatives are
waiting for you in the Land of the Day."
"Yes, yes!" she moaned. "I dream a lot. Soon I'll join the
Ublurmeun, the People of the Day. They have been waving at me
in my dream."
Each day that the weather permitted, we returned to the
nets. Gradually the catches got smaller and smaller. Finally,
Kakagun said, "The fish are scarce. The ice is getting thicker. We
are going to take out our nets and move to Taheriuak for the rest
of the winter. But first we want to do some trading at Burnside
post. What do you want to do, *Fala?*"
"I have been thinking of returning to the Mission. I have
enough fish stored for my dogs now. Will you give me a ride
there! I'll come back with my team and pick up my supplies."
'Yes, *Fala*. And I want to get some traps and ammunition. We
shall all go tomorrow."
Despite Kakgun's heavy load, it took us only an hour to reach
Burnside over the reasonably smooth ice of the frozen channel.

20

Four Years Later

During the next four years I heard little of Kakagun and Nokadlak as I traveled far beyond the normal orbit of the Fine Sewing People of Lake Kiluitok and the Musk-ox People. So closely knit that they could really be considered one, these two groups traditionally inhabited the Bathurst region. Their nearest neighbors were the People at the Far End who lived on and around the Kent Peninsula at the eastern entrance of Bathurst Inlet. All three groups shared the same hunting grounds, meeting in the spring at the small trading post of Ungevik on Wilmot Island for the seal hunt.

To the Western and Eastern Eskimos these people were known as the Krangmalit, derived from the word *krangma* meaning "beyond." They mixed freely with the People of the Rich Fishing Grounds at Cambridge Bay on Victoria Island, and also the People of the Berry around Ellice and Perry Rivers on the mainland coast of Queen Maud Gulf.

All these groups spoke with a slightly different accent from the Western and Eastern Eskimos. The former's distinguishing characteristic was a smoother, less guttural manner of speech wholly lacking the "s" sound which they replaced with an aspirate "h." Their word *nathek* (a seal), for example, was pronounced *natsek* by Western and Eastern Eskimos. A more important difference between these groups and other Inuit was the energetic and more venturesome spirit, backed by a pleasanter disposition and a livelier native intelligence.

For various purposes—such as census taking, Mission building and replacement duties—my travels took me to Coppermine, Minto Inlet, Holman Island, and Tree River, occupied by diverse groups. The Western Eskimo influence was readily noticeable in their manner of speech which accepted both the "s" sounds and the aspirate "h."

Wherever I went, I found distinctively descriptive names attached to the various local groups. At Minto Inlet and Prince Albert Sound on the west coast of Victoria Land dwelt the People at the Back of the Land. At Dolphin and Union Strait, which separates Victoria Island from the Arctic's mainland, I met the Tomcod Eating People and near them the People of the Cape. During my stay at Coppermine I mixed with the People of the Falls and with some of them visited their friends across Coronation Gulf on Richardson Island, favored by the People of the Caribou Antlers.

Although these groups stuck to their respective camping and hunting grounds, they were all acquainted and I found little to distinguish between them or their nomadic life-style. In small clusters of families—usually three or four at most—they were scattered over a vast frozen land that had seen their ancestors struggle for mere existence in much the same ways for thousands of years. Except for modern firearms and such utensils and provisions as they were able to acquire from the White Man's trading posts, their way of survival had not changed since the glacial period. Severed from the outside world since time immemorial and almost entirely free from outside influence, they remained primitive in all essential respect.

Theirs was a world of flat marshlands in the summer and of frozen tundra for the rest of the year. Of stony hills and eroded mountains. Of snow and ice over frozen seas. Of awe-inspiring gales and blizzards. It was a world of dead monotony. Of hardships and sufferings inconceivable to the White Man. An unconquerable sense of self-preservation and an immense longing for an unclouded happiness must have set the tone for every day of their lives. What else could have driven them ceaselessly on through the ages? Only that and an unswerving determination, bordering on inflexible obstinacy, to preserve their customs and language for themselves. Geography and climate—which accounted for most of their physical hazards, miseries, and discomforts—also aided them in perpetuating their isolation from the rest of the world. Detached from their original hordes, they nevertheless responded to the same instinctive gregariousness that characterizes the musk-ox and the caribou by banding themselves in small nomadic groups and wandering together in a neverending quest for sustenance.

It was this perpetual pursuit of game—animals, birds, and fish—that brought me face to face with an old friend at the delta of the Hood River in the Arctic Sound. I had spent weeks on Kent Peninsula and along the southeastern shores of Melville Sound, visiting Inuit families mostly in the vicinity of Hope Bay and at the mouth of the Angnimayok River. The terrain was rough and hilly, spotted dominantly with granitic rock, rising sharply to an elevation of at least a thousand feet above the Sound. I was heading back to Burnside when I thought I'd see if there was anyone at the usual campsite of Kattimanek near the Hood River Rapids. From the steep bank of a frozen, winding stream I could see a kneeling native using his snow knife to cover up a set trap with snow, and smooth it over with the back of his mitt. A pebble chanced to slip from under my boot and rolled downwards. The hunter's acute sense of hearing caused him to turn and glance up in my direction. And we were both relieved to recognize each other.

"*Fala, hey!*" he cried with unconcealed surprise. "Where did you come from? Did you drop from the sky?"

"No, Nokadlak, I don't think I'll ever deserve that high abode! Actually, I left Ikalulik Island this morning by moonlight on my way from Kent Peninsula."

He studied me briefly as I approached. "You look cold, and your dogs seem tired, *Fala*. My igloo is up by the rapids. Let's go there. I can look at my traps tomorrow."

"I certainly won't say no to that! I'm as tired as my dogs."

At the foot of the steep descent in the riverbed two snow houses nestled in a cover. Beyond them lay grizzled hills reaching up to 1,150 feet. The rock formation was of the coppermine series found in most of the mainland coast of Coronation Gulf. The forbiddingly desolate scene reminded me of imaginary lunar landscapes. But the resemblance vanished as the tiny camp sprang into exuberant life. Hearing our teams, the dormant dogs jumped up and started a dissonant chorus of warning and welcome. The youngsters and their parents ran out of the igloos' porches, waving and shouting at us as we climbed the intervening distance.

Their mittens off, Kakagun, Kablunak, Naodluak, Angivrana, Kudnanak, and a young lady of seven—all smiling and laughing—fervently shook hands with me. "The Little Father has come back!" they kept repeating happily to one another. No conquering hero I knew of was ever accorded a more affectionate reception. Their friendliness was so overwhelming, I almost forgot my tired, half-frozen limbs.

"And who is the pretty girl?" I ask rhetorically. "Can she be the baby that had a bad tummyache a long time ago and slept on my lap like a newborn pup?"

"My name is Naoyak," she identified herself with inherent dignity. "And I know who you are, *Fala!* Everybody has told me about you."

"I've heard a lot about you too, Naoyak. Only good things, though." She laughed and hugged me, saying, "You must stay with us now. Never go away."

"Tell me, Naoyak, where is your Grandmother Manerathiak? Is she waiting for us in the igloo?"

"No, she is dead."

"That's too bad!" I exclaimed. "I was very fond of her. She was a good woman."

Kablunak broke the uncomfortable ensuing silence. "Come and have some tea, *Fala!*" she said. "The men will look after your dogs."

It was heartwarming to see the flame of the blubber lamp reflected on the snowy dome. "Thanks, thanks!" I said. "It's wonderful to be inside. It's so cold outdoors. The ground wind blew all day on the sea ice and at times I could only see the high bluffs of Iglooruak Island."

Still smiling, Kablunak took my parka and shook off the last clinging snow. She scanned my face momentarily, then said hesitatingly, "Your whiskers are full of ice, *Fala*. Under them you look thin!"

"I've been traveling a good deal, Kablunak. When I return to my Mission post, I'll shave off my whiskers. They're always collecting icicles."

"The Little Man likes to learn through hardship. Why don't you puck your whiskers out the way the Inuit does? Then your face won't hurt."

"I have too much hair on my face to pull it out. But look at the top of my head. All my hair is gone there!"

"What happened to it, *Fala?*"

"I got sick when I was staying with the People at the Back of the Land at Minto Inlet." She laughed, finding it amusing that such a thing could happen to a man.

Naoyak moved closer to where I sat on the *iglek* and rubbed my bald head as some pitchers do a baseball before they wind up for the throw. "It feels like the breasts of my mother!" she smiled. Then, without prompting, added with a sweet shyness, "*Fala*, give me your boots. I'll put them on the rack to dry."

With serious mien she beat each boot with the *anaotak* (a stick used to remove snow) and placed them above the blubber lamp to dry. Turning to Kablunak, she said solicitously, "*Fala*

331

must be hungry. I'll fill the pan with meat and fish, and call the people to eat."

"That's fine! Everything is ready! Go and call everyone for tea."

The response to Naoyak's musical "*Teatorithe!*" was immediate. Kakagun, Nokadlak, Kudnanak, and Naodluak hurried in. Behind them, leaning forward to counteract the weight on her back, shuffled in Angivrana. She had aged visibly and tiredness was apparent in her every step.

"My Little Boy is heavy," she explained to me with a smile, despite her burden.

"When was the Little Man born?" I asked her.

"Last spring during the caribou hunt," she said proudly. "His name is Angun." Knowing that *angun* meant a man in his prime, I replied, "That's a good omen. Perhaps he will be as great a hunter as his father!"

Honored by the comparison, Nokadlak beamed and added his own prediction, "My son Angun will kill many musk-oxen and maybe bears, too!"

Perhaps because I was only too conscious of my bald pate, I quickly noticed that the hair on top of Nokadlak's head now almost concealed the deep scars left there by *akhak*, the bear, as the permanent reminders of his close brush with death. However, his friend Kakagun, our host, promptly diverted everyone's attention to me, his guest, "*Fala*, drink some hot tea, eat, and rest yourself!" His normal adult voice had strangely changed to a deep and raucous sound in the intervening years.

Naoyak placed a basin full of frozen fish and caribou meat on the floor of the igloo, where everyone could help themselves and then made the rounds with mugs of hot tea. Biting eagerly into the meat, my friends began to stuff themselves to full capacity. What they couldn't get into their mouths, they cut off with upward strokes of their sharp knives or with the half-moon-shaped *ulon*. A large pot of caribou broth, brought in by Kablunak, completed the filling meal. I had been sampling the victuals in silence along with the rest, studying my friends after our lengthy separation. Somehow I couldn't help feeling the void left by the Grandmother's death.

"When did Manerathiak die?" I couldn't resist asking Nokadlak.

"It's two or three years since she died—during the summer. She was getting too old and useless."

Characteristically an Eskimo's description of the passage of time was vague. If Manerathiak had died the previous year, Nokadlak would probably have said "*aipagane*" or possibly *"ukkior"* (winter), since the Arctic year is mostly a long winter, anyway. For a two-year period or so, he'd use the word *"aypago,"* and for the distant past *"ignilrat."* To fix an Eskimo's past date with any degree of accuracy was difficult at best.

And just as the past, so the distant future doesn't really interest the average Eskimo either. If he has to set a date for tomorrow, he'll accurately say *"arkago,"* or for the day after tomorrow it'll be *"arkagoago."* But for a few weeks or months ahead he'll use less definite expressions like *"opingrakhak,"* i.e. before spring; *"aoyakhak,"* before summer; *"ukkiakhak,"* before winter; *"opingrame,"* during the spring; *"aoyame,"* during the summer; and *"ukkiame,"* during the winter. To an Eskimo that's patently close enough for all concerned. Perhaps the most typical Eskimo word for the indefinite future is *"illani,"* which translates into "some day in the future." But, then, who can or wants to delve precisely into the unpredictable unknown, anyway?

"What happened to Manerathiak, Nokadlak?"

"Who knows? We had pitched our tents at the mouth of the Hiorkretak River. It was a rainy, windy morning. Manerathiak walked along the shore towards the cliffs overlooking the bay. She did not come back."

"And you don't know where she went?"

Everyone stared at me in astonishment. Nokadlak chuckled, "She went to the top of the highest cliff facing the sea. The weather was stormy. The waves angry and high. She simply disappeared, *Fala.*"

"That's too bad!" I commiserated. "Grandmother Manerathiak certainly knew the way of your ancestors. She was a true Krangmalek woman!"

After that eulogy no one mentioned her name anymore.

"Kuptana, the wife of Haala, died too," volunteered Kablunak. "You remember, *Fala,* she had a bad sore behind her ear? She died at Taheriuak during the winter. "It's truly hopeless."

Kakagun put a prompt end to these mournful recollections by asking, "Where did you travel, *Fala?* Whom did you see? What have you done since you left Burnside?"

I sensed that a long evening was in store for me. Many more questions would be asked as my friends were starved for news. But I didn't really mind that, having propped myself against my sleeping bag on the *iglek,* content to be out of the bitter cold and comfortable in the relative warmth of the igloo. I began to fill them in on a few highlights of the intervening years.

"After my visit with you at Kubiortorvik, *Fala* Delalande came from Coppermine to tell me that I was needed at Minto

Inlet where dwell the People at the Back of the Land. Before spring an airplane came and flew me to a place called Big Skull. *Fala* Buliard was sick there, so the big bird carried him back to the distant Land of the White Men.

"Among the people I met at Big Skull were Nokadlaaluk and his wife Oviluk. Because they had been starving, they ate the dead bodies of their friends to survive. At Kagneriuak I got to know an Alaskan Eskimo named Natkusiak, whom the White Men called Billy Banksland. A great traveler, Natkusiak guided the Stefansson expeditions around Banks Island and beyond. On Banks Island where the winter nights are very long, there are many polar bears and seals. Seals are usually so plentiful there that the sea ice is covered with them as they lie basking in the sun. But that spring's end the ice cracks appeared surprisingly late on the frozen sea, so we all came very close to starving. That's when I got sick and lost my hair, as you can see." My listeners nodded understandingly. "Now there are only a few caribou left inland and they are very small," I continued. "All the musk-oxen are gone. They died long ago when the rains came and froze on the land, covering the grass with a mantle of ice and leaving nothing for them to eat. It's a good place for foxes and hares, though. But I wouldn't like to live there, for it's always cold and the great wind storms blow across the land day after day.

"About that time, when I was with the People at the Back of the Land at a place called Krasingortarvik, there was a lake nearby full of big red fish. That's were Naneroak killed his brother Kapulak."

"I know Naneroak," cut in Kakagun. "But I don't remember his brother Kapulak. He must have been much younger than Naneroak."

"Naneroak was married, wasn't he, *Fala?*" asked Angivrana.

"Yes, but his wife died a long time ago. She had adopted a young girl and Naneroak brought her up."

"Why did Naneroak kill Kapulak?" Kakagun wanted to know.

"The brothers were visiting their trap line when a storm arose. They built an igloo and stayed in it for three days. On the third night Kapulak had a bad dream. Still half-asleep, he tried to kill Naneroak with an axe. It is said they fought for the axe. Naneroak managed to get hold of it and stunned his brother with a blow on the head. Kapulak did not recover. He died before morning."

"Did you see Kapulak's body, *Fala?*" asked Nokadlak.

Yes, I did. One day as I came out of my igloo I saw a *krepik* (sleeping bag) lying on the snow on the riverbank, not far away. I went over to it to satisfy my curiosity. Inside, on his back, with his knees bent, lay Kapulak, dead and frozen."

"Naneroak told you how he died?"

"Yes, Nokadlak. He said his brother's forehead turned soft where he hit him with the axe, and he died during the night."

"Did you say Naneroak is still living with his adopted daughter?" Kakagun asked me pointedly.

"I did. They are always together, but they stay away from other people. When I left, they had moved to Lake Niarkronasuk." Everyone laughed understandingly. It was time to change the topic.

"One summer day," I continued, "I noticed many round hillocks just behind my house. Because I didn't know what they were, I asked Nokadlaaluk if he knew.

"Long, long ago," he explained, "Inuit came here from where the sun goes down at the end of the day. They built igloos of driftwood and covered them with peat moss. Later they moved away towards the rising sun."

"To satisfy my inquisitive nature, I dug out some of the mounds. Under them I found arrow and harpoon heads made of copper and some made of chipped stones; also needles, scrappers made of bones, skulls of musk-ox and caribou. Nokadlaaluk said that long ago men and women lived there in great numbers."

"What else did you do, *Fala*?" Kablunak inquired.

"I often visited the trading post at Fort Collinson in Walker Bay. The White Man trader there was Jack Kilgour.

He must have been lonely, because he went away to his land and married a White Woman. When they returned, he began to trade with the Seal People. One day he took his wife out in a kayak. But he didn't know how to paddle it, and he drowned. His wife was saved by the Inuit.

"At Fort Collinson I also saw the R.C.M.P. schooner *St. Roch*, which was wintering there. Christmas came and the policemen on the boat were homesick, missing their wives and children. But *Falas* Buliard and Delalande arrived by dog team from Coppermine and brought them mail from their families. There was jubilation on the schooner and Captain Henri Larsen was very happy for his crew."

My Eskimo friends smiled. They, too, seemed happy and relaxed. More tea was served by Kablunak while Naoyak went into the snow porch and returned with large slabs of dry meat and caribou fat.

After exchanging several minor experiences with them, I recounted my near-drowning when crossing the Minto Inlet in

335

my jolly boat. "I was returning from the trading post at Fort Collinson with some supplies. When I reached the middle of the inlet, a big storm suddenly struck, raising huge waves that drove my helpless boat to the entrance of the inlet. Late in the evening, when I had almost given up hope of survival, the merciful Great Spirit tossed me ashore at a place called Hikoshuilak. The boat had been full of water and I was soaking wet and very cold. But I was lucky, for I saw people running towards me. They were old friends from Banks Island: David Bernard, Andrew and Bob Diamond, Ikey Bolt, George Porter, Sam Carter, Edna Klinkenberg, and their families. I forget their Eskimo names. They were skilled half-breed trappers—their fathers were White Men—and I'm sure you've heard of them all. So astonished were they to see me emerge from the mountainous waves, they first took me for some spirit rising from the sea. When they discovered it was me, they displayed their excitement with such peculiar expressions as "Be very happy, *Fala* has returned from the dead!"

"I left Minto Inlet that summer for Holman Island were *Fala* Buliard was building the Mission of Christ, the King, and I helped him for a while. The trading post, too, was moved from Fort Collinson, Holman Island. Then a new trader arrived. His name was Bill Calder, but he didn't know that Inuit children had nicknamed him Biscuit, because he frequently gave them biscuits covered with jam.

Naoyak, who now sat with Kablunak, laughed heartily and murmured audibly to her, "What a name to give a Man!"

"From Uluksartok I went back to Cambridge Bay. I stayed there only one winter, because I had to visit the people along the coast of Victoria Land at Wellington Bay and also at Richardson Island. Everyone there was hungry that winter. The caribou had not come and great snowstorms kept the men inside their igloos for days and days. Many dogs died of starvation and the people promptly ate them. It was at Richardson Island that I heard the story of two children who changed into thunder and lightning. It was told by Niptanatiak who had married a women from King William Land. Would you like to hear it?"

"Yes, *Fala*," said Nokadlak for the rest, "Tell us the story!"

"Long ago, there were two children, a brother and a sister. They had been abandoned by their parents and nobody cared about them. Thus, when the time came for the people of the village to move across a big river, they left them behind to die. The children sat on the shore and cried because they were alone and hungry. Then they decided to search the old camp for food and anything that might be of some use to them. All they found was a firestone and a piece of caribou skin with its fur shaved off.

336

The children didn't know what to do with their find, although they thought about it for a long time. Finally the boy said, 'I have an idea! Why don't we change from human beings into something else? What do you think of that, little sister?'

"The girl pondered the idea before answering, 'I'd like to be a caribou cow.'

" 'No, no!' her brother protested. 'You'd soon be killed by a hunter!'

" 'Then I would like to be a seal.'

" 'Silly girl! You'd soon be eaten by the bear!'

"They thought of many other animals, but remembered they were all hunted by man. Then the sister said brightly, 'I know what I'd really want to be—thunder or lightning!'

" 'Ah, that's much better!' her brother readily agreed.

"So they changed into Thunder and Lightning, two mighty Spirits of the Sky. By striking the firestone, the sister produced huge sparks of lightning, while her brother beat the stretched piece of dry caribou skin like a taut drum, thus creating great noises and lights that were heard and seen by people below. The siblings then moved across the river, stopped over the camp of those who had abandoned them, and made so much thunderous noise and sent down so many lightning sparks that all the people in the camp died. Eventually when some travelers arrived on the scene, they found lifeless men, women, children, and dogs in various sitting or lying positions, but they couldn't understand why they had all died. Mysteriously, too, when they tried to move the corpses, they fell to pieces.

"That is the way, 'tis said, that the Inuit discovered that the Spirits of the Air cannot be trusted."

"*Fala*, I heard this story a long time ago when I was a child and my parents lived on the Back River," Kablunak recollected. Feeling that her frank disclosure wasn't intended to deter me from continuing my account of recent experiences, I continued, "From Richardson Island I visited the people of Kidlinek (at the Far end of Kent Peninsula). It was spring then and I was traveling with Kununahuk. You all know him because he came from Taheriuak. Anyway, we got lost for four days in the thick fog of Melville Sound." If someone had thrown a cream pie in my face I don't think my audience would have laughed more heartily. When their merriment subsided, Angivrana said comfortingly, "Everybody gets lost once in a while in our land, *Fala.*"

"That's right," agreed her husband. "A man should never travel alone for long distances. Anything can happen to him on a long trip. He might get hurt. His dogs might run away. Or the Spirits of the Land could try to mislead him."

"But I wasn't alone, Nokadlak. I had Kununahuk with me."

"I know, *Fala*, but Kununahuk has always been as useless as a blind woman and wouldn't be able to help you find the way."

"You may be right, Nokadlak. In fact, when I told him we were lost, he almost stopped eating for a couple of days. Instead he kept repeating, 'What will happen to us? We cannot see anything round us. The Spirits are against us. They have put the land to sleep in the white night of the fog and silence. Whatever will betide us?!' "

"What did happen to you, *Fala?*" asked Angivrana out of genuine concern.

"One evening, as I tried to fall asleep, Kununahuk went out of the igloo. Shortly after I heard several rifle shots. I ran outside to see what was going on. Rifle in hand, he was standing on the sled, looking around and listening. I asked him what he was shooting at. He said, 'At the spirits, *Fala*. I heard them whispering! At first I thought of shooting you because you are a Kablunak and the Spirits don't like White Men. Then I heard them talking to each other and laughing. So I fired my rifle to make a loud noise and scare them off. You see, now they're gone!' "

My listeners nodded approval of Kununahuk's behavior as Nokadlak expressed their consensus, "He could not do anything else!"

"But he did do something else!" I retorted. "He was so scared during the night that he relieved himself in my frying pan. When the resultant smell woke me up, I asked him, 'What did you do that for? Why didn't you step outside!'

"His reply was, 'Because I was afraid,' "

"He should have put that frying pan outside. Its smell would have kept every Spirit away from your igloo!"

They all laughed appreciatively at Nokadlak's wise crack. But he further surprised me by conceding amiably, "Maybe you were right, *Fala.*"

"How did you find your way again?" Kakagun wanted to know.

"When the fog slowly lifted on the following day, I took my rifle and climbed the nearest hill. In the distance I recognized a place called Mallehiorvik where I could see an igloo and dogs," I told him.

"You see, Kununahuk was smart," concluded Kakagun. "Sometimes, when we stand up to them, the Spirits fear us and depart. Whenever I hear a murmur or a hum of conversation coming from the land, I throw rocks around or shoot the air with my rifle. Other times I sing the magic song of the *tunrak* (sorcerer):

> O Spirit, take a good look, a long look at me!
> I am not afraid of a worm, a creeping worm,
> Hungry for my blood, gnawing at my flesh.
> You are like a Fox—afraid of Man.
> O Spirit, Spirit, Bad Spirit of the Land,
> You're like a ground Squirrel afraid of a Child.

During the three days I spent at the rapids, the men didn't bother with their trap lines. They busied themselves skinning the foxes they had caught earlier and drying their pelts, stretched on a wooden frame, above the blubber lamp. Between their other household chores, Angivrana and Kablunak worked on their clothes and fancy trimmings for their parkas and boots. When curiosity over their feverish activity got the better of me, I asked Kablunak where they were getting ready to go.

"Didn't Kakagun tell you, *Fala?* We've decided to go to the trading post with you."

So that was it! I had casually mentioned that I wanted to be back at Burnside before Christmas, and now I was going to have plenty of company all the way. "That's very good news, Kablunak! Traveling alone isn't much fun. Besides, I wouldn't like to get caught in the fog all by myself! By the way, your new clothes look very pretty, and I hope you will have a good time at the Post!"

All the while Naoyak followed me about the camp like a friendly kitten. "Why don't you play with Naodluak?" I asked her.

"I like to play with him. But he is always hunting ptarmigans along the riverbanks with Kudnanak."

"Won't they take you hunting with them?"

"No, *Fala.* Naodluak says I am too young. He says it's dark most of the time now. The spirits might take me away into the mountains."

"Never mind, Naoyak. The boys will be back soon and maybe Naodluak will play with you then. In the meantime, let's visit Angivrana. You can take care of her baby while she is sewing."

"No!" she replied adamantly, puckering her nose. "I'll play with Naodluak when he comes back."

Before I could utter another word, she turned and scampered off like caribou fawn towards Kakagun's igloo. On impetus I followed her in. The unexpected scene is still vivid in my mind. Crowding her adoptive mother Kablunak, trying to get at her breasts, Naoyak kept repeating, "I want a drink!"

"You're a big girl now, Naoyak. You don't need my milk anymore, like a newborn child," the woman said patiently.

Sitting cross-legged on the *iglek*, Kakagun stopped skinning a white fox he had in his lap long enough to tease the youngster, "Naoyak may be a girl, but she is more like the calf of a musk-ox. All she wants is milk, milk!"

Ignoring her adoptive Father, Naoyak resumed her plea, "Let me drink, Mother!"

In the end it was Kablunak who gave in. "There it is!" she said reluctantly. Her breast was surprisingly round and firm for a woman who apparently had not had any children for several years. "Or were they perhaps all girls?" I asked myself.

As if she had read my mind, Kablunak sighed and mused aloud "I had a girl. Kakagun promised her to a hunter. I wonder where she is now."

Her thirst manifestly quenched, Naoyak resumed playing with Kablunak's breast as if it were a toy, drawing this smiling protest, "What have I done to you that you should bother me when I am so busy getting ready to leave tomorrow?"

Naoyak chose not to answer, but presently stopped her play, put on her mitts, and announced, "I'm going out to see if Naodluak is coming."

Kablunak and Kakagun took her whims in their stride. In fact, their composure never wavered. They remained ever cheerful and gentle with her. Marveling at their unfailing patience, I said to them, "Naoyak has changed a lot since I saw you people last, but in some ways she is still a child."

"She doesn't cry so much now, *Fala*," Kablunak said kindly. "She is learning to be a woman."

"Sometimes she still wakes up at night, but she is better now," acknowledged Kakagun.

"Did she keep you awake much before?"

"Yes, after her sickness at Kubiartorvik, she used to wake up often, whimpering and even screaming. At first we wondered if she had pains. Then we found she wanted hot broth. So Kablunak would get up, light the lamp, and put the pot with broth over it."

"Then I'd crawl back into the *krepik* and wait for the frozen broth to melt and warm up. It was cold going back and forth," Kablunak admitted.

"Do the White Men try to please their children as we do?" Kakagun asked me.

"Not as much. Some White parents even spank their kids when they keep asking for impossible things or do not listen to them."

"We leave them alone," Kablunak said. "That is the way of our forefathers."

Moments later Naoyak bounced in excitedly. "Naodluak and Kudnanak are coming! They're crossing the river. Come and see!"

When neither Kakagun nor Kablunak stirred from their work, I stepped outside to humor the girl. Moonlight glittered off the ice on the river and off every snow-covered slope and ridge. Sharp gusts of an icy wind from the east tore across the unearthly stillness, whipping up a gossamer curtain of snow. Nothing moved around the camp except for an occasional puppy that wandered with its tail signaling friendship among the motionless dogs strapped to the line.

"There they are, *Fala*!" Naoyak pointed towards two moving shadows on the glare ice mid-way across the half-mile-wide river delta. Between snow curtains I could see them sliding expertly over the treacherous surface, despite the bulging hunting bags on their bent shoulders.

We walked towards them slowly and cautiously along the sloping bank. When only a hundred yards remained between us, Naoyak ran out to greet them. "You have killed many ptarmigans!" she exclaimed with radiant admiration. The young hunters acknowledged her compliment with ready smiles.

"We went up to the large willow patch behind the rapids. We found many birds there and we killed all we could," said Kudnanak. "It was cold, but it was fun!" Naodluak, to whom Naoyak was promised, added cheerfully.

"Let me see what you got," Naoyak insisted, prancing around the two youthful hunters.

"Wait till we get inside," Naodluak said firmly, and the girl did not repeat her request.

Kudnanak walked off to his father's igloo as I followed Naodluak and Naoyak into theirs. "It's cold up the river," said Naodluak, as he deposited his heavy bag near the blubber lamp and flicked the hoarfrost off his light eyebrows. Naoyak dipped impatiently into the bag and brought out a white ptarmigan, chubby but smaller than a grouse. She held it up for all to admire.

"I'll make my good hunter some tea and we will eat the gizzards of the ptarmigans" said Kablunak. "Give me your parka. I'll place it on the rack to dry."

We all sat down on the *iglek* and began to strip the ptarmigans. It was an easy task. We made incisions under their tails to help pull off their skins and feathers in a continuous motion toward their heads. Then we extracted the birds' innards

341

and put them aside to be fed to the dogs later. Only the gizzards were placed in a bowl for immediate consumption. The remaining parts, including the birds' heads, would be kept for future snacks. Cups of hot tea were passed around as we helped ourselves to the gizzards, first ridding them of half-digested willow buds with our knives. Their thick, muscular walls and tough lining sounded like crackers under our teeth.

"You must have shot many ptarmigans, eh?" Kakagun suggested to Naodluak.

"We should have bagged more. But we ran short of ammunition. There were many hare and fox tracks, too. We will go after them tomorrow."

"Tomorrow, if the weather is good, we're all going with *Fala* to the trading post."

"Fine! I have a few foxes I can trade for ammunition. And maybe we will see some friends there."

"You can get me some candy, Naodluak!" Naoyak hinted coyly.

Out of my insatiable curiosity I asked Kakagun if he had lately seen the White Man who used to live at the bottom of Baillie Bay on the old campsite of Kattimanek, about five miles from the mouth of the Hood River. Little was known about him except that his name was "Ship" Leonard and that he had arrived alone aboard his schooner from the West to trap in this region. I'll never forget what happened only hours after I first met this Norwegian at Coppermine two years before. He had come by dog team to get his mail—which was brought to Coppermine once a year, during the first week of January—from Yellowknife by bush pilot Ernie Boffa. "Ship" Leonard strode into the Mission that afternoon to relax for the rest of the day with Fathers Delalande, Le Mer, and me. After supper, "Frenchy" Chartrand and Corporal "Red" Abraham of the local Mountie Detachment likewise dropped in for a chat and a few drinks (which were also delivered by the mail plane) to help us celebrate belatedly the start of another New Year. Then a few trappers and traders, including "Big Slim" Semmler, Art Watson, and Bill Storrs, unexpectedly appeared on our doorstep. They were already feeling no pain. In short, almost the entire allowable supply of whisky was consumed that night to the accompaniment of some pretty tough, tall tales.

Well after midnight, for no special reason, "Ship" Leonard challenged "Frenchy" Chartrand to an arm wrestling contest. That was when the trouble began. Both men were over six feet tall and powerfully built. They strained, groaned, and swore in a surprisingly even match-up. Suddenly, "Ship" Leonard somehow

342

lost his balance and fell to the floor, yelling something incomprehensible in his Scandinavian tongue. Everyone guffawed. But "Ship" neither smiled, nor laughed. He rose grim-faced and went after "Frenchy" with his fists. The policeman wasn't about to back away. He counterattacked, outyelling his opponent in native French, "*Mon cochon* (my pig), I'll show YOU, *mon cochon!*"

The rest of the men didn't interfere for a while, blatantly enjoying the battle between the two white giants. Finally Corporal Abraham asked the onlookers to help him break up the combatants. By then our kitchen was a thorough mess, with broken glasses, bottles, china, and ashtrays littering the floor.

Eventually, when both "Ship" and "Frenchy" had calmed down, Father Delalande formally proposed a toast for a Happy New Year. Everyone shook hands and "Frenchy" even hugged "Ship," patting him on his back with "No hard feelings, *mon vieux* (my old friend). Compliments of the season to you!"

They were all basically good men and true—the real toughs of the Far North—who knew how to share comradeship and who brought a measure of benevolence to an otherwise cruel land.

"I have not seen the Kablunak you call "Ship" Leonard since last summer," Kakagun told me. "But I heard he is trapping far inland along the Hood River hills."

343

21

Christmas At Burnside

"We'll take the short cut to Portage Bay," Kakagun proposed as we prepared to leave camp by the light of the morning stars. The wind had dropped during the night, but it was still raw and cold on the sled. On the bleak, desolate land itself there was truly nothing to cheer the human soul. But one had only to glance at the heavens above to be fascinated by nature's indescribably beautiful shimmering curtains of colorful lights made all the brighter by the exceptional clarity of the Arctic air.

Kakagun took the lead, followed by Nokadlak's team and mine. Naodluak sat next to me, apparently pleased to be on the move again. Almost at once we began to climb. When we reached the first plateau above the Hood River, Naodluak doffed his outer parka, retaining the inner one. "It is warmer here," he said. "It's always colder down by the river."

"I've noticed that, too. You know why? Because cold air is heavier than warm air and flows down the mountain slopes to take the place of the warm air going up, settling in the valleys." Whether he understood me or not, Naodluak readily agreed, adding, "Sometimes when I visit my trap line I feel colder in the coves and narrow inlets than on the hills around them. It's like going outside from a warm igloo."

Towards noon we gained the summit of the portage at about 1,050 feet. We rested our dogs while we made tea behind blocks of snow which served us as a temporary shelter against the cold air and a nagging ground wind. Around us was a scene of winter desolation on a grand scale. Far below to the southwest, the frozen Hood River—to all appearances like a sleeping white serpent—hid its head in a rocky canyon of the coastal hills. Beyond them to the northwest the silvery ice of the Arctic Sound stretched to the bleakness that was Cheere Islands. To the north lay Aligak, Iglooruak (Like a Big Igloo), Kanuyak (Copper), and the Ikalulik (There Are Fish) Islands of the Barry Islands group at the entrance of the Bathurst Inlet. To the east the Umikmatok Hills formed the backdrop across this inlet. Down below to the southeast we could discern Portage Bay, and beyond it the bluffs, shielding the ice-bound Kiluitok region around Bathurst Lake. Except for us and our dogs, the drifting snow, and the moaning wind, nothing moved or uttered a sound in the dusky twilight of the polar night.

Kakagun finished his tea and dry meat, surveyed the elements, and pronounced, "Hilla, the Spirit of the Air, is disturbed. I can hear Narhuk, the Storm Child, weeping with the drifting snow. Come, let us move! Burnside is still far away."

The descent was dangerous. We rode the crests of eroded hills with gaping half-snow-filled canyons on both sides. Once Kakagun missed the trail. To avoid backtracking, we would have to go down a steep slope to a rocky creek below. After a brief consultation with Nokadlak, Kakagun told Kablunak, his wife, to hold the dogs while he pulled the sled to the edge of the incline. It balanced there for a moment, then started to slide backwards downhill, gathering momentum and dragging the scrambling dogs after it. Kakagun promptly dropped to the snow and slid alongside on his posterior. He came safely to rest at the frozen creek just as the sled ploughed into a snowbank. Helped by Kudnanak, Nokadlak sent his sled down backwards in like fashion, and I did the same while Naodluak held my dogs. Our huskies yapped excitedly at this unaccustomed maneuver, but they and their sleds all managed to land unscathed.

"Come down! It's your turn," Kakagun shouted to Kablunak who stood hesitantly with Naoyak at her side. The girl descended first. She was doing well until the halfway mark, when she lost her balance, turned over and rolled the rest of the way like a sack of flour. Kudnanak and Naodluak in particular thought it a grand joke, infecting everyone with their laughter. "Now you look like a small white bear," they teased her. Evidently none-the-worse for the surprise experience, Naoyak extricated herself from the snowdrift that ended her progress, stood up, and laughed good-humoredly with the rest.

Gallantly Kakagun offered to climb up and help the women navigate the tricky slide, but Nokadlak put him off with a smile, "Let them try. They can't get hurt."

With the baby still asleep in her hood, Angivrana squatted down, pulled the back of her long parka forward between her legs, held the hem tightly, and was off. She negotiated the course so well that Kablunak seemed to gain added courage. But it still took a little urging on her husband's part before she cautiously lay down on her back and skidded downwards, braking with her outstretched arms. As soon as she reached the bottom of the incline, she lifted her long parka and brushed off the snow that had accumulated on her breeches up to her waist, all the while smiling and repeating "It's cold! It's cold!"

Late in the evening we finally reached the Burnside Post. Tiny lights from the domes of five igloos built in the deep snowdrift of the channel's bank outlined the campsite, but the Hudson's Bay Company's buildings were totally dark. The resident dogs had already announced our arrival, but kept howling in unison for an added reason. Not far off, toward the Burnside River, we could hear the unmistakable long, mournful wails of wolves.

Since the wind was rising into a storm, I left my friends with the other natives and hurried to the Mission. My sled dogs lay down thankfully to rest as I removed their harnesses and attached them to the line. I fed them dried fish and blubber, then went into the house. It was like an ice cavern! I lit the two coal stoves and in due time their warmth made itself felt throughout the small building. In the interim I warmed my inner self with several cups of steaming coffee in the little kitchen. There, too, I found a heartwarming note from Father Delalande, written in his beautiful, witty French, "My dear traveler, now that you are back home, after burning many icy trails, you are entitled to a good rest. I have made some apple pies for you (sorry, with dried apples only!), as well as a bunch of French loaves (I mean with a little French taste in them, if you still remember what it's like). You'll find them on the shelves in the porch. Do give them a try! Also, I left a bottle of wine with the new Hudson's Bay trader, Leo Manning, for your Christmas Mass. It's not strong enough to be left here in the cold, you know! I hope Leo didn't fall for it and toast all the Irish saints in the meantime. Keep up the good work and God bless you! Happy Christmas!

P.S. I'll be at Coppermine until spring, then on the trail again.

I savored the friendly message several times, but couldn't think of any means to thank Father Delalande for his thoughtfulness. So I prayed for his continued good health and happiness before turning in for the night.

I was getting things straightened around in the forenoon when Leo Manning, whom I had never met before, came over from the trading post. We shook hands warmly and settled down in the kitchen for a chat. He was a handsome man in his mid-thirties with a kind, smiling face and light-blue eyes. His outstanding feature, I thought, was his curly, golden blond hair.

"I'm the new trader, Father," he introduced himself simply in unmistakable Irish accents. "I came last summer from the Eastern Arctic. I like it here."

"So did your predecessor, Billy Joss, whom I knew. Have you any idea where he might be now?"

"He was transferred to the trading post at Read Island on Dolphin and Union Strait."

"Father Delalande thoughtfully left me a note in which he gave me your name. That's why I wasn't surprised when you came."

"He's a fine man, full of fun! I'm of your faith, Father, and I would like to know what you might have in mind for Christmas. If you need any help, I'll gladly serve at the Midnight Mass."

"Wonderful! For a real change I won't be alone to perform the service."

"If you'll pardon a personal remark, I can tell you are French, but your accent is different from Father Delalande's."

"That's probably because Father Delalande hails from Paris, while I came from the island of Corsica. And what about you, Leo?"

"Oh me? I was born in Ireland at a little place called Mulrany, on the west coast. I came to Canada as an apprentice for the Hudson's Bay Company. I was only sixteen years old at the time. And, you know, Father, to this day I can't figure out why they gave me this job, me being Irish Catholic and they strong Protestants!" he said, laughing. Then added, "Well, I must be getting back to the store. The natives are anxious to trade their furs. Besides, I'm sure you've lots to do, too, after your long absence. I just thought I'd pop over and make your acquaintance; and I'm glad I did."

As Leo Manning was leaving, I asked him if he still had the bottle of wine Father Delalande had left with him for the Midnight Mass. "I surely do!" he answered with a smile.

"In that case, Leo, if you don't mind, I'll pick it up this afternoon and we can then decide what to do for tomorrow's Midnight Mass."

Outside a strong wind was raising curtains of snow across the land. Hilla, the Malevolent Spirit, was taking charge of his domain. I could tell by listening to the distant rumbling of the wind in the hills above the Burnside River that a major storm was approaching. It was that time of the year when the last throes of the struggle between the sea and the cold air usually took place. The energy involved in these atmospheric conflicts was enormous. Freezing winds, moving from the Heart Mountains and the two-mile thick ice cap of Greenland, roared down to the vacuum created by the rising warmer air of the Arctic Ocean. Normally the titanic struggle would be over by mid-January. With the ocean frozen, the blustering tempests would arise less frequently, giving the intense cold full dominion over the land and sea.

Leo Manning was in the kitchen when I knocked on his door. "Come in, please, Father! Only a White Man knocks on the door in this country," he smiled his welcome as I entered. "How would you like to start with a wee celebration? I have some pretty fair stuff in my bedroom," he offered when we sat down.

While he was gone, I glanced about from my kitchen seat. The house had not undergone any visible changes since trader Billy Joss was its occupant. Adjacent to the kitchen and separated by an arch was the combined dining and living area. A table and chairs still occupied center stage while under a wide window a sofa and an end table continued to grace the rest of the room. At its far end a door led to the bedroom.

"Here's something special you might enjoy, Father," my host said on return as he poured generous amounts of the bottled liquid into two glasses. "I'd like your opinion of it."

I took a sip, coughed involuntarily, and blurted, "Boy, oh boy! That's really good and strong!"

"Aye, so it is," my host agreed with deep satisfaction.

"What is this potent potion, Leo?"

"It's a whisky we Irishmen call poteen. Look in your glass. What do you see? Just pure white mountain dew from the Old Country! My Ma used to give us kids a shot of it in the winter before we left for school After Pa died, she kept stilling poteen in our cellar, hiding it from the Royal Irish Constabulary and Excise Tax collectors, so she could sell it to the good Catholics of the parish and help keep our bodies and souls together."

"Your poteen reminds me of a liqueur my parents served after dinner when I was home in Corsica. But they gave us children tastes of it soaked in lumps of sugar. No wonder they called it a *canard*, which in French can mean either a duck or a hoax! That delicious brandy was made from distilled crushed grapes and was usually referred to as *eau-de-vie*, or water of life."

Since Leo was in no rush to get back to his store, I told him what I had in mind for the Midnight Mass and asked him if he could play a small organ I had in the Chapel. "Not too well,

Father, but likely well enough to please the audience," he chuckled.

I ran back to the Mission with the bottle of wine for the Mass, keeping an eye on the flickering light of the Coleman lamp in the living room window, as the storm had increased noticeably in violence. Kakagun, Nokadlak, their wives and children had meantime made themselves comfortable there, some of them resting on the floor, their backs pressed against the wall, others sitting on benches provided for visitors. A tin of tobacco was being passed around, each guest rolling his or her own cigarette.

"It's drifting hard!" I panted.

"Yes, yes!" They repeated in unison, "*Pirkrilertok!*"

I asked Kablunak if she would like to make some tea in the kitchen. Naoyak went with her. With the help of Naodluak and Kudnanak I took out a big basin of thawed fish for the dogs. Blurred outlines emerged like threatening shadows in the drifting snow. My faithful four-legged friends of many travels and lonely days were glad to get their rations. We hurried back to the warmth and comfort of the Mission house. Mugs of tea and a bowl of sugar were waiting for us on the living room table. From the porch I brought in a case of Scandinavian hardtack, pilote bread, and a can of jam. As we ate, I told my friends that the following night we would have a special Church service and that food would be served to all comers immediately after. I asked them if they knew any of the people living in the igloos down the channel. Kakagun answered for the rest, "Kirluayok, the sorcerer, came with some people from Aniarhiurvik at the end of the inlet. They will visit you tomorrow. You know them all, *Fala.*"

Little Naoyak came and sat beside me. I hugged her and asked if she was enjoying herself with all her new friends. "Yes, yes," she beamed. "We played all morning with the pups and slid on the bank of the channel. But the wind became too strong. We had to go back to the igloos. Men and women were visiting each other and telling stories. Then we all went to the trading post. Kablunak got me a pair of scissors, needles, and calico. She will teach me how to make a dress to cover my parka."

"Do you remember any of the stories you heard, Naoyak?"

Nokadlak promptly answered for his natural daughter, "Come on, come on! Tell *Fala* the story of the two hares who were attacked by *Orkpik* (an owl). You laughed when the woman told it to us, remember?"

"Yes, yes, I'll tell it to *Fala*. There was a big owl who was tired of eating little lemmings. One day he went hunting for bigger game. Just as he flew above the side of the hill, he saw two hares rubbing each other's noses. 'At last,' the Owl said to himself, 'I'm going to have a really good meal!' As he dived down on the hares, he grasped one in each claw. The hares were very frightened. In fear they leaped in opposite directions and pulled the owl's legs apart until his body split in two and he dropped dead.

" 'That's what happens,' the woman who told us the story said, 'to people who are too greedy.' "

Everyone laughed at Naoyak's retelling of it, and more tea was passed around to everybody.

Suddenly a great howling of dogs was heard above the turbulent storm, followed by enthusiastic shouts of "Travelers, travelers, many of them!"

Keen to welcome the new arrivals, my friends ran down to the channel towards them, but I couldn't even see them in the pelting snow. Yet, mixed in with the doleful cries of the dogs, I could hear unmistakable human wailing—the travelers' customary way of announcing the recent death of a relative when they approach a native settlement. Traditionally, too, the camp's inhabitants joined in by shouting the name of the dead one whose soul might still be wandering in search of a living being to carry on the deceased's name.

Two sliding doors separated our large living room from the small Chapel. On each door panel Father Adam had masterfully painted a man-sized Angel with developed wings. The Eskimos descriptively called the Angels *Iharolik Munarhie,* the winged Guardian Spirits. Upon the platform in the center of the Chapel stood an altar with two *prie-dieu* for kneeling at prayer. Framed pictures of the Stations of the Cross adorned the walls around the room.

Kakagun and Nokadlak had asked earlier if they could use the living room for a dance on Christmas Eve. I told them they could use it whenever they wished, but that I would conduct the midnight service in the adjoining Chapel. The influx of my friends and their families began about six o'clock, possibly because I had asked them to come early to enable Kablunak and Angivrana to get a head start on cooking caribou meat and rice for serving right after the Midnight Mass. Naodluak and Kudnanak gave me a hand in transporting the loads of Arctic char from the fish house, as well as the big, pungent land-locked Arctic char which had fermented in the sand during the summer. We carried them to the porch where we sawed them into man-sized chunks for the festivities. Kakagun and Nokadlak filled two 45-gallon barrels with ice and placed them on each side of the stove to melt in anticipation of the copious consumption of tea during the long evening. In addition, I provided two crates of pilote bread, plus several cans of jam and tobacco. We had to fight every proverbial inch of the way against the wrath of the storm to get at my supplies. By the time we finished our preparations, we were understandably tired. We had just sat down to rest over cups of tea, when the first group of Eskimos came in. We shook hands and the women brought them tea. To break the silence, as well as to satisfy my curiosity, I asked the arrivals where they had come from. Their apparent leader, round-faced Kudlek, a man in the prime of life, tall and powerfully built, said agreeably, "We came down from Lake Taheriuak."

"How did you manage to find your way in the *pirtok* (snowstorm)?"

"We were lost for a while. But yesterday morning we followed a light which moved ahead of our dog teams until it came to rest in the evening above your abode. All the others in Kudlek's group nodded in their silent endorsement, while one of them, Angivralukhak, elaborated, "We saw a brilliant halo. Some Good Spirit led us to your big house, *Fala*."

Next to Angivralukhak and his wife sat a strikingly pretty young girl of about ten, who had brown hair, a white complexion, and large almond-shaped blue eyes. In her small voice she said hesitantly, "I was really frightened when I saw the moving light!"

"This is my daughter Itorkrana," Angivralukhak's wife hastened to add with pride. I didn't need a second glance at the youngster to tell that she was the image of a White Man I had known at Coppermine.

By eight o'clock most of the local natives had found their way to the Mission. They were all dressed in their very best. Their parkas were lined with trimmings of various designs, wolverine and white weasel strips adorning their sleeves. Their boots were of a silvery white caribou hide, embellished with beads and cuttings of wolverine fur. A few of the hunters haughtily wore parkas made entirely of rare dappled caribou fur, while others resembed masquerading dominoes in white and black checks. The women's fashions were even more colorful than the men's. Ingeniously their wearers had trimmed the hoods of their long parkas with gray, white, or blue wolf fur; they hung two or three white weasel furs from the bodice and the shoulders; and they wore slippers of bleached sealskin decorated with caribou fur. Additionally, the men's, women's, and children's parkas were all adorned with the same pattern that distinguished the Krangmalit from the Eastern and Western Eskimos—two half-moon strips of white caribou fur descending from the wearers' shoulders to their breasts.

To everyone's delight, trader Leo Manning arrived with a

gramophone and records, determined to teach our assembled Inuit guests the intricacies of square dancing. He was accompanied by a young Eskimo couple. I barely recognized the woman as Pokiak, the sensuous drum dancer, who uninvited came to sleep in my tent one beautiful spring evening almost four years ago when the People of the Berries had camped on the Ellice River. We shook hands, her eyes resting shyly on my face as she introduced her young man, "This is Mituk, my husband, *Fala.*" She had changed noticeably since our previous meeting, Arctic hardships and the constant exposure to its winds and merciless cold making their indelible imprint on her face, too.

Leo began by arranging men and women in couples around the room, taking the center himself with Pokiak. "Now, everybody try to do exactly what we do!" he instructed the expectant gathering in Eskimo. They all laughed at his mixed Irish-Nathilit accent, but readily emulated his and Pokiak's example to recorded background music. It was definitely a dance to remember! While the younger children sat goggle-eyed on benches backed against the walls and babies slept or cried in their mothers' hoods, Leo and Pokiak led their pupils through promenades, allemande right and left, do-si-dos, and swing your partners. They caught the spirit of the square dance with surprising rapidity. Soon Leo was able to stop demonstrating, mount a chair, and act as the caller. The older couples didn't join in the dance, being too shy to try.

Later, as everyone took time out for tea, Leo announced that the *kattuk* (big drum) was ready and Kakagun was about to start the Inuit dance. In anticipation of his forthcoming challenge, a long, hopeless shudder twisted the great hunter's frame as he began to beat the short stick against the drum's stretched skin, crying hoarsely that he would drive away Hilla, the dreaded malevolent Spirit of the Storm:

> "Aya, aya, ayhe. . .Hilla, Hilla, where are you?
> Hiding behind the hills and in the clouds?
> Hilla, Hilla, where do you run to?
> To the end of the seas, or to the heavens?
> Aya, aya, aya, ayhe. . .
>
> I know where you are,
> I know where you go,
> I know where you run,
> And I won't give you peace!
> Aya, aya, aya, ayhe, e, e, e. . ."

His voice trailed off as he seemed to debate what to do next. Then, deciding to hand the drum over to Pokiak, he urged her with, "Come on, dance!"

It was a heavy drum to handle, even for an average man, but pretty Pokiak did not seem to mind. She side-stepped towards me, bending and twisting her body with the rhythmic pounding of the drum. Her soft voice had a lulling quality as she sang:

"My heart be happy, aya, aya, ya, ya. . .
I shall never forget the tent on the frozen river
And the Little Man sleeping beside me.
And many nights did I weep
For he wasn't meant for me.
Aya, aya, ya, ya, ya, ya. . .
I'll never forget! I'll never forget!. . .

Towards midnight, as I began preparations for the Mass, Leo stopped the drummer and declared that the dance was over. Amid much hilarity most of the dancers trooped outside to cool off before the church service. We closed the partition between the two rooms in preparation for it.

While only a handful of the natives were converts, nearly every family crowded into the Mission as I tolled the steeple bell. It was one White Man's show they didn't want to miss!

Outside the wind continued to scream and howl, but as I surveyed the quiet assemblage before me in the light of the swaying kerosene lamp suspended from the ceiling, a feeling of comfort and security filled my heart. I offered a silent prayer for my friends at home and across the Barren Land. Then I spoke to the gathering before me on the meaning of Christmas and the celebration of its Mass.

My friend and erstwhile opponent Kirluayok, the sorcerer, sat in the front row, subdued but ever watchful. There was a sense of bewilderment in his eyes and many questions must have occurred to him. Who knows? I thought to myself. "There is something unique and unaccountable in the heart of every man or woman and it cannot be explored simply by taking apart his or her tissues or glands. There is a consciousness that only the Good Lord can enlighten."

Leo Manning contrived to play the little organ sufficiently well enough to receive loud, though discordant support from the unrehearsed choir. And the congregation showed its appreciation by giving the entire service quiet and undivided attention.

After the Mass a hot entree of caribou with rice, followed by frozen fermented fish, pilote bread, and jam was served to all present by Kablunak and Angivrana. Leo and I sat together meditatively sipping tea, when Pokiak unexpectedly joined us. None of us referred to the theme of her song during the earlier drum dances. Instead I politely inquired how she and her husband Mituk were doing.

"We're fine. But our baby girl died during the summer. It's truly hopeless," she sighed, then added brightly, "But I'm glad to see you again, *Fala*. Will you stay here now and not go away again?"

"I hope so, Pokiak. And some day I'll visit you and your husband. Maybe you will have a little son by then! Anyway, I'll always remember you," I smiled back.

All our Eskimo visitors having departed, Leo invited me to his place for the richest Christmas spread I'd seen since I left my Corsican home. While I shook the snow off my parka on his porch, he lighted two tall read tapers on the dining-room table to reveal a Christmas pudding, surrounded by plates of cheese, crackers, salami, olives, and cookies. Above all, there was a bottle of Chartreuse! I could not imagine how Leo knew that this was the drink my family invariably served on festive occasions. But the mere sight of the familiar wine made me homesick.

Concurrently, although he put on a good front, I sensed that Leo's mind was far, far away. Finally, he confirmed my feeling, "I guess it's silly of me to keep my cherished secret to myself. The fact is, Father, I'm in love with a wonderful girl in Winnipeg, Manitoba. We plan to be married this coming summer. Aye, that seems like a long way off at the moment. She is not of our faith, but I don't care. Her name is Mary Carpenter, and I'm sure you'll like her. After the wedding we'll come back and live here for a while."

"That sounds wonderful, Leo! Congratulations! Just keep thinking how lucky you are, and time will pass faster, you'll see! Now bring on your poteen and we'll celebrate a wonderful, beautiful Christmas!"

22

Kakagun's Traps

There were nine good reasons for my decision to spend the toughest part of the winter with my friends at their Hood River camp—my nine sled dogs. Until the caribou poured down to the sea from the tree line in May, there would be no food for my canine friends around Burnside since my Mission predecessor had not cached sufficient meat and fish supplies to last all winter. So now I had but one choice—to move in with someone who had enough victuals to go around. Fully aware that few Krangmalit hunters were as well provided as Kakagun, I told him of my intention.

"You can stay with us as long as you like, *Fala*," he replied without hesitation. "We'll get food for your dogs. And if we don't find any caribou inland, we'll hunt seals on the sea ice between visits to the trap line."

"I'll set traps, too, Kakagun, besides giving you ammunition, tea, and tobacco for any dog food you supply."

"What you want to give, *Fala*, I'll take."

Although his family and Nokadlak's had obviously enjoyed their current visit to the trading post, they seemed eager to return to their own camp and its familiar routine. Having only partially replenished their stores at the trading post, the two hunters now looked forward to the big trading session in the spring when they would have many more foxes with which to bargain for Leo Manning's merchandise and at the same time impress their fellows.

Apart from numerous fresh tracks of foxes and wolverines all over the campsite, we found the place unchanged. Nevertheless, despite burning the blubber lamp all evening, Kakagun and Kablunak were unable to warm up their igloo. "It's worn out," Kakagun concluded resignedly. "The snow blocks have turned into ice. Tomorrow I'll build a new one."

"I'll help you," I volunteered. "And attached to your igloo I'll build my own, so as not to crowd you during my stay here."

"I'm glad you are going to spend the winter with us," little Naoyak said sleepily. She was lying in the *krepik* next to Kablunak, fondling a doll I had not seen before.

"Where did you get that beautiful doll, Naoyak?" I asked.

"I bought it for her!" Naodluak, to whom the girl was promised, said proudly. "It was the only doll in the trading post." Propped up on his elbows in the sleeping bag next to mine, he lay watching the flickering flame of the lamp. Kakagun could not sleep, either. He didn't complain, curse or rebel as a White Man might under similar circumstances, but accepted the temporary discomfort as an inevitable part of life with the time-honored explanation of the People Beyond, "There is nothing one can do about it."

A dry, hollow cough bothered him, however. I asked him if he had caught a chill. "No, *Fala*. My throat is sore. It has been sore a long time. It started after a piece of fish-bone got caught in my throat."

Our breath steamed up in the cold air, condensed and fell back in snowy flakes over our *krepiks*. Restless and possibly thinking of the trapping days ahead, Kakagun began this sad, slow tune:

> All day I search for you.
> Where are you, Roamers of the Sea?
> *Aya, ya, ya, a, a, ye, e, e. . .*
> All night I search for you.
> Where are you, Roamers of the Land?
> *Aya, ya, ya. . .*
> Flee not the hunter, Beasts of the Sea,
> Beasts of the Earth!
> Don't be afraid, don't go away.
> Bring your skins and your fat flesh
> To the abode of a great hunter.
> *Aya, aya, ya, ya, a, a, ye, ye, e. . .*

His song went on unvaryingly, endlessly. It was so monotonous, it helped me fall asleep despite the cold surroundings.

Kakagun, Naodluak, and I took the better part of the morning to build a large igloo with a short passage connected to a smaller one for me. Nokadlak and Kudnanak did the same for their own families. This done, the women transferred all their household implements into the new quarters, then served us hot tea with dry meat and frozen fish. After these refreshments, while Kakagun was having a smoke, I took the opportunity to look at his throat with a flashlight. Sure enough, it had an inflamed swelling at the back. In addition each side of the sturdy neck appeared tense and swollen. But there was really nothing I could do to help Kakagun since I had no idea of what actually ailed him, nor any drugs that might benefit him. Maybe an abscess formed around a fish bone, I surmised silently, and promptly ridiculed myself, maybe, maybe. What a diagnosis!

With mixed feelings of inadequacy and superfluity I followed the hunters to their meat caches they had wrapped in caribou skins and placed on boulders out of the reach of passing predators. Kakagun sniffed at the prevailing light wind and predicted in a worried tone: "The warm moist breeze of winter has come. By tomorrow there will be a great storm!" Arriving annually in January and lasting merely a few hours, this relatively gentle southwesterly is the last breath of a Chinook wind, now almost spent after crossing the great plains and sub-arctic forests from the leeward side of the Canadian Rocky Mountains.

"Hilla, the Spirit of the Air, doesn't like the Chinook," confirmed Nokadlak. "He is going to send Uyaluk, the Great Wind Storm, to chase it away."

How right my two friends were! By early evening the wind— now blowing from the northeast—began to increase in intensity. No longer the gentle Chinook, it was turning into the cold, cruel, fearsome Uyaluk. We trooped outside to pile insulating snow on our newly fashioned igloos to protect them from the impairing effect of the storm. We also fed our dogs before returning to our respective snow houses. Once inside them we settled down to a relatively comfortable evening. From my iglek I could see a good part of Kakagun's abode through our connecting passageway. I went there in answer to Naoyak's lilting call that tea was being served. Her adoptive mother Kablunak had anticipated our increasing appetites with chunks of meat and fish displayed in a basin. We ate in comparative silence, listening to the furious pounding of the wind outside our haven of rest, reassured by the provident sight of frozen caribou carcasses and fish stacked against the wall behind the blubber lamp.

I used the rest of the evening to ready the fifty traps I had brought with me from Burnside. For each ring at the end of the chain attached to the trap I inserted a small peg of willow, and checked for broken links. I had also brought along several old coal-oil cans filled with fermented herrings and rancid blubber

357

for baiting the traps. In short, I was ready, except for my outer garments. I asked Kablunak to look them over with her practiced eye.

"Your parka has a few small holes, *Fala*. I'll patch them."

"Thanks, Kablunak. That should stop the wind and the snow from coming through as it did at the end of last winter. I wore poorly sewn breeches then. The stitches came loose between my legs. When the storm caught me on the trail, the skin of my testicles froze and it took a long time to heal." Kablunak laughed heartily, and all the others joined in the merriment. Kakagun added to the general hilarity by asking me, "Did your penis get caught in the storm, too?"

"Yes, Kakagun, but it wasn't too bad."

"That won't happen again, *Fala*," Kablunak smiled. "I am going to make sure that your clothes are properly patched."

Naoyak, who was unconcernedly playing with her new doll on the *iglek*, saved me from further embarrassment by asking me to tell her a story. "Certainly, Little Seagull," I readily agreed. "I'll tell you a tale I heard when I was visiting the People of the Berries at the Kulugayuk River. Long ago there was a family with a father, mother, and two sons. Their name was Orkpikut, the owl family. The sons were good hunters. They usually returned from hunting with ground squirrels and lemmings. So there was always food in their igloo.

"One day a human, who was passing by, heard Father owl asking his wife to 'Go out and see if our sons are returning with some food, because I'm very hungry.'

"Mother owl went outside, looked around and yelled to her husband, 'Yes, they are coming back! And it looks like they are bringing us something!'

"'Quick, quick!' Father owl said excitedly. 'I'll take my team and meet them!' But in his rush Father owl couldn't find his dogs' harnesses.

"'Where are the harnesses, Mother owl?' he cried impatiently at his wife.

"'Just there, behind the snow porch. But I didn't have time to mend some of them.'

"'You are a good-for-nothing woman!' Father owl told her angrily.

"'Our newborn child kept me so busy, I didn't have time for anything else,' she explained.

"That is how Father and Mother owl talked to each other, Naoyak. They snapped and quarrelled over silly things, just like human beings, while their two sons trudged home with the ground squirrels they had caught."

Although this Eskimo story ended in a characteristically anticlimactic moral, little Naoyak appeared to enjoy its imagery.

The early morning sky was overcast and an Arctic grayness enveloped everything around us when we left our camp. The great storm had passed, sweeping back the warm air to the south. Naodluak rode with me on top of my steel fox traps that I had bundled under a canvas on the sled along with my food supplies and bedding. When we reached the frozen Arctic Sound, I noticed that Nokadlak and Kudnanak swung their sled to the right. "Where are they heading?" I asked Naodluak.

"They will follow the coast to Banks Peninsula, heading north. Then they will turn south to Portage Bay. In a few days they will go back to their former camp by the portage."

"Does Nokadlak have traps all the way?"

"Yes, *Fala*, he has many."

We left Nokadlak to his conquest of the Banks Peninsula and continued along the west coast of the Sound. "Where does your Father's trap line end, Naodluak?" I inquired.

"At Cape Barrow."

A good fifty air miles away and probably more than twice that distance along the irregular coastline, which protrudes into the Coronation Gulf, held at least one advantage: there Father Adam had built a one-room shack in which he stored emergency rations and fuel. I was gladdened by the thought of spending a night in the little wooden structure that was comfortably heated by a coal stove.

Meanwhile on a small promontory Kakagun pulled up his team. He climbed to its rocky top, looked around, then stooped down. I joined him while Naodluak kept an eye on our dogs. "The fox is gone!" he exclaimed, pointing to the white forepaw in the closed trap and bloodstains in the snow.

"You've been away too long, Kakagun," I rationalized. "The fox has had time to chew his frozen paw."

"Yes, and I expect to find more like this one. Besides, wolverines and wolves have had time to wander around and eat some of the caught foxes. This always happens when I don't visit my traps often." Kakagun opened the trap in question, tossed away the paw, and reset it. He pulled on the chain to make sure it was still firmly anchored in the hard snowdrift. Satisfied, he cut a hole in the snow, just deep enough to contain the snare, and laid it in. Then he covered it over with a slab of hardened snow which he scraped almost to paper thinness with his snowknife. The camouflage was perfect, yet brittle enough to break at once under the weight of an unsuspecting fox. As bait Kakagun sprinkled bits of rotten fish to encourage the fox to walk about until it stepped upon the center lid that would spring the trap. As he did so, he asked me to cut him a block of snow. "I'll place it right by the trap. It will be easier to find it when I come back again" he explained.

"And it will also attract the curious fox," I contributed.

"That's right! Especially when I spread a little blubber over it. The fox will play around it, piss on it like a dog, and eventually jump on the trap." For extra insurance Kakagun scooped out several handfuls of snow from the base of the foot-high pyramid on the side nearest to the trap and put a piece of fish into the recess. Not even the smartest fox in the Arctic could possibly get at it without treading on and springing the trap!

The canny hunter had placed his traps a quarter of a mile or so apart, and we checked out as many of them as we could during the daylight hours. Here and there, along silenced creeks, on hilltops, and in other likely-looking spots, I set some of my own traps.

By late afternoon, while a ground wind moaned among the snowdrifts, we drove past Kater Point, southeast of Cape Barrow and facing the Stockport Islands. We built a small igloo, fed our dogs with dry meat, and crept into our overnight shelter. Kakagun sealed its doorway with a large block of snow, Naodluak got the small blubber lamp going, while I lit my Primus stove for extra warmth and made a pot of tea. As we relaxed on the *iglek* after dining on chunks of frozen meat, I asked Kakagun, "When you were smoothing the snow around your traps, I heard you say something I did not understand. You did not speak to me, but to the land. Remember?"

"Yes, they were magic words, *Fala.*"

"To whom were you speaking?"

"To the soul of my dead Father. His body was left on a spit of land were I set a trap. He was a *tunrak* (sorcerer). He had great powers over all animals—caribou, foxes, wolves. His soul is still around because he died not long ago."

"What did you say to your Father?"

"I said, 'Father, Father, talk to me and say the magic words you taught me when I was only a boy.' These were my Father's magic words: 'Wanderers of the Land, come, come and place your paws on this fresh snow!' "

"Why does the soul of your Father remain so long around this part of the land?"

"Who knows? It's there, and it goes up and down the coast, helping those who ask for help. Some day his soul will move to live forever in the Land of the Day."

"How many foxes did you and Naodluak catch today?"

360

Thoughtfully counting on his fingers, Kakagun said, "I got ten foxes: three cross foxes, one red fox, and six white foxes. That reminds me, Naodluak. We should skin those that aren't frozen." The youngster got off the *iglek* and put his parka back on. "I forgot to bring them in," he said. "I'll get them now." He let himself out by cutting around the entrance block and kicking it forward.

"There are not many white foxes this winter," observed Kakagun as Naodluak crawled back in with three of them and one red. Their feet were stiffly frozen, but otherwise they seemed soft enough for fleecing.

"Why is this a poor winter for foxes?" I asked Kakagun.

"Last spring I saw females with their young. They had only two or three pups each. During the summer while I was hunting caribou, I saw fewer foxes than before."

"How many pups does a female fox usually have?"

"Four, five, or six."

"How do you account for the small litters?"

"Maybe it's because the lemmings are scarce and the undernourished foxes get sick and die."

The first fox that Kakagun skinned showed no fat on its bright red carcass. "See, Fala, this one didn't have much to eat! The lemmings are disappearing."

"But foxes feed on more than lemmings."

"That's right. Sometimes they will eat a ptarmigan or find the remains of caribou killed by wolves. And far out on the ice pack they'll eat carcasses of seals abandoned by the bear. But lemmings are their main food, *Fala*."

"You mentioned seeing foxes in the summer. Where do they live then?"

"After the ice break up, all white foxes hide in their holes on riverbanks and in sandy mounds, near places where there are plenty of fowl and eggs."

"I've heard that white foxes are easier to trap than the others. People on Banks Island often don't bother to put any bait at all around the traps."

"They are not as sly and suspicious as the red fox, *Fala*. Many times I have seen him following my team, staying around my camp, watching people moving about."

"I know what you mean. There were a couple of white foxes under my shack at Cambridge Bay. They emerged periodically to see what I was doing. They weren't shy, just curious."

Kakagun's son Naodluak was an expert in skinning foxes. With a pocketknife, he made an incision on the inside of one hind leg to the other, freeing each paw from the bones; he then cut all along the tail, trimming away the fur. Similarly he cut the skin from one front paw to the other. He peeled off the skin like a glove from the tail to the snout, making incisions around the ears and mouth to free the skin. Now only the carcacass remained. Having skinned another fox, Naodluak said critically, mostly for my benefit, "This one is lean, too. If it had been fat, we could have boiled and eaten it. As it isn't, I'll give it to the dogs."

"I dislike fox meat because it has such a strong flavor," I told him. "Moreover, I ate too much of it when I visited the People at the Back of the Land at Minto Inlet.

"We don't usually eat it. Only for a change," said Kakagun. "We like to try everything except the raven."

"Why not the raven?"

"He is taboo. My father used to say he is unclean."

Before piling into our *krepiks* for the night, we stepped outside to inspect our dogs and fill our lungs with fresh air. Seldom had I seen the Northern Lights in a more spectacular display. Like a glittering *corps de ballet* they glided over nature's immense stage, now rising, now falling, ever colorful, never still. The ground wind having died completely, it was so quiet I imagined I could actually hear the celestial show. To me it sounded like the delicate rustling of silk tresses, yet as I bent down to the frozen ground I knew that the gentle noises came not from the heavens above but from the snow particles expanding in the intense cold.

At Daniel Moore Bay next day, Naodluak and I were astonished to see two wolves caught in Kakagun's traps. Even the great hunter himself beamed with special pride. Still alive, the platinum blue *arluk* and the plain gray *amakro* wolves were clearly more surprised than we at the encounter. They cringed in fright, tails between their legs, like beaten dogs.

But there were natural cowards among our dogs, too. While the wolfish scent enticed most of the huskies into a sprint for the traps, some of them showed their reluctance to approach the enemy by skidding on their rumps. Kakagun wasted no time. Within ten yards of the traps he anchored the sled to discourage the more venturesome dogs, then with rifle in hand, squatted in the snow, and fired. The handsome Arluk rolled over, blood gushing from his mouth. Again Kakagun took aim and shot, sealing the *amakro's* fate. In a few moments he and Naodluak considered it safe to remove the pair from the powerful traps.

The wolves weren't there by chance. Nearby another trap held the paw of a white fox, its fur scattered about the gravelly pit in silent eloquence. And partly buried in the gravel, only a few feet away, were the ravaged carcasses of four seals.

"How did these seals get here?" I asked Kakagun.

"I hunted them last summer. Got more than I could carry in my canoe. I cached them in the gravel. They made big bait!"

I wondered what Kakagun would do next with them. As if in answer to my thoughts, he said, "The wolves are too heavy to haul to the next camp. I'm going to skin them right now."

"I'll reset the traps while you do that," added Naodluak.

I helped Kakagun. It didn't take us long. We made an incision the length of the belly, from tail to lower jaw and across from leg to leg, front and back, pulling the skin off on each side. My guess was the wolves weighed about ninety pounds each. There certainly was no fat on their carcasses. "How old are they, would you say, Kakagun?"

"Two winters. They are young males from the same litter, *Fala*."

"How can you tell they're from the same litter when their coloring is different?"

"Their muzzles are both long for their heads. See how their forehead slopes the same way? Compare their eyes, their ears. Notice how long their fur is over their bellies and their legs. They are alike, but for the color of their fur."

Each time Naodluak glanced in our direction, he smiled and paid compliments to the *arluk*'s fur: "It's beautiful! It will make wonderful hood trimmings for Kablunak and Naoyak!"

"Don't you get *arluks* very often, Kakagun?"

"No, *Fala*, *amakro* is the common one. Sometimes we get black and white wolves. But, like *arluk*, they are scarce."

"That's strange! When I hunted with the Tunuarnermeun people, all the wolves we saw were white. Even in the summer they were white. Is that because their islands are more northerly?"

"Yes. I've hunted them far inland at Prince Edward Bay. But in our land there are only a few white wolves."

"Do you find that wolves like to hunt in packs?"

"Sometimes they like to hunt alone or in pairs. Mostly in winter they travel in packs of one or two families, rarely more. By doing so, they can corner a caribou more easily."

"Last spring, while I was watching a herd of caribou crossing the ice at Kent Peninsula, I counted fifteen wolves traveling together."

"Probably that was a two-family pack. Fala. Maybe two bitches, their mates, yearlings, and two-year-old cubs."

"What's the biggest pack you've ever seen?" Naodluak asked his father.

"One winter, when I was at Hanimor River visiting my trap line, I saw about twenty *amakro*. In all my life I never again came across such a large pack," Kakagun replied.

"Have any of your people been attacked by wolves?"

"No, *Fala*. Singly or in a pack, the *amakro* may follow or circle a hunter and his dog team at a distance, but not for very long."

"Why?"

"The first rifle shot, and sometimes just the hunter's scent—if it is strong enough—will scare the *amakro* away."

"What about dog scent?"

"That doesn't frighten the *amakro*. In the gloom of the winter night many a dog on the dog line has been attached and killed by him. Of course, some dogs can take care of themselves. But if a dog, or a whole team, runs away from camp, sooner or later it will fall prey to the *amakro*."

"I thought the wolves were after caribou and musk-ox the year round."

"Not always, *Fala*. In summer they will eat anything—birds, squirrels, hares."

"Wolves look so much like dogs that I suppose they breed like dogs, too. Do they?"

"No, *Fala*. Dogs breed almost any time. But the *amakro* bear their young only in the spring."

"Where do they hide at that time?"

"They seek only natural dens. Usually among fallen rocks in the hills. They like to watch all the approaches without being seen themselves."

"That's pretty clever! How many cubs are there in an average litter?"

"Anywhere from five to ten."

"Who provides food for the cubs while they are still too young to fetch for themselves—the male or female parent?"

"The *amakro*. While the bitch watches over the cubs, he hunts alone and drags part of his kill to his family. Sometimes the parents hunt together, but they go away for short periods of time only, and always come back the same day. The fittest cubs survive, grow up, go hunting together, make with other *amakro*, and part—You ask a lot of questions about the *amakro*, *Fala*. Have you not hunted them yourself?"

"I went hunting a few times with Nerreok, a clever wolf hunter, when he was at Umikmatok one fall. We ran trap lines on high ground and across passes, setting traps around caribou carcasses. We used to lie in ambush, sometimes waiting for hours before we could get a shot at the *amakro*. I remember Nerreok got so tired of waiting one day that he fell asleep. Concealed by rocks, I kept up the watch. While he slept, I saw five wolves cautiously approach the caribou we had killed earlier that day. I nudged Nerreok, saying 'Hey, wake up, the wolves are coming!' He rubbed his eyes, half-asleep, 'Where, where?' I pointed to the wolf pack. They were sniffing at the carcass, licking the dried blood, and biting lazily at the soft parts. They were not hungry.

"As we took up our positions, Nerreok whispered, 'Let's shoot together, *Fala*!' We fired at the same time. Then quickly again. Three of the wolves bounced up and two of them fell dead. The third tried to run away on three legs, but Nerreok broke his back with a well-aimed shot. The other two escaped. Those we killed we skinned and left their carcasses to the roaming foxes and wolverines."

"Did you get any bounty for their furs at the trading post?" Kakagun asked me.

"No, in those days, at the start of the White Man's big war, the police were not paying bounty on wolves. I know they do now again."

"Yes. I remember, *Fala*. When the bounty payments stopped, most of my people did not bother to hold their summer and fall hunts for the *amakro*."

"That's not why your people call the policeman an *amakro*, is it?" I said, tongue in cheek.

Kakagun and Naodluak laughed heartily, and Kakagun replied, "No, *Fala*. You were here before the Kablunan started their war. You must have heard our people calling the policeman an *amakro* then. It's because he goes after men like a wolf stalking caribou."

Later, as we looked across Detention Harbor from Galena Point, Kakagun mentioned that few White Men had ever visited this part of the country. "Even we Inuit seldom come here," he added pointedly.

"Why is that?"

"Because long ago the hunting failed our forefather. The few caches of caribou meat they had were eaten by wolverines. Many of our predecessors died of hunger. Their descendants haven't forgotten."

"If the hunting is so poor in this area, why did we come here?"

"It's good ground for foxes, *Fala*. My trap line follows the shoreline to the foot of the harbor. Let's take a look at it!"

In the ensuing ten miles we snared seven foxes, one of them a handsome platinum blue that was very much alive. Kakagun smacked the doomed animal on its nose with the handle of his snow knife. It flopped over and lay unconscious. He finished it by crushing its ribs and heart under his feet. Then he picked it up by its hind legs and examined its fur. Finding no fault, he smiled with satisfaction and reminisced, "When I was a young boy, fox were a mere pastime for women. They used their fur for children's garments, parka trimmings, and cleaning themselves. Now I can trade one at the trading post for a .22 rifle or for two steel sled runners."

"How did the women hunt foxes?"

Both hunter and son looked incredulous as Kakagun spoke, "How is it you don't know, *Fala*? Didn't you ever see the kind of traps my people used before the Kablunak came?"

"I can't remember, Kakagun."

"We used to make traps with heavy flat stones. We set them like a box, with the lid on and an opening with a stone slab above, so that it would fall and close the trap if the bait inside was touched."

"Oh, yes! I've seen those old traps here and there, even up in the Land of the Tunuarnermeum along the Kogariuak River. But I paid little attention to them."

By noon next day we reached Desbarats Inlet, which lies a couple of miles south of the tip of Cape Barrow. There, dwarfed between six hundred-foot bluffs surrounding it like a horseshoe, nestled Father Adam's little shack—a welcome halfway shelter for the Missionaries traveling between Burnside, Coppermine, and Cambridge Bay. It consisted of a twelve-foot square room, equipped with a coal stove, a table and chairs, and three wooden bunks. In its tiny enclosed porch the considerate priest had stored a dozen bags of coal, a case of kerosene, and a crate of large tins containing dehydrated vegetables.

Silently blessing my colleague and friend, I started a fire with the coal and cooked the vegetables in a pot. Quickly the snug cabin warmed sufficiently for us to devest ourselves of our outer garments and relax in comfort. I poured some water from the kettle into a pan and washed my hands and face for the first time in many days. Feeling wonderfully refreshed, I asked my companions if they would like to do the same. From the bunks they looked up at me and laughed in concert. Presently Kakagun summed up their perspective: "When you wash your face, you take out the fat. Then your nose and cheeks will freeze more easily. If you Kablunan listened more often to the Inuit, you would avoid a lot of trouble in our Land!"

It was indeed a treat to sit down to a potful of boiled meat and vegetables after a steady diet of frozen or dry fish and meat. Kakagun and Naodluak, both of whom downed enormous quantities of the stew, expressed their approval with loud belching and the polite "My belly is full, thanks!"

Cape Barrow was the anchor point on Kakagun's trap line. Apart from that, it held no attraction for him. We left after a restful night in the warm hut to face a bitterly cold ground wind on the sea ice. Kakagun chose not to retrace our steps by Detention Harbor and Daniel Moore Bay, following instead the western shores of Chapman Islands down to Stockport Islands.

Two of his older dogs developed badly frozen flanks and had to be left behind at the mercy of the Barren Land. I was thankful that my own dogs were all in good shape. Actually I began making sure they would be strong and well-conditioned from the time they were six-month-old pups. Gradually working them into the team to temper their growth and steel their muscles, I had them thoroughly prepared for long-distance travel by the end of their first year. Concurrently careful not to overburden or overstrain them, I always tried to keep them well-nourished and content. Not surprisingly, Kakagun's shorthanded team soon began to fall behind mine. He had only seven dogs left, against nine of mine. He motioned me to stop and caught up to me. "I'm too heavy for my dogs. I'll ride with you, *Fala*. Naodluak can take over."

There was little for us to do at most of the traps. Only a dozen foxes were caught in all of them. Kakagun's thought dwelt understandably on one of the Eskimo hunter's favorite topics— dogs. Following several unexpected flattering remarks about my huskies, he paid me the supreme compliment by asking if I would let him have some of my pups next spring. "You can certainly have them, but you'll have to feed them every day if you want them to withstand the constant cold and the long trips you like to take."

"Yes, *Fala*, I'll do that, although we Inuit raise our dogs differently. We don't want their stomachs stretched because we don't always have the food for them. When they're young, we feed them little, never too much. Later, we give them enough food for the work they have to do and no more. They get used to that."

Despite his seemingly heartless talk, I knew that Kakagun— like all good hunters everywhere—loved his dogs. It was a great pity, but inevitable that, at best, sled dogs last a mere four or five years in the Barren Land. Then would come their unrewarding doom, one of the saddest features of Arctic life, for no man in the far North destroys a faithful dog without a pang of guilt and grief. Inhuman as it may sound, the native hunter would sooner lose one of his own family than a dog, since a female child or an old woman represents an extra mouth to feed. But for a man to lose a

367

dog—where would he be if he couldn't go hunting or trapping by dog team? I presumed that these might have been some of Kakagun's dark thoughts as he sat moodily and silently on my sled. If my presumption was correct, then he had my fullest sympathy and understanding for I, too, had known such moments of defeat and doubt caused by similar circumstances—moods as gray as the low-hanging clouds, void of all color, drained of all life. There is no telling how long they could affect a man, nor what it would take to shake them off.

A string of small islands sheltered us from the crosswind as far as the Stockport Islands, but still Kakagun said nothing. It was only when we entered the narrow passage between an island shaped like Napoleon's hat and Kater Point that he dramatically broke his silence, "Stop, *Fala*, stop!" he cried anxiously. "The ice is smoking!"

"Where, Kakagun?" I demanded from fright, automatically throwing the anchor to halt our progress.

"Look just ahead!"

Not fifty yards away a light vapor hung over the ice. It was the danger signal Father Delalande had once warned me about between Koagiuk Island and the mainland: "When you see that, it means open water in the ice floor. Don't ever try to cross it! And be exceedingly cautious!"

"True enough, worn down by the strong currents of the narrow gap, the ice had reluctantly given way, and now—above the suddenly free, fast-flowing water—hovered a gray fog. Kakagun jumped off the sled and waved his hand to Naodluak behind us, yelling, "Stop! The ice is smoking!" Naodluk also obeyed at once.

Kakagun now turned to me, "Little Father, I'll lead the teams to shore. We'll follow it until we reach the end of the gap. It should be safe then to use the sea ice again." Relieved of the vital decision, I readily nodded agreement.

We navigated the quarter-mile detour safely and it took us an additional hour to get past the danger area, so rough was the ice along the shore. We forced ourselves to build an igloo and crawled into it for a much-needed rest.

Out on the open sea ice next day we were overtaken by a gusty wind which whirled fine powdery snow in clouds that sifted through everything in sight. The dogs, the sleds, and we upon them all turned a ghostly white. As if this wasn't enough, the snow not only glued down our eyelids, it melted on our faces only to freeze again and burn the skin. The cold wind blasts seemed to penetrate our skulls, lowering our mental capacities. But we were determined to reach our camp, and if the dogs could do it, we would too. The huskies did not let us down. Late in the evening we were greeted by Nokadlak and Kudnanak, who had arrived earlier and stood waiting for us outside the igloo with Angivrana, Kablunak, and little Naoyak.

Both families crowded into Kakagun's igloo that night to hear how Nokadlak had brought back a musk-ox from Kanuyak Island. "I was resetting a fox trap when the dogs scented something unusual," he began. "Kudnanak stopped them just in time from running away. Then we saw a lone musk-ox coming down the hillside towards us."

"It must have been an old bull looking for a fight," opined Kakagun.

"Yes. But the Spirits of the Land were good to me. They helped me shoot him in his tracks."

"Did you see any more musk-oxen on that island?" I queried.

"Yes. After we fleeced the musk-ox, we climbed the nearby hill to reconnoitre. We saw a herd of about thirty traveling west. They were on the alert for three wolves that followed them, trying to snatch away their calves," Nokadlak said, pausing to puff on his cigarette. "The wolves made a rush for their calves only once, for the big musk-oxen formed a circle around their young ones," his son Kudnanak broke in. "Standing shoulder to shoulder, with their horned heads sticking out in all directions, they left no opening for the wolves."

"We started down the valley to shoot the wolves, but they turned and fled," Nokadlak resumed. "This signal led the musk-oxen to disappear out of sight, too. "

"Did you bring back the musk-ox hide?" inquired Kakagun.

"Yes. Angivrana will scrape it and shave off the fur."

"I'd like to trade a piece of the hide. Kablunak needs some to make boot soles," Kakagun explained.

"You can have it, and some meat, besides," said Nokadlak.

"I'd like to have some musk-ox meat, too," piped up Naoyak. "It tastes better than caribou meat!"

"Of course," Kakagun acquiesced. Then he added as an afterthought, "There is so much meat in one musk-ox that it's a great pity to see so many of them get away."

"Perhaps it's better that way. We aren't starving and the police from Coppermine won't come after us!" I said smiling.

Kablunak and Angivrana chuckled softly while trading pungent witticisms at my remark. They knew as well as their menfolk did that it was the law of the land to leave the musk-oxen alone.

Later in the night Kudnanak called us from his igloo, "Come and have tea and musk-ox meat!" We went. Contrasted with our earlier harrowing experiences, it turned out to be a delightful evening.

23

Hirenek, The Sun

"Let's go up to the hills and greet Hirenek, the Sun!" suggested Nokadlak one morning. "He should be back today— the sky is brightening." It had been intensely cold for the past two weeks, so cold that even the foxes stayed in their lairs and our traps remained empty. But now the long Arctic night was on the wane and once again the benevolent sun was about to gladden our hearts.

Carrying our .22s in case we encountered small game, Nokadlak, Kakagun, their two sons, and I climbed the height of land above the Hood River rapids. The moment they saw the pale golden rays of the sun slant over the frozen desert, my companions removed their mitts, tossed back their hoods, and blissfully waved their arms at the low-hanging Hirenek as if they had suddenly been transported to sunny Arizona, California, or Florida. They smiled, laughed, jumped about and otherwise saluted the mighty sun.

"For us it is a sign of good luck and prosperity, *Fala*, to greet Hirenek on his first return," Kakagun justified their spontaneous demonstration of genuine delight. "He is the Good Spirit who harbors many helpful spirits and we must welcome them back to our land."

"It was easy for me to understand how the same sun that I had always taken for granted on the shores of the bright blue Mediterranean became a near-deity in the Barren Land. Its long-awaited reappearance brings cheer and hope to the People Beyond. It beautifies their dreary existence. It adorns their monotonous surroundings with a crown of glittering light and dancing colors. It transforms the most desolate stretch of ice and snow into a scene of transcendent beauty.

No wonder, I thought, the casual visitor to the Arctic often carries away with him little else besides memories of vivid sunrises and sunsets in a setting of dazzling whiteness. "The Arctic is picturesque beyond description," he will say enthusiastically and in all sincerity to his eager listeners at home. But how deceived and disillusioned he would be if he remained in the same land for years instead of days! Then imprinted permanently on his mind would be a shadowy world of man and beast at continual grips with sub-zero temperatures and monstrous snowstorms, a world so primitive and savage that the struggle to keep from freezing and from starving is their main and often their only concern.

I glanced at my Inuit friends facing the sun and at their long, grotesque shadows on the snow floor. Their ecstatic salute to the reborn sun was summarily over. Their faces resumed their customary serenity. They were resigned to their lot because they knew no other land, no other climate, no other way of life. The Barren Land was theirs from birth till death. No other people wanted it; no one would attempt to take it away from them. This was their sole security. Yet it gave them a contentment that our world has always sought, but has never found.

"We didn't see anything except a few hare tracks," Kakagun reported later in the day when he and his son Naodluak rejoined the rest of us in camp.

"*Ukadlek* and *Akreliek*, the Ptarmigan, are hiding in the creeks," explained the game-wise youngster. "It's too cold for them today."

"Yes," agreed Nokadlak. "Until spring we won't get much game inland. We'll have to hunt *Nathek*, the Seal."

Kakagun looked at the women busy with their sewing, at Nokadlak and Kudnanak (who was straightening a willow stem over the blubber lamp in anticipation of the seal hunt), then said decisively, "There is little food left for the dogs. I'm going after seals tomorrow." The great hunter turned to me, "*Fala*, will you help us look for his breathing holes?" Knowing I would acquiesce he hardly bothered to wait for my answer, so anxious was he to sharpen his spear on a piece of slate and tie a long, narrow strip of sealskin to its detachable head.

Not having any special preparations to make, I joined Naoyak and Naodluak in their frequent evening indulgence—cat's cradle game. Like most Krangmalit I've met, they were skilful at it, using their imagination in throwing string patterns of animals and people over their fingers, perhaps as a concrete means of transmitting their inner thoughts. In a sense, too, these creative patterns compensated the People Beyond—and especially their youngsters—for the non-existence of illustrated books or graphic art in their primitive, nomadic society. In effect, the string game provided almost unlimited possibilities for their alert minds, bringing about a harmonious adjustment through a series of complex movements with their fingers. Admittedly, I couldn't keep up with them. Their practical fingers were simply too fast for me.

"This is a fox running," Naodluak was saying to his promised Naoyak. "Pick it up and transfer it into a sled."

The girl passed her agile fingers through the mesh of string and triumphantly held up both hands with a passable sled outline.

"*Fala*, it's your turn!" she exclaimed. "Make some dancing children. I'll tell you how to weave the strings. "Like this, make intertwisted loops," she demonstrated.

"I made an honest attempt to follow Naoyak's instructions, but when I held up my clumsy effort, Kakagun took his curious eyes off his own work to look at my creation and snorted, "It looks like the testicles of a dog! Give it to me, *Fala*. I'll finish it for you."

Introducing his thumbs and little fingers under the stretched strings and picking up others, he produced another design. "What do you think this is, *Fala?*"

"I couldn't guess, Kakagun."

"It's a man and a woman embracing in a *krepik* (sleeping bag)." Swiftly he made a few passes to astonish me further. "This is a woman breast-feeding a child! I can make many more patterns like those!" he bragged.

But I had got the general idea and excused myself on the pretext of getting some fresh air. I strolled along my dog line and spoke reassuringly to my canine friends. They sniffed at me and wagged their friendly tails. Above, the sky was clear, and it was intensely cold.

Although I was tired, I couldn't fall asleep. I closed my eyes and tried to relax in the furry sleeping bag, but my impressions and thoughts of recent events kept my mind churning.

With unsuppressed yawns, Kakagun and Kablunak began undressing for bed. I could not help overhearing their whispered words about their son and his betrothed. "Naodluak is almost a man now," said Kakagun. "He should start sleeping with Naoyak."

"She is not very old yet, but she can learn to please her man," agreed Kablunak.

Aloud to the playing youngsters Kakagun said, "We are going to sleep. Make room for Naoyak in your *krepik*, Naodluak. She will keep you warm. And some day she will be your wife."

Naodluak reacted with a smile, but the girl, now ten years old, showed no emotion. They divested themselves and squeezed their young bodies into the boy's sleeping bag. Somehow, in those surroundings, this arrangement didn't seem lascivious or even incongruous. It was more an act of affection or even of friendship than a performance of passion.

"Have some meat and fat, *Fala*," said Kakagun. "You'll get cold standing on the ice if you don't fill your stomach now."

"It was raw and windy on the frozen Arctic Sound where we had driven early that morning under a cloudless sky. Only Angivrana remained in camp, ten miles to the south, to mind her baby. We had anchored our three sleds and Kablunak was dishing out food from her grub bag, while Kudnanak and Naodluak melted snow in a large kettle above their Primus stove.

As I munched bits of frozen musk-ox meat and caribou fat, I let my gaze wander across the rigid sea to the gray horizon. There wasn't a sign of life as far as I could see. The only sound was the ceaseless swishing of drifting snow along the glassy ice floor.

"Let us go now and look for the seal's blowhole," said Kakagun, unharnessing one of his dogs and attaching a leash to its collar. "This is one of the best I've ever had for scenting them."

"Mine is good at it, too," rejoined Nokadlak. "I had a better one last spring, but he was killed in a fight." Like Kakagun, he slung a seal bag with his hunting implements across his shoulders and picked up a five-foot harpoon.

Just before we walked off in search of seals, Kablunak, who was staying behind with Naoyak to look after the teams told Kakagun that they would make a windbreak for themselves out of snow blocks while we were gone. "We won't be too cold, and we'll have hot tea ready for you when you return with seals," she added with a dutiful smile.

Our dogs strained against their leashes, sniffing into the wind, stopping, then trotting off again, their muzzles barely skimming the snow. The hunters' sons also let the huskies choose their own direction, and they responded like trained bloodhounds. Suddenly Naodluak's dog froze in its tracks, vigorously sniffing the snow beneath it. From several yards away, Kudnanak's dog swerved to the same spot. Highly excited, both dogs began to dig the crusty snow. Covered by a drift of hard snow and totally invisible even at close range, the seal's tiny breathing hole now became apparent. Kakagun raised his hand to signal for silence, then whispered to me: "Can you smell it? This breathing hole was made by a bull seal."

I sniffed hard at it. "Yes, it smells strong," I replied. An unmistakable odor, like the mustiness of rotten onions, escaped from the blowhole.

Lest the dogs' ardent digging warn an approaching seal, the boys pulled them off a safe distance while Kakagun prepared to mark the give-away hole. "Nokadlak and Kudnanak are going to look for others," he said as they walked off quietly to the left. He knelt down and began to scrape away the top layer of snow, smoothing the rest noiselessly with his mittens. Then out of his tool bag he took out a yard-long, pencil-thin whalebone with a pronounced curve and lowered it through the hole. He rotated it systematically, probing the shape of the breathing hole under the snow to determine its exact center. Evidently satisfied, he grunted, "This one will do, *Fala*. Cut me a block of hard snow."

With my trusty snow knife I chopped a large slab out of a snowdrift and brought it over to Kakagun. He placed it on edge, stood up and urinated on it. "You, too, *Fala!*" he urged me. "It will be easier to see this marker from a distance."

As I obliged him, I recalled the kidney pills I had in my medicine bag. They contained a certain amount of methylene blue, a bluish-green dye. The first time I gave one of these pills to a young Eskimo who complained of a backache, he nearly had a fit. "I'm dying! I'm dying!" he yelled. I asked him what was ailing him. "I'm urinating colored water!"

"Oh, I forgot to tell you that the medicine I gave you would change the color of your urine."

My young patient must have wasted no time in spreading the word around the camp, for within the next few days men, women, and even children came to ask me for the pills, (safe for adults and children) while the snow around the Mission buildings and their igloos began to sport a variety of designs in blue-green. Subsequently an innovative native hunter showed up on my doorstep, saying, "I would like to have some of your medicine, Fala, to mark the snow blocks when I set my traps or go seal hunting. It's easy to see them from far away." Good thing my mind wasn't thinking commercially or I might have been tempted to enter the vivid dye market with a "Rhapsody in Blue" pill and substantially revolutionize the Arctic's bleak monotony.

Our first breathing hole marker ready, Kakagun, Naodluak, and I marched off with the two dogs in the opposite direction from Nokadlak and his son. The dogs led us to four other blowholes within a half-mile radius. Each of these we packed so thoroughly with snow that no seal would ever break through. By the time we had sealed off (no pun intended) the last hole—or so we hoped—we had gone around in a semi-circle towards Nokadlak who, in turn, had done the same to meet us.

"We found a few more breathing holes and kept one of them open," Nokadlak told us.

"If we are lucky," replied Kakagun, "the seal has only those two marked holes left for breathing. Let's try them out!"

As the two boys continued to look for additional holes, Kakagun and I retraced our steps to the one he had marked. Nokadlak proceeded to his own.

"Keep a little away from the breathing hole *Fala*. And don't make any noise. *Nathek*, the seal might hear you," cautioned Kakagun. He pulled out the willow stem he had prepared the night before and knelt down silently by the blowhole. The dried willow rod was forked at one end so as to spread inside the foot-wide blowhole. Its other end was topped with an eider duck feather that fluttered gaily in the light breeze, as if it sat upon an Easter bonnet.

Having first gently swept the crust off the hole with the back of his mittens, Kakagun pushed the forked end of the rod about a foot down into the hole. He attached a string to the stick and pegged the loose end to the snow. This sensitive marker was now so set that the least pressure on it from below would start the feather quivering. Kakagun took one more precaution. Out of his bag he drew out a piece of polar-bear skin which he spread on the snow as a rug to stand on. It would insulate him from the freezing floor, as well as deaden any creaking sound he might make by moving his feet. Finally, he picked up his harpoon and held it waist-high, bending forward slightly over the feather to await its decisive signal.

Once he mounted guard, Kakagun stood immobile. The next move would be strictly up to the seal. Till then the hunter's eyes would be rivetted upon the bright plume. At any moment it might be nudged by the unsuspecting seal. On the other hand, the wily seal might not show for hours, using other breathing holes that we may have overlooked. No matter how long his vigil, though, a hunter of Kakagun's caliber would remain as motionless as a snowman for the duration.

Almost a half-mile away, Nokadlak stood poised for action in like manner. Beyond him the two boys maintained their breathing hole search. And far behind us, against the grayish twilight of a wintry sky, Kablunak and Naoyak resembled two tiny pebbles on a sea of white.

Although it was bitterly cold, no one would have suspected

it merely by looking at Kakagun. He appeared oblivious to the elements and to the seemingly reluctant passage of time. His life and the welfare of his family depended upon his patience and endurance. Only the hoarfrost on his eyebrows and chin told the real story.

I stood a few yards off, watching him, trying to keep still, yet warm. But it was impossible not to feel the icy wind. It pervaded my entire body, benumbing my muscles and making me ache all over. I hoped and prayed that the seal would come soon and end this misery.

It seemed like an eternity, but it actually took only a half-hour by my watch, for the feathered indicator to move upward. Immediately Kakagun's body stiffened. Slowly he raised his right arm, tightening his grip on the harpoon. Then, with a grunt, he thrust his weapon down along the willow rod dead through the center of the hole. I heard the dull thud of the harpoon's spur against the seal's head. Quickly discarding the shaft of the harpoon, Kakagun began pulling on the rope connected to the metal spur. The seal splashed and snorted in his determined attempts to plunge down its escape hatch, but the rope held.

"Help me!" yelled Kakagun.

Miraculously my numbness vanished and I was at his side in an instant.

"Hold it tight!" he commanded, as I took over the line with both hands, pulling for all I was worth against the struggling seal. Kakagun went down on his knees to cut the blowhole wide open with his snow knife. As he labored, water and blood spurted from the enlarged aperture. Obviously delighted, he kept encouraging me in my all-out effort to outlast the powerful, twisting amphibious mammal.

Led by their sniffing, yapping dogs, Kudnanak and Naodluak came running towards us as Kakagun kept chipping away the ice around the breathing hole with his ice chisel to make it wide enough for hauling in his prey. Together we pulled up the bleeding seal onto the ice, and the dogs leaped for the warm blood oozing out of its neck wound. Kakagun promptly kicked the huskies away and said, "Let's eat the liver! It will warm up our stomachs."

"Just then we heard faint shouts. Instinctively we all looked in Nokadlak's direction. Pulling on his harpoon rope with one arm, he was frantically waving to us with the other.

"Father got a seal!" Kudnanak voiced the obvious.

"Let's run!" reacted Kakagun.

We dropped our catch and sprinted. I could see Nokadlak straining like the anchorman on a tug-of-war team. He was backing up, using his weight for every possible advantage. Then he was suddenly down, flat out on the snow, sliding towards the breathing hole. Next moment he was struggling to stand up and pull his unseen adversary in the opposite direction. Now he was sitting on the snow, involuntarily skidding forward.

"Must be a big seal. Maybe an *ugiuk!*" Kakagun panted as we raced side by side to aid our mutual friend.

The moment we grabbed the rope from Nokadlak, we felt a powerful pull. No wonder he couldn't handle it alone, I thought. As fast as he could, Nokadlak opened and enlarged the blowhole. Then, smiling proudly, he said, "There's an *ugiuk* down there! I'll use your rifle, *Fala.*"

I had seen a few of these bearded or square-flipper seals before, but had never pulled one out of its breathing hole. Slimmer than the adipose walruses and sporting no tusks, the *ugiuks* are readily recognized by their length (up to ten feet), and their weight (up to eight hundred pounds), rather than by their "beards" which actually consist of long hair that hangs sparsely from the upper lips of both males and females. Feeding mostly on seaweed—unlike the hair, ringed, or common Arctic seals who favor fish in their diet—these huge, normally solitary amphibious mammals gather in small groups at breeding time in the fall, then disperse to their chosen territories. The females' pups are usually born in late March. As for breathing holes, the *ugiuks* prefer their own, but are quite willing to use those of the ordinary seals.

Aided by the boys, we drew back the rope until the bearded head of the huge seal appeared above the bloodied water. Nokadlak fired twice, point-blank. The turbulent water grew redder, then quietened. The fight was over. But we still had a job on our hands. The giant seal must have weighed a good five hundred pounds, and to hoist it up was a problem in itself. Nokadlak solved it by passing the rope through an incision in the animal's lower jaw and securing its snout in a loop. It took the combined strength of the rest of us to drag the massive *ugiuk* onto the ice floor while Nokadlak guided it through the suitably enlarged hole.

"The good spirits have been kind and helpful to you today, Nokadlak," said Kakagun charitably. "If the *ugiuk* had backed up under the ice floor, he would have swum away with your harpoon and maybe one or two of your fingers." Accepting this as a compliment, Nokadlak happily extracted the seal's liver and passed it around for each of us to sample. But I didn't take a bite because I had been warned in the past by Father Buliard that the *Ugiuk's* liver is often inhabited by long, white worms and could also be the home of trichinae, tiny, hair-like worms whose larvae infest the intestines and muscle tissues of man, causing diarrhea, stomach and muscular pains. Polar bear liver carries the same parasites. So I simply cut a large piece of the seal's liver and threw it on the ice floor, saying, "This is for the spirits who have been good to us." My friends all murmured their appreciation of my thoughtful gesture.

As she had promised earlier, Kablunak had tea ready for us behind her rampart of snow, when we rejoined her and young Naoyak. Kakagun's wife could see that our hunt had been successful, but Kudnanak surprised her and the little Seagull by announcing that his father had shot an *ugiuk*.

"You are certainly skilled!" Kablunak praised Nokadlak. And, admiringly, Naoyak echoed her adopted mother's words.

That evening, while we were resting in Kakagun's comfortable igloo, Naoyak came and sat beside me on the *iglek*. "Little Father," she began, "when you were helping Kakagun and Nokadlak hunt seals my mother Kablunak told me a story about a young man who could not catch seals. Would you like to hear it?"

"Certainly, Naoyak. I like stories."

"My mother said this man was a member of the Seal People group from King William Island. The strange thing about him was that when he went hunting seals, he had no luck at all. His wife got so tired of it that one day she told him, 'If you don't bring back a seal from your next hunt, I won't give you any water to drink.'

"This scared the man. He went out looking for seal breathing holes all over the sea ice. He walked and walked all day and all night, but never found a single blowhole. Instead he came across a big igloo. He went inside and found it belonged to a family of polar bears. After resting with them a few days, he returned to his own igloo. When his wife saw him, she asked, 'Where are the seals?'

" 'I didn't see any sign of a seal. They must be afraid of me,' he answered.

" 'Well, then, I won't give you water or broth to drink!' she said angrily.

"As the unlucky man sat sorrowfully on the *iglek,* he heard a big noise outside. Then, all of a sudden, part of the igloo caved in and a polar bear stood in the breach. It was the Good Spirit who had followed the man. The wife was so scared, she at once took the kettle off the rack and poured water for her husband. Seeing this, the big bear left, looking very pleased.

"From that day on, the husband always got water, broth, and

tea after hunting. Not only that, but after the polar bear's visit the man (who had been so unlucky in the past) now always returned from the hunt with seals. What's more, he became the greatest seal hunter of King William Island. He was called and is still remembered as the Great Seal Hunter."

"We'll try another trick on the seals," Kakagun told me a while later when I inquired why he and Nokadlak had prepared nearly three dozen three-pronged hooks. "Are you planning to place two or more of them in each blowhole?"

"No, *Fala*, only one in each."

"Then you'll probably have far more than you can possibly use."

"No. The ice is thick now and seal cows carve out resting chambers for their young at the top of the breathing holes. It's easier to set three-pronged hooks in many holes than to spear a seal in one of them."

"But how can a seal cow build a chamber in the solid ice, Kakagun?"

"She goes above the ice into the snowdrift protecting the breathing hole. There she scrapes out a small igloo. In it she takes care of her pup, or sleeps and rests herself. If the spirits are good to us, *Fala*, you will see for yourself."

It would have been an enjoyable hike had it not been for the ubiquitous cold and wind. I followed Kakagun and Naodluak, his son, with their leashed dogs, while Nokadlak and Kudnanak went their own way. It was understood that we would meet later by the dogsleds which were guarded, as before, by Kablunak and little Naoyak.

Whenever we discovered a breathing hole, Kakagun inserted a three-pronged hook through it, about a foot below the water line. Then he anchored the free end of the attached rope in the hard snow, placed a snow block, urinated on it, and the trap was ready.

Setting the three-pronged hook in the only three chambers took a little more effort and skill. In each case Kakagun had to cut open a hole in the roof of the hidden compartment large enough to pass his arm through it so he could lay the triple-pronged hook exactly the way he wanted it. Because I couldn't really see how he did it, a likely problem occurred to me, so I asked Kakagun, "When the seal cow enters the chamber, won't she notice your hook and avoid it?"

"No, I've covered it with fresh snow. The seal will come up head first from the hole and will glide over the hook without feeling it. But when she begins to back out, then she'll get caught by the prongs."

"So from what you say, it should be easier to catch a seal which has no rest chamber, but only a breathing hole."

"That's right, *Fala*. In the hole the pronged hook hangs straight down. It doesn't bother the seal as he comes up for air, but often catches him on the way down because the hole is narrow."

"Can't a hooked seal free himself when you're not around?"

"He will struggle and try to dive down, but he won't succeed. He will starve and eventually freeze if the hunter does not return to that breathing hole in good time."

There was still some daylight left when we returned to camp. Naoyak and Naodluak took advantage of it to check some traps the girl had placed near weasel holes along the riverbank. When they returned she proudly exhibited five small animals, less than a foot long but with beautiful short white fur. I was curious. "What are you going to do with the ermine fur?" I asked Naoyak. "Are you going to put it on the sleeves of Naodluak's parka for good luck, so he can say, 'Weasel, weasel, come and fight bad luck to its death!'?"

"No, *Fala*, I'm going to trade it for calico."

"Why?"

"To make a nice dress for spring. That's when we go for the big trading."

Too bad, I thought, these handsome ermine furs won't bring you much more than a dollar or two in kind at the trading post!

I was awakened next morning by Kakagun, who was the first up. *"Fala,"* he said, "Nokadlak and I are leaving early. Do you still want to take a good look at the three-pronged hooks with us?"

"How's the weather?"

"You can hear the wind. It's also misty. But it's passable."

"I'll be ready soon."

From marker to marker Kakagun and I went, stopping at every blowhole in the four-mile circle. We gave each line a tug to see if there was anything on it. Two of them rewarded our efforts. As we hauled in the first seal onto the ice, Kakagun turned the struggling mammal on its back, saying "Here's the way to kill a seal *Fala*." With his left hand pulling on a flipper, he raised the animal's forepart, then sharply snapped its head against the middle with his right hand. I heard the muffled crack of breaking bones in the seal's neck, but that was all. Without so much as a cry, it lay limp and dead at the great hunter's feet. He insisted that I deliver the same merciful *coup de grace* to the other seal, and I found his method easy to execute and thoroughly efficient.

"That's a fair catch for one day," Kakagun said contentedly as we loaded the seals aboard the sled. His gaze went past the sealskin, picturing food for us all, as well as fuel for the blubber lamp. "We'll come back tomorrow and look for other breathing holes," he added smiling.

With the wind lashing us from the southwest, we hurried back to camp. I couldn't share Kakagun's delight. The chilling blasts seemed to penetrate to the center of my skull.

Nokadlak returned a little later. He had managed to get one seal, and bagged several ptarmigans in the bargain. He joined the rest of us in Kakagun's ample igloo where Kablunak passed around meat, fish, and boiled seal blood until a chorus of belches announced that our appetites were satisfied.

A renewed feeling of happiness and good humor pervaded the shining white abode, accompanied by a general upsurge of confidence. Only those who had gone cold and hungry could really have understood how we felt that night. While we were enjoying the warmth and comfort of the igloo, and the children were playing the cat's cradle game with strips of calico and teasing one another, Kakagun surprised me with, "Little Father, you came to our land to tell us about the Good Spirit of the White Man. Will you tell us about Him now, just as we told you about the Spirits of our Land in the past?"

"Only too gladly, Kakagun. After all, that's why I left my country and my family to come here and tell your people about this wonderful Spirit."

Under the flickering light of the blubber lamp, I recounted the never-ending search of all the earth's peoples, tribes, and groups for the Great Good Spirit who would satisfy their hunger for total happiness.

"The search went on everywhere and in countless ways," I continued. "Between their joys and sorrows, hopes and fears, people tried to influence the higher world, even as you do to this day, by magical rites, by offers of food, or by invoking the spirits. Until one day a Man came and said He was God, the Chief of all Good Spirits. He came from the darkness, as the sun rises at the end of the long winter night. And people from all over the world began to turn to Him because He was like a great light. That's why I came to your land Kakagun. To let you and your people know that there is Someone above us all Who cares for you and me and everybody else."

24

Interlude

My friends accompanied me back to Burnside for their spring trading splurge. The morning after our arrival there, I had an unexpected visitor at the Mission. It was Naoyak, the young Seagull. She sat down on a bench in the living room and informed me that some travelers were coming.

"Aren't you going to greet them?" I inquired.

"I came to ask you to come with me."

"First let me give you some tea and bread I just made, Naoyak. Then we'll go." She drank her tea hurriedly and took a slice of bread with jam on it. "Thank you, *Fala*. Now let's meet the newcomers! They should be getting close."

We walked within sight of the fifteen igloos and tents, including Kakagun's and Nokadlak's, strung out along the channel's shore, and sat down on a drift of hard snow. "Look, look! Many travelers!" she cried with roused feeling as six dogs teams came into view around the bend of the channel while the entire village population poured out to watch them cover the last quarter-mile across the snow floor.

"Do you know any of these people, Naoyak?"

"Yes, I have seen them all before inland. They are from Lake Beechey and Hanimok (a confluent of the Burnside River). Look they all have big loads! They must have caught lots of foxes."

All the new arrivals wore well-trimmed clothing, as if they had just left their igloos to attend a dance. But their tired, weather-beaten faces spoke silently of storms, hardships, and fatigue. Incongruously, their lordly handshakes and broad smiles intermingled with loud sorrowful wails that reechoed on the sloping banks of the channel.

"Somebody died inland," Naoyak, my young "godchild" correctly surmised.

Nevertheless the moans and laments—polite expressions of sympathy for relatives who had died recently—were readily supplanted by the excitement of renewing friendships after months of near-isolation.

Knowing how busy Burnside trader Leo Manning would be with this crowd that day, I purposely avoided the H.B.C. trading post until he could catch his breath. Instead I took advantage of the warm sun to browse through the camp, to find out exactly who had arrived, and learn their latest happenings.

Characteristically, the campground was untidy, if not revolting. Strewn with litter of dog and man, the area had been used as a latrine by both. As a partial grace, though, human excrement had been disposed of by the ever-present Husky pups. Around each igloo the snow floor was strewn with caribou skins, firearms, bundles of traps, harpoons, scoops, and ice chisels. Piles of frozen caribou carcasses and bundles of dried fish lay close to the dwellings. The sleds were partially covered with snow to prevent the peat runners from melting in the sun. Amply exposed to the wind, boots, fur socks, caribou and seal hides, and anything else that needed drying or bleaching hung on ropes strung between poles.

In response to repeated, loud tea calls, I dropped in on several families. Everywhere the story was happily the same. Their trapping had been good, starvation was avoided, the past was forgotten, the present was theirs to enjoy. Meat and fish, dry or frozen, were generously passed around and consumed with gusto. Every family shared their bounty with those who weren't even related to them, as had been their immemorial custom. Their strong herd instinct brought them together in much the same way that prompted musk-oxen, wolves, or caribou to band together for survival in the dangerous Land Beyond.

Outside his tent, Nokadlak was unwrapping the furs on his sled. "Go in, *Fala*" he said. "Angivrana will give you some tea."

I asked him who had died inland during the winter.

"It was Karonak, the hunchback."

Karonak, I knew, had experienced back problems for several years. He had come to the Mission complaining of constant pain in his spine. There was a kind of overgrowth between his shoulder blades, and the last time I saw him it had developed into a large mass of fibrous tissue which forced the poor fellow into

384

his grotesque posture. On that occasion Karonak, who was a good storyteller, sat down on the floor of my living room, his deformed back against the wall, his hands around a tea cup, and said to me, "You remember I told you some stories about a man we call Kiviuk. I have not seen him, but it is said that he visited Taheriuak many times. Nobody really knew where he came from. Some claimed he came from the Bottom of the Sea; others, from the Land of the Day.

"Anyway, when he came to Taheriuak the last time, he saw an igloo that had no porch and apparently no door. (He simpy didn't realize it was an overnight 'traveling' igloo whose entry was closed with a block of snow from within). Curious, he climbed atop the igloo and and made a hole in it with his snow knife. Below he saw a woman scraping human skin. She could hear someone moving above her and could see some snowflakes float down before her. But when she looked up, she couldn't detect Kiviuk because her eyelids were so big they wouldn't open when she tilted her head back. This made her so mad, she cut off her eyelids with her *ulon* (half-moon shaped knife), and Kiviuk saw two bleeding eyes staring at him.

"While he descended from the top of the igloo, she quickly removed the block of snow from the door, emerged outside, and invited him to enter her igloo. Once they were both inside, she asked Kiviuk to undress and place his clothing on the drying rack above the blubber lamp. Then she took her *ulon* and told him she was going out to fetch more blubber for the stone lamp. Unbeknown to Kiviuk, the woman was a sorceress who intended to make a big fire in which to cook Kiviuk and eat him.

"Looking around the igloo, Kiviuk saw many human skulls, all clean-picked without a trace of flesh on them. To his added amazement, one of the skulls opened its mouth and said: 'Run away, run away! Or the sorceress will eat you when she returns. Look at us! She devoured our bodies. Nothing is left of us, but our bones. Run, run for your life!'

"When Kiviuk tried to grab his clothing off the rack, he could not do so because they were jumping up and down and sideways. Fortunately Kiviuk had a helpful Spirit—Orkpik, the Big Owl—whom he invoked at once: 'Orkpik, Orkpik, fly over here and help me!' The Bird Spirit flew in through the opening in the roof and with wings pushed Kiviuk's clothing into his arms. Dressing as speedily as he could, Kiviuk darted through the door and sprinted down the sloping seashore to his kayak.

"The sorceress spied Kiviuk and chased after him. But he had a good start on her and was already paddling in deep water by the time she reached the water's edge. Aware that she could not now reach him, she became so angry that she slashed her *ulon* at a large rock, cutting the massive stone into small pieces, like chunks of caribou meat. Meanwhile Kiviuk seized his harpoon and plunged it into an even bigger rock which stuck out of the water. Seeing how strong Kiviuk was, the sorceress yelled to him, 'Come back and be my husband!'

"But Kiviuk was too scared to trust her and paddled away. In her rage the sorceress threw her *ulon* in his direction, but the knife failed to reach the target. Instead it skidded over the water, creating many ice floes. It is said among our people," Karonak, the hunchback, concluded, "that the ice on the seas, the lakes, and the rivers was created by the sorceress at that moment. Before Kiviuk met the sorceress, there had never been ice on our waters."

Having picked up an armful of furs from his sled, Nokadlak followed me into his tent. "I'm going to see if they are in good shape and then trade some of them," he told me.

His wife Angivrana sat on the *iglek*, putting on her boots. Her baby rested comfortably in her parka hood. Nokadlak tossed the furs to Angivrana, "Have a look through these. We can trade them now."

Instead of sorting the pelts, she replied, "The *Kablunak* (White Man, i.e. the trader) will look at them all. But we must remember to get something in exchange that we really need." In the silence of their igloo in the Arctic Sound she had decided long ago what they should obtain at the trading post. But from previous experience she knew that once Nokadlak was confronted with the wealth of the trading post, her advice would be quickly forgotten—unless, of course, she was right there beside him to remind him of their prime needs.

Together we walked up the hillock to Leo Manning's emporium. Like a King Eider displaying his colorful plumage, Nokadlak entered the warehouse with his bundle of fine furs. And fluttering like a goose about to take flight, Angivrana was close on his heels. They glanced around quickly. A dozen hunters with their women and children had preceded them. Here was the moment Nokadlak and Angivrana had looked forward to all winter. Here was their one great opportunity to show off in front of their friends.

Nokadlak's eyes kept shifting from side to side. He had come with the intention of making a brilliant impression on everyone. Yet now he stood speechless, almost breathless, before the awesome array of the *Kablunak's* ingenious merchandise. Sparkling hardware shone at him from the shelves or dangled tantalizingly from the rafters. Beautiful new rifles, boxes upon boxes of ammunition, dog harnesses and tools of every kind, crates of tea, sacks of sugar, flour, glassware, enamel cups, bundles of calico—the choice seemed endless. He was thrown off balance, as a child in a toy shop. Mechanically he pulled the furs out of his bag and dumped them on the counter. "Give me this! That!" he began pointing indiscriminately at a variety of articles, and Leo obligingly fetched and laid them before him.

Ever practical and self-possessed despite the strange surroundings and glittering temptations, Angivrana stepped in to rescue her bewildered spouse. "Why do you choose what you don't like? I don't think you'll really want a dog collar. We need a kettle, some enamel cups, a pot, needles."

Entranced by the seemingly limitless commodities on display Nokadlak hardly noticed his wife. But Angivrana wasn't so easily discouraged. She knew precisely what she wanted, and she meant to get it. "We have only a little tea and tobacco left. I thought you would want to get some," she wheedled him.

"It doesn't matter," he countered impatiently. "If you would only leave the thinking to me."

They stayed in the store literally for hours, arguing back and forth over each item, trying to get the most out of the Kablunak they were set on outwitting. Thoroughly wise in their ways, Leo left them alone while he attended to other customers like them, who were closer to reaching a final decision.

When Nokadlak and Angivrana ultimately left, shorn of the furs, but laden with bags and boxes of White Man merchandise, they paused outside the store and I heard Nokadlak complain, "We have no matches!"

So back they went and Nokadlak told Leo as soon as he got his attention, "It's too bad, but we didn't get any matches. How are we going to light fires without them?" He rummaged through his purchases and brought out a roll of twine. "Look, White Man, I don't need this. Will you exchange it for matches?"

Leo accommodated him without protest. To me he said in English with a wink, "They'll be back again!"

Visitors swarmed into Nokadlak's tent almost as soon as he and Angivrana returned from their shopping spree. He spread his purchases flamboyantly, with the triumphant smile of the shrewd and successful bargainer. As his guests picked over the newly acquired articles with various complimentary exclamations and gestures, one of the men held up a watch and asked: "What are you going to do with this, Nokadlak?"

"I don't know. The baby might like to play with it."

"I'll trade you a newborn pup for it. How's that?"

"Good. I need more dogs!"

An hour earlier Nokadlak had paid two foxes for that watch. Now he was exchanging it for a puppy worth one fox at most. But it was spring. He was happy. And at the year's end he would have a new, trained member for his dog team.

Before the last of Nokadlak's visitors left, his former watch had been successively traded for a snow knife, then for a beautiful parka, a dozen traps, and finally for a night with the successful bidder's wife. Through the rest of the day similar exchanges of goods and services were negotiated between the holidaying hunters.

On subsequent days more families arrived from different parts of the Land Beyond, until by the end of the week a hundred dancers crowded nightly into the large communal igloo. Among them I spotted my former guide at Cambride Bay, the self-centered hunter Kunak. After exchanging greetings, I asked him if he had found himself a wife in the interim. A cocksure laugh preceeded his confident reply, "I have a better time without a wife, *Fala!*" Later that evening, when Kunak took up the drum, his boastful nature came through loud and clear:

> I'm still a young man. *Aya, aya, ya, ya. . .*
> Caribou and seals are no match for me.
> On the sea ice I hunt the great Polar Bear—
> Nothing is impossible for me! *Aya, ya, ya, ya. . .*

Kunak continued his song with vainglorious claims of his remarkable prowess in hunting and in lovemaking, as well as the matchless speed of his dogs. His last claim could not go unchallenged. Towards the end of the dance when the women had brought in their steaming kettles of tea to accompany the meat and fish, everyone squatted restfully on the snow floor, Kakagun's husky voice rose above all others: "Hey, Kunak, you said your dogs can beat anyone's team here. How about a race tomorrow?"

"My dogs brought me here from Cambridge Bay in four days. They are a little tired. But they're still good enough for a race. I'll bet a fox that I'll win!"

"I'll take that bet!" Kakagun rejoined eagerly. "It will be easier than catching a fox with a trap!" His audience laughed appreciatively.

When news of the coming race reached his trading post, Leo Manning wasted no time in putting up five foxes for the first prize, three for second, and one for third. In addition, the public relations conscious Hudson's Bay Company's local representative offered to stage a party for everybody following the big race. The dogs themselves must have sensed their masters' excitement, for their howling now drowned out everything while the hunters went about icing up their sleds and harnessing their teams. The contestants had earlier agreed to use only five dogs to a sled, and to carry no extra weight on it.

I accompanied Leo to the starting point at the entrance of the channel where a noisy, joyful crowd had already gathered. Presently the competing teams drove up to their positions on the starting line. We counted forty-five entrants (plus their two hundred twenty-five lively huskies).

"Better tell the drivers the rules now, Father," Leo suggested. "Once around Koagiuk Island and back here. No running alongside the dogs. No whips. Then start them off with a rifle shot."

Walking behind the sleds so that all the drivers could hear me, I kept repeating the rules in Eskimo. That done, I stood back, waited briefly for them to get set, and fired into the air. Amid a roar from the partisan spectators, the startled dogs scrambled in all directions. Some actually turned right around and headed back for camp, despite the insistent *"gee"* (right) and *"ha"* (left) commands of their respective masters. Several teams managed to tangle, resulting in a monstrous dog fight. Bystanders ran to break it up, while dogs left behind on their lines contributed to the general tumult with their furious yelping. The complete commotion was indescribable.

"What a start! What a shambles!" Leo roared delightedly as he, too, tried to restore a semblance of order in the proceedings.

The hubbub subsided only when the last of the contestants was finally off and running, with the teams now strung out on the seafloor among the snowdrifts.

"How long do you think it'll take them to get back, Father?"

"The course is a good twenty miles. I'd imagine the winners will cover it in about three hours."

"That's a pretty long wait. Why don't we organize something for the young folk in the meantime?"

The Krangmalit boys and girls took naturally to sprinting races and to tug-of-war between the sexes. In the latter event, while their parents screamed encouragement with "Come on, come on!" the boys suddenly slackened the long rope. Unprepared for this crafty maneuver, most of the girls lost their balance, landing on their seats. Taking immediate advantage of their adversaries, the boys gleefully hauled them across the middle line to win the contest butts down. Loud praise for the cunning little men and suggestive comments about the frailty of little women filled air. Everybody laughed heartily, and Leo gave out his candy prizes.

"Maybe the women can do better than the men," I suggested.

That was all the incentive they needed. The men expected little resistance from the weaker sex and almost let their cockiness defeat them. On the opposite end of the rope the women proved tenacious, if nothing else. And for a truly dependable anchor they had picked the tallest and strongest woman in the camp. She wasn't fat—for no Eskimo woman has a chance to get plump in the Barren Land—but she was built as solidly as a man. Planting her feet in a snowdrift, she dug in her heels and refused to be budged. Disconcerted by their ineffective initial attempts, and goaded by the explicit taunts of the children and old people on the sidelines, the men could gain no ground. Neither would they surrender an inch. Very gradually, however, the strain proved too much for most of the females and they summarily surrendered. That "war" was also over.

We were in the midst of foot races for women when someone sighted the first of the returning dog teams a couple of miles away. To get a better view of the home stretch, we all climbed the sloping bank.

"Who's in the lead?" was the question on everyone's lips. "He's well ahead of the rest!"

I noticed Kablunak and Naoyak standing close together, watching intently. Tense moments passed. Then the girl's excited voice rang out, "The lead dog is white. It must be Kakagun's team!"

"It's Kakagun! It's Kakagun!" the word flew round.

Nearly everyone shook hands with the great hunter as he crossed the finish line. He beamed a smile becoming the victor. When I had a chance to congratulate him, he laughed. "The race was won before we started, *Fala!*"

"What do you mean, Kakagun?"

For the last few days I fed my dogs caribou meat. They liked it. Yesterday I didn't feed them at all. Today they were furious because I let them smell the meat, but didn't give them any. To earn it they ran like wolves!"

And the boastful Kunak? He placed neither second, nor third. Two other young men from Hanimok did that. Kunak, the braggart was sixteenth.

When all the teams were in, everybody headed for the trading post, milling outside the helper's shack where Leo served tea, *pilote* bread, and jam. I had contributed caribou meat and rice, which several women volunteered to cook for the hungry multitude.

Nearby Leo set up a block of snow and placed a target on it. He paced off a hundred yards and waited for the rifle marksmen. Each hunter was allowed three rounds, courtesy of the Hudson's Bay Company, which also provided the prizes—several cartons of .30-30 ammunition.

Again Kakagun emerged the winner. But now I thought I sensed a hint of jealousy or resentment among the other participants. This gave me some concern. With the hunters being primitive, impulsive men, perhaps my friend Kakagun was taking unnecessary chances by showing off a little too much, I silently conjectured. In some remote camp or corner of the Land Beyond his present stellar performance might eventually invite a mortal rifle shot or stab by an envious competitor.

Finally, there was an archery shoot to divert the assembled crowd. This time my old freind Nerreok, the lone wolf hunter, proved to be the outstanding performer. His arrows not only hit the thick snow target at thirty-five yards, they went right through it and landed well beyond. No wonder I had not been able to draw his bow when he offered it to me at Melville Sound! And I wasn't the only one amazed by Nerreok's power and archery skill. Waiting his own turn to shoot, Nokadlak told me with apparent awe, "Nerreok killed two caribou that were running side by side with only one arrow!" Thus the archery championship was never in doubt as Nerreok triumphantly carried off the prize—two one-pound tins of tobacco.

Inevitably the great excitement of fur trading and visiting each other subsided after a few days when the mundane problem of dog-food supply became a worry for most hunters. Some of them, in fact, were getting ready to leave for the entrance of Bathurst Inlet, noted for its spring seal hunt. Therefore I was hardly surprised when Kakagun and Nokadlak came to the Mission early one morning and asked me if I'd like to go seal hunting with them for the day. "We don't have much blubber left for our lamps, *Fala,* and we're low on dog food," they chorused.

"I'll gladly go with you, but I'll take a small sled and only five dogs. That should be enough to carry a few seals—if we're lucky enough to get them."

We had reached a reef north of Koagiuk Island when Nokadlak stopped his dogs and pointed to a dark spot on the white expanse about a half a mile ahead. As Kakagun and I also halted our teams, Nokadlak said, "The snow is crackling under our feet. I'll go afer *Nathek* alone." Out of his hunting bag he drew a long white sealskin parka and put it on. It fell to his knees, and its hood hid not only his head, but also part of his face. Thus camouflaged, he ran forward in a crouch with the sun at his rear, while Kakagun and I watched from behind rocks.

"*Nathek,* the seal, is short-sighted," said Kakagun. "He will think Nokadlak is a piece of rough ice and will let him come close."

When he was a mere fifty yards or so from the seal, Nokadlak fell prone and waited for the seal to raise its head. When it had gone back to sleep, he ran a few more steps, flopped on the sea ice, and uncovered his rifle. Fully armed, he continued to worm his way closer to his prey until he lay ready to shoot. The seal's head came up. There was a loud report. *"Nathek's* dreams are over forever!" said Kakagun approvingly. Then he added, "I'll show you I am as good as Nokadlak. Let's find another seal!"

We drove up to Nokadlak, his dog team willingly following ours, and resumed the hunt. Every few minutes Kakagun stood up on his sled for a better view of the frozen sea. "There!" he finally exclaimed, pointing. "This one is not too far away. And there are many more in the distance. Let's stop now. Otherwise he may hear or scent us."

Kakagun quickly attached a four-foot square white canvas sail to a tiny sled, whose runners were intentionally wrapped in strips of polar-bear skin to deaden sound. Only three-feet long and not much more than a foot wide, somewhat like a child's sleigh, it served merely to support the small sail that concealed his movements from the vigilant seal, whom he could observe the while through a peephole in the canvas screen.

"Keep the dogs from howling, *Fala,*" Kakagun said quietly. He gazed around, sniffing at the breeze, plucked a few hairs from his parka and tossed them in the air to check the wind's direction. "I'll have to walk a long way round, or the wind will waft my scent to the seal," he soliloquized. Stooping behind the sail, he walked off, pushing the tiny sled before him with the barrel of his rifle. Half an hour later I could barely discern him stalking the intended prey. Kakagun was crawling now, getting within firing range. The unsuspecting seal didn't have a chance.

It was natural that both hunters should offer the third seal we sighted to me. "Lets see if a Kablunak can be as good as an Inuk," Kakagun teased me. "Go ahead, *Fala,* try it!" added Nokadlak.

I borrowed the latter's white parka, and used his tactics to approach the seal from the rear. When I was some thirty yards from it, I let its eyes get used to my prostrate white form. It seemed to me that *Nathek* stared unduly long in my direction and I was about to shoot when another seal raised its head out of the same blowhole. I took a potshot at the latecomer, then fired quickly at my original quarry before he could dive.

"You are like an Inuk, *Fala!*" Kakagun complimented me as he and Nokadlak brought up my team. "But we heard two shots. Why?"

"Look in the blowhole. The reason may be there."

A quick glance down the breathing hole was sufficient for my friends. "You're certainly capable *Fala!*" they chorused, pounding my shoulders in approval.

The news of our successful seal hunt brought about a marked change in the attitude of even the most lackadaisical hunters, serving as a reminder that their dog food, too, was dwindling and it was the right time to move to the hunting grounds. Several hunters left the next day for Taheriuak in the expectation of encountering caribou there, but the majority headed during the next few days for the entrance of Bathurst Inlet, some eighty miles to the north. There, on Wilmot Island, seals would be plentiful about this time of the year and hunters would congregate from as far as Cambridge Bay, Richardson Island, and Tree River, only to disperse in all directions two or three weeks later before the summer ice break up.

The last to leave Burnside were the families of Kakagun and Nokadlak. With their impending departure for Wilmot Island, there was no point in my remaining at the Mission. My duty was to keep in close touch with the People Beyond.

25

Snowbound

A mass of whirling snow granules drifted over Wilmot Island when we arrived there, bucking a cold northeaster. It was a foretaste of the miserable weather that was to dog us almost daily for the next two weeks.

Tents were pitched all around the main cove, which faced out of its horseshoe of surrounding cliffs. Each tent was protected by five-foot snow walls, with only its top exposed, flapping in the wind. A small trading post, once the domain of a White Man named Jim Eccless, was now closed. Set on an inclined gravel beach, the old building looked over a splendid natural harbor.

So preoccupied were earlier arrivals with minding their own tents and equipment in the howling wind, that our coming was virtually unnoticed. No dance was held that night. The men were too tired to build a hall, and it was too cold for open-air frolicking.

Howling dogs woke me up late next morning. Another team was pulling into the camp. I breakfasted on coffee and started my rounds. The wind had grown stronger overnight, hurling snow on the sea, the beach, and on the distant bluffs whose tops were rounded by centuries of erosion. Only a few hunters were outside, checking their dogs and sleds.

Kakagun's tent was crowded. His wife, Kablunak, was serving tea to the newest guests, a young couple whom I readily recognized as Pokiak, the seductive dancer who came to my tent one evening at Ellice River, and her husband Mituk. A child's head showed from Pokiak's hood. I shook hands with them and asked Mituk conversationally what kind of weather they had faced on the trail. He wrinkled is nose before answering, "We had wind every day after we left Tree River. Yesterday we couldn't even see this island, and camped on the sea ice."

Politely Pokiak added, "We are glad to see you again, *Fala*. Look at my baby boy sleeping in my hood. His name is Tupek, the Tent. I thought of you when I conceived him."

In due course, when I told Kakagun and Kablunak I was going to visit the other people in camp, Naoyak, the Little Seagull, said, "You'll find everybody in, *Fala*. It's too stormy for hunting. I'll come with you." She slipped on her outdoor parka and put on her warm mittens. Without saying a word, Naodluak (Kakagun's son and her betrothed) followed us.

"Which tent do you want to visit, *Fala?*"

"Any one will do, Naoyak."

Confidently she guided us from tent to tent. She seemed to know everybody in camp. Her excellent memory certainly spared me the incivility of asking my future hosts their names or where they came from. The few times that she hesitated, Naodluak was able to help out. He, too, was proud of his intimate knowledge of the families we called on, and his fund of stories about them was unending. "That tiny, chubby woman we just saw, *Fala,* is Ikayaluk. She has passed from man to man. Five, perhaps more. She stays with one hunter, then another. And always some stranger comes along and takes her away."

"What's her present husband's name?"

"It's Krihuk. He is a great fighter with his fists."

"I didn't see children near their tent. Have they any?"

"Ukayaluk never had a boy. She bears only girls. She is childless."

In another tent we saw a tall, lean man who stood off by himself, acting in a peculiarly restless fashion. He kept hopping from foot to foot, shaking like a dog just out of the water, and laughing continuously at everything and everybody in sight. "That's Kaotak," Naoyak said quietly to me. "He's from Ellice River."

Outside I asked Naodluak what he knew about Kaotak. "I heard he killed two men, *Fala*. He took away the wife of his first victim, but he ill-treated her and she soon died. Then he lived with the young wife of the other murdered man. She bore him a child. But she ran off with another hunter. Since then he has been shaking like that. He has lost control of his mind, it is said."

In another tent Naodluak introduced me to a couple in their late twenties who hailed from Melville Sound. The young man's name was Alikamek; his wife's Mangaluk. After leaving them I told Naodluak that I had heard (from Scotty Gall, the H.B.C. trader at Cambridge Bay) of an Alikamek who had killed two White Men at Tree River. His immediate reply sounded reassuring, "This is not the same Alikamek. He is the son of the murderer."

I couldn't remember the full details of the killings, nor even the names of the two slain White Men. But I did recall that late in 1922 there had been a lot of trouble among the People at the Far End of Melville Sound, brought on largely by the local shortage of women. Two young men, Alikamek and Taptamikana, had tried to take away a woman from her husband. In the ensuing struggle five Eskimos were killed, including that woman and her spouse. Alikamek and his friend were picked up a few weeks later by a corporal of the Royal Canadian Mounted Police from Tree River. At the R.C.M.P. station, where they were temporarily held, Alikamek managed to seize the corporal's rifle while he was resting and shot him on the spot. The Hudson's Bay Company's trader heard the fire and rushed over to the scene. Alikamek killed him, too.

Within an hour of the shooting, two teams arrived at the post, one of them carrying the stricken corporal's companion, a young R.C.M.P. constable returning from a routine patrol to Coppermine. Alikamek and Taptamikana were arrested by the new arrivals without a fight and taken without delay to Herschel Island, site of the main R.C.M.P. Station in the Central Arctic, roughly a thousand miles to the west, near northeast Alaska's Demarcation Point. There the two murderers waited two years to be tried. Meanwhile they were allowed to move in perfect freedom within the confines of the police station. Finally, after a further investigative delay, they were condemned to be hanged. Both went to the gallows without apparent fear or remorse, smiling to the end.

For the next three days Wilmot Island's weather steadily deteriorated. Powdery snow fell continuously. With the wind's help, it sifted through every tiny hole in our tents and buried our sleds, the dogs, and any equipment left outside. We spent much of our time digging out and cleaning our belongings. It was an exhausting, unproductive, endless task. The hunters were becoming growingly impatient. Here it was May, yet still no sign of early summer. Supplies were dwindling fast, but it was impossible to replenish them under these atmospheric conditions.

Towards the end of the week, the winds gradually dropped and everybody emerged to remove some of the drifts around the tents and generally resume more normal activities. Suddenly someone shouted, "Look, *aangnek!*" Overhead a flock of ducks was flying north.

"They're looking for open water," said Nokadlak, "But they'll find nothing but ice."

"At least we know that warmer weather's coming," Kakagun observed more optimistically.

Some of us couldn't help chuckling when an hour or so later the ducks were back overhead, flying lower but faster in the opposite direction towards the bottom of Bathurst Inlet where open water was now forming at the mouths of the rivers.

To soothe their habitual restlessness, the hunters and their families exchanged frequent visits, despite the dangers and extreme discomforts of venturing out during blizzards.

"Come on, *Fala!* Come with us. You won't get lost with us," Nokadlak or Kakagun would say to me whenever they decided to call on their friends in various parts of the camp. It was like preparing a full-scale polar expedition. Outer parkas, breeches, and a snow knife were minimum equipment for everybody but the babies, who took the chance in their mothers' hoods. The hunters and their wives realized that losing their way in the swirling, blinding snow meant possible death, unless someone had an implement for building a small igloo to wait out the storm.

The women held sewing bees, which kept them cheerfully occupied and afforded them added opportunities for small talk, gossip, and occasional songs. A woman might start to sing and her friends would join her in the refrain:

> "Certainly we all desire a strong man, *yai, yai, ya.*
> I knew such a man; I have seen him
> Running across the hills like a caribou.
> By my tent I stood, impatient,
> Wishing he would come and lie beside me.
> Certainly we all desire a strong man,
> *Yai, yai, ya, ya, a, a. . . .*

With Kakagun and Kablunak I happened to be detained one evening in one of the largest tents in camp where half a dozen women had gathered with their sewing. They chatted and laughed as they scraped, rubbed, and chewed the caribou skins they would later fashion into handsome parkas. Kakagun shifted his large frame uncomfortably and said to me, "Let's go and see the menfolk. These women sound like a flight of ducks!"

Overhearing the comparison, a chubby, elderly woman with a pear-shaped face retorted, "Your wife had brought in lots of skins. Why can't a big strong man like you help her scrape them?"

When Kakagun chose to ignore her, Pokiak, with her baby in the hood, spoke for all to hear, "Men will give their urine to dampen the skins, but they don't want to touch them with their hands!" While there was more truth than humor in her remark, everybody laughed as if it was a great joke, adding their own ribald comments. It was Kakagun's cue for a string of lewd remarks on women in general. Surprisingly (to me) the women enjoyed the insults immensely, and kept looking at me to see if I would join in. I pretended not to understand the mutual off-color defamation, and the talk eventually returned to sewing.

"Who made your parka, *Fala?*" asked Pokiak with an admiring look.

"Kablunak did, when I was at the Place of Reunion, or Arctic Sound."

"It's beautiful!"

Kablunak smiled self-consciously as I said, "She is a very clever seamstress."

"Do the White Women also make clothes as we do?" asked the chubby one.

"Yes, they, too, make clothes, but they use mostly calico because it's never cold in my country. And their dresses are of different shapes and colors."

It was virtually beyond their imagination that somewhere was another land where ice and snow did not exist, and they would look at each other openmouthed, whispering, "No kidding! How could such a place exist? Even in summer, when the sun warms our land, we feel the cold."

Aloud one of them added, "Our clothes are the same because we use only caribou skin for protection from the wind and cold."

"Why don't you use other animal skins for variety?"

"We don't use seal, *Fala*, because it isn't warm enough in winter. Besides, it stiffens in cold weather. The white bear and the musk-ox are too warm and too heavy. Wolf and fox fur is warm and light; but it's too weak and snow sticks to it and cakes it into ice."

It was during one such session that I was able to renew my acquaintance with Kirluayok, the sorcerer. We had not seen each other since he had tried to cure little Naoyak's stomachache at Kubiartorvik, but he spoke to me now as if there had been no interruption in our friendly relationship. "You are too much by yourself, *Fala*. Why don't you take a wife like everybody else here?"

"Many White Men live without wives, and I'm one of them.

If I was married, I wouldn't be here to help your people."

This simple explanation didn't satisfy Kirluayok. Besides, he liked to have the last word. "*Fala*, look at the beasts. They are like us, male and female, and they always mate. It is good to have a wife. It is no good to live alone."

"You and I know many young men here without mates, Kirluayok. And you yourself have no wife, either."

"I had a wife, but she died. I could have one now. But I like to sleep with a different woman wherever I go. That's what young men do. There are too few women among my people to go round."

"Yes, I know, Kirluayok. That's the reason you and the young men like to move from camp to camp."

"But whenever a young man finds a woman, young or old, he marries her," interposed Kakagun.

"Yes, they must marry," Kirluayok repeated automatically.

"Yes, yes," cooed an old woman squatting forlornly in a corner of the *iglek*. "I always trained my children how to mate when they were young. Now they are all married and have their own children to teach."

"And I have already taught Naodluak and Naoyak," echoed Kakagun. "Now they always sleep together. Naodluak doesn't have to look for a wife, unless he loses Naoyak by being a poor hunter."

"We gave Nokadlak a rifle and three dogs for Naoyak," Kablunak reminisced. "When I was a girl, my parents handed me over to the parents of my first husband for nothing. They were good friends and good hunters."

"I was a good hunter when I was younger," said the sorcerer. "I got my wife for nothing, too. I tried her out for two winters. She was good. Then she became pregnant. I don't know whether I made her pregnant for I had many good friends. But I knew I had to take care of her. She bore me three sons. Then one day I found her dead in the *krepik* (sleeping bag). You're a White Man, *Fala*. I can tell you that many of our women would like to sleep with you."

"You can have my wife, *Fala*," offered Kakagun. "Kablunak told me that she likes you." Trying to appear unaffected by Kakagun's remark, she gave me a quick smile and stood up to serve tea. I deemed it best to hold my tongue.

The unbroken stormy weather was getting on everyone's nerves. On several occasions the men set out to build a communal igloo for a dance, only to see the gusty winds either eat away the friable snow blocks as fast as they could cut them, or pile up drifts to hamper their progress. Apart from the

399

uncooperative elements, their own hearts were clearly not in the job at hand. Even the visions of wild nights of dancing and carousing didn't help them shake their lethargy as if the numbing cold and their protracted inactivity had penetrated all their senses.

Then there was the business of finding food for the dogs—a problem I shared with the rest. Much as I hated to face the storm, I went out with Kakagun and Nokadlak after tomcods, the only fish available at the time. If they did nothing else, however, these excursions to a comparatively protected cove on the west side of the island helped shake me out of my sluggishness. Like my friends, I was smothered by the well-known "Arctic mania" brought on by worry, loneliness, and bitter cold. We walked along the shore and across a narrow strip of land to the fishing spot where, in the lee of the sloping bluffs, earlier arrivals met behind blocks of snow and jigged for tomcod.

"I'll make a hole for you first, *Fala*. Then you can help me scoop out the chips of ice," said Kakagun. It didn't take us very long to ready a couple of holes, even though the sea ice was five to six feet thick. Half an hour later, warmed by our efforts, we sat down to dangle our hooks in the dark water beneath the ice, using bits of white calico for bait. Luckily the tomcods were both plentiful and gullible.

Nokadlak's fishing hole turned out to be the best producer. In the two hours we spent jigging, he pulled out no less than thirty fish. Kakagun and I between us caught forty-five, many of them weighing from six to ten pounds. There was little nourishment in the tomcods but at least they would keep our dogs fed until we could provide them with something better.

By the time we returned to our tents, we were half-frozen. Kakagun's cough sounded worse than usual—and, for the first time, I heard him complain about the weather. "It's cold, it's freezing. Winter lasts too long in our land." Intermittently his wheezing cold made him gasp. After one extended spasm he cleared his throat and admitted, "It's painful. It gives me a headache. My throat is hard and swollen."

As often in the past, I wished with all my heart that there was something I could do for my friend, but the symptoms told me otherwise.

That evening, as I called on several neighbors, I noticed that a placid air had replaced the customary verve of Krangmalit gatherings. They had reverted to the tranquil resignation imposed upon them by winter's rigors and dull surroundings. Once again they were in a state of partial hibernation, their minds and souls seemingly suspended in a vacuum.

Circulating among them, Kirluayok, the sorcerer, solemnly advised his listeners out of his vast knowledge of the Barren Land: "When Hilla (the malevolent spirit) decides to change his course, the southern wind will bring a fast thaw. It would then be wise to move to your winter camps."

Even the children, normally as lively as the husky pups they played with, were subdued. With the rest of them, Naoyak spent most of the time standing idly in the tent, her face glum, her ears half-listening to the sparse talk of the elders present.

At times the adult conversation degenerated into a dis-jointed, stammering monologue with the bystanders hardly listening at all, yet automatically nodding their heads in tacit agreement. Nokadlak's half-hearted effort was a typical example, "I was just jigging for tomcod with *Fala*," he began slowly, lifelessly, then paused. "We found a good spot along the cliffs." He paused even longer. "My bitch had a litter of five pups." He fell silent again, gathering his thoughts. "*Fala* hooked a big tomcod. He pulled it up. The line broke. As I said, my bitch bore five pups. Two are female. Should I keep them?"

Accustomed to the mental processes of the People Beyond, I listened patiently to the simple, often disconnected observations of Nokadlak and his friends. Nevertheless, I could imgaine what a complete outsider would think of them. "Tell me, Father," he would probably ask, "are they people of average intelligence, or are they simpleminded?"

In such an event I would promptly leap to the defence of the Inuit. "No! They're not simpleminded! They may not have our powers of logical description, but their way of thinking has its own wisdom. Though they may not grasp the antecedent and the sequence of a given topic, their minds remain alert and keen-witted whenever they are with friends. Their memory is exceptional. It compensates them for the lack of written language. Since they communicate strictly by the spoken word, every detail and action, every unusual occurrence in their daily round is stored away in their minds to be recalled at leisure for their relatives and friends during the long polar nights and the great storms in the comparative seclusion of the igloos.

"It is only when they are alone, separated from other families by distance, weather or both, that they sometimes appear drowsy and stultified. But as a rule their innate sense of humor supersedes their oppressive boredom and they laugh off their problems.

"I must concede, though, that on such occasions of mental depression, their better natures are sometimes overshadowed by incomprehensible acts of brutality. These reveal their primitive

401

temperament, hardened through the centuries by the cruel, frozen world about them and dulled by their monotonous routine and the lack of varied distractions. Habituated from childhood to natural and violent death, they are not in the least troubled by an act that puts an end to a person's life, no more than the slaying of any animal, bird, or fish.

"Also, because their entire concept of life differs from ours, they cannot be understood on brief acquaintance. To know them thoroughly and to understand them fully, one must live with them and among them, take part in every phase of their daily routine for years on end, speak their marvelous language, and only then judge them; but not before!"

When the storm finally diminished, the hunters quickly spread out on the sea ice in search of seals, just as their ancestors had done for countless generations. Soon the various families would be separated for several months, and this fact made them lose interest in their friends and neighbors and think more in terms of their own family groups.

Their seal hunt proved so disappointing that many of the hunters began to pack and leave the island the following day. Kakagun and Nokadlak were among them, realizing that they, too, must go their separate ways to avoid possible starvation. "My dogs are almost starving," I told my two friends, "and the caribou have probably arrived. So I'm leaving in the morning for Burnside."

"Nokadlak's family and mine will travel by way of the Kulugayuk River," responded Kakagun, whose cough seemed worse. "We shall winter at Taherkapfaluk. Will you be coming to see us there, *Fala?*"

"I don't think so, Kakagun. I intend to revisit the People on the Back of the Earth." The latter were so called because their land is the ultimate limit of inhabitable tundra. Beyond it lie longer Arctic nights, greater storms, stronger and more dangerous currents under the ice floor. From the Parry and Sverdrup Islands northward to the ice cap, this frigid area remained mysterious to them in the belief that it was inhabited solely by unfriendly spirits.

During my previous sojourn with the People on the Back of the Earth from March to September in 1939, there were only twenty-one families in the group living around Minto Inlet and Holman Island. They seldom mixed with other groups of Eskimos and that occured only in the spring, mostly with hunters from Banks Island.

This time around I spent nearly two years visiting the People on the Back of the Earth and other groups in Prince Albert Sound,

402

Dolphin, and Union Straits, again finding their life-style even more stark and harsh than that of the groups with whom I associated in the Land Beyond. For one thing, they adhered more closely to the ways of their ancestors. For another, animal life was less varied and less plentiful in their territory. Caribou were few and of relatively smaller size. The herds of musk-oxen had died of starvation when the rain froze on the land. Fish and seals consequently became their basic food. Countering these conditions head on, they followed a more limited pattern in their hunting and fishing endeavors, keeping almost continually on the move.

For two additional years I helped the resident Fathers at Coppermine and vicinity, as well as in Tuktuyaktuk and the Mackenzie Delta, minister to some two hundred families gathered in those areas. Both years presented rewarding experiences, not only with the nomadic Inuit, but also with members of the Royal Canadian Mounted Police, local Hudson's Bay Company traders, and occasionally with transient white trappers.

I returned to my Burnside Mission in late May 1948, feeling that I had seen Arctic life stripped of its grimmest essentials and that I had acquired a far deeper understanding and appreciation of the People Beyond.

At Burnside, too, I learned from trader Leo Manning that Kakagun and Nokadlak were planning to winter at Gordon Bay, about thirty miles to the northeast. I decided to join my old friends there come September.

26

Tuktuk Drive

Surprisingly no one greeted me on the beach when I arrived at Gordon Bay, although four tents stood guard on a lovely sandbar at the mouth of the river.

Hior—the first part of the bay's Eskimo name, *Hiorkretak*—translates into sand, while *kre* stands for anything fine or beautiful, and *tak* is a body of land. By joining its name's prefix, infix, and suffix, one gets a fair description of that campsite on the shore of the Hiorkretak River.

Dwarf willows spotted the sloping hills on both sides of the winding river, providing a pleasant contrast to the bare rocks jutting out of the riverbanks.

The sound of my outboard motor prompted several dogs to rise for a better view of my sixteen-foot-long jolly boat built with over-lapping cedar boards. The others set up or remained lying, to watch me with a boredom born on the dog line.

I had left the Burnside Mission early that morning and made good time crossing the Bathurst Inlet between several small islands. But now my friends were nowhere to be seen. As I walked up to the tents, I listened for their vocal sounds. Hearing none, I peered inside each tent. They were all empty. I sat down on a nearby rock and pondered the situation. As I waited perplexed, I heard faint human voices and laughter upstream. The reassuring sounds grew louder. Yet I still couldn't see anyone, for the river curved sharply behind huge boulders, concealing the approaching company. Finally I heard someone exclaim, "Boat has come!" Several natives rounded the bend, running towards me and shouting their welcome. A couple outdistanced the rest and headed straight for me. I rose to greet them.

"It's *Fala*!" cried the young woman, rushing to shake hands with me.

"Naoyak! How you've changed! And this must be Naodluak. How big you've grown since I last saw you!"

"Yes, *Fala*, I'm Naodluak. At first I didn't recognize you. You have taken off your beard."

Four intervening years had done much for the handsome young couple. Naoyak had grown as tall as I. No longer the little girl I remembered, she had filled out and her pretty face carried a promise of maturity, though it still retained its red cheeks and smiling eyes. And Naodluak, now as tall as his father Kakagun, simply towered over me. He regarded Naoyak with such tenderness and possessiveness that I couldn't restrain my curiosity, "Are you married?"

His answer was definitive and proud: "Yes, we are married."

During my years among the People Beyond I had noticed early that their views on, and observance of marriage differed fundamentally from its counterpart in America and Europe. Among other dissimilarities, in my time, Krangmalit marriages were not preceded by formal engagements, neither were they marked by any church or civil weddings, nor followed by honeymoons or reasonable facsimiles. A girl or woman could be purchased or exchanged for something of value—such as a rifle, for instance. Or she might be given away without any strings attached to another family, even as Naoyak was, to be reared as a future "bride" of that family's younger male member.

Because of a continuing shortage of females for reasons of their secondary status, a member of the weaker sex could be "married" many times (i.e. live together with different men) before settling down for good with one "husband" or family provider. Also because of their comparative scarcity, women were not considered as mere chattels without any personal feelings. To an Eskimo hunter a "wife" was a practical necessity and, therefore, rarely ill-treated or abused. And, as everywhere else, a couple's own children served to bring their natural parents closer together. But all Inuit children, natural or adopted, were given a vital priority: they had to be fed and taken care of first. Especially so if they were boys—tomorrow's providers of food and shelter.

Kakagun, his old friend Nokadlak with his son Kudnanak, and Kudnanak's pal Agleroitok now surrounded me. Then came the puffing women, who had been slowed down by the weight of their caribou bags. Greetings mixed with shouts of laughter, accompanying such good-natured observations as Kablunak's "*Fala* has cut off his whiskers. His face looks like a young girl's!"

Agreeing with Kakagun's wife, Angivrana stroked my bald pate, adding, "But his head feels like a woman's breast!"

When the resulting laughter and Kakagun's coughing abated, the great hunter suggested, "Women, make tea! We're all thirsty and hungry. *Fala* must be, too."

Picking up armfuls of fuel from the piles of willow twigs by each tent, the women went willingly into the tents to fire the stoves. I sat down on an overturned sled with the men. Nokadlak patted his bulging carrying bag. "We got many fish at the traps, *Fala*."

"Where are your traps?"

"By the rapids, in a small creek off Hiorkretak River."

"Agleroitok and I didn't fish. We went looking for his dogs," Kudnanak interposed, glancing at his friend from Wilmot Island. He was massively built, thick folds of flesh almost concealing his slanted eyes.

"What happened to the dogs, Nokadlak?" I asked.

He smiled. "They ran away yesterday when we were looking for *tuktuk* (caribou). Agleroitok had four dogs with him to pack the meat. He tied them to a willow when we saw two caribou bulls grazing. We went after them. But as we fired on them, three more caribou emerged from a creek. The dogs saw them. They're still chasing them!"

"My dogs will not catch the caribou," Agleroitok drawled. "And if they don't turn back, the wolves will get them."

Kakagun nodded silently. Then a coughing spell hit him. His thin, leathery face showed his pain. He was still tall, erect, and handsome. His movements expressed his enviable energy. His eyes were still piercing. But his cropped hair showed some gray and his aquiline face was drawn and more deeply lined than the last time our paths crossed.

"I cough a lot," he said apologetically. "Sometimes it chokes me, setting my head on fire."

"It's too bad," sympathized his buddy Nokadlak. By contrast, the intervening years had hardly left a mark on him. Long-legged and broad-shouldered, he still wore that indefinably mixed expression of mirth and sadness peculiar to mature Eskimos as yet unbroken by their cruel surroundings. Only the crow's feet about his eyes were more pronounced now, especially when he laughed or spoke.

"Tea should be ready soon," said Kakagun, noting the wisps of smoke rising from the stovepipes that signaled hot willow fires in former ten-gallon gas barrels below, and listening for the clattering of enamel cups within the tents. Expert fire and tea makers that they were, the women did not keep us waiting long. Exuding good cheer, they brought us steaming tea along with meat and half-dried Arctic char. Only when all the menfolk had been served, did the ladies squat down on the sand to enjoy the food and drink with us.

Naoyak stood out among them. In the youthful bloom of life, she flitted back and forth with the kettle, smiling, refilling the cups, joking with everybody.

Politely I prompted Agleroitok, "I don't know your wife's name." He was so pleased with my expressed interest that his eyes seemed to disappear for a moment. "Her name is Komayak." Then, pointing to a girl of about eight, sitting on the ground with a young boy, he added, "That's my daughter Ikhorina. She is promised to Kudnanak."

"Is the little boy yours, too?"

"No. Mine died at Taherkapfaluk. This one is Nokadlak's."

Eyeing Agleroilok's wife, who seemed older than he was, I tried to recollect where, or in what connection I had heard her name before. She appeared conscious of my scrutiny, and old scars on her thin cheeks showed up more prominently in her embarrassment. Suddenly I remembered. It was she who several years before had fallen for an Arctic Mountie and wanted him all to herself! Komayak, the jealous one, who refused to be the plaything of a White Man known to be having affairs with other native women, and who shot him down instead.

Uncannily guessing my thoughts, Kablunak, the wife of Kakagun said with a giggle, "Komayak was kept prisoner at Coppermine for a whole winter. She cooked there for another policeman. Then she went away with Agleroitok."

I was to learn no more. Abruptly Kakagun changed the subject with his flat assertion that the caribou were returning from the north. Nokadlak picked up the hint, "Let's prepare the pathways for them tomorrow!" he said enthusiastically.

"We haven't much caribou fat for the winter," Angivrana added encouragingly.

"Last fall we hunted caribou for their fat. We got a full sled of caribou fat one day. That was the time Naoyak became a woman," Kablunak reminisced.

"I remember now," said Angivrana. "When I learned that, I told Naodluak that Naoyak was his and he could live with her in his tent."

"Kablunak and Angivrana helped me make the tent," joined in Naoyak. "Afterwards I sewed clothes for Naodluak all by myself."

407

Apparently another memory caused Angivrana to laugh. "What is it?" Kakagun asked inquisitively.

"Nokadlak's brother was hunting with us at that time. His son Kublurinak tried to sleep with Naoyak. He didn't know it is taboo among cousins," she laughed, as if she were recounting an unusually funny story.

Leaving the fine sandbar of the Hiorkretak River, we climbed its north bank to reach a narrow valley lying between eroded hills. Over the centuries, boulders of all sizes and shapes had detached themselves from the bluffs and rolled down to the valley floor, making our passage along it difficult. In the distance several indistinct shapes almost blended into the green-gray of the granite.

They were the vanguard of the caribou herds to come.

We walked the length of the mile-long valley until it opened up like the top of a funnel onto the wide rolling plain that ended in a marsh. "Any day now the caribou will be passing here in small herds on their way south," said Kakagun.

"What are you going to do? Build cairns or wait for them behind rocks?"

"They are too cautious now to be stalked, *Fala*. The wolves are after them. To get the caribou we'll have to drive them into the valley and down towards the river by the camp."

Quietly Kakagun conferred with Nokadlak before announcing for all to hear, "We can start erecting man-likenesses. I'll go with *Fala* and the women to the left."

"We will follow you on the right," Nokadlak spoke for the men and boys.

I helped Kakagun build a pile of rocks nearly five feet high and watched him apply the finishing touches with moss to give it a vague resemblance of a human form. The women were doing the same, joking and singing verses appropriate to the imminent hunt, such as:

Caribou cow, I know your fate:
The great caribou bull will chase you
Until the time comes to mount you,
Or you fall prey to the hunter. *Eye, ya, eye, ya, eye...*

One by one we built these crude man-like cairns about fifty yards apart, while Nokadlak and his helpers did the same along a parallel line two hundred yards away. It was hard work for us all, stooping, carrying, laying rocks all day long, stopping only twice to refresh ourselves with tea and food. But our labors were made infinitely worse by swarms of little black and sand flies, which increased in numbers and ferocity as we came closer to their swamp. They clung to our sweaty faces, necks, and hands, crawling stealthily inside our sleeves. They bit into our flesh and sucked our blood, leaving our skin in itching, burning bumps. My only consolation was that it was now late August and the overwhelming clouds of enormous Arctic mosquitoes had vanished two or three weeks earlier. Otherwise I doubt I could have endured the task.

By the time we reached the marsh, fifty cairns stood strung out behind us like a casual file of soldiers. Kakagun pointed to a well-trodden path along the edge of the bog. "Many caribou will come this way, *Fala*," he prophesied confidently.

Totally unexpectedly, a solitary shot rang out over the plain and reverberated through the valley. We looked about, but saw nothing unusual. Everyone was visible, except Kakagun's son Naodluak. His pal, Kudnanak, son of Nokadlak, smiled knowingly, "Naodluak saw a fawn and went after it. He must have got it."

That was sufficient notice for the eager women. They at once gathered clumps of Arctic heather and resinous moss, piled them into a heap over flat rocks, and set fire to them in anticipation of the feast. Naodluak did not disappoint them. He appeared presently from behind a knoll, carrying the young caribou straddled on his shoulders. Proudly he tossed his prize on the ground, flayed it, and shoved its skin into his hunting bag. Naoyak and Kablunak sliced off long, thin steaks and passed them to Angivrana and Komayak, who drew a flat rock out of the fire to use it as a frying pan.

While I savored the tender meat, my eyes picked out several caribou bulls grazing at a comfortably safe distance among the rocks. Quite apart from them, out on the open land, a number of caribou cows and their fawns were also feeding. It was as peaceful a scene as one might find on a well-regulated farm, and it readily brought smiles of joy to my friends, whose appetite for caribou had only been whetted by the fired fawn.

On the slope of a hill, a mile away, female caribou stood by while two bulls battered each other so furiously that we could hear the thuds of their clashing antlers. Though fierce, the battle was brief. What looked like the smaller of the gladiators turned and ran off, shaking his antlers like a stunned boxer trying to clear his head. The victor recovered his breath, strutted over to a cow, and topped her. Everybody around me laughed while Kablunak, sitting cross-legged on the ground, said to the other women, "Seeing the bulls playing their game, all bloody and covered with foam, makes me feel like a young woman again!"

The ladies walked ahead of us as we retraced our steps through the valley. They chattered and laughed, pausing only for potshots with their .22s at ground squirrels that peered curiously at us from all sides. "Soon they'll have enough squirrels to feed each one of us," said Kudnanak with a smile.

"That's good! At least, it'll be a change," rejoined Naodluak, his chum.

Past the valley's throat we built additional cairns as directed by Kakagun, who led us close to the camp where the river flowed, at once wide and deep. With the cairns all ready, Kakagun and Nokadlak brought over their kayaks and hid them behind large boulders for the closing stage of the hunt.

Still our preparations were far from over. Until late that evening we toiled over our hunting equipment. Rifles were cleaned and checked. Bows were strung with new twisted caribou sinew. Arrows were feathered. Short-shafted spears were made with chunks of loose copper found inland. The women sharpened their *ulons* (half-moon knives) and skinning knives on flat stones, mended the sealskin boots, and filled hunting bags with ammunition.

A cheerful atmosphere pervaded our gathering. Sipping his umpteenth cup of tea, Nokadlak put his feelings into words, "Caribou are plentiful. We shall not go hungry!"

"Yes. I was thinking the same thing," echoed Kakagun. "This is a good place for wintering. Tomorrow we will kill as many caribou as possible." For the time being, at least, they knew they were secure from the evil spirits of their land.

"*Fala!* Wake up!" Kablunak was saying as she shook me from sleep. "We'll be going soon." Kakagun, her husband, was dressing and coughing. I was the last one up.

The sun was just rising when I stepped outside. It was cold and the ground was hardened by frost. Naoyak was walking down her dog line, checking the huskies. When she saw me, she waved and shouted, "It's cold! But the sun will soon warm up the land."

Kablunak poked her head through the little door of the tent and said invitingly, "Come in, *Fala*. Have some tea before we leave."

Nokadlak and Kudnanak did not come with the rest of us. "They are going to hide near the kayaks and wait for the caribou," explained Kakagun. "We'll join them afterwards."

As we entered the valley, Naodluak and Agleroitok, his friend, left our party to climb the north side of the rising cliffs. We waited for them to wave to us upon sighting the caribou. We could see them scanning the land from their vantage point, but the pre-arranged signal did not come. Instead they ran down leisurely towards us. When they were within hearing distance,

Agleroitok yelled, "Caribou—many of them—coming slowly!"

"They are still far away, but they are heading for the marshes!" Naodluak elaborated exuberantly, and everybody laughed for joy.

"You can go and make a lot of noise to frighten the *tuktuk*," Kakagun told the women. They left eagerly, almost on the run, Angivrana carrying her young son on her shoulders. As they disappeared in the folds of the rolling land, Kakagun said with a smile, "Women are good for this work. They can scare any animal in the tundra!"

As Agleroitok and Naodluak walked slowly up the valley, Kakagun turned to me, "Let's find a good hiding place, *Fala*." He eventually drew my attention to what looked like a soldier's foxhole with a windshield of rocks. There were many of them along the beaten caribou paths. "These hiding places were made long ago by our ancestors. They lay in them and shot arrows at passing caribou."

"Yes, Kakagun. I've seen them at Holman Island and Cambridge Bay. Hunters still use them to save ammunition."

"It's easier to shoot lying down in a hole than standing behind a boulder."

More than an hour passed before the women started their ear-splitting noise, baying like wolves in high-pitch tones. Their contribution was immediately effective. First, half a dozen caribou, then ten times that number stampeded along the trail prepared for them. Terrified, they veered off the edge of the marsh, clear of the menacing cairns, and straight into the valley of no return.

Naodluak and Agleroitok let the first wave enter the narrow valley before opening fire. From his foxhold Kakagun shot arrow after arrow with amazing accuracy. Only when his quiver was empty did he resort to this rifle. Caribou tumbled all around us. Those which escaped raced out of the valley towards the river where we knew Nokadlak and Kudnanak were waiting for them. Subsequent waves of the bewildered caribou met the same fate. It was no sport, it was butchery, not aimless or wanton slaughter, though, but the vital provision of food for the fast-approaching winter.

When only a few straggling caribou remained on the valley floor, Kakagun shouted to Agleroitok and Naodluak, "Come on! Let's go back to the river!"

Several caribou were swimming midstream, and Nokadlak in his kayak was down on their necks, spear in hand. Confused and terrified, other caribou milled on the bank where Kudnanak, unobserved, picked them off with his rifle. We opened fire on them, and before long none remained alive. The water turned red as they floated downstream.

Kudnanak hopped into the second kayak to help his father retrieve them one by one with a rope. When the last of the caribou had been towed to the shore, Nokadlak said, "I'll stay behind to empty their bodies while they are still warm. The rest of you had better go with Kakagun to help the women skin the other caribou."

Here and there, amid the boulders of the valley, we came across wounded caribou lying helplessly and silently. A final shudder went through them as the hunting knife ended their misery.

We found women beyond the marshes flaying caribou they themselves had managed to shoot down. Sweating freely over their work, they had replaced their parkas with shapeless Mother Hubbard calico dresses. Naoyak's arms, I noticed, were caked with blood up to her elbows. She pointed to the caribou she had just skinned, saying to Naodluak, "Look how thick the fat is!" True enough, the white fat extended to the top of the animal's back. Thin between the shoulders, it thickened gradually to a depth of nearly three inches at the rump.

"The caribou is fat," agreed her young husband. Then he added with a boastful smile, "We killed them all!" Naoyak's natural response was to jump and dance with glee.

It didn't take long to skin and empty the rest of the caribou the women had killed. Then laboriously we cut out chunks of half-frozen peat with our hunting knives to conceal the piles of caribou from foxes and crows who would have plenty to eat for awhile with caribou entrails strewn all over the place. The peat would freeze during the night and make a protective shell for the carcasses until the hunters required them.

The women worked exceedingly hard. Testifying to that, sweat streamed down their necks, matting their long black hair. "It's too hot!" was their recurrent complaint. Nevertheless they sang happily:

> "How shall I speak, aye, aye, ye
> To the caribou who came to me,
> Running across the land to our tents? *Aye, ye, ye, ye*
>
> How shall I speak to the Guardian Spirit,
> *Aye, aye, ye, ye*
> Who rushed the wandering caribou
> Across the valleys to our tents? *Aye, aye, ye, ye, ye*

Everyone repeated the refrain, their monotonous rendering of it echoing between the hills.

Where Naodluak, Agleroitok, Kakagun and I had been lying

412

in ambush, dead caribou were scattered all over the ground. I counted more than fifty. Some of those shot down by arrows were still breathing. Kakagun finished them with his trusty knife and plucked his arrows out. A few stragglers came within firing range and promptly paid the maximum penalty for their curiosity.

At last the critical part of our work was over and we lounged on the rocks, sipping hot tea the unflagging women had prepared. I watched Nokadlak slice one of the caribou stomachs. The skin around the raw pouch was a dirty yellow, but inside it was all green. The hunters and their wives scooped out handfuls of cud and began to lap it up like porridge. It was the only vegetable I ever saw them eat in quantity.

I would have preferred not to sample it, but Angivrana insisted I should while she spoon-fed her child. With a flat stone I took a small helping of the greenish paste. It tasted rather like spinach, but it stunk like fresh cow-dung. For that reason I wasn't exactly enthusiastic. So to avoid being thought a spoil sport, I pretended it was as delicious as they themselves found it.

We spent the remainder of the day cutting up the carcasses and packing the life-sustaining meat to our camp. Between us, we had killed scores of caribou, yet each hunter knew exactly how many he personally had accounted for and kept that number of skins for himself and his family. As usual, with all the surrounding excitement of the hunt, I was the only one who had not kept score. So, when fifteen skins remained unclaimed, I gathered them as my own.

It took us several days to slice the meat and hang it up to dry in the wind and sun. All skins were dried by being stretched and pegged to the ground. Some of them would end up being traded at the H.B.C. Post. Even bones with some meat on them were placed on flat stones to dry. Later they would be used for making broth or given to the dogs. Thus almost every part of the caribou—from hoof to head—was used in some way.

Although the meat, the skins, and the bones surrounded every tent, I knew they would be consumed before the long, cold winter set in. And yet, aside from fish (that would be difficult to catch under the ice) there was nothing else my friends could hope to obtain in quantity during the freeze up. Besides, caribou meant not only more nutritious food, but also warmer clothing, better shelter, and stronger dogs. To the People Beyond, in short, the caribou formed the foundation of their precarious existence.

Following the big hunt and its consequent chores, everybody in camp relaxed for a few days, mostly outdoors in the afternoon to take advantage of the ever-waning sun. Agleroitok, Naodluak, and Kudnanak challenged each other in wrestling bouts to the delight of the women, and led the others in playing games. Actually Agleroitok was far too strong for his two pals and even gave Kudnanak's father Nokadlak a tough battle in the various man-to-man bouts.

One of everybody's favorite tests of strength and agility was the neck string pull. Participants lay prone head to head facing their respective opponents and placed a caribou thong around their heads, just above the ears. They then raised themselves up on their hands by extending their arms as if doing push-ups, while pulling away their heads from each other. The one who allowed the thong to slip off his head became the loser. It was a painful game for the adversaries, whose faces showed a mixture of strain and comic expressions as they strived for victory. But it was fun from start to finish for the onlookers.

The most interesting game for all concerned was a shooting match with bows and arrows. A one-foot-square piece of caribou skin mounted on a five-foot post served as the target. No bull's eye or brightly colored concentric circles showed on it. Each contestant was allowed three arrows. At a distance of one hundred feet, it took inordinate skill to place them all in the target and be declared the winner. There were no prizes for anyone. Accomplishment and good fun were ample rewards. But there was happiness and a sense of security among my friends. They were living for the day, enjoying it in their traditional way, without a thought of the approaching winter playing its own waiting game.

"It's freezing! I'm going back to the Mission at Bathurst tomorrow," I informed Kakagun and Nokadlak. They were not surprised. Kakagun gave his approval, "The seagulls and ducks have left. Snow will fall and winds will blow harder and more often. You are wise to go while the weather is still good, *Fala*." Kakagun had been increasingly troubled with coughing attacks, but maintained his usual friendly composure.

"Are you people coming after the freeze up?" I asked.

"Kakagun and I will come to trade some caribou skins," Nokadlak answered for both of them.

"When we come, *Fala*, maybe you can give me something for my throat," Kakagun added. "It is more painful now. Sometimes I choke at night."

"Do come as soon as you can, Kakagun, and I'll see what I can do for you." I tried to make my words sound full of hope, but my heart felt heavy in the knowledge that I possessed no magic remedy for his debilitating malady.

When Naoyak heard that I would be leaving the following day, she came over with Naodluak to Kakagun's tent. "You are

414

going away," she said softly. "Here, I made a pair of slippers for you, *Fala*. Take them."

Their tops expertly sewn of black and white fawn hide, and their soles of bleached sealskin, they were a beautiful pair. Deeply touched, all I could say was, "They're very pretty. Thank you, Naoyak!"

She beamed, flattered by my praise. Naodluak added a little commendation of his own with a smile of understandable pride, "She is skillful!"

27

Disaster

I reached Bathurst Mission just as the bad weather set in. Sleety northwest winds whipped up the seas as never before. They rose seven feet in a land where tides are almost unknown. The squalls brought frost without dry snow, together with damp, penetrating cold that chilled every living being. Thick snow followed closely on the heels of the departing sleet. It fell continuously for several days and nights, covering everything in sight except Bathurst Inlet, which was still free of ice. The scene resembled the negative of a photograph—white land against black sea.

It took only three consecutive nights of comparative calm and dropping temperatures to change the heaving black water into a motionless frozen mass of white. Then the wind came flying back. Day after day, in undiminishing fury it tore in from the northeast. Clouds of powdery snow raced across the plains, swept into the creeks and the valleys, rolled over the mountains, until it was impossible to distinguish the land and the sea from the sky. Everything was gray twilight.

Not a single Eskimo came to the local trading post where, relatively safe and comfortable, Leo Manning, his wife Mary, and I jointly hoped for a quick turnaround in the weather. I peeked out their window at the gray expanse and the raging elements around my Mission shack and prayed that my friends at Hiorkretak (the Land of Beautiful Sand) were being spared from Nature's winter violence.

Mary Manning had come by plane from Winnipeg, the

Manitoba capital, with two executives of the Hudson's Bay Company, shortly after my return from Hirkretak. She was a friendly, kind person whom Leo affectionately called "my city girl." Her deep black hair, held in a loose knot at the back of her neck, emphasized her delicate oval face, which was further enhanced by her gem-like, widely spaced dark eyes. With his golden hair, and blue eyes, Leo presented a complementary contrast. More importantly, he and Mary were obviously very much in love. I felt truly privileged to enjoy the company and the kindness of this wonderful couple.

In early December the restless winds decided to calm down. After weeks of unrelenting turbulence, the silence of the frozen land and sea was overwhelming in its own way. Only the melancholy howling of passing wolves, or the yelping of my dogs on their line broke the perfect stillness of the long Arctic night.

Then one day the temperature slid down to -45° in a matter of hours—a most unusual occurrence at that time of the year, which prompted Leo to predict gloomily that there were more and worse storms ahead.

Later that day Kakagun, Nokadlak, Naodluak, Kudnanak, and Agleroitok arrived at my Mission house. They all looked tired and gaunt, a yellow tinge of sickness showing in their faces. Kakagun's eyes were bulging, and a dry, grating cough contorted his strong features as we shook hands. I now knew what I had suspected before: the big man, the great hunter, was slowly dying of strangulation from some malignant growth in his throat. And I was powerless to help him.

"Where are your women?" I asked Kakagun, trying not to show my deep concern for his hopeless condition.

"Still at Hiorkretak. They are jigging tomcods and hunting in the creeks for ptarmigans and hares." His voice sadly lacked its usual vibrant vitality.

"We came only to trade foxes and caribou skins," explained Nokadlak. "And we are going back tomorrow," his son Kudnanak added.

"Did you get many foxes?" I asked conversationally, and at once wished I hadn't.

My question merely brought sardonic smiles from the men and the answer I deserved from Nokadlak: "Foxes, like us, don't travel during storms, *Fala*. And we had storms all the time."

"It really couldn't be helped," Agleroitok asserted in a conciliatory tone.

"We were hungry. We lost some dogs." Naodluak elaborated.

"Can you give me something for my cough, *Fala?*" asked

Kakagun. "My throat hurts. Sometimes I can't even talk. I'm getting older and weaker by the day." He coughed again.

"Don't worry! I'll try to get you some relief."

After partaking of some tea and food, my visitors decided to call on Leo Manning.

"If you'd like to sleep here, bring in your *krepiks* (sleeping bags)," I told them. "Don't build an igloo. It's too cold outside."

"Thank you, *Fala*. We'll sleep with you," Nokadlak answered for the rest.

When they returned an hour later, I had a pot of meat and steaming rice ready for them. They ate their fill, then, drowsy with food and the warmth of the Kablunak's igloo, unrolled their *krepiks* on the floor and stretched out. For a long time that night I heard Kakagun's raucous cough above their snores.

"The moon has a ring around it. We'll have to hurry," Nokadlak told his friends when they rose early next morning.

"Our dogs have had a good rest. We may have time to reach Hiorkretak before the storm," said Kakagun wishfully.

"I'll visit you soon," I assured him in parting. "Meantime keep your throat warm day and night."

"Yes, *Fala*. But warm or cold, it's always painful."

As they left, I glanced at the thermometer that hung by the entrance porch. It had climbed during the night and now read only -15° F. But in my living room the barometer had dropped several millibars, indicating a change. Towards noon it dropped still further and the wind was gathering force. By two o'clock a squall swept the snow off the frozen ground with such force that visibility was simultaneously reduced to zero. Despite the four-foot thick protective wall of hard snow around it, the Mission building shook under the powerful blasts. I was imprisoned by the elements.

For several days the terrible tempest continued, with wind velocity reaching one-hundred miles an hour, according to Leo who had an anemometer mounted near his house. I worried about my friends at Hiorkretak. Had the women and children enough food? Had they sufficient blubber for their stone lamps? Did the men return safely to their camp? I wasn't to know the answers for several weeks, for there was no quick way to communicate.

Though the storm center eventually moved on, the wind did not subside completely. In fact, we were exposed to such a succession of violent northeasterly gales just before Christmas that only Leo, his wife Mary, and their helper's family attended Midnight Mass. No one else came to Burnside either to pray or to trade.

In mid-January the temperatures dropped to a frigid 45° below and rested there. The wind disappeared, however, and I thought it safe to go and see my friends. I took along coal oil for their Primus stoves, several pounds of tallow for the stone lamps, and flour. I encountered no problems on the way to Hiorkretak, but although I found them thinner than ever and somewhat subdued in manner, they were as hospitable as ever. Naoyak had lost some of her characteristic cheerfulness, but she didn't complain. Kakagun's condition had visibly worsened. Only a dozen dogs were still alive. Canine tails scattered on the ground near the dog lines explained the fate of the rest who were sacrificed to keep their stronger teammates alive. Scorning these and other reverses, the Eskimos' resigned reaction was always the familiar philosophical *"Ayornaronarevok*—there is certainly nothing one can do about it; it's truly hopeless!"

Everyone agreed it had been a terrible winter. Even when the long, stormy polar night gave way to the spring sun, the weather continued to be treacherous, with sudden gales sweeping over the snow-covered tundra and driving every living being to the nearest shelter. Scorning the inherent dangers and inconvenient travel under such circumstances, the restless natives converged on the trading post at Bathurst from all directions. Yet trader Leo Manning somehow managed to find time to come over to my Mission hut one morning to tell me that a plane, chartered by his employer, the Hudson's Bay Company, was due to arrive that day to pick up his wife who was now in her fourth month of pregnancy. "Mary's getting lonely around here. And she worries about sudden complications while carrying our child so far away from professional help. So I contacted Yellowknife by shortwave and my boss is sending Ernie Boffa, the bush pilot, to fly her in. From Yellowknife Mary will take a plane to Winnipeg to stay with her folks. She won't be homesick any more and she'll worry less in her home town, especially as it has a modern hospital with a good maternity ward."

I thought how fortunate Mary was to have such a kind and understanding husband, but refrained from putting it into words. Instead I asked Leo if the Eskimos had been successful in their hunting around Bathurst. He sighed and shook his head. "Trapping's been atrocious! Most of them starved off and on through the entire winter. I'm really amazed to see them looking so cheerful and outwardly composed. But they're a sorry lot, just the same—gaunt and aged before their time, much like their pitifully skinny dogs."

It was still so cold outdoors that most of the hunters had built

419

spacious igloos instead of pitching their caribou tents. But none of them bothered to put up a large communal igloo for dancing. That effort would have taken energy they could ill afford to spare.

The few foxes brought in by the hunters were soon traded for such essentials as ammunition, tea, and tobacco. "No dispensable merchandise was wanted," Leo summed up. "It was definitely the worst business year I experienced in my entire trading career. Even the few pelts they bartered with were of relatively poor quality because the foxes themselves had been starving, too."

"The Big Bird has arrived!" went up the cry when the plane appeared above the post, flying low, looking for a smooth ski landing on the frozen channel. I recognized the aircraft as a single-engined amphibian Norseman that could carry a pilot and three passengers. This time the pilot was alone. As soon as the Big Bird coasted to a halt, the curious natives encircled it. Some of them had never seen one before—certainly not at such close range.

Ernie Boffa climbed down from the cockpit to shake hands with Leo, Mary, and me. Formalities over, he promptly announced to the Mannings: "We must leave right away! It's a long haul to Yellowknife and the weather's unpredictable."

No one attempted to detain him, although a look of heartfelt sadness spread over Leo's face. When Mary was safely aboard the Norseman, I tried to comfort her husband, "Before you know it, she'll be back with your child. Come and have a cup of coffee with me at the Mission."

As we walked, I broke the silence to divert Leo's thoughts, "One can easily tell that most of the natives had an exceedingly tough winter. Did you notice how little life is left in some of them?"

"Sure, Father. But they'll get back to normal as soon as the caribou come. Oh," he added hastily, "with Mary's imminent departure I forgot to tell you about a radio message from Coppermine the other day. Seems a police patrol is headed this way, but they didn't say why. Should be here any time now."

"Do you know who's coming?"

"Yes, a fellow named Yates. He had never seen the Arctic until last summer."

When Leo left my premises, I went down the channel where the igloos were arranged like giant white beehives. Meeting some of the natives, I informed them that a policeman was coming soon and that he would probably ask for the usual gathering of all the hunters. Although they seemed uninterested

420

in the news, one hunter quipped pointedly, "Is he going to count the foxes we trapped, or the caribou we shot on our land?"

"No," I replied in the same ironic tone, "but he might ask how many musk-oxen you left inland." It was grim humor, but they squeezed every ounce of laughter they could out of it before they turned back to mending their sleds, dog harnesses, harpoons, and other life-sustaining equipment.

Upon return to the Mission, I was pleasantly surprised to find my living room taken over by several friends, among them Kakagun, Naodluak, and Naoyak. My old acquaintance Kirluayok, the sorcerer, was also there, and I greeted them all warmly. Although he complained of getting older, I thought Kirluayok's ageless features remained the same. Politely I assured him that everyone else was aging, too, but he took little solace from my trite remark.

Having treated Kakagun's throat two days earlier, I was anxious to know how he was. His disappointing answer came in a choking whisper, "I can't swallow solid food anymore, *Fala*. Soon I shall die from hunger."

Pooh-poohing such thoughts, I asked Naoyak to make tea for us all. She rose willingly. As she brushed past me on her way to the kitchen, I suddenly realized how dreadfully thin she was. I hoped that Leo Manning was right when he predicted that the coming caribou would bring my friends back to normal.

For lack of other drugs, I put a few drops of iodine in Kakagun's tea and gave him a couple of aspirins with the admonition: "Swallow these now, Kakagun, and stay with me for a while. It's warm here and it will do you good."

"What are you giving him, *Fala?*" the sorcerer asked suspiciously. "Something to make him die quicker?"

With the little vocal force at his command, Kakagun came to my defense, "You're an old man yourself, Kirluyaok. Soon flies will be laying their eggs in the sockets of your eyes. Why don't you let *Fala* alone? Can't your ancient eyes see he is trying his best to help me?"

Late the following day the dogs' cacophonous howling announced the arrival of the policeman. In bright moonlight I saw his team coming up the slope towards the trading post. I walked out to meet Constable Yates. He was a tall, pleasant-looking young man of about twenty-five, with jet-black hair and a mustache. He hadn't shaved for days and his thin face reflected the hardship of the trail. I introduced myself and asked him if he had had a good trip. "Would've been fine, Father, if Nathit here hadn't got the flu a couple of days after we left." I recognized his young guide and interpreter from Coppermine. He had earned the reputation of a fearless traveler, but at the moment he could hardly stand up by himself.

Leo Manning emerged from the trading post to welcome the young Mountie, and the Eskimos began to crowd around the two newcomers, shaking hands with the Inuit guide and the Amakro (the Wolf, or Policeman). Spontaneously they helped unharness the panting dogs and unloaded the sled while Leo invited Yates to make himself at home in his quarters.

"What about Nathit?" he asked with concern.

"He can stay with my helper. And I'm sure Father Raymond won't mind taking care of his cold."

"I'll be only too glad to give him a good dose of anti-grippe capsules, but I'm afraid that's about the extent of my medical supplies at present."

When I reached Leo's helper's house, it was jammed with Eskimos. Nathit lay fully dressed on his sleeping bag, coughing and talking to his friends. The air was blue with cigarette smoke and, I suspected, thick with flu germs. I got Nathit to take the pills, admonishing him, "Rest and keep warm. Drink a lot of tea. You have been taught what to do when you were in school in Aklavik. But your friends are not immune to the flu and will be very sick if they catch it from you."

Constable Yates did not waste time. He had Leo warm up his commodius warehouse with a large coal heater and held meetings with the natives for the next two days. With the aid of all present he brought his census figures more or less to date and then through Nathit, his interpreter, painstakingly explained pertinent sections of the Game Ordinance and such welfare items as emergency rations to be obtained from the trading post in time of starvation. That was about the extent of federal government help to the remote Eskimo groups scattered in the High Arctic.

Apart from sending the Mounties to the Barren Land in those days, Canada's government largely ignored the immense north and its people beyond the Arctic Circle. When the "cold war" brought on the Distant Early Warning (DEW) Line's radar trip wire against Soviet attack from over the pole around 1947, Ottawa's politicians began to show more interest in the condition and culture of the Eskimos. Still, it wasn't until 1953 that Canada set up a Northern Affairs Department. Significantly, too, in that year Prime Minister Louis St. Laurent admitted that "apparently we have administered those vast Territories in an almost continuing state of absence of mind."

His job done, Constable Yates hurried off to other camps at Gray's Bay, Tree River, and along the mainland Coast, taking the

422

ailing Nathit with him. At noon the day they departed, Naoyak and Kablunak called at the Mission. Both were coughing and miserable. "*Fala*, I'm sick," said Naoyak, "I don't feel at all well. My head and my throat ache. My body feels cold."

"The same with me," echoed Kablunak. "I cough all the time. Many of our people are coughing now."

After administering the "cure-all" cold capsules to them, I suggested they go back to their respective igloos and rest, adding "Drink lots of tea and broth and try to keep warm. I'll come and see you later."

During the afternoon other Eskimos beat a regular path to my door. But except for first aid supplies, aspirin, and anti-grippe capsules (in which I was rapidly losing faith), my medicine shelves were bare.

All my shivering patients complained of the same distress: "We are coughing. And we are cold."

Two boys came early next morning, saying, "People are sick, *Fala*. They are asking for you."

It had snowed during the night, and now a ground wind whipped the powdery snow in our faces. Apart from the sleeping dogs, there was no sign of life outside the thirty igloos. Nor could a stranger have guessed all the misery they contained within their round walls. More than a hundred people—men, women and children—were in various stages of the debilitating disease, tossing about listlessly, moaning, coughing, and spitting where they lay.

I found the flu epidemic truly terrifying. It attacked some enfeebled adults so violently that they succumbed to it within a day. Those who survived longer, kept coughing up excessive amounts of slimy yellow-green mucus not unlike pus exuding from a boil. Yet their lungs sounded like dried leaves crushed underfoot. They were being choked with a mixture of phlegm, foam, and thick black blood resembling grape jelly. Their faces were tinted yellow and their lips purple. The smell of their expectorations and of surrounding decay was nauseous, if not overpowering.

I took the temperatures of some of the sick. It was around 104° F. Strangely, children seemed to react better to the flu attacks than their elders, and none of them died, perhaps assuring the continuation of the People Beyond.

I didn't read everybody's temperature, knowing that by now they would all have the fever. Instead I gave them cold capsules and aspirin, advising them to stay put in their warm sleeping bags, and drink plenty of boiled water or tea.

Finding several igloo entrances blocked by snow, I dug my

way in, wondering if their occupants were still alive. Even though the only light in each igloo came from its blubber lamp, that was sufficient in most cases to spot the greenish-yellow mucus hanging frozen on the walls and messing up the snow floor. Some of the older Eskimos didn't waste their sputum—they spat it into their cupped hands and sucked it in to regurgitate it later. It wasn't a sight for a queasy person.

No matter whose igloo I entered, its tenants were either moaning or coughing as they lay in their sleeping bags on the raised platforms of snow. Some had enough strength to crawl into the porch at varied intervals to relieve themselves.

In Kakagun's igloo Naoyak was coughing fitfully on the iglek. "I feel too hot," she wailed, her face burning red with high fever. Naodluak lay prone beside her, spitting down on the floor. He kept saying, "I'm getting weak."

Stretched out in the *krepik* close to Kakagun, his wife Kablunak courageously tended the blubber lamp. The great hunter was a shocking sight. Air hissed through his throat like steam out of a boiling kettle as he fought for his breath. I could barely understand what he was trying to tell me, but it sounded like "I'm choking. I'm finished."

"You are all coming with me to stay at my house where I can take better care of you," I told them as cheerfully as I could.

"No, *Fala*," Kakagun mustered a faint, but determined protest. "I'm going to die like a true Inuk in my own igloo!"

"And I shall stay with Kakagun to the end," Kablunak added resolutely.

Sick as they were, Naoyak and Naodluak didn't hesitate to accept my invitation, however. They dressed warmly and followed me. As we trudged to the Mission building, a familiar figure crawled out of one of the igloos. His parka embellished with the magical symbols of his trade, Kirluayok, the sorcerer, paused to eye me curiously. Then his tired old face cracked at the mouth as he spoke with authority: "People are coughing. They are sick. It is because they have displeased the spirits of the land."

"I'll do my best to keep the spirits away," I said helpfully.

His deep gray eyes flashed angrily. "You'll help much more by keeping your Kablunak nose out of my people's lives!"

If he was looking for a fight, I thought it best to disappoint him in his ugly mood by moving silently on with my two young patients. Once inside the Mission hut, I made them comfortable in their sleeping bags which I laid on a pile of caribou skins. I gave them tin cans to spit into and shoved more coal into the heater. Then I served them hot tea with a strong dose of anti-grippe capsules, and bade them rest while I went back to see Kakagun.

On my way over, I thought it advisable to speak to Trader Manning about supplies for the ailing natives. "The flu is getting out of control, Leo," I told him. "All but a dozen are stricken with it. And what worries me, too, is that most of them have little fuel left for their lamps, and their stock of dog food is meagre at best."

"Well, I've plenty of coal oil, Father, but that's not much good because only a few of them have Primus stoves. Those who can use it, of course, are welcome to it. But as for dog food, I'm afraid I can't give them any more than you can. I'd like to help them any way I can, though. I know what this flu can do to an Eskimo. Actually I don't feel too good myself, and I hope my wife didn't catch it on her way home."

Kakagun's eyes bulged wildly and his puffed veins protruded on his temples, as he was torn by convuslions. Making desperate efforts to get enough air into his lungs, he hissed faintly when he saw me, "Let's get it over with, *Fala!* Give me something to make me die!"

I diluted aspirins in warm water and fed the mixture to him, a few drops at a time. It didn't help at once. He begged me repeatedly to shoot him or strangle him. "I can't fight anymore. I've come to the end," he murmured pathetically.

In one of his worst fits, when with wide-open mouth he gasped for air like a fish out of water, his wife tried feebly to pull his tongue. With tears in her eyes, Kablunak implored him not to leave her. "Come back, come back!" she wailed like a lost child. It was the first time I saw an Eskimo woman shedding genuine tears of utter grief.

When the mild drug began to take some benign effect, I told Kakagun I would return after visiting the other families. There was a noticeable change in their attitude towards me now. Many would not speak to me and all refused to take any of my medicine. Knowing Nokadlak better than the rest, I expected and received an honest answer from him to my oft-repeated question, "Why do you refuse my help?"

"Because Kirluayok warned us that your medicine would kill us. He said the Spirits of the Sea and Land told him in his dreams that we must avoid touching or receiving anything from you, or we shall all die."

Just as I was about to accept defeat, from the other *iglek* of the double igloo unmistakably came Agleroitok's brave request, "Give me some of your medicine, *Fala*. My wife Komayak and I will take it."

"Where is your daughter?" I asked the couple whom I first

met at Wilmot Island. "Is she ill, too?"

"No, she is visiting her friends."

I invited them to come to the Mission, adding, as an inducement, that their friends Naodluak and Naoyak were already there. After a brief consultation they decided to come along with me. Kudnanak, the other mutual friend, wavered for a while, but finally said he would follow us.

None of my arguments, however, could budge his parents, Nokadlak and Angivrana. Steeped in Krangmalit customs and superstitions, they were as adamant as Kakagun and Kablunak, their best friends.

28

Ayolerama

Constable Yates and his guide Nathit had picked up the flu bug from shaking hands with some White Men who had flown to Coppermine. The flu this pair unwittingly transmitted to the Eskimos at Burnside turned into a virulent form of pneumonia that had devastating effects on the poor natives who had never been exposed to it.

Almost everyone in camp was prostrate. Although the weather continued cold and windy, so low were the indisposed natives' stores of blubber that in many of the igloos the stone lamps were lit only when it was necessary to melt snow for drinking water or making tea. Dog food was all but gone, too, but there was an ironic twist to that predicament. More than half the huskies out of a total of about 450 had developed distemper, an infectious and contagious viral disease which—among other complications—brings on a complete loss of appetite, thereby eliminating its victims' feeding problem. But the gamut of distemper symptoms unfortunately includes several other disastrous complications besides pneumonia, such as dysentery and chorea (a form of paralysis) which frequently supervenes and is generally fatal. Not only did the ill-fated dogs stop eating, therefore, but in a matter of a few days most of them perished. As for their survivors, many were left more or less to starve in the snow and/or to subsist on the bodies of their dead counterparts.

Even in the Mission building, with its contrasting comfort and care, the condition of my youthful patients grew steadily worse. Flushed and breathing with extreme difficulty, Naodluak told me he couldn't stand the suffering much longer. Hardly feeling any better than her husband, Naoyak tried bravely to smile when she complained of an aching head and pains in her chest. I did the little I could for both of them.

Later in the day Naodluak became delirious. I couldn't make any sense out of his mutterings, but Naoyak stoically insisted that he was trying to say he was nearing his life's end and wanted water to help him go to the Land of the Good Spirit. I talked quietly to Naodluak and baptized him, but there seemed to be no understanding in his feverish eyes. When approaching death suddenly lifted him out of his morbid state, he spoke softly to no one in particular: "*Ayolerama*, I am truly without hope. But why must I leave this wonderful land?"

"Your soul will find a much better place in the sky above," I said. "I told you about it often when I stayed with you at Kattimanek. Remember?"

"*Illa, Fala.* And I remember the song we used to sing about it." His eyes closed as he began to hum the refrain of a Christmas hymn:

> "*Kuvianartorle. . .* How wonderful for us that
> God was born
> To make us friends of His
> In a Land of Happiness. . ."

His voice grew fainter. He licked his fevered lips and said hoarsely, "*Teatorlanga*, give me tea with lots of sugar." I raised his sweaty head with my left arm, and brought the sweetened drink to his mouth. He tried to sip it, but couldn't. Like a whipped puppy, he looked up at me and whispered: "Will there be a lot of sugar in the Land of the Good Spirit?"

"Yes," I answered. "And many more joys than just sugar."

"*Goanna*, thank you, *Fala*. Take care of Naoyak." He did not speak to me or to anyone else again.

"*Anerneyertok*. He has lost his breath," Naoyak cried softly.

"*Anerneyertok*," repeated the others unemotionally.

I went out and asked two hunters who were still miraculously free from the flu to help me bury the boy. We wrapped his thin body in a caribou skin and carried it out to the waiting sled. Slowly we pulled it for some 300 yards to the Mission's burying-ground, and laid the remains on a snow-covered knoll. We placed blocks of snow all around the corpse and I said prayers for his departed soul.

As we trudged back, Agleroitok's daughter ran up to me. "Kakagun is dying! He wants you," she said bashfully, avoiding my eyes. I dropped the sled rope and hurried over to my old friend's side. Kakagun had all but crawled out of his *krepik* and sat almost naked, gasping for breath. I took his pulse. It was

428

racing. I dissolved some bromide tablets in water and attempted to spoon the liquid down his throat. He spat out every drop. "I can't swallow!" he explained hoarsely, adding "Give me my *attige* (parka). I'm freezing!"

Kablunak pointed to Kakagun's best parka and I helped him put it on. He stretched out in his sleeping bag as if to sleep, but his difficult breathing kept him twisting and shuddering. I took his hand. "Kakagun, you tell me you are going. Would you like to go to the Land of the Great Good Spirit—the one I told you about?"

"*Illa, Falanuak.* Yes, Little Father. Baptize me! I have been thinking about it a long time."

"I'll be gone tomorrow, too, *Fala,*" moaned his wife Kablunak. "I also want to see the Land of the Great Good Spirit."

I proceeded to baptize them both with a little water from the kettle. Kakagun was quieter now, thinking. Finally he whispered: "Are you going to put my body in the ground?"

"I can't while the ground is frozen."

"But are you going to when summer comes? I'm afraid of lying in the ground."

"There's nothing to be afraid of. Burial in the ground is protection against foxes and wolverines."

"My people never put bodies under the ground."

"Yes, I know, Kakagun. I'll do as you wish."

He fell silent again, except for his laborious breathing. Suddenly it, too, stopped.

Kablunak shrank into her *krepik.* She knew her great hunter would never rise again. And whatever will to live she might have had was now gone.

Three other bodies were removed from the camp to Burnside Harbor, just a mile away from our post.

While their dogs died from starvation, distemper, or exhaustion on the dog lines, whole families crowded together in the same sleeping bags, spitting their lungs out.

In the entrance of one igloo I found a group of fever-ridden natives standing completely naked in the sub-zero temperature. Others, young men in the prime of life, were pacing back and forth in front of their igloos, with only their breeches on. The exception among them was Iharoitok, who could not walk, of course, because he had cut off his frozen feet years ago. His bare torso covered with perspiration, the poor cripple sat moaning in the snow.

"Why didn't any one of you listen to me?" I demanded. "Why didn't you try to keep warm, as I asked you to do to help yourselves feel better?"

429

But I was simply wasting my own breath, as they chorused back: "Kirluayok, the *Tunrak*, told us to go outside to lose our sweat."

"Tomorrow you'll all lose your lives!" I countered bitterly.

Some of them laughed at me through their shivers. Others coughed in my face.

"Where is the Sorcerer?" I asked in desperation.

"*Nauna.* We don't know."

It wasn't difficult to locate Kirluayok. He was crouching in his *krepik*, shivering, coughing, and moaning, like the rest. Regarding me blankly, he blurted: "Leave me alone, *Kablunak* (White Man)! The Spirits will help me."

"They are powerless now to help you or anyone else. Your people are dying right and left and you are hastening their deaths."

"*Ayornorman.* There is nothing one can do," he said resignedly and, for once, his tone was subdued.

That night I woke up in a cold sweat. Someone was calling me from the living room. By the dim light of a storm lantern I saw Naoyak propped up against her folded parka. "I can't stand it anymore," she sobbed, her wasted body torn in agony. She was choking now, and her formerly pretty face portrayed nothing but pain and hopelessness.

Agleroitok's wife Komayak, who lay coughing next to the suffering Seagull, said dispassionately: "She can't pull through."

I slid a cushion behind Naoyak's head and tried to cheer her up. "You'll feel better when I get you some tea."

"*Immana, Fala!* No, Father! Don't leave me!"

I sat down on the floor. "I won't leave you, Naoyak. Don't be afraid."

As I wiped the sweat off her thin face and neck, she asked, "Am I going to see Naodluak soon?"

"Yes, and Kakagun and Kablunak, too. Then some day I'll come and we'll all be together again, never to be separated."

"We'll all wait for you, *Fala.*"

I kept talking to her quietly, recalling all I had tried to teach her about the Good Spirit over the years, and filling her heart with Christian hope. I baptized her. Towards dawn the smile I knew so well returned to her sunken cheeks. "I'm not afraid anymore," she murmured calmly. "Go to sleep, *Fala.* I'll be all right."

"No, I'll stay with you. Just close your eyes and rest."

Courageously Naoyak tried to relax, but her breathing became labored. Like a wounded fawn, she lay staring at me with imploring eyes, waiting for the final merciful moment. It came at sunrise. Without a word or gesture of emotion, she passed on beyond, the true Eskimo to the end. I wrapped her slender young body in her sleeping bag, the one she had shared with her husband, and laid it close to Naodluak's. . .

Leo Manning was gazing through the kitchen window when I called at his trading post. He had shaken off the flu, but wisely stayed indoors as much as he could.

"Say, what's going on out there?" he greeted me, pointing to a commotion among loose dogs coming and going from Tikerak, the point of land about a mile away, protruding like a forefinger into the sea.

"Those are some of the surviving dogs, Leo. They had lived so far on their weaker brothers. Now they're feasting on the corpses at the point." Even as I spoke, several huskies lumbered back to camp past us. Their bloated paunches hung low, like toy balloons filled with sand. I shuddered, and walked over to the window in the living room which looked out in the direction of the Mission's burial ground. I was relieved to see no dogs there. The blocks of snow provided enough protection against them for the time being.

Curled up and stiff, Kablunak lay dead in her *krepik,* just as she had predicted. There was no one else in Kakagun's igloo. I tried to stretch her body out to wrap it for burial like the rest, but rigor mortis proved stronger than me. Covering her in caribou skins, I took her away as she was.

Nokadlak died stoically, without a murmur. And so did his son, Kudnanak, as well as the latter's friend, Agleroitok. All three might have survived if they had not passively surrendered to an enemy they could neither see nor understand. I buried them all side by side.

Left without their husbands, Angivrana and Komayak put up a surprising fight—as did their children—and slowly recovered from the disease. They would soon readjust their lives with other hunters who had lost their wives.

The biggest surprise of all proved to be Kirluayok, the old Sorcerer. Only a few days earlier he had been plagued with a terrible cough, his cheeks swollen enormously with pus exuding from the extended pores. But now he seemed almost completely recovered. While I marveled at his stamina, I could not help criticizing him for turning the people against me.

"They must listen to me, their Tunrak, and no one else. Otherwise a greater calamity still may befall them," he threatened. "I told you before, White Man," he added defiantly, "there's no room here for both you and me!"

A frightful coughing fit shook his Spartan frame. He doubled up, throwing his arms across his chest to allay the pain. Blood gushed from his mouth, dark and thick, and splattered over the snow floor. He reeled like a drunkard and fell in his own blood while I watched, horror-stricken.

In all, 41 men and women perished in our camp as a result of innocent handshakes between the virus carrying visitors and the friendly, unsuspecting People of the Land Beyond. . . .

It was like the raising of a siege when the caribou came at last and the stronger hunters were able to kill several dozen of them for the depleted camp. Slowly the other survivors and their dogs picked up strength. In fact, by the second week in May most of them were able to disperse to their winter camps at Taheriuak, Krimakton, and Taherkapfaluk.

Members of some families, whose numbers had been severely depleted, rode along with others. Several men and women replaced the fallen dogs in the latter's harnesses and pulled their sleds and belongings like beasts of burden. Children reduced the load by walking alongside the sleds instead of riding on them. Everyone was glad to move away from the scene of horror and death.

In their fresh surroundings they soon forgot the recent disaster. Not unlike their ancestors who were oppressed by countless centuries of privation and failure against the Evil Spirits of their land, they were too concerned with their daily fight for existence to worry about the recent past. . .

When—at long last—Bathurst Inlet became free of ice, and Leo Manning's wife Mary had returned from "outside" with her first-born child, I took them along on several enjoyable excursions in my trusty whaleboat. We gathered flowers and ore-bearing rocks, and generally idled away the sunny, care-free days. Their friendly company helped restore my undermined health and morale.

Later that summer, when it grew too windy and cold for those pleasant outings, I asked Leo if he would help me bury the dead at the Mission cemetery. "Sure, Father," he said. "How many are there?"

"Fifteen. But there isn't much left of them. The ground should be sufficiently thawed to a foot or so to make digging comparatively easy."

Still packed in caribou skins, now bleached by the sun, the corpses lay on the mossy ground. "The foxes and wolverines have been here," observed Leo, pointing to scattered bits of caribou fur and human bones with flesh still attached to them. Clouds of bluebottle flies swarmed over the remains, and even with the wind behind us, the stench of decaying flesh was overpowering. I strode right up to the gruesome bundles for a closer look. Foxes and wolverines had dragged out the bodies from the caribou skin sleeping bags and feasted on them. Leo was right: the scavengers had done a thorough job of stripping the skulls of all their soft parts, half-chewing the arms and legs, and leaving the torso bones exposed and crawling with maggots.

Our shovels bit readily into the top few inches of mossy soil, but it wasn't long before the gravel and clay layer gave way to permanent frost. We shoveled the remains into the common shallow grave, covering them with what we had dug out.

Using long spruce logs brought in by the Missions' supply boat, *Our Lady of Lourdes,* I made a plain cross and Leo helped me plant it in a hole dug in the permafrost. The cross stood nearly fifteen feet high and could be seen for miles around. Silently we prayed for the departed souls from the Land Beyond.

Epilogue

Raymond de Coccola was born in Corsica in 1912 in the village from which his ancient family takes its name. Educated in Corsica and at a Jesuit College in France's Haute-Savoie (bordering on Switzerland), he chose to be trained as an Oblate missionary. In 1937, at his own request, and even though he spoke no Eskimo nor English, Father de Coccola was sent to live among the Eskimos of the Canadian Central Arctic. From then, until he was invalided out in 1949, he visited the outside world only once.

Since his recovery from the effects of twelve years in the Barren Land, Raymond de Coccola has lived in the much gentler climate of the British Columbia coast. It was as an assistant parish priest at Powell River that he met public relations man Paul King, who helped him write this book. It is to his Quebec-born wife Suzanne, that the co-authors have also dedicated this book. A contemporary of Raymond de Coccola, Paul King was born in Manchuria and educated in North China and Western Canada. A graduate of the University of British Columbia, he has been an athlete, journalist, soldier, teacher, and weekly newspaper publisher and editor.

Upon leaving Powell River for the Greater Vancouver area in the mid-fifties, Raymond de Coccola was given his own parish on the border of the sprawling Burnaby Municipality and the City of New Westminster. With the enthusiastic help of many dedicated local parishioners, he was eventually successful in building two (Catholic) churches, two schools, a manse, and a nuns' convent

434

there.

Owing to the scarcity of priests at the time, Father de Coccola was prevailed upon by his superiors to remain at St. Michael's Parish for an additional five years after customary retirement at sixty-five. Hundreds of his parishioners honoured Father Raymond at a surprise farewell gathering upon his long-awaited move to his scenic hideout on the shore of a little mountain lake in the lush Fraser Valley east of Vancouver, B. C.

Hancock House Publications

19313 Zero Avenue, Surrey, B.C.
Canada V3S 5J9   (604) 538-1557

New Releases & Famous Backlist

Quest for Empire
Kyra Petrovskaya Wayne
This historical novel traces the struggle of Governor Baranov and his men to colonize Russian America. From Sitka, Alaska, to Fort Ross, California, the Russians try to establish permanent New World colonies. The bloody Tlingit massacre nearly wipes out the fort, and the harsh winters and relentless sea take their toll. But through it all the men, and women who love them, persevere and prosper.
5½x8½ 415 pp ISBN 0-88839-191-9   sc

ISBN 0-88839-193-5   hc

By The Same Author—A New Edition

Shurik
Kyra Petrovskaya Wayne
In the horror of war, love and humanity persevere. This drama is set in Leningrad during the 900-day siege—the story of an orphan, Shurik, befriended by a Red Army nurse. Death and destruction is everywhere, yet people reaching out to others alleviates some of the suffering and makes existence during the war bearable.
5½x8½, 209 pp. ISBN 0-88839-198-6   sc

Hancock House Publications

My Heart Soars
Chief Dan George
Drawings by Helmut Hirnschall
The philosophy of the Indian people
expressed eloquently by a great and
wise chief and enhanced by evocative
drawings.
8½x10½, 96 pp, ISBN 0-919654-15-0 hc

My Spirit Soars
Chief Dan George
and Helmut Hirnschall
Chief Dan George died in 1981 at the
age of 82. At his burial an eagle flew over
in silent circles, a symbol of his departing
spirit. The title of this book was inspired
by that event. Fully illustrated.
8½x10½, 96 pp, ISBN 0-88839-154-4 hc

Vander Zalm's
Northwest Gardener's Almanac
Bill Vander Zalm
All your gardening questions answered in this month-by-month
guide to gardening in the Northwest.
When to prune, what to do about pest problems, soil problems
and—just about everything else you need to know, in order to
grow more beautiful and productive plants. Be the envy of your
neighbors with the help of your "green thumb" and *Vander
Zalm's Northwest Gardener's Almanac.*

5½x8½, 256 pp, ISBN 0-88839-163-3 sc

Hancock House Publications

COOKBOOKS

Cross Can. Cooking

Let's Dry It

GARDEN BOOKS

Garden Perennials

Vader Zalm's NW
Gardeners Almanac

WESTERN
GUIDE BOOKS

Alpine Wildflowers

B.C. Our Land

Coastal Lowland
Wildflowers

Exploring Outdoors
Southwestern B.C.

Indian Herbs

Mooching Salmon

NW Wild Berries

NW Wild Harvest

Orchids of N. America

Rafting in B.C.
Lower Thompson R.

Sagebrush Wildflowers

Steelhead
Trophy Trout

Upland Field &
Forest Wildflowers

Western Mushrooms

Western Wildlife

EASTERN
GUIDE BOOKS

Eastern Mushrooms

E. Rocks & Minerals

Fish of the Atlantic

Indian Artifacts of NE

Introducing Eastern
Wildflowers

INDIAN TITLES

Argillite

Artifacts of NW
Coast Indians

Art of the Totem

Coast Salish

Haida

Indian Healing

Indian Tribes of NW

Indian Weav. Knit.
Basketry of NW

Kwakiutl Legends

My Heart Soars

My Spirit Soars

The Providers

The Song of Creation

Totem Poles of NW

Those Born at Koona

We-Gyet Wanders On

West Indian Basketry

GENERAL TITLES

Ethnic Vancouver

Falconry Manual

Guide to Vancouver's
Chinese Restaurants

How Come I'm Dead?

How to make Money In
Blue Chip Stocks

Ingram's Income
Tax Guide 1986/87

Ingram's Invest.
Guide

Ogopogo

The Ships of B.C.

The Ships of B.C.

Shurik

HISTORY TITLES

Barkerville The Town
That Gold Built

B.C.'s Own Railroad

Early History of
Port Moody

Fishing in B.C.

Fraser Canyon Hwy.

Gold Along
the Fraser

Gold Creeks &
Ghostowns

Guide to Gold Panning

Living With Logs

Logging in B.C.

Mackenzie Yesterday
& Beyond

Mighty Mackenzie

Nelson Island Story

Old Wooden Buildings

Quest for Empire

Quest for Empire

NORTHERN
BIOGRAPHIES

Alaska Calls

Fogswamp

Incredible Eskimo

Lady Rancher

Nahanni

Northern Man

Novice in the North

Ralph Edwards

Ruffles
on My Longjohns

Sasqatch

Wings of the North

Yukon Antics

Yukon Lady